Regimes of Legality

Regimes of Legality
Ethnography of Criminal Cases in South Asia

Edited by
DANIELA BERTI
and
DEVIKA BORDIA

OXFORD
UNIVERSITY PRESS

OXFORD
UNIVERSITY PRESS

Oxford University Press is a department of the University of Oxford.
It furthers the University's objective of excellence in research, scholarship,
and education by publishing worldwide. Oxford is a registered trademark of
Oxford University Press in the UK and in certain other countries

Published in India by
Oxford University Press
YMCA Library Building, 1 Jai Singh Road, New Delhi 110 001, India

ISBN-13: 978-0-19-945674-1
ISBN-10: 0-19-945674-7

Typeset in Dante MT Std 10.5/13
by The Graphics Solution, New Delhi 110 092
Printed in India by Rakmo Press, New Delhi 110 092

Contents

Acknowledgements

This volume is part of a broader research programme that was funded by the *Agence nationale de la recherche* (ANR programme 08-GOUV-064) for the period 2009–2012. The programme, entitled 'Justice and Governance in India and South Asia' (http://just-india.net) was coordinated by Daniela Berti and Gilles Tarabout and was hosted by CEH, *Centre d'études Himalayennes* (Centre for Himalayan Studies), a CNRS *(Centre national de la recherche scientifique)* unit. The programme is particularly indebted to the *Foundation Maison des Sciences de l'Homme* (FMSH), Paris, and to its Franco-Indian Exchange Programme, which was run by France Bhattacharya and Véronique Bouillier, for hosting the workshops and for receiving scholars from abroad. We are also grateful to the *Centre d'études de l'Inde et de l'Asie du sud* (CEIAS) and to the *Réseau Asie* for their support.

For this volume, the editors have drawn on the expertise of many scholars with whom they regularly collaborated, such as Antoine Garapon, Werner Gephart, Catherine Clémentin-Ojha, Kalyanakrishnan Sivaramakrishnan, Christophe Jaffrelot, and Joëlle Smadja. Special thanks go to Gilles Tarabout who provided us with his insights from the inception of the project to the preparation of the manuscript for this volume. We would also like to acknowledge the work of Bernadette Sellers and David Jobanputra who proofread some of the chapters included in the volume. Lastly, we would like to thank Oxford University Press for showing an interest in our manuscript and for agreeing to publish it.

Foreword

While reading the following chapters and their introduction, I found myself constantly casting my mind back to my own periods of field research in South India. Ostensibly these were not at all concerned with crime, but in retrospect criminal incidents gave rise to what are still, after almost forty years, some of the most vivid memories of my initial stay there, while the context in which my second period of extended fieldwork took place was shaped by a criminal case almost a century earlier. The various discussions in the present volume help me to see these events in a fresh light.

During my doctoral work in the 1970s in the Tirunelveli District of Tamil Nadu state, there were several murders in the locality, two of which impinged directly on the village in which I and my family were living. About one month into our stay, our landlord suddenly fled the house and went to hide at the home of his mistress (*vaippaatti*) in a nearby village (he was a widower). There had been a murder in Kovilpatti, the nearest sizeable town. The actual murderer, we were later told, was a local Maravar man who allegedly had several previous contract killings in his *curriculum vitae*. The police, however, were looking for the man who had supposedly instigated and paid for the murder. Both the victim and instigator were close relatives of our landlord. He was not at all involved in the murder, but his flight was precautionary; the wanted man was absconding and—our neighbours explained—it was normal police practice under such circumstances to take close male relatives into custody, holding and allegedly beating them until the fugitive gave himself up.

That night we were woken in the early hours by the village dogs, who began a cacophony of barking lasting a full twenty minutes. The cause of this hullabaloo proved to be a detachment of police, whose approach had been detected while they were still several kilometres away. They arrived at our house, the other half of which was by now empty, and peered in at us through the open, barred windows. We feigned sleep. Next morning, our neighbours crowded round: 'What did the police say?' 'Why did they leave?' We explained, to general merriment, that the police had been taken aback to see us there. They had whispered frantically to one another, '*vellaikkaaran, vellaikkaaran* (white man, white man)', and had not felt able to enter and question us.

In the final week of our stay there was a murder in our village itself— the first in twenty years, I was told. It happened soon after dawn in the Paraiyar quarter, but the ostensible cause was a seemingly trivial incident the night before, when the murderer (or his brother; accounts were confused because the two had the same name, and were commonly differentiated only as 'Big A' and 'Little A') had asked K, the victim, for a *beedi* (cigarette) during a drinking and gambling session, and had been refused. In the morning, Big A attacked K with a sickle, inflicting about 20 blows on the head and arms. Big A himself had an almost-severed forearm, and their respective younger brothers were also wounded, though less seriously. I did not go to the far end of the village to view the scene, though many others did. The police were sent for, and one constable arrived by mid-morning, followed by a stream of motorcycles and jeeps, coming and going for the rest of the day. The wounded men were taken to hospital by bullock cart, and the police took into custody those remaining relatives of the main protagonists who were unable to buy them off, a task made easier by the fact that all those involved were local residents.

Later that day, our landlord's family fed the dead man's brother-in-law. Rice and a piece of fish were served to him in two coconut shells. He ate on the verandah, and afterwards our landlord's son kicked the shells out into the street. I asked why he was being fed, and was told that he was a good man, but very poor. He was a day labourer, and because of today's events he had not worked or been paid, and had no money for his family's food. Furthermore, he had no money to hire the bullock carts, or to pay off the police. I was asked for Rs 50 to cover this (a considerable sum in those days, equivalent to ten days' wages). The money was described publicly as a loan, but our landlord's son took care to check, in private, that I realized I would never be paid back. That evening groups of men sat around discussing the incident and recalling other murders in the locality. The prevailing view, articulated so widely and uniformly that it seemed a stereotyped response, was that it was a great misfortune (*paavam*); for the sake of a few *paisa*, people said, shaking their heads with a kind of grim glee, the cost of the *beedi*, one man was dead and three wounded. The ensuing trial would cost those involved anything from Rs 5,000 to Rs 10,000, which needless to say the protagonists did not have.

This is in fact the classic form of interpersonal violence in this region, and all murders are referred to locally as 'cuttings (*kaatutal*)' whatever the actual weapons used. This lends them a quasi-sacrificial element, in that the harvesting of rice, the decapitation of goats at the annual goddess festival, and the killing of one's human enemies, are all performed using the same implement, the sickle (*arivaal*).

It is important to note, however, that my roles in these two incidents were those of a mere bit-part player, whose awareness of the overall course of events was highly fragmentary and partial. To some extent, therefore, my perspective resembled that of many of the protagonists in the chapters to follow, caught up in legal processes that are only partially visible or comprehensible to them. What is more, I never discovered the outcomes of these cases because they were still pending by the time I left the field.

By contrast, in my later fieldwork in the mid-1980s, centring on the substantial Murugan temple at Kalugumalai, my vantage point was sometimes that of the legal proceedings themselves, to the extent even of several weeks spent in the archives of Madras High Court. Temples are highly litigious institutions, whose acephalous organization encourages perennial and interminable disputes among their trustees, priests, temple servants, worshippers, and benefactors. In the case of Kalugumalai temple there was the further complication that its hereditary Trustee, the Raja of Ettaiyapuram, had been fighting in the courts for decades to prevent an administrative takeover by the Hindu Religious and Charitable Endowments Department. Those were all civil matters, of course. Yet it became increasingly clear during my fieldwork that the present character and even the modern geography of Kalugumalai town had been shaped by a criminal case almost a century earlier, whose ramifications included convictions for murder, later overturned at appeal; an official enquiry by the colonial government; and even—though it would be too much of a digression to discuss it here—an appeal to the Privy Council in London.[1]

The context, briefly, was a long-running dispute between local Nadars and the temple, represented by the Raja, over the Nadars' claimed right to take wedding processions through the main car streets around the temple. Such cases were widespread across Madras Presidency in the late nineteenth century, as Nadars sought to pursue their long-lasting status claims through the fresh avenues seemingly provided by the newly reformed court system. These attempts were uniformly unsuccessful, however, because the courts at that time—in line with Freitag's analysis of the North Indian context, as discussed in the introduction to this present volume[2]—routinely refused to interfere with practices that could be shown to accord with established local 'custom'. Even so, the resentments stirred up by these legal challenges posed a severe threat to public order throughout South India, and Kalugumalai witnessed one of the bloodiest episodes.

In 1894, by which time the Raja had died and his estate was being managed by the Court of Wards on behalf of his juvenile heir, the Nadars' claim was finally and decisively rejected by the Court of Appeal. The Nadars' response, which even local French Jesuit missionaries admitted was strategic rather than motivated by faith, was to convert *en masse* to Catholicism. They began building a chapel on a plot of land adjacent to East Car Street, purchased for them by the local missionary leader, Fr. Caussanel. This generated violent Hindu protests, arson attacks, and several arrests on both sides for breaches of the peace.

Matters came to a head during the Pankuni Uttiram festival in April 1895, which also happened to be Palm Sunday. At Pankuni Uttiram the mobile images of the main temple deities are taken in procession around the car streets, riding on a huge wooden temple car pulled by hundreds of devotees. When the car reached the chapel on this occasion, the Hindu side claimed that there was no room to pass and the decorations in front of the chapel would have to be demolished. Subsequent events were highly disputed. It is at least clear that the Estate Manager appointed by the Court of Wards, a senior Indian member of the civil service, tried to persuade the Nadars to remove the decorations just long enough for the car to pass. Stones were thrown. As the Manager tried to restore order he was stabbed to death. Others in his party were wounded and two later died. That afternoon Hindus mounted a concerted attack on the Nadar quarter. Houses were burned and business premises looted, Nadar women were stripped and abused, seven Nadars died, and several other people, including children, were horribly burned.

Of those arrested, only 24 of the 70 Hindus even faced trial in the Sessions Court, and all were released on the spot. By contrast, 34 of the 42 arrested Nadars stood trial for murder and rioting (Tinnevelly Court of Sessions, Case No. 41 of 1895). They were even accused of burning down their own church. Two Nadars were sentenced to death for the manager's murder, and all the others received short sentences for rioting. The failure to convict, or even charge, anyone for the murderous attack on the Nadar quarter caused widespread public outrage throughout Madras Presidency, especially in view of allegations that this attack had been led by the local Head Constable himself. As a correspondent in the *Madras Mail* asked sardonically, on 5 June 1895, 'these gallant guardians of the peace who captured 40 [Nadars], could they not capture even one Hindu?'

The interminable delays that characterize South Asian legal proceedings nowadays were hardly in evidence here. Judgment on the Nadars' appeal was delivered by the Madras High Court on 4 December 1895, less than eight months after the riot itself (Referred Trial No. 74 of 1895). The judges subjected the evidence to far greater forensic analysis than had been the case for the Sessions Judge, whom they accused of accepting the prosecution evidence 'in an indiscriminate fashion'. Their reasoning displayed far greater awareness of the possibilities for contamination of evidence resulting from the delayed taking of witness statements. In such an emotive context, they noted, 'we do not think it safe to trust the evidence of any of the witnesses who did not make their statements immediately'. They strongly censured the Sessions Judge for failing to realize 'how great the risk was that spectators at the [riot] might after some interval of time … be led to believe that they could point out among the prisoners the men who did particular acts most especially if rumour had already fixed itself on certain names'. Whether or not a Nadar had been guilty of the Manager's murder—which was by no means clear when the evidence was carefully assessed—it was certain that neither of those convicted of the murder had been identified as the culprits by anyone interviewed at the time. All the prisoners, including the two supposed murderers, were ordered to be acquitted and discharged.

This case had significant ramifications both within the colonial government and on South Indian public life. The government's review of the legal debacle exonerated the local police and judicial officials entirely, and blamed the acquittals wholly on the Sessions Judge and on Mr Powell, the Government Pleader in the High Court (*G.O. No. 1189 [Judl.] of 16th July 1896*). As an assessment of this review by a senior British Jesuit noted, this whitewash was hardly surprising: 'As a matter of course Government are bound by ties of self-interest to defend as far as possible the acts of their own servants. To admit corruption and mismanagement and blundering on the large scale in which they appear ... in this case would be to admit a serious blot in their ... administration' (provenance unknown; held within Fr. Caussanel's file on the case, file 217/71 in the Jesuit Archives at Shenbaganur). Nadars everywhere greeted the verdict as a great victory over higher castes, and even Hindus credited the Catholic church with overturning a serious miscarriage of justice. Fr. Caussanel became an overnight celebrity and was paraded through the streets in triumph when he visited the nearby towns of Sivakasi and Srivilliputtur soon afterwards. In Sivakasi, 2,000 people declared a wish to become Catholics. The two condemned men themselves toured the villages preaching, and drew huge crowds.

Rethinking these events in light of the chapters to follow, it is immediately clear that despite the very drastic changes in both the legal system and the political context since that time, this century-old case makes manifest several themes arising in these contemporary accounts too: for example, caste discrimination, acts of atrocity, the alleged incompetence and partiality of the police, the changing of testimony by key witnesses, and the role of public opinion in shaping and being shaped by high-profile legal proceedings. More generally, the fact that I have been able to study this case from several different perspectives and to analyse the political, cultural, and socio-temporal factors at work—to say nothing of my amateur sleuthing in attempting to work out what 'really' happened in Kalugumalai's Car Streets in April 1895 (Good 1999b)—reveals the considerable strengths of the court case-based approach that characterizes this present volume. Legal processes provide unique sources of documentation for historians or historical ethnographers: how else, for example, could I have gained access to the views of nineteenth century Kalugumalai residents except through their detailed printed testimonies and cross-examinations held in the archives of Madras High Court and the Jesuit Mission?

It is true, obviously, that the fact that a case follows one particular course rather than another, forecloses as well as opens insights into the events under dispute. Because no Hindus ever stood trial in connection with the Kalugumalai riot, for example, the alternative Nadar version of events—that the Estate Manager's murder was an opportunistic act by a disgruntled hanger-on in the Raja's entourage, whose privileges had been curtailed by the Manager's reforms and who used the riot as a cover for his actions—was never tested in court. On balance, though, the strength of the insights offered by such methods far outweigh such drawbacks. After all, a court hearing provides a unique opportunity for both sides to present their arguments systematically, and for those arguments and the supporting evidence to be considered in balanced fashion. This latter ideal may not, of course, be realized in practice. In the Kalugumalai Riot case, proceedings in the Sessions Court were attacked by all parties. Nadars complained that the Judge ignored his Assessor's recommendation of 'not guilty'; the High Court identified at least one 'serious mistake' by the Sessions Judge; and the Madras Government accused him of a lack of 'proper thoroughness and care'. It is true that the Government took an equally jaundiced view of the High Court proceedings, no doubt largely because of its embarrass-ment at the outcome; nonetheless, the analysis by the two High Court judges, Messrs Shephard and Davies, clearly provides us with the most thorough and least partisan examination of the evidence that is ever likely to become available.

If such insights are possible solely from studying the 'entextualiza-tions' generated by legal proceedings of more than a century ago, how much richer will be those gained by the direct ethnographic observa-tion of court cases taking place in the here and now?

★ ★ ★

On the day I began writing this foreword, in late May 2014, the interna-tional news headlines were filled with reports of crimes in South Asia. A pregnant woman on her way to court in Lahore had been stoned to death, allegedly by her own family, for marrying against their wishes. It was claimed that the police stood back during the attack and did nothing, though the local police chief denied this. The girl's father was arrested soon afterwards, while other relatives were absconding. Within days, allegations emerged that the dead woman's sister had been poi-soned by the family four years earlier—ironically, for refusing to leave an arranged marriage after a dispute between the two families. It also transpired that the dead woman's husband had murdered his first wife but had not gone to prison because his son had 'forgiven' him in return for the payment of 'blood money'.

Next day in Uttar Pradesh two teenage girls were found hanged, having first been subjected to gang rape. Again it was claimed that local police were slow to act, having allegedly ridiculed the initial complaint because of the low caste background of the complainants. Within a few days, however, as public outrage against the police and the state's Chief Minister mounted, three persons had been arrested for the crime, two policemen had also been arrested, and two more dismissed. A few days later still, there was yet another twist to the story. Uttar Pradesh's police chief claimed that post-mortems showed only one girl had been raped; he asserted that their deaths seemed in fact to be examples of so-called 'honour killings' by their own families, and claimed that the three men who had actually confessed to the murder might be innocent after all.

Clearly these two cases, with their international coverage and complex, rapidly evolving scenarios, represent merely the visible, sensational tip of a huge iceberg of largely unreported crime. All over South Asia, every day, thousands of criminal actions great and small lead to arrests, charges and legal proceedings. In India alone, for example, the National Crime Records Bureau recorded almost 750 violent crimes per day in 2012, including nearly 100 murders and 100 attempted murders (*Crime in India 2012*, Table 3.1: http://ncrb.gov.in/; accessed 3 June 2014). In total during that year, a staggering 3.3 million Indians were arrested for offences under the Penal Code, and over 3 million were actually charged (*Crime in India 2012*, Tables 12.1 & 12.10).[3] Those involved come from all walks of society. Following the 2014 General Election, for example, political commentators noted that the newly constituted Lok Sabha (Lower House) in India was not only the richest ever to be elected, on average, but also contained an unprecedented number of MPs against whom there were outstanding criminal charges.

And yet, as the editors of this volume point out in their introduction to the present volume, court cases in South Asia have received astonishingly little anthropological attention. What actually happens in practice to all these people who are arrested, charged, or appear before a court? What is the role of the police in all this? The legal profession?

The judiciary? What happens when (or if) a case goes to court? Who gives evidence and how is that evidence assessed?

There are two kinds of answer to such questions, focusing respectively on what the editors term 'the official representation of south Asian legal traditions and the everyday practice of justice-making'. The official picture is a technical one, accessible through official documents and treatises on black letter law: all these activities are regulated by legislation, rules of procedure and codes of professional conduct. As regards everyday practice, however, legal processes depart markedly, and crucially, from their official representations. They reflect local culture in the form, for example, of customary dispute settlement procedures being conducted in parallel to the formal legal proceedings, through caste councils or by quasi-religious means. Perhaps even more importantly, they are shaped by local and supra-local structures and inequalities of power, that help explain, among other things, the ubiquitous influence of processes of extra-legal mediation and negotiation out with the court itself, and the startling propensity of key witnesses to change their earlier stories when actually called to testify in court.

These are the kinds of everyday practices and complex inter-relationships examined by this ethnographically rich and path-breaking collection of essays. They lay the foundation for what promises to be a fruitful new trend in the legal anthropology of South Asia.

ANTHONY GOOD
University of Edinburgh
June 2014

Notes

1. For more detailed accounts and analyses of all these events, see my articles: 'The Burning Question: Sacred and Profane Space in a South Indian Temple Town.' *Anthropos*, 94: 69–84 (1999a); and 'The Car and the Palanquin: Rival Accounts of the 1895 Riot in Kalugumalai, South India.' *Modern Asian Studies*, 33(1): 23–65 (1999b).

2. Freitag, Susan B. (1991). 'Crime in the Social Order of Colonial North India.' *Modern Asian Studies*, 25(2): 227–61.

3. Given the huge populations of several South Asian countries, it is perhaps more informative to look at crime rates rather than absolute numbers. For example, the latest UN *Global Study on Homicide* gives homicide rates (generally

for 2012) in India and Pakistan as 3.5 and 7.7 per 100,000, respectively, compared to 1.0, 1.0, and 4.7 for France, the UK and the USA (http://www.unodc.org/documents/gsh/pdfs/2014_GLOBAL_HOMICIDE_BOOK_web.pdf; consulted 16 June 2014).

DANIELA BERTI

DEVIKA BORDIA

Introduction

This book provides an anthropological approach to examining the way criminal cases are dealt with by courts in South Asia. It takes criminal cases as a framework to study how power dynamics and individual strategies either comply or clash with a legal setting. The case-study approach that is used here allows us to examine a set of state and non-state institutions and the practices of people associated with them. It helps to analyse the underlying tension in institutional contexts between legal practitioners such as police officers, lawyers, and judges who orient their claims towards neutralism, objectivity, and equality and a set of everyday interactions and decisions where cultural, social, economic, and political factors play a major role.

Our argument is that criminal cases offer a means of studying a wide scope of social issues from the vantage point of litigation and negotiation. The contributions to this volume focus on acts that the state has classed as criminal, ranging from those that were defined as a crime when the Indian Penal Code was first drafted in 1860 such as murder and rape to events that that have more recently been criminalized, such as atrocities against Scheduled Tribes and Scheduled Castes and violence against women. Laws that criminalize practices like domestic violence and caste atrocity have enabled activists to garner attention toward certain issues and to build networks within police and court institutions. Activists have approached the legal institutions and advocated for legal reform based on different motivations and intentions, and this has shaped the discourse and idioms that animate different social movements. Other cases reveal some resistance within society to conform to the changing definition of crime that is introduced by legislation subsequent to new state commitments. They also show how judicial procedures at play in a given society succeed in enforcing unpopular social and cultural reforms or, on the contrary, how resistance to these reforms impacts the judicial process.

From a methodological point of view, the ethnography of court cases proposed here mainly relies on narrative constructions. Its aim is not to reconstruct facts but to see how opposing parties try to uphold contrasting versions of these facts. These 'stories' that are strategically built in accordance with procedural constraints are eventually legally proven or ultimately challenge the opponent's version. The official version of the story produced at the time of the trial is often the result of more informal, under-the-table interactions and negotiations which may have occurred well before the trial itself and are based on power relationships, political pressure or, sometimes, monetary transactions. This book focuses on formal and informal interactions between the various actors involved in a criminal case: the accused, police officers, lawyers, judges, prosecutors, witnesses, local leaders, and community members.

Court Case Approach

The heuristic potential of court cases to provide an understanding of the society in which they occur has been widely explored in the field of history. Court documents have been used by historians as a way to capture cultural tension which lends an in-depth understanding of the crucial transformations at work in a society over a given period. One example is a double volume entitled 'On Trial: American History through Court Proceedings and Hearings' (Marcus and Marcus 2006), where the authors collected edited transcripts of trials for use in American history classes. Starting with the transcriptions of hearings for a series of criminal cases, students are taught about important topics in American history, such as the American Civil War and Reconstruction, the Ku Klux Klan, and the beginning of protective labour legislation.

Similarly, historians specializing in Europe have traditionally used trials as a historical source. Subsequent to Ginzburg's works on witchcraft trials in particular, it is now current practice for historians to draw on court documents to provide information not only on the history of judicial institutions (Farge 2011) but also on aspects of everyday life which, being rather commonplace, are not mentioned in other sources. Court documents have in fact been used to study how the body was perceived and how emotions were expressed by witnesses testifying before tribunals during the Inquisition in the thirteenth century (Cheirézy 2009); or to analyze the perception and the definition of incest in nineteenth-century France (Giuliani 2009); or even to document the unknown sleeping habits of French working classes in the eighteenth century (Garnier 2009).

Historians have not only used judicial documents as sources for their research. They have also developed an epistemological reflection on the nature of these sources. They have questioned the kind of voices expressed by these sources and the way they are to be used, the research strategies that have to be followed in dealing with them and the way to interpret these sources. One major issue is whether it is possible to extract from these judicial sources a testimony (Farge and Cerutti 2009) that has not already been structured by a juridical language or if, on the contrary, these sources are entirely shaped by juridical forms of knowledge and power. More specifically, historians have argued that the voices heard in court reports—that of the judge, of witnesses, of experts—are all distorted by a deforming mirror: the transcription by the court clerk; the witnesses' attitude towards the judge; understanding justice as a system of authority (Giuliani 2009: 21). In other words, they have underlined the need to take into account the relationship between written documents and the situational framework in which these documents have been produced: the fact that the witness report is the result of an interrogation; that the witness report may also be influenced by the attitudes and personalities of the judicial officers; or by the way the witness regards the justice system, and many other contextual factors. In spite of being an 'imperfect archive' (Giuliani 2009) judicial documents are an integral part of historical research and they are even considered to be one of the only ways many people in past societies had to express themselves and to be heard up to the present time (Garnier 2009).

The importance attributed to the oral nature of court interactions has been at the very heart of the research carried out over the last decades on American and European trials by ethnomethodologists and conversational analysts keen to study the linguistic mechanisms through which legal power is achieved. These authors have looked in detail at oral interactions and examined the mechanisms that lie behind courtroom talk, the power relationships between protagonists, and the strategies used by judicial professionals to turn the situation to their advantage (Atkinson and Drew 1979; Conley and O'Barr 1990; Drew and Heritage 1992; Gnisci and Pontecorvo 2004). Most of these works have treated the courtroom as an empirical setting where power can be observed in action through language (O'Barr 1982; Conley and O'Barr 2005 [1998]). Here, power means what emanates from the linguistic mechanisms of talk in the courtroom, from institutional legal roles, from professional speech styles. It is power to control a setting where the rules and turns of speech are very different from those used in everyday conversation (Conley and O'Barr 1990: 21), where some are authorized to speak and others are restricted to giving answers, where by using a legal question-ing technique, professionals transform a dialogue into a self-serving monologue. Some authors have also examined the social values behind courtroom conversations. One example is Matoesian's work on rape where the author argues that talk in the courtroom not only enacts the power of legal institutions but also reproduces the social value of patriarchy and male hegemony in society (Matoesian 1993: 215; see also Conley and O'Barr 2005).

Anthropologists working in non-Western countries recently adopted this method (Hirsch 1998; Dupret 2006; Chang 2004; Richland 2008; Stiles 2009; Svongoro 2011), with the exception of those work-ing in India and other South Asian regions where very little research is done on courtrooms. In fact, while historians specializing in India have often drawn on trial reports as precious sources of information (Singha 1998; Freitag 1991), court cases have received little attention by anthropologists. Besides the pioneering works by Marc Galanter, in the 1990s, studies on South Asia started to take into account district court (Das 1996; Agnès 2004) or appeal court judgements which had had repercussions on various aspects of contemporary Indian society. These studies have, however, mainly focused on the content of the judicial decision and on the implications that this decision could have from a political science, juridical, or sociological perspective.[1] What has been neglected is not only the form in which these judgments have been drawn up (from a linguistic and 'discursive' point of view) but also the complex and long-term judicial story of the case; this includes a multitude of professional and non-professional actors, of official and non-official interactions and has produced a number of legal (written) documents and contrasted (oral) narratives.

The argument put forward in this volume is that courtroom ethnography has to take into account not only the official reports provided by courts, but also the ways in which these documents are produced in the first place and the discourse that is held inside and outside the courtroom by the actors involved in the case. On the one hand, judicial reports and official documents may help to recreate the 'texture' by which the court and society have exchanged, formulated, negotiated, or opposed conflicting opinions on a register that is 'rule-oriented' (Conley and O'Barr 1990). On the other hand, the ethnographic investigation of courts and the collection of narratives and practices outside courtrooms may provide a more 'relation-oriented' version of legal facts—a version expressed by the parties actually involved in the case, whose logic and points of view are deeply entrenched in social ties, economic interests, feelings, conflicts, or loyalties (Berti 2011).

Anthropological research carried out in the field of legal practice in South Asia initially focused on village disputes and on the tactical possibilities offered by the coexistence of 'indigenous' and official laws. Srinivas' idea of 'bi-legality' (Srinivas 1964) by which he wanted to describe villagers' attitudes to using both 'indigenous' and official law in accordance with their own estimations of propriety and advantage was developed by Cohn (1987 [1965], 1987 [1959]) who insisted on the importance of analysing both what may induce villagers to choose between one or another system of justice-making, and what kind of consequence the choice may have on relationships in the village. Cohn emphasized villagers' attitudes to using the court not to settle disputes but to further them, so that most of the cases that go into courts are 'fabrications to cover the real disputes' (Cohn 1987 [1959]: 90).

Ethnographic fieldwork has highlighted, on the one hand, the existence of local procedures of justice-making (Hayden 1984) and, on the other hand, the complex interaction between the official representation of south Asian legal traditions and the everyday practice of justice-making which is often informed by the pragmatic combination of older and newer legal procedures (Moore 1998).The emphasis these authors lay on the contradictions and oppositions between 'state' versus 'indigenous' customs has been partly criticized by Anderson (1990) who, by referring to recent Indian medieval historiography, underlines the fact that the coexistence of a centralized political power with local dynamics of loyalty and authority existed even during the pre-colonial period. It is not therefore a consequence of the post-colonial period. He also criticizes the fact that these studies emphasize cultural differences to the detriment of an understanding of 'how the structural distribution of political authority is related to processes of production and social reproduction' (Anderson 1990: 163).

Yet again from a perspective of legal pluralism, the disparity between law on paper and law in action has been highlighted by Marc Galanter. Many works by this author deal with the relationship between state and non-state regulations—especially in studying the emergence of distinctively modern legal institutions (Galanter and Khosla 1987). One example is his study of Nyaya Panchayat that was created by the state in village areas—partly as an 'ill-conceived aborted revival of traditional dispute settlement bodies to divert minor cases from courts and partly as a means to displace existing or potential mechanisms for dispute settlement' (Galanter and Baxi 1979; Galanter and Krishnan 2004).[2]

Drawing on Galanter's postulate that courts of justice provide a window onto significant facets of Indian society (Galanter 1972), the chapters presented in this volume explore the relevance of analyzing criminal cases from an anthropological perspective. The volume relies on the theoretical assumption that the study of these judicial cases in all their multifaceted complexity provides a pertinent and original angle from which to access some issues of contemporary India, as well as a variety of frameworks where the interactions between different forms of operative power and authority may be observed.

Courts Proceedings and Legal Narratives

The question raised by the afore-mentioned historians regarding the way judicial documents are recorded is of crucial import in the context examined here. In fact, although Indian criminal procedures apply the so-called principle of orality according to which evidence against the defendant must be presented by witnesses in court and must be subject to cross-examination, the judicial practice attributes a crucial role to writing because what witnesses say before the judge is recorded in writing during the trial. Oral evidence is produced in court mostly so that it can be put on record. The observation of a criminal trial highlights the creative process of legal transcription similarly to what Stiles (2009) wrote in her ethnography on Islamic courts in Zanzibar. The author refers to the work of the historian Leslie Peirce who noted that the different ways in which the litigant's testimony was recorded in documents in sixteenth-century Ottoman Islamic courts was to be interpreted both as a consequence of restrictions on procedures and as a way of preserving communal well-being. Using the linguistic notion of 'entextualization' (Bauman and Briggs 1990), of creating 'extractable' texts from oral discourse, she shows how Zanzibar court narratives are framed differently throughout the proceedings by litigants, by clerks, and by judges, each of them emphasizing different legal issues by building on previous entextualizations of the dispute (Stiles 2009: 35).

Interactions in Court

The process of entextualization is particularly relevant to the judicial settings studied here. In fact, contrary to what Dupret observed in reference to Egyptian courts for example, where the evidence has already been written by the lawyer and by the prosecutor before the trial, and where court hearings are 'weakly interactive' (Dupret 2006: 153), in Indian courts the examination and cross-examination of witnesses and the transformation of question-answers into written documents occur at the trial itself. The production of court documents in India is the result of oral exchanges which are often extremely tense and where, as in other common law systems, questioning is carried out with the aim of suggesting something rather than of obtaining an answer (Conley and O'Barr 2005: 26).[3] The writing process enables legal professionals (the lawyer, the prosecutor, or the judge), who master the relevant writing techniques to transform the questions into witnesses' self-narrations[4] and put on record the crucial points which they wish to suggest.

The long and meticulous recording of evidence in Indian trials (Annoussamy 1996: 78) strongly contrasts with the French procedure described by Bouillier (in this volume) where nothing of what witnesses say during the hearings is transcribed by the court. Similarly, the eloquent nature of the French *plaidoirie*, is markedly different from the way 'arguments' are conducted in India, which mostly consists in reading aloud before the judge (who follows on his file) passages of the previously recorded evidence.[5]

The role that writing plays during a trial in India and in France needs to be understood in relation to the different ways the verdict is reached and formulated. As noted by Bouillier in this volume, and like other jury-based systems, the verdict is given in France Assize Courts by ordinary citizens—the jurors—who have no legal background and who are asked to decide according to their own 'intimate conviction' on the basis of what they have heard during the trial.[6] Even though jurors have recently been ordered to provide a short report, they do not have to justify their decision in writing. The 'intimate conviction' according to which French jurors are asked to pronounce the final verdict contrasts with the technicality of the reasoning process through which the judge in India arrives at his verdict. The decision here is taken by the judge alone on the basis of his own interpretation of what has been 'put on record' and by taking into account contradictions, procedural mistakes, and previous rulings. The role played by the recording of the hearings comes across even more clearly during the appeal process when the judge decides 'according to facts and law' by mainly relying on the evidence recorded by the trial court years before.

Settlement Negotiations

Observations of the oral and written procedures applied in court provide the social anthropologist with an interesting setting for studying the way state power is concretely implemented and how people organize themselves when faced with the state's legal constraints. Some of the chapters in this volume show how the judicial process is constantly bent by different kinds of out-of-court negotiations that take place between the parties from the time the case is filed to the trial itself, all of which ultimately undermines the rule of evidence once the judicial process gets under way.

In the narcotics case discussed by Berti, the negotiations prompted witnesses to deny before the judge what had been written in the police report at the time they gave their statement. Such repudiation led the prosecutor and the judge to declare the witness 'hostile', which insinuated that they had reached some form of compromise with the accused. The police officers themselves were eventually blamed by the judge for having turned the case around in favour of the accused by giving contradicting statements during the hearings. In other cases, an out-of-court compromise between the parties is tacitly accepted by the court or it may even be explicitly requested by the judge—somewhat questioning the criminal nature of the case. Baxi's chapter presents an inter-caste love story which was initially falsely filed as a rape case by the girl's parents and in which the accused, who was asked by the court to reach a compromise with the plaintiffs, was happily married with the alleged victim when the trial took place. The trial itself then became a form of fiction, which was played out by the prosecutor and the judge even if there was no longer a case to try. Baxi shows the extent to which these dynamics inform the legal procedure not only during the investigation, but also inside the courtroom when procedures are adjusted to ensure that the verdict is in keeping with the compromise that the parties reached a long time ago.

While in Baxi's case, a compromise is accepted or even encouraged by the judge and the prosecutor because of their awareness of the non-criminal nature of the case, in other cases involving allegations of corruption from the victim's party, the judge's reasons for encouraging a compromise may be more difficult to analyse. In the case discussed by Jaoul, for example, the judge's alleged request that a Dalit reach a compromise with the accused from an upper caste was presented by a lawyer activist as proof that the judge had taken a bribe. Here, far from being condemned by the court, an out-of-court compromise is allegedly imposed on the victim under the authority of the judge.

Fictional Scenarios

Verbal exchanges in court are not merely used to contradict previous versions recorded during the investigations. They also produce new narratives which are formulated in anticipation of their prospective use, providing the judge with an alternative narrative for the case. One issue that is addressed in this book is how narratives are formulated during or in view of the trial. In some cases multiple overlapping strategies are used by the parties (with the help of lawyers) to play around with the different legal sections according to their focus of interest. Legal narratives and the effects they have during the trial may also follow a rather conventional scenario familiar to and often produced by legal professionals (Basu, Baxi, and Berti in this volume).

This raises the issue of fiction and plausibility in the judicial process. The case discussed by Letizia (in this volume) about a Hindu extremist in Nepal accused of placing bombs in the city shows how the arguments put forward by the defence—use of torture by the police, frame-ups, political intervention, weak prosecution—appear to be plausible scenarios which guarantee a lenient sentence for the accused. The author also analyses how the charisma and religious/political position of the accused and the context of uncertainty within the Hindu majority owing to secularist reforms in Nepal might have influenced the decision to have a Chief District Officer (instead of a District Court Officer) try the case and have ensured full respect of court procedures (for example, the lawyers being present).

Judicial procedures may also be strategically shaped by the police and the prosecutor according to the social status of the accused or in relation to a specific religious or cultural setting. In the case presented by Bordia in this volume, concerning a Girassia woman accused of killing her husband, the author interprets the judge's attitude towards the case as a consequence of a parallel that non-tribal people make between the perceived immorality of tribal practices—in the case at hand, the possibility for a Girassia woman to have an extramarital relationship—and the culpability of the accused. The impact that the social status of the accused has on the case also emerges in Redding's chapter on a criminal case in Pakistan that was filed against transgendered individuals where the police's method of identifying individuals corresponds to and eventually clashes with the way these transgendered individuals are identified in Court (Redding in this volume).

Although, occasional reference to the personality of the accused or to their cultural or social background is made by the judge or prosecutor during hearings, these references are never recorded in the official transcription of the evidence. In fact, in Indian judicial procedures, as in other common law countries, the personality of the accused or their moral behaviour is not explicitly taken into consideration by the court. This aspect of the procedure yet again contrasts with the context described by Bouillier for French courts where psychologists and psychiatrists may be summoned to the court to give their opinion. The jurors' perception of the personality of the accused and their social/ cultural background, along with the circumstances of the offence, play a significant role in the jury's verdict.

Legislation Through Court Archives

Court reports have also been used by historians to study the reforms the British introduced in legal codes and judicial procedures. Freitag (1991), for example, has analysed how attitudes toward criminality may throw light on what she calls the 'social order' of a particular place and time. She draws attention to the transformation which the British introduced regarding the perception of crime and in particular to what she considers a fundamental distinction in the way the raj dealt with what they perceived as crimes committed by individuals ('ordinary crime') and crimes committed by communities ('extraordinary crime'). By relying on annual records of crime and police statistics, she shows how in spite of legal codes and of police forces to deal with individual crime, the British were much more concerned with what they believed to be collective criminal actions aimed at weakening the authority of the state (Freitag 1991: 229; see also Yang 2003).

Singha's work is particularly worth mentioning here as it touches upon an issue that is addressed in this volume concerning the definition of the line between civil and criminal jurisdiction during the early colonial period (Singha 1998: 137 sq.). On the basis of court documents, this author shows how a major issue emerging from the cases she studied was an attempt to narrow the public dimension of certain norms of moral regulation by relegating them to the sphere of the domestic and personal. The shifts in the commitments and priorities of the colonial and post-colonial state had a significant bearing on what would be counted as a criminal act. Singha notes that the colonial state wanted to 'communicate the idea that the criminal act affected the interests of all, i.e. the public interest which the state represented, and punishment would be meted out in those terms' (Singha 1998: ix). While the colonial state excluded some issues from the criminal process or therein assigned them secondary status, the post-colonial policy has gradually further extended the category of 'crime' to encompass a number of social or gender discriminations. Therefore, since the 1980s in particular, a number of Acts, for instance regarding narcotics, caste atrocity, and violence against women, have been passed which have officially criminalized practices and some relationships that were previously culturally approved (or tolerated) and legitimated by law.

The chapters in this volume highlight the different contrasting dynamics in the way this legislation is concretely and even strategically implemented in court. In the case of the Narcotics Drug and Psychotropic Substances Act, for example, the state's attempt to enforce legislation provokes opposition from villagers who defend their cannabis-related practices as their cultural right to assert their traditional multiform domestic use. This cultural argument may also adopt an ideological tone and turn into criticism of the state's inefficacity to propose an alternative for villagers' economic subsistence. The state's efforts to enforce drug legislation are explicitly or implicitly challenged here. However, it would be reductive to interpret these challenges in terms of a simplistic form of opposition between the state/urban elite and village/ rural people: firstly, because the economic stakes in narcotic practices in certain regions concern many different people—from villagers to the international mafia network, and even corrupt state representatives (police, land officers, and sometimes even legal professionals); secondly, because the Court may provide an arena for expressing contrasting social dynamics—of both corporatism and antagonism. In fact, the idea that a criminal case may be falsely registered to settle a village dispute is commonly suggested by both villagers and judicial professionals (Berti, in this volume).

The manipulation of the law by plaintiffs appears to be a common aspect of the colonial and pre-colonial period, which according to Cohn (1955) and Benton (2002: 135) would be due to the existence of a plural legal landscape and to the tactical possibilities that such a legal plurality offered. This plurality of choice also occurs within the state system where people navigate within state law, between civil and criminal sections (Sharafi 2010). However, what seems to characterize the current situation is the multiplication and diversification of mediators between state and non-state institutions that contribute to translating the plaintiff's issue and framing social facts into official legal texts (Chatterjee 2004; Eckert 2006). A number of actors take part in transforming the voices of litigants, reformulating accounts to satisfy the requirements of legal categories, and exploring alternative parallel options among official legal provisions. Apart from lawyers who put the law at the service of a wide variety of groups in society (Galanter 1972), court professionals, police officers, NGOs, feminist groups, and mediator counsellors experiment with legal provisions, determining the form strategic negotiations take, legitimating 'competing constructions of reality through which the conflict may be expressed' (Comaroff and Roberts, in Rosen 2008:18). The court's decision about the case may be based on the specific section that has been chosen to frame the case and on the judge's personal attitude towards that section (Basu, in this volume).

The question of the 'reputation' under which a law is submitted particularly emerges in the case of the 'Scheduled Castes and Scheduled Tribes (Prevention of) Atrocity Act' which is often presented in upper-caste court milieus as being misused. According to this discourse, the Act would be used by Dalits as a way of exerting pressure on a member of an upper caste or of having him arrested immediately by filing a false case against him. The idea of being involved in a false case is commonly used in court as a defence strategy and Dalits themselves use this argument when they are involved in cases filed against them. However, as the case presented by Jaoul in this volume shows, victims may be persuaded to look for an out-of-court compromise in order to settle the case, paradoxically making the court a site of resistance against the anti-discriminatory legislation that it is supposed to implement.

These examples show how judicial procedure has to contend with social dynamics.[7] However, as presented in the next section, law also constitutes a crucial modality of participation in state governance, reconciling the legislative process and the activism of civil society representatives.

Law and the Public Sphere

Legal reforms in South Asia have led to vibrant debates and discussions among litigators, legal practitioners such as police officers, judges, and lawyers, civil society institutions, and political leaders. The dialogue that has emerged around legal and constitutional processes has a long history in South Asia and can most recently be located in efforts towards writing a new constitution in Nepal; judicial activism in Pakistan; law reform in India, Public Interest Litigation, and the passing of new legislation have been motivated to a large extent by the efforts of social movements. The dialogue, political activities, and the relationships that have been formed around the law and practices of legality have led to the constitution of public spheres.

The Habermasian notion of a public sphere—where people come together to engage in rational critical dialogue and where a person's argument rather than their social position determines the course of dialogue—has been assessed in several ways, particularly in terms of who has access and can participate in the public sphere (Frazer 1990; Warner 2005). The way in which scholars have critically engaged in a Habermasian notion of the public sphere raises two sets of questions about the publics that are constituted around legal processes in South Asia. The first set concerns those who have access and can take part in these publics. How do people develop the competencies to become involved in debates and discussions around legal and constitutional reform? Who ends up excluded from these forms of engagement? The second set of questions pertains to how new ideas and dialogues that emerge from the implementation of laws, Supreme Court directives, or constitutional amendments circulate and are revised in different localities. How do people revise and resist new ideas, particularly those that criminalize existing social practices? How does constitutional law and judgments passed by higher-level courts impact practices at police stations and district courts, and the attitudes of legal practitioners, political leaders, litigators, and litigants?

The themes and issues that emerged around the protests following the gang rape of a girl on a bus in December 2012 shed light on the link between social movements and the law. During these protests, men and women came together to demand stricter laws pertaining to violence against women, specifically reforms in the rape law and better implementation of the law. Along with an overwhelming turnout at public protests, a large number of citizens were actively involved in debates both during the protests and on the internet, in newspapers, on the television, and radio about intricacies of the rape law and its implementation, the death penalty, marital rape, and women's safety in the city. The language and ideas about legal reform that accompanied these protests are rooted in the campaign, protests, and advocacy of the women's movement since the 1980s that has addressed the laws and legal practices legitimizing women's subordination. Over the last three to four decades, women's groups have campaigned for the revision of laws or advocated for new laws pertaining to crimes against women, including rape, sati, dowry, domestic violence, and sexual harassment at the workplace. The social mobilization and campaigns around legal reform set a precedent and created a discourse in the public sphere about violence against women and gender inequality, which shaped the contours of the debates and dialogues around the 2012–2013 protests and the events that led to the passing of new anti-rape laws.

Within the women's movement there has been a vibrant debate about whether focusing on mobilization around legal reform enables the participation of women from different backgrounds. For example, critics have noted that the anti-rape protests in Delhi in 2012 were limited to the concerns of women in urban areas and that forms of political action were not framed in ways that address sexual violence faced by lower-caste, Dalit, and tribal women. These criticisms point to broader questions and issues: whether focusing on legal reforms restricts participation in the public sphere; the actual efficacy of implementing progressive legislation; and whether the latter can be applied to other social movements. In the context of the Dalit movement and the environmental protection movement, scholars have shown how the centrality of legal reform and court activism restricts people's engagement in the public sphere and also co-opts political activism into the agenda of the liberal state (Rao 2009; Sundar 2009; Sivaramakrishnan 2011). Some of these scholars have simultaneously noted how legal reforms have changed the discourse in the public sphere and how a larger number of people now participate in protests, campaigns, and the making, passing, and implementation of the law (Sundar 2009; Sivaramakrishnan 2011).

As mentioned above, in this volume, Jaoul describes the interactions and networks between Dalit activists, Dalit lawyers, and judges with respect to the Scheduled Caste and Scheduled Tribe Prevention of Atrocities Act. While the conviction rate of those accused under this act may be low, the political mobilization and social activism around cases that are being tried under the Atrocities Act provide a momentum for Dalit activism. For example, Jaoul notes how local activists encourage villagers to file complaints and ensure that the police record them so that the offenders can be challenged in court. Furthermore, activists link specific cases of atrocities against Dalits to the demands made during protests that include dharnas (sit-ins) and gheraos or sequestering lower-level courts. Litigators are often integrated into the movement and in some cases they assist Dalit lawyers. Jaoul's contribution shows how ideas and discourses pertaining to atrocities against Dalits that animate court interactions are then channelled through the networks and associations that are formed between activists, police officers, and lawyers. This process is facilitated when Dalit activists themselves become lawyers and by the presence of Dalit judges.

While cases involving atrocities against Dalits provide a moral dimension that enables a particular kind of mobilization around the 'atrocity' category, the focus of cases pertaining to violence against women is often about charting the best course of action that will ensure institutional and family support for individual cases. In the wake of legal reforms pertaining to violence against women, government and non-government organizations, activists, and ad-hoc groups have emerged, which may or may not be associated with the women's movement, and which address family disputes and cases of violence against women. Individuals linked to these organizations mediate between disputants and legal practitioners at the police station and at court. Basu's contribution demonstrates how a range of organizations in Calcutta, whether affiliated to the then ruling left party or to autonomous women's groups, assist women by providing counselling services and, as mentioned above, strategizing on how to address cases most effectively by drawing on both criminal and civil law. For years, the rule of the Communist Party of India (Marxist) in West Bengal created a situation where the concerns and commitments of women's groups were shaped by the priorities and commitments of the CPI (M) (Ray 1998). Basu shows that organizations which provided mediation services for people at court were often either directly linked to the CPI (M) or were able to draw on resources and connections with party members in order to assist disputants. However, together with party ideologies, the circulation of the ideas underlying legal reforms regarding violence against women, for example criminalizing domestic violence, was also crucial to informing the everyday practices and strategies employed by various organizations that assisted women in the court (Basu in this volume).

Legal reforms and constitutional amendments have led to a circulation of new ideas and concepts in the public sphere. The activities of social movements, lawyers' movements, NGOs, and political parties provide networks and channels of communication that facilitate how new ideas circulate and are employed by different institutions. For example, Redding demonstrates how the Supreme Court in Pakistan responded positively to litigation prepared by a group of lawyers and concerned individuals who sought to protect the rights of transgendered individuals. The terms used to describe these individuals changed from the more colloquial term 'hijra' used in the report following the police raid to the more gender-neutral term 'unix' in the Supreme Court petition. The shifts in terminology impacted the groups of people who were actually categorized as 'hijra' and 'unix,' thereby also changing the meaning and political implications of what these terms imply. Redding's contribution demonstrates how the languages and ideas of the state and the law revise and re-shape the meaning of concepts and terms in ways that may not have been previously anticipated by social movements.

The contributions to this volume also demonstrate how new concepts and languages that emerge from the Supreme Court and constitutional directives are interpreted locally, and how criminal cases also become an arena where actors resist new state policies and constitutional directives. Letizia's contribution about a person accused under the Arms and Ammunition Act in Nepal, and who was also suspected of being a part of a Hindu fundamentalist underground association, is framed in a larger context of ideas emerging from a newly declared secular state. The direction that the case took was shaped by the ways in which right-wing Hindu groups mobilized public sentiments of fear among some members of the Hindu majority who were also uncertain about what secularism entails. Letizia shows how these sentiments of fear were articulated by police officers and lawyers who admired the courage of the person accused in standing up to the policies of the secular state, thereby leading to a light sentence, given the nature of the evidence produced.

All the contributions in this volume in some way demonstrate how criminal cases shape public opinion. The discourse around a criminal case reflects existing ideas in the public sphere and a case can also shape the ideas and languages around specific issues. The manner in which a criminal case leads to the formation of public opinion around new issues or reinforces widely held biases and prejudices depends on two inter-related factors. First, activists, lawyers, and judges are able to use political ideology and public commitments arising out of new laws and constitutional directives to build networks and public opinion around a particular case, which often shapes the direction the latter takes. Second, police officers, lawyers, and judges reflect widely held biases and prejudice regarding gender, caste, and religion. They use their authority to resist and to revise the issues arising from specific cases and legal practices, and court documents can reinforce existing biases and prejudice. There is therefore a disjuncture between, on the one hand, the ideas and values underlying new laws, constitutional amendments, and state policies, and on the other hand, histories of accumulated institutional practices and the training and preparation of police officers, lawyers, and judges.

Mediation and the Production of Authority

The contributions to this volume reveal how there is a discrepancy between the legal procedures outlined for example in the Code of Criminal Procedure and the Indian Penal Code and 'law as process' or the everyday practices of different legal institutions. This discrepancy manifests itself in the ways in which local realities, community norms, individual concerns, and histories of accumulated institutional practices motivate each stage of the legal procedure. Negotiation and mediation between, on the one hand, police officers, lawyers, and magistrates and on the other hand legal practitioners characterize legal practices; for example, the way in which local leaders exercise control over how to police officers gather evidence and register a case, or how activists instruct disputants on what kind of testimony they should deliver in court. The contributions in this volume refer to how legal practitioners in different regions of South Asia explain to ethnographers how and why negotiation is an unavoidable aspect of the legal procedure. In some instances they refer to the constraints they face in their work as a result of the deficiencies and glitches in the ways institutions work. In other cases legal practitioners assert that communities and various groups of people are incapable of adhering to the legal procedure, for example, by not providing adequate evidence and testimony.

Legal practice that consists of negotiation is commonly viewed as a corruption of the ideals of the law and of the proper legal procedure where unmediated face-to-face interaction between legal practitioners and disputants is seen to ensure impartial fact finding, evidence gathering, and passing a verdict. In India the practice of relying on local leaders and community-based institutions for everyday governance has been central to forms of state-making since the colonial period. Colonial officers relied on village panchayats, landlords, and headmen for governing communities that were seen as vast and impenetrable. These forms of everyday governance varied from one region to another and depended on specific conceptions of people and place. For example, in his work on jungle mahals or the frontier regions of Bengal, Sivaramakrishnan (1999) demonstrates how the colonial state drew on a 'discourse of frontiers', depicting certain areas as intractable and 'zones of anomaly' that shaped ideas of intransigence and difficult-to-administer places in order to justify relying on headmen and landlords for everyday governance. Such analyses reveal how mediation and negotiation, rather than an aberrant or anomalous ruptures to otherwise rule-bound practices, were crucial to state-making practices during the colonial period.

Local leaders, middle men, and activists milling around the police station and the court perform a number of different roles. Mediators bring different parties to the police station and the court, confer with police officers and lawyers, and carry information back and forth between legal practitioners and litigators. They make the law accessible; they are capable of bending legal procedures; they act as go-betweens explaining the intricacies of a case to the police and lawyers; and they translate and simplify the law and legal procedures for disputants. Local leaders and activists who act on behalf of disputants organize meetings between legal practitioners and litigants, strategize about the best course of action, and they prepare and train people, including witnesses, on how to respond to lawyers in court. These leaders also facilitate negotiations in and around the police station before a case is registered, and during the trial's proceedings they may facilitate out-of-court agreements or may attempt to coax the accused into pleading guilty. In some cases what is at stake for disputants are the networks and associations that emerge during the interactions and negotiations between leaders and legal practitioners, rather than the court verdict or achieving justice.

Social scientists have pointed to the intentions of local leaders, middle men, brokers, fixers, and 'big men' who assist people in accessing resources, negotiating with state officials and legal practitioners, and in addressing neighbourhood and village disputes (Hansen 2001; Eckert 2004). These leaders wield power and influence in their communities and often draw on their vast network of connections and associations at critical moments, for example at the time of elections. The contributions to this volume demonstrate similar intentions among leaders who become involved in the work of mediation in the context of legal institutions. Bordia's analysis (Chapter 6 in this volume) of the events around a murder case among Girassia tribals in Southern Rajasthan demonstrates how tribal leaders assist villagers involved in a case in order to gain authority in villages. Tribal leaders gain visibility by establishing associations and networks with other leaders in different villages and by demonstrating their connections with police officers and lawyers. Therefore, the direction that a case takes depends on whether tribal leaders are willing and successful in undertaking negotiations with other tribal leaders, panchayat leaders (or leaders of the village council), and legal practitioners. As mentioned above, Jaoul and Basu reveal different processes around mediation and negotiation pertaining to progressive legislation for Dalits and women respectively. In such instances, activists and social workers draw on litigation to mobilize people around issues of violence against women and atrocities against Dalits and involve litigants in wider social movements.

In some cases in the South Asian context, police officers, lawyers, and judges also often perform the role of mediation. Headley (Chapter 7 in this volume) demonstrates the case against panchayattars or panchayat leaders who were accused of meting out unfair punishment to a woman in the context of a matrimonial dispute. The judge did not convict the panchayattars but condemned their practice in the harshest terms. He also convinced the woman to withdraw her case against her husband and in-laws. Headley reports that while reflecting on the court proceedings, the judge stated that he conducted a panchayat between the husband and wife by making them reach a compromise. By describing the court proceeding as a panchayat, the judge echoed popular ideas that are reflected in short stories, films, and other descriptions of village life, where panchayat leaders understand their community, personally know disputants, mediate between the people involved in a dispute, and above all attempt to arrive at a compromise in order to ensure village harmony. Such forms of justice are perceived as different from state law where the focus is on objectivity; the judge delivers a verdict, and there are winners and losers. When judges describe court practices or verdicts as 'panchayati justice', they justify mediation and compromise within the courtroom and deviation from statutory legal practice by evoking forms of justice that are often represented as the ideals of community life in India as in the case above. In other instances, commentators have used the phrase 'panchayati justice' to condemn a particular verdict as partial and catering to the sentiments of specific communities.[8]

The forms of mediation that are associated with a criminal case depend on popular perceptions about different legal systems and how various communities are seen to access either state law or non-state law. Cases outlined in this volume reveal how legal practitioners believe that particular groups of people are incapable of providing sufficient evidence, of adhering to court procedure, and are better governed through their own customs and panchayat institutions as the latter are more equipped to understand the sentiments of a community. Litigators often believe that police and court practices are dense and complicated and that they can only navigate these procedures with the assistance of mediators and community-based leaders.

Contributions in this volume demonstrate that legal practitioners describe their work in terms of ideas of objectivity, impartiality, neutrality, and equality. And yet, they claim that local constraints and social contexts prevent them from actualizing these values in everyday practices at the police station and the court. Litigators and mediators seldom expect to encounter these ideal values of the law when they access legal institutions. People are well aware that police- and court-specific procedures have been shaped by local history, culture, and politics, and litigators and mediators must attune to these procedures in order to navigate these institutions.

Notes

1. One remarkable exception is the work of Pratiksha Baxi which focuses on the ethnography of rape cases in Gujarat Session courts (Baxi 2014). Jayanth Krishnan recently headed a comparative study on the function of District Courts in three Indian states (Krishnan et al. 2014).

2. Aside from social science literature on Indian justice, there are numerous Indian jurists and university professors of law who regularly publish material in specialized journals devoted to Indian legal studies. The number of socially

committed studies of this kind has recently increased with a number of recent works exploring the social, political, and socio-legal implications of legal texts, judges' decisions or other judicial reports, with the intention of denouncing either social injustice or the dysfunction of the system in order to suggest possible ways of improving it. This commitment to socio-legal activism tends to blur the distinction between jurists and committed social scientists, for instance in debates on a unified civil code versus personal law, or on the reservation policy, gender inequality, human rights, or environmental protection (Sathe 2002; Baxi 1982; Agnes 2004; Larson 2001; Menski 1998).

3. Tag questions are often preceded by a statement that makes the answers almost irrelevant (Conley and O'Barr 2005: 26).

4. Furthermore, the passage from speech to writing is most often a shift from the vernacular language to English, a language that most people involved in the case—the victim, accused, witnesses—do not even understand.

5. Nowadays, the practice of transcribing verbal interactions in court does not seemingly depend on the difference between common law and Romanist procedures as was the case in the past where Romanist procedures stipulated that all the evidence be compiled into a full written report (Shapiro 1981: 38).

6. Similarly to what happens during Anglo-American trials, this implies that when the case goes to appeal everything has to be done all over again (Bouillier in this volume).

7. See Baxi (2003) and Guha (1989). For an historical analysis of these theories see Wardhaugh (2005), Ludden (2001), and Sivaramakrishnan (2008).

8. This was the case when Rajeev Dhawan described the judgment on the Ayodhya issue as 'panchayati justice' as he said that it takes away the legal rights of Muslims and converts the moral sentimental entitlements of Hindus into legal rights.' See http://www.thehindu.com/todays-paper/tp-national/panchayati-justice-that-takes-away-legal-rights-of-muslims-rajeev-dhavan/article805552.ece.

References

Agnes, Flavia. 2004. *Law and Gender Inequality: The Politics of Women's Rights in India*. New Delhi: Oxford University Press.

Anderson, M. R. 1990. 'Classifications and Coercions: Themes in South Asian Legal Studies in the 1980s', *South Asia Research*,10(2): 158–177.

Annoussamy, D. 1996. 'La justice en Inde', *Les cahiers de l'IHEJ*, 3: 1–34.

Atkinson, John M. and Drew, Paul. 1979. *Order in Court: The Organization of Verbal Interaction in Judicial Settings*. London: Macmillan.

Baxi, Pratiksha. 2014. *Public Secrets of Law: Rape Trials in India*. New Delhi: Oxford University Press.

Baxi, Upendra. 1982. *The Crisis of Indian Legal System*. New Delhi: Vikas Publishing House.

———. 2003. 'The Colonialist Heritage', in P. L. Munday and R. Munday (eds), *Comparative Legal Studies: Traditions and Transitions*, pp. 46–75. Cambridge: Cambridge University Press.

Bauman, R. and Briggs, C.L. 1990. 'Poetics and Performance as Critical Perspectives on Language and Social Life', *Annual Review of Anthropology*, 19: 59–88.

Berti, D. 2011. 'Courts of Law and Legal Practice', in Isabelle Clark-Decès (ed.) *A Companion to the Anthropology of India*, pp. 355–70. Delhi: Blackwell.

Benton, Lauren. 2002. *Law and Colonial Cultures. Legal Regimes in World History, 1400–1900*. New York: Cambridge University Press.

Chang, Y. 2004 'Courtroom Questioning as a Culturally Situated Persuasive Genre of Talk', *Discourse & Society*, 15(6): 705–22.

Chatterjee, Partha. 2004. *The Politics of the Governed: Reflections on Popular Politics in Most of the World*. New York: Columbia University Press.

Cheirézy C. 2009. 'Crainte et dépendance: le pouvoir sur les corps en Toulousain au XIIIe siècle', in Maria Eugenia Albornoz Vasquez, Matteo Giuli and Naoko Seriu (eds) *Les archives judiciaires en question, Centre de recherches historiques*, CRH Electronic Journal, 9 July 2013 (http://acrh.revues.org/1537).

Cohn, B. S. 1987 [1965]. 'Anthropological Notes on Disputes and Law in India'. In Bernard S. Cohn (ed.), *An Anthropologist among the Historians and Other Essays*, pp. 82–122. New Delhi: Oxford University Press.

Cohn, B. S. 1987 [1959]. 'Some Notes on Law and Change in North India', in Bernard S. Cohn (ed.), *An Anthropologist among the Historians and Other Essays*, pp. 79–93. New Delhi: Oxford University Press.

Cohn, E. J. 1955. 'The Board of Review: A Novel Chapter in the Relations between Common Law and Civil Law', *The International and Comparative Law Quarterly*, 4(4): 492–507.

Comaroff, John L, and S. A. Roberts (1981). *Rules and Processes: The Cultural Logic of Dispute in an African Context*. Chicago: University of Chicago Press.

Conley, John M., and O'Barr, William M. 1990. *Rules versus Relationships: The Ethnography of Legal Discourse*. Chicago: University of Chicago Press.

———. 2005 [1998]. *Just Words: Law, Language, and Power*. Chicago: University of Chicago Press.

Das, V. 'Sexual Violence, Discursive Formations and the State', *Economic and Political Weekly*, 31(35/37): 2411–23.

Drew, Paul and Heritage, John. 1992. *Talk at Work: Interactions in Institutional Settings*. Cambridge: Cambridge University Press.

Dupret, Baudouin. 2006. *Le Jugement en action: Ethnométhodologie du droit, de la morale et de la justice en Égypte*. Geneva: Librairie Droz.

Eckert, J. 2004. 'Urban Governance and Emergent Forms of Legal Pluralism in Mumbai', *Journal of Legal Pluralism*, 50: 29–60.

Eckert, J. 2006. 'From Subjects to Citizens: Legalism from Below and the Homogenisation of the Legal Sphere', *Journal of Legal Pluralism*, 53–4: 45–75.

Farge, A. and Cerutti, S. 2009. 'Introduction' in Maria Eugenia Albornoz Vasquez, Matteo Giuli and Naoko Seriu (eds). *Les archives judiciaires en question, L'Atelier du Centre de recherches historiques*. CRH Electronic Journal, Accessed at http://acrh.revues.org/1476 on 9 July 2013.

Farge, Arlette. 2011. *Un ruban et des larmes. Un procès en adultère au XVIIIe siècle.* Paris: Éditions des Busclats.

Frazer, N. 1990. 'Rethinking the Public Sphere: A Contribution to the Critique of Actually Existing Democracy', *Social Text*, 25/26: 56–80.

Freitag, S. B. 1991. 'Crime in the Social Order of Colonial North India', *Modern Asian Studies*, 25(2): 227–61.

Galanter, M. 1972. 'The Aborted Restoration of 'Indigenous' Law in India', *Comparative Studies in Society and History*, 14(1): 53–70.

Galanter, M. and U. Baxi. 1979. 'Panchayat Justice: An Indian Experiment in Legal Access, in Mauro Cappelletti and Bryant Garth (eds), *Access to Justice, Vol. 3: Emerging Issues and Perspectives*. Milan: Guiffre.

Galanter, Marc and Khosla, Dinesh. 1987. *Myth and Reality of the Protection of Civil Rights Law: A Case of Untouchability in Rural India*. Delhi: Hindustan.

Galanter, M. and Krishnan, J.K. 2004. 'Bread for the Poor: Access to Justice and the Rights for the Needy in India', *Hastings Law Journal*, 55: 789–834.

Garnier, G. 2009. 'Le recours aux archives judiciaires pour étudier les habitudes de sommeil', in Maria Eugenia Albornoz Vasquez, Matteo Giuli and Naoko Seriu (eds), *L'Atelier du Centre de recherches historiques* CRH Electronic Journal, accessed at http://acrh.revues.org/1554 on 9 July 2013.

Ginzburg, Carlo. 1983. *The Night Battles: Witchcraft & Agrarian Cults in the Sixteenth & Seventeenth Centuries*. Baltimore, Md.: Johns Hopkins University Press.

Giuliani, F. 2009. 'L'écriture du crime : L'inceste dans les archives judiciaires françaises (1791–1898)', in Maria Eugenia Albornoz Vasquez, Matteo Giuli and Naoko Seriu (eds), *L'Atelier du Centre de recherches historiques*. CRH Electronic Journal, accessed at http://acrh.revues.org/1582 on 9 July 2013.

Gnisci, A. and Pontecorvo. C. 2004. 'The Organization of Questions and Answers in the Thematic Phases of Hostile Examination: Turn-by-Turn Manipulation of Meaning', *Journal of Pragmatics*, 36: 965–95.

———. 2004. *Ecstasies: Deciphering the Witches' Sabbath*. Chicago: University of Chicago Press.

Guha, R. 1989. 'Dominance without Hegemony and its Historiography', in R. Guha (ed.), *Subaltern Studies VI: Writings on South Asian History and Society*, pp. 210–309. Oxford: Oxford University Press.

Krieken, R.V. 'Law's Autonomy in Action: Anthropology and History in Court', *Social & Legal Studies* 15(4): 574–90.

Krishnan, J. K., Kavadi, S.N., Girach, A., Khupkar, D., Kokal, K., Mazumdar, S., Nupur, G., Panday, A., Sen, A., Sodhi, and Takale Shukla, B. 2014. 'Grappling at the Grassroots: Litigant-Efforts to Access Economic and Social Rights in India', *Harvard Human Rights Journal*, 27.

Hansen, Thomas B. 2001. *Wages of Violence: Naming and Identity in Postcolonial Bombay*. Princeton: Princeton University Press.

Hansen, Thomas B. and Stepputat, Finn (eds). 2001. *States of Imagination: Ethnographic Explorations of the Postcolonial State*. Durham and London: Duke University Press.

Hayden, R. M. 1984. 'A Note on Caste Panchayats and Government Courts in India: Different Kinds of Stages for Different Kinds of Performances', *Journal of Legal Pluralism*, (22): 43–52.

Hirsch Susan F. 1998. *Pronouncing & Persevering: Gender and the Discourses of Disputing in an African Islamic Court*. Chicago: The University of Chicago Press.

Rakshak. 2013. Fighting Barriers to Justice and Equality. An Investigative Report. Accessed at http://www.498a.org/contents/Publicity/498aBooklet.pdf on 22 July 2013.

Lazarus-Black, M. and Hirsch, Susan F. (eds). 2010. *Contested States: Law, Hegemony and Resistance*. New York, London: Routledge.

Larson, G. J. (ed.). 2001. *Religion and Personal Law in Secular India: A Call to Judgment*. Bloomington: Indiana University Press.

Ludden D. (ed.). 2001. *Reading Subaltern Studies: Critical History, Contested Meaning, and the Globalisation of South Asia*. New Delhi: Permanent Black.

Marcus, Robert, and Marcus, Anthony (eds). 2006. *On Trial: American History through Court Proceedings and Hearings II*. New York: Brandywine Press.

Matoesian, Gregory M. 1993. *Reproducing Rape: Domination through Talk in the Courtroom*. Chicago: University of Chicago Press.

Menski, W. (ed.). 1998. *South Asians and the Dowry Problem*. New Delhi: Vistaar.

Moore, Erin P. 1998. *Gender, Law, and Resistance in India*, Tucson: University of Arizona Press.

O'Barr, William M. 1982. *Linguistic Evidence: Language, Power and Strategy in the Courtroom*. New York: Academic Press.

Philips, S. U. 1998. *Ideology in the Language of Judges: How Judges Practice Law, Politics, and Courtroom Control*. New York: Oxford University Press.

Ray, R. 1998. 'Women's Movements and Political Fields: A Comparison of Two Indian Cities', *Social Problems*, 45(1): 21–36.

Rao, Anupama. 2009. *The Caste Question: Dalits and the Politics of Modern India*. Berkeley, Los Angeles, and London: The University of California Press.

Rosen, Laura. 2008. *Law as Culture: An Invitation*. Princeton: Princeton University Press.

Richland, Justine B. 2008. *Arguing with Tradition: The Language of Law in Hopi Tribal Court*. Chicago: University of Chicago Press.

Sathe, Satyaranjan P. 2002. *Judicial Activism in India: Transgressing Borders and Enforcing Limits*. New Delhi: Oxford University Press.

Sharafi, M., 2010. 'The Marital Patchwork of Colonial South Asia: Forum Shopping from Britain to Barod', *Law and History Review*, 28(4): 979–1009.

Shapiro, Martin M. 1981. *Courts: A Comparative and Political Analysis*. Chicago: The University of Chicago Press.

Singha, R. 1996. 'Making the Domestic More Domestic: Criminal Law and the "Head of the Household", 1772–1843', *Indian Economic Social History Review*, 33(3): 309–43.

Singha, Radhika. 1998. *A Despotism of Law: Crime and Justice in Early Colonial India*. Oxford: Oxford University Press.

Sivaramakrishnan, K. 1999. *Modern Forests: Statemaking and Environmental Change in Colonial Eastern India*. Stanford, California: Stanford University Press.

———. 2008. 'Some Intellectual Genealogies for the Concept of Everyday Resistance', *American Anthropologist*, 107(3): 346–55.

——— 2011. 'Environment, Law and Democracy in India', *The Journal of Asian Studies*, 70(4): 905–25.

Stiles, Erin E. 2009. *An Islamic Court in Context: An Ethnographic Study of Judicial Reasoning*. New York: Palgrave MacMillan.

Wardhaugh J. 2005 'The Jungle and the Village: Discourses on Crime and Deviance in Rural North India', *South Asia Research*, 25(2): 129–40.

Srinivas, M. N. 1964. *A Study of Disputes*. Delhi: University of Delhi.

Sundar, Nandini. 2009. *Legal Grounds: Natural Resources, Identity and the Law in Jharkhand*. New Delhi: Oxford University Press.

Svongoro, Paul. 2011. *Linguistic Features of Courtroom Discourse: A Zimbabwean Study*. Saarbruücken: Lambert.

Warner, Michael. 2005. *Publics and Counterpublics*. New York: Zone Books.

Yang, A.A. 2003. 'Indian Convict Workers in Southeast Asia in the Late Eighteenth and Early Nineteenth Centuries', *Journal of World History*, 14(2): 179–208.

1

SRIMATI BASU[*]

'3 punishments for 3 mistakes'

Negotiating between Courts, Police, and
Mediation in Family Law and Family
Violence

In the summer of 2006, the World Cup in Germany was the subject
of many intense conversations in Kolkata, where football is an excep-
tionally passionate way of life. The Kolkata Family Court was no exception. France's loss in the World Cup Final was commonly attributed to a
penalty brought on by superstar Zenedine Zidane's aggressive headbutt
(allegedly in response to an Italian player's racial slur). Zidane's poor
impulse control led him to lose sight of the big picture. 'You've played it
excellently like Zidane, so far; don't ruin everything at the end like him,'
Family Court 'counselor'[1] Sudha advised her enraged client Shibaji.
Shibaji, agitated about getting back with his wife and children, also had
a flair for melodramatic language: '*Tintey bhuler tintey shaja, bishshash
korey chchilam boley 498, bhalobeshe chilam boley 125,*' he declaimed. My
translation—'[These are] 3 punishments for three mistakes I made: 498

* This chapter draws on the author's ethnographic work published in
part as *The Trouble with Marriage: Feminists Confront Law and Violence in India*
(Oakland: University of California Press and Delhi: Orient Blackswan, 2015).

because I trusted her, 125 because I loved her'—does little to convey the perfect rendition of his film hero speech and performative pitch.[2] Having slapped his wife in the court corridor after the last hearing for alimony in the presence of several witnesses, thereby potentially turning the legal case against him, he had merited scolding from the counselor who was trying to get him a favorable reception from the judge.[3] He was defending himself by citing the multiple legal fora within which he felt himself to be cornered.

Significant here is Shibaji's reference to some of the common legal nodes approached by people encountering problems with family law and domestic violence: the controversial Section 498A of the Indian Penal Code (IPC) pertains to 'domestic torture', while Section 125 of the Criminal Procedure Code pertains to maintenance for some categories of relatives in penury. Along with S304 of the IPC pertaining to dowry related crimes, the former is a criminal matter managed by police and criminal prosecutors. The latter is a criminal provision, but is most often deployed in divorce or separation cases, in lower-level civil courts or in special set-aside Family Courts dealing with civil family law, alongside maintenance awards falling solely under civil law. Shibaji was also involved in a divorce dispute, managed by the Family Court, and a custody claim in the same court.

Counselor Sudha and litigant Shibaji's interactions exemplify the ways in which performance is foregrounded in formulating legal strategies related to family law and family violence. But most significant for our purposes here is Shibaji's reply about the three punishments and mistakes to demonstrate the multiple, often dissonant, levels negotiated by litigants in Family Law. These include formal and informal legal norms, civil, and criminal laws, mediators of various persuasions, and sanctions of varying authority. Notably, the affect and performance surrounding the conflict—the couple's anger and frustration, the counselor's scolding, the judge's reprimand—draw much substance from the confusion and contradiction surrounding the multiple charges. As Shibaji's iteration of the number 'three' indicates, pluralities are routine in the ways potential clients are urged to progress: ideally by leverage of temporalities, differences in criminal enforceability, and sanction, and monetary settlements (monthly alimony or lumpsum) depending on the perceived strength of the case.

When trouble breaks out in a marriage, I observed,[4] people choose a number of different strategies based on the resolutions sought, and the relative power and influence of the two families involved, including their access to community and political organizations. Based on the advice they get, they must then navigate between invariably difficult choices based on the economic and social outcomes they deem preferable. Typically, solutions explicitly weigh formal and informal, civil and criminal, and social options against each other, in recognition of their contradictions and limitations. Litigants then play off existent civil and criminal provisions to optimize socioeconomic bargains. However, moving between available sites is not a mere instrumental manipulation of legal provisions; through their choices, litigants also shape the meanings of violation and harm, often differently than envisaged in formal legal intent. These manoeuvres, in other words, exemplify not just the 'weak' legal pluralism of the availability of parallel adjudicatory fora, but 'strong' legal pluralism in the sense that people make complex and strategic choices about courts and their alternatives by weighing cultural tradeoffs (Engel 1980; Merry 1988; Williams 2006). In particular, in the cases from legal and quasi-legal venues of marriage and domestic violence mediations followed in this chapter, violence is either elided in order to preserve marriage for social and economic security, or contrarily, evoked deliberately in order to enforce economic settlements. While legal provisions open up new possibilities for strategies and subjectivities, they generate systemic difficulties of preventing routine violence and enforcing post-divorce maintenance awards.

The following cases delineate some of the contradictions and tradeoffs involved in these choices. The first two sections describe informal and quasi-legal venues, with varying degrees of access to the power of the State. Here, domestic violence is acknowledged, but used as currency in the terrain of negotiation, without being the focus of action. In the latter two sites of formal enforcement, of criminal and civil law respectively, domestic violence is readily treated as an available (if disapproved) strategy for settling economic issues in marriage, rather than as a gendered crime. It is typically ignored or treated with suspicion, and rendered invisible in working out economic and residential contracts.

Combating Domestic Violence: Law and Mediation

Violence against women, notably custodial rape and domestic violence (often connected to dowry) was a central organizing force of the Indian women's movement especially in the 1980s, reflected both in feminist writing and in innovative public actions and legislative demands (Gangoli 2007; Kumar 1993; Menon 2004). The foundational report *Towards Equality: Report of Committee on the Status of Women in India* prepared for the UN Decade of Women, authored by many academics and activists who were part of the women's movement, both echoes and institutionalizes this force: the strong indictment of the patrilineal family as generative of violence against women, related to women's lack of access to economic and cultural resources (CSWI 1974) was pursued later in several State directives (Gopalan 2001). The institutions profiled in this chapter (laws against domestic violence, Women's Grievance Cells, Family Courts) are all shaped by that influence, if also by trends of alternate dispute resolution and NGOs as a mode of service delivery. This chapter, in tracing some of the crises and contradictions that have emerged in enforcing and institutionalizing these changes, echoes the analyses of other scholars who have examined the effects of feminist legal reform (Hautzinger 2007; Lazarus-Black 2007; Rajan 2003).

In cases of emergent marital problems, people often start by involving extended kin to draw attention to any trouble (including violence or harassment) and warn or shame the parties into early modification. They then seek other informal solutions like approaching organizations that function as fictive kin, including neighborhood associations, local branches of political organizations, non-governmental organizations (which may nonetheless function through political networks), or autonomous women's organizations. Civil courts are approached at a much later stage, most often to negotiate questions of alimony before, during, or after divorce; families may engage lawyers in this process, but are also encouraged by Family Courts legislation to frame their issues in their own words and work out matters directly with judges through counselors.

Domestic violence complaints, commonly evoked in marriage troubles, follow related and sometimes contradictory paths. Beyond family or community negotiation, and the mention of violence in the course of civil divorce proceedings as grounds of cruelty (in seeking alimony, separation, or divorce), there are also several criminal law options. These typically include making a GD or 'General Diary' at the local police station as a way of creating a track record of the complaint (this requires no investigation or corroboration), approaching a Women's Grievance Cell in a police station to make a complaint about domestic violence and/or dowry recovery under S498A (which might well lead to a mediated financial settlement rather than a criminal case), or more recently, going to Protection Officers who administer the Domestic Violence Act (PWDVA 2005) and are able to work out civil remedies including property and residence options. When engaging facets of the State with varying financial and carceral punitive sanctions, or involving feminist or political organizations in intimate family negotiations, people are expected to have some recognition of the valences and hence the possible social outcomes.

Section 498A of the Indian Penal Code is the most direct provision for addressing domestic violence and criminalizes 'cruelty,' including physical violence and mental harassment such as dowry demands or other psychological forms of intimidation. An expansive provision enacted in 1985, it emerged from feminist mobilization against murders and suicides connected to family violence, and is stern in its punitive scope: it allows for extended family (not just husbands) to be held accountable for violence, and holds offences to be non-bailable, non-compoundable (cannot be withdrawn by the petitioner), and cognizable (police are bound to investigate). Complaints under S498A have carried exceptional public notoriety and been the focus of ire for many men's groups, alleged to be excuses for leveraging large alimony settlements given the threat of imprisonment of husbands and extended family under the provisions of the Act, thus convenient tools for avenging wives. Alongside hegemonic notions of domestic violence as minor conjugal conflict, and marriage as the optimal social location with or without violence, judges, police, and mediators are thus often loath to enforce the punitive provisions of S498A. As the following sections demonstrate, they are more likely to use the potential charges to negotiate marital reconciliation or financial settlement. Litigants are carried along in this process as well. 'Cruelty' has thus emerged as an overdetermined legal category that both highlights domestic violence, and helps deflect its sanctions.

The range of institutions delineated above is meant to facilitate people's direct access to law, but Rayna's case illustrates the difficulties of doing so without a concerted strategy. Rayna was highly unusual in going to the police and asking to make a GD of the violence she was facing in the extended family, that is, to document it for future use. The officers told her they would not pursue the matter as a S498A domestic violence case, though they did not explain why: it was unclear whether

the husband's family's political influence was in play here, or whether
a woman showing up by herself at the police station without an
organizational representative accompanying her made the difference.
Dissatisfied with this outcome, Rayna took the extraordinary solution
of finding a lawyer herself, who drafted a S156.3 petition, asking for
the lower-level civil court to initiate a case, and obtained a court order
directing the police to investigate. But this move seemed to have landed
her in a legal situation so complicated that the mediation organization
was holding a special late strategy session for her. Rayna recounted to
the mediators that she had married against her parents' wishes, with no
wedding costs or dowry. After they mended this rift, her husband often
asked his in-laws (through her) for money to fund various projects,
which had added up to Rs 4 or 5 lakhs from her father. She reported
much physical violence both within the nuclear unit, and in an extended
household with his brother's family.

Suraha, the organization she had sought out, founded by a prominent member of the then ruling Left Party, was often able to marshal
political connections and resources to help its clients in ways that an
autonomous women's group could not typically do (as the following
section makes clearer). Here, though, the mediator-counselors were
worried about Rayna's case because her lawyer's petition referred only
to coerced and repeated payments (that is, a form of extended dowry
harassment), with no mention of any physical torture or violence. This
was likely an effect of the lawyer having decided that dowry laws were
a more surefire way of pursuing a criminal case than domestic violence
laws, because of the latter's notoriety. But, as one counselor explained
passionately, given the usual police reluctance to prosecute domestic
violence under S498A, the police were unlikely to add an investigation
of violence if not explicitly directed to do so in the petition. He thus
doubted that they would be able to proceed on the question of violence,
even as the group strategized about possible ways to add an amendment
to the S156 petition, and reassured her, 'remember this case is only one
thing, it is not your life, whatever happens with the case, you need to
take care of yourself.' Rayna's case, thus, demonstrates the problems
of pursuing domestic violence as a crime: despite the political clout of
the group from which she sought help, her efforts were thwarted by the
confusion between dowry claims and domestic violence among police
and lawyers, the rigid nature of petitions, and the cultural atmosphere

of suspicion against S498A cases. In other words, her lawyer's strategy reflects the common perception that filing a domestic violence claim directly under S498A case had little success; S498A cases were perceived, rather, as paths to other solutions such as alimony, return of marriage gifts, or reconciliation.

Choosing Paths: Negotiations in Mediation Centres

As alternate dispute resolution methods become increasingly popular, and the boundary between governmental and non-governmental organizations becomes increasingly ambiguous (Sharma 2006), a dizzying array of organizations in Kolkata have taken on mediation, including, for our purposes, marital mediation. Between neighbourhood associations, local branches of political organizations (most prominently in West Bengal, the women's wings called *Mahila Samitys*), non-governmental organizations which function through political networks, or autonomous women's organizations, there may be little commonality in political ideologies, or in connections to the women's movement. However, these organizations work in a 'political field' (Ray 1999) whose discourse is shaped by laws launched in response to (national and global) women's movement demands, including recognition of the criminality of domestic violence and the economic entitlements of women. In the context of West Bengal, organizations associated with almost four decades of the then-ruling Left Front coalition were able to access more resources and influence, if constrained in the kinds of demands they could make and the priority they could assign to gender; autonomous women's organizations, on the other hand, are able to be more critical or radical, but have to strive harder for making their way through the system (Ray 1999).[5]

Nari Nirjaton Pratirodh Mancha ('Forum against Oppression of Women,' most often called *Mancha* or 'Platform/Stage') is a long-standing autonomous women's organization, explicitly feminist, which foregrounds anti-violence work as central to its identity, through public awareness campaigns as well as support and counseling for individual cases. The mediators, largely women with some male allies, come from a range of socioeconomic classes, with occupations ranging from low-level office work to lawyers, professors, and journalists, many of the senior set having had long histories of radical political work. Mediation sessions are held once a week in their offices, where the members of the collective advise clients as a group; as needed, members then accompany clients to police or courts. The organization is committed to centering women's agency in its modes of operation. However, as the following example shows, it may have to set questions of violence strategically aside for more fluid solutions per clients' wishes.

During the weekly counseling session one evening in 2006, Madhumita narrated to the *Mancha* counselors that she had left her marital home in Kolkata without her one year old child, frightened by the behaviour of her husband who allegedly had a 'bipolar mood disorder'. Asked what outcomes she would prefer, she said she wanted to be back with her child, to have some money to live on, and be back in the extended family home despite their collective verbal, financial, and emotional violence and the erratic behavior and impotence of her husband, if only they could be warned to behave a little better. In this case, her parents had initially been loath to get the extended kin to inter-vene, given the greater wealth and connections of her in-laws, and had later tried this with little change. They had also felt hesitant to approach women's wings of the locally powerful political organizations, the most common solution, because her mother-in-law was believed to be a powerful member herself, and had thus come to Mancha because of its reputation for being politically autonomous.

In response, the counselors at Mancha laid out the various facets of the state she could engage, with escalating intensity and consequences: to make a GD at the local police station as a way of creating a track record, to approach a Women's Grievance Cell to file a S498A case, or to file a divorce or maintenance case at the Family Court. The mediators cautioned her, however, that each of those needed to be launched with a precise recognition of the consequences, though they would accom-pany and assist her with each. The subtext here was that bringing an avowed feminist organization to intercede or threatening criminal or civil proceedings might well be perceived by already dissatisfied in-laws as a point of no return. Expressing an urgent feeling to be back in the affinal home before her child's birth day a few days later, Madhumita ended up taking the quickest and most pragmatic step: she simply called her mother-in-law and asked to move back. However, she let the organization know that she would file a GD at the local police station sometime when she was over at her parents', in case they needed a paper trail for a later S498A or divorce case. We had no knowledge of whether she did so, but the message seemed as an indication that she knew her longer-term problems had not been resolved.

Here, civil and criminal venues function as alternate and parallel options. Each is seen in terms of its potential to obtain certain goals: money to live on, access to a child, social respectability. Bringing up violence is a delicate calibration: it carries some social leverage when brought up by women's kin to work out matters without going public, but tips the scales when women's organizations or police or courts are involved. Respectability and shame are emphasized as critical currency for these middle-class families, in contrast to the example in the next section, where problems of providing subsistence are the main source of shame (and domestic violence is prosaically acknowledged). In both, Madhumita's and Rayna's cases, several seemingly woman-friendly options (neighborhood associations, Mahila Samitys) were closed off because of the in-laws' influence, a reminder that some women (here mothers-in-law) may also use community networks to deflect charges of violence. Madhumita's chosen strategy hedged all these options: it took the quickest and least intrusive path (if the least transformative and most dangerous one), while leaving open a formal remedy and the possibility of initiating a criminal record in anticipation of future legal leverage, as well as continuing the relationship with the organization. Rayna, having foregone these networks initially, was more vulnerable to legal jeopardy. In contrast to Madhumita, who seemed to temporarily have found shelter in marriage, Rayna was also socially vulnerable in having stood by her resistance to violence and financial extortion.

Using Violence: Mediation Boards in a 'Family Protection' Centre

Community mediation or *shalishi* purports to offer culturally sensitive and precise solutions while offering efficient alternatives to law. The then-ruling party in West Bengal thus began enthusiastically supporting a wide network of such forums in 2004, promoting them as optimal modes of alternate dispute resolution as well as indigenous forms of mediation.[6] Unlike local adjudicating bodies such as *panchayat*s (Moore 1999) or village *salishes* (Shehabuddin 1999), the new organization profiled in this section was headed by professionals, including several in law enforcement, who often invoked their powers in formal legal realms to design informal solutions. The members negotiated resolutions on matters of women's economic sustenance as well as violence, using the sanctions of criminal law to exert pressure, even though the long-term enforcement of these resolutions remained unclear. However, they worked through paternalistic scripts of gender even as they explicitly attempted to help women, thereby reflecting patterns of patriarchal authority similar reported for *panchayat*s and *salish*es (Moore 1999; Shehabuddin 1999).

At the *Paribarik Paramarsho O Shahayata Kendra* ('Family Advice and Assistance Center' would be a rough translation) in a medium-sized town about an hour from Kolkata, arbitration sessions lasting about 3–4 hours were held every Friday. The unit was actually located inside one of the police posts in the town, advertising the *Mahila Pulish Tadanta Kendra* ('Police Investigative Center for Women');[7] a different police station across town functioned as a Women's Grievance Cell of the kind described in the following section, where criminal complaints were to be investigated. The center profiled here focused on *shalish* or arbitration and sent people off to the other police unit when necessary. As a constable said to an NGO representative who had arrived there with a woman client, '*Ekhaney, jara shongshar korben tader jonyo*' (my translation, 'this place is only for those who want to pursue marriage' does little to capture the sense of *shongshar/sansar* as embodying notions of family, domesticity, worldliness); for registering a complaint she needed to go to the other police station. To approach this unit, thus, is to foreground reconciliation as a putative outcome. While almost every case I observed here dealt with domestic violence, this violence did not even figure in the record-keeping of the local Women's Grievance Cell where criminal complaints were to be lodged. In this town, the two venues involving similar cases and crimes occupied mutually exclusive spaces.

The 'counseling' (their term) board consisted of a local female magistrate (of the lower courts), a male doctor, a female lawyer, the male supervisor of the Center, and the female Officer-in-Charge [OC] of the Cell. The 'board' had been given the authority to summon witnesses and draw up arbitration agreements but had no civil or criminal enforcement authority beyond that. However, given that the OC and a magistrate served on it, they seamlessly invoked these other formal roles during proceedings. The board members sat on a row of chairs behind a wooden screen, across the table from a bench for the couple.

Every other available seat was occupied by family members and even neighbours, and over the top of the screen was a continuous row of heads peering in. In this setting, these families and community members were allowed, indeed encouraged, to attend.[8] This Center, thus, deployed formal legal provisions even as it circumvented them, and deliberately incorporated community sanctions and surveillance to extend its reach.

Domestic violence allegations were often front-and-center in women's complaints here, not merely obliquely evoked as part of legal strategy as described in later sections. Nor was the violence contested by the accused or their families. The counselors/arbitrators also took the violence seriously, perhaps because denial was impossible. The formal position was to condemn it in the strongest terms and emphasize its criminal nature. And yet, while their solutions contained provisions to reduce violence, the focus was on social and economic solutions, which the professed outrage and sanctions against violence helped enforce.[9]

Mirza came to an afternoon's hearing brashly defiant, readily admitting to drunkenness, drug use, battery, and bigamy (the last being legally valid for Muslim men). His wife, Fariza, listed her complaints about 18 years of marriage as follows: 'nesha bhang, khisti, maar, bochor bochor jomi bikri' (being drunk/drugged, cursing her, beating her up, selling off their [family] land each year). In her framing, notably, the physical violence was seen as part of a linked chain of behaviour, at least on par with economic abuse. She identified two main triggers of Mirza's violence: her objection to her husband's family marrying off their daughter too young and to the particular groom; and her everyday complaints upon his return that there was no food at home. Bigamy did not feature in her list of complaints. Mirza, on the other hand, foregrounded equitable treatment of his two wives and the need to provide for his second wife as well, possibly in parts of the same house if the children agreed.

The adjudicatory board responded to a variety of issues rather than keeping a narrow focus, in line with their stated purpose of working towards a holistic community solution. For example, various members expressed much regret about the daughter's marriage: 'She could have got a good job as a Muslim girl, have you seen the [good] jobs other girls are getting?' They began with the proposition that they would try for a mimangsha or solution, but that if they failed to resolve matters, there would have to be a legal case. Mirza said he didn't want a legal skirmish at all costs, whereupon the doctor reminded him that in that case he should attend to what they said, suggesting that it would be in his best interest to do so—because he had admitted to domestic violence, the very first step in a legal case might be a jail sentence. Occasional bouts of strong-arm negotiation followed from this, with a defiant Mirza saying 'Fine, jail's what I want', and the police OC, the magistrate, and the doctor making moves as if to put him away immediately, saying that a night in jail would do him a lot of good. These transactions underline that the criminality of domestic violence was explicit to everyone, an imminent threat whose sanctions provided an illusory yet capacious space for negotiating other needs related to subsistence, property, and parental authority.[10]

The solution involved economic sustenance for Fariza by recourse to landed property that Mirza had been selling off systematically, such that only six bighas (about two acres) were left. Mirza was notionally willing to let his children from Fariza, though not Fariza herself, have access to half of his land, claiming the other half would be for the other wife and his business. The board examined the land documents closely, rejected his proposal of making an informal transfer mediated by his father, and instead, came up with a strongly patrilineal solution (far below the *de jure* gender division of Muslim property law in India). Mirza was to formally pay to register two-thirds of the land in his son's name, with his daughter having access to the income until marriage, and his wife in her lifetime. He was to return to the Board with legal documents showing he had completed the registration in his son's name. Other conditions included: the second wife was not to be brought back to this marital residence; Mirza was to be responsible for providing food for the household; and Fariza was to be able to choose or consent to her daughter's marriage partners. Both the husband and in-laws protested vehemently at this last condition, among other reasons saying 'what if she picks a dark person?', but the Board prevailed, at least in writing.

The Board gave Fariza overt support to use their resources, and asked her to come back whenever there were problems, also urging relatives on both sides to report any domestic violence to them. But they simultaneously negotiated a set of conditions which buttressed patriarchal authority over her mobility and decision-making. While Fariza was to have access to the land, and a monthly maintenance amount, this was on condition that she return to her marital residence immediately, that she stay there peaceably (*shantimoto*), and that thereafter she get permission from her husband or in-laws when she wanted to visit her natal home. Mirza protested by claiming that Muslim wives were not to leave home by themselves, but promptly followed that up by refusing to shop for food for her, saying she could go to the market herself. He was roundly berated for the latter and told he was liable for providing food, but the former injunction was never directly challenged. Even as the magistrate said to Mirza, 'Remember you've signed things here, if you beat her up again you'll find out what the results are for you (*petaley bujhbey ki phol*),' she followed this up by advice to Fariza to 'get along with others (*maniye nao*)' and 'be less agitated/rambunctious" (*lompho jhompo kom diyo'*).

Despite these complicated contractual exchanges, uneasiness prevailed as the group left. Fariza said that she was afraid he would beat her a lot because she had brought these issues to the Board. 'Why did you do it then?' a married female neighbour chimed in, even as Fariza was urged by the Board to calm down and seek help when necessary. The magistrate commented wistfully at their departure: 'Let's see them "united" first, let them stay together first—there are a lot of problems from "broken families"'. I asked in the interlude between cases whether they thought their intervention was going to stop Mirza's domestic violence, 'It may decrease a bit', the doctor responded.

The possibilities and circumscriptions of community mediations through official boards are exemplified here: the board had the skill and police resources to leverage criminal legal sanctions, and the civil authority to design a contract about maintenance and property that mirrored remedies available in venues such as the Family Court.[11] The Board articulated righteous if jaded outrage at domestic violence, consistently condemning it in all public declarations (and hoping some injunctions would stick as a result). The optimal conjugal family and the companionate marriage where partners have an equal say in family decisions, as imagined in post-colonial Family Law, was reflected in their negotiations to allow women a say in their children's marriages, and to imagine that sharing a home with a co-wife is humiliating to a first wife (also a mark of Hindu hegemony). But the correlates of their vision of conjugality included: a 'united' family being optimal for mental health and social harmony, women needing to defer to authority structures in their affinal homes, and women faring best when they acted without undue agitation or strident claims. While domestic violence was undeniable, and the formal position was to condemn the violence in the strongest terms, emphasize its criminal nature, and include solutions to reduce violence, the primary focus was on social and economic issues, enforced through the professed outrage.

'Be Clever, Don't Be Stupid': Police Counseling

One might imagine that police units handling rape, domestic violence and other crimes against women would be outside the realm of mediation, but the Women's Grievance Cell of the Kolkata Police, the central post of Kolkata's clearinghouse for violent crimes against women, enthusiastically embraced 'negotiation' as an effective and efficient mode of operation. The Officer in Charge (OC) narrated that they added mediation to their array of tactics soon after they opened in 1995, apparently independent of women's movement demands for more humane and less intimidating forms of legal access. The Deputy Commissioner (DCDD) came up with the idea that counseling would be a good idea for some violence cases: as the OC remembered, 'He said to us, "listen to them, hear their problems"; and I soon understood too when I applied my own smarts to it that a third party intervention often resolves things (*mitey jai*).' The staff of four took on both investigation and counseling, but narrated the reconciliations they had brought about with special pride. They were candid about and indeed pleased with their un-police-like tasks, recounting the number of couples they had reconciled, proud of the statistic that they had registered only 4 of the 470 petitions that came to them in 2004 as S498A cases. 'We prefer counseling because you can't have a home if there is a 498' (*498 case holey arghar-ta hoi na, tai counseling prefer kori*), the OC Samaddar claimed, a statement often iterated by her staff as common-sense knowledge. Samaddar framed S498A cases in terms of performance and manipulation—'let me tell you how the game works' (*khelata apnakey boli*)—insisting that S498A cases are used by litigants 'to apply pressure' (*pressure debar jonyo korey*). In a small number of exceptional cases, they acknowledged, they helped couples draw up agreements that would become the basis for mutual consent divorces. Even more rarely, they filed formal S498A charges.[12]

As the following case reveals, both the litigant and investigator acted within a fairly well understood orchestration of claims. The primacy of economic needs in the dissolution of marriage was foregrounded here again, with the police treating claims of violence primarily as a discursive strategy for framing such needs. I met Rekha one morning sitting with the OC, describing her five year long marriage (they had a three-year old child) to a pilot at a foreign airline (hence a very good income). With a father-in-law who was a bank manager and a brother-in-law a dentist in the US, her husband's family was considerably better off than her natal family, her father being a retired college professor in a small town. She claimed that her husband's family had been very opposed to the marriage, and that when they eventually moved to live with his extended family, her father-in-law became increasingly verbally abusive: he often said that she came from a bad (*kharap*) family, cursed her as ill-behaved and unruly (*oshobhbho beyadob*), preferred her to be confined to her room, and insisted on an abortion of her second pregnancy. By her account, her husband had changed from being caring in the last few years, and during his brother's visit had joined his family in demanding she leave. Rekha had been at her parents' since then, locked out of the matrimonial home.

The OC checked and confirmed that there was actually a divorce case under way, wherein her father-in-law had accused her of 'behaving badly' (*kharap byabohar*) in his plaint. The police, she said, had called the husband's family to come in three times, without success. Here, the OC's interrogative mode suddenly changed physically and verbally: looking too casually at her ring, she asked Rekha, 'what do you want out of this?' (*ki chaichchen?*). Rekha replied with the English word 'settlement.' The word seemed to imply divorce by mutual consent (including an alimony agreement), because in response Samaddar reminded her that it took a year for the divorce, and that 'settlement' was difficult in cases such as this where she had an 'irritative' [in English] nature and where there had been disputes (*jhograjhanti*).

Rekha's only allegations of physical violence emerged at this point. She said she had been thrown down in the bathroom, and had not told her parents she cracked her head. But the OC went on with her earlier thought: 'Your case is legally weak, so now all we can try is counseling.' It emerged that there was no substantive record of any violence, other than the 'GD' recorded shortly before the divorce was filed. Rekha's father who had come in recounted: 'The local police station wanted to use counseling to make him less rigid, that's why they recommended filing a case.' The response at this point illuminates the Cell's pride of place in the hierarchy of criminal justice, as well as the power assigned to criminal over civil measures, as Samaddar rebuked, 'The *thana* (local police station) don't know these things, they don't need to know, but *we* know that filing a case creates more rigidity'. Another staff member chimed in: 'When you make a report at the *thana* that means the husband promptly puts in a 'mat suit' [matrimonial suit or divorce case] to counter the police claim.'

Both these police officers asserted, in other words, that Rekha's mistake lay in leaving a formal record with the local police station in the form of a GD; this lower-level station, which they depicted as less sophisticated in these matters, had by its insistence irretrievably damaged any possibilities of reconciliation and thereby made divorce inevitable. Samaddar interrogated Rekha about whether she had been rough with her father-in-law and postulated that this might have turned her husband against her as well—'If you reacted [badly], the son will not go against the father, I would not either.' This hypothesis further underlined the officers' evaluation that Rekha's divorce case had gone beyond the possibility of an amicable outcome, with the in-laws' ire provoked as much by her putative aggression at home as by her summoning the law/police. The final advice to Rekha and her father, accordingly, invoked the strategic powers of legal fora, and imagined women as having new agency if they put it to use in the right way, such as under the Cell's guidance: 'You can't just start a criminal case in a naïve way (*bokar moto*), you have to win it. She should have been more 'intelligent' and patient (*shohonshil*), now she has poisoned her husband's mind against herself.'

The OC's scant offer of help was that they would try to 'set up the home again, since there is a child—but everything has been delayed because of the case.' Rekha and her father asked the police to talk with the other parties before the court hearing in two weeks, since they could not talk directly while the matrimonial suit was under way. She promised they would try, and that a 498A case could be filed later if the counseling failed, but that this would not go well if the divorce judgment went against them in court. The final question from Rekha's father, seemingly in response, was: 'How much could maintenance be?'

Again, the answer was deeply circuitous: 'Time will be needed. If the police try to achieve something good then it takes time, we have to show the police are involved in "social welfare"'.

This case exemplifies the contradictions around civil and criminal provisions for divorce, and the linkages between domestic violence, alimony, and divorce. Divorce and criminal suits appeared here as a carefully choreographed set of call-and-return responses. The Police Cell entrusted with monitoring S498A claims put forth the analysis that launching a case under S498A delayed matters, precipitated divorce proceedings and wreaked irreparable damage. The only good S498A case was one that did not quite become a S498A case; the only smart reason to file a S498A case was when all other mediation and reconciliation objectives had been exhausted. Rekha's father's question about maintenance at the end was thus not, as it seems, a non sequitur to Samaddar's suggestion about a S498A case down the line, but at the core of the whole conversation: the audience with the police officer was primarily driven by the need for a home and financial sustenance for Rekha and her child, with the narrative of violence driven not so much by a need for amelioration or sanction, as by the need for leverage.

Whether OC Samaddar's questions about Rekha's nature were interrogation of facts or merely narrative strategy, Rekha's behaviour was held to be responsible for the demise of a marriage, the implication being that self-effacing pleasantness was a condition for having claim to matrimonial resources. Notably, there was remarkably little discussion of the details of violence throughout the whole interview. The police officers discussed it merely in terms of relative strategy and never queried the facts. Even Rekha invoked physical violence only incidentally, implying that it would worry her parents. This interview was held in her aging father's presence, after all, making a narrative account of her violence possibly more difficult. The whole legal apparatus, in other words, was constructed around the awkward, double-edged articulation for better terms in divorce.

Defying the Judge's Plan: Family Court

Family Courts (in cities where they have been established) serve as the primary venue for the adjudication of civil matters relating to marriage disputes, maintenance/alimony chief among them (constituting 43 per cent of the caseload of the Kolkata courts) (Agnes 2004). In India, these courts were put in place with strong advocacy from the women's movement. They were imagined as lawyer-free venues providing less intimidating legal access to women, sites of Alternate Dispute Resolution both in the sense of being set-aside courts dealing with family matters that would lessen the burden of regular civil courts, and in the sense that they emphasized mediation and 'conciliation' rather than adversarial process. But as I have explored elsewhere, these venues also show contradictions as sites of feminist legal reform (Basu 2012): notable among these contradictions is the ambivalence towards divorce in the Family Courts Act (1984) in the phrase 'protection of the family,' and the confusion over whether the word 'conciliation' refers to non-adversarial legal process or to 'reconciliation'. Moreover, despite the notion of these courts as a changed mode of delivering law, Family Courts are in fact lower level civil courts, where the case-record serves as the base of appeals in higher courts, and as evidence for other civil or criminal cases. While lawyers are discouraged (though more in theory than in practice) and litigants are urged to frame and conduct their own cases, in fact judges preside over trials in ways undistinguishable from other kinds of courts, moderating the cross-examinations of litigants, summarizing litigants' words into the legal record, insisting on formally correct petitions and evidentiary documents, and regularly invoking their own authoritarian roles.

Judges and counselors in these courts, drawn respectively from the judiciary service (with no particular background in family law) and from women's wings of political parties (in the case of Kolkata), may differ in their backgrounds and skill sets, but are fully committed and scrupulously attentive to women's economic maintenance, consonant with the protective ideology of the Act. They described this task as one of their principal responsibilities, and would work hard to come up with financial settlements, even when they regarded the female litigants in negative light, such as a case where a woman had left her husband and was living with another man, and another of a querulous and highly confrontational woman who screamed at everyone including the judge. However, both judges and counselors were correspondingly outraged when litigants actively attempted to manipulate economic settlements outside their authoritative direction, particular ire being reserved for those who had been to other criminal or mediation venues to allege family violence.

Such steps were regarded by the judges as moves to influence the maintenance settlement, or in other words, to flout their authority and reject the ways in which the judges' negotiation skills could have ensured litigants a more felicitous outcome. A stark example is provided by the following case involving a revised maintenance claim from the wife Shibani, and an opposing claim of restitution of conjugal rights by her husband Hemanto. Judge K said to Shibani with visible contempt, having learnt that she had filed (and lost) a S498A case: 'What a blow [you dealt your husband]! He was just about to lose his job, and such a good senior job in the Railways. If I sent a qualified young man to you now, could you find him that good a job?' Then with a pause and a very sarcastic smile, 'But you want maintenance from him all right, and he has the job so he can pay it.' That is, the criminal complaint of violence was deemed to be not just vindictive but self-defeating for Shibani, a form of legal assertiveness at odds with her role as an economically vulnerable entity in need of the court's protection.

Judge K, one of the two judges of the Kolkata Court (typically a male and female set), was known for her long inquiries and passionate directives, by turns marshalling her identities as empathetic woman, concerned elder, savvy urbanite, professional, and authority figure. In this case, she foregrounded her knowledge of government jobs and urban housing to try to evaluate whether Hemanto had made a good faith effort to find a home for Shibani away from his extended family, and if he could afford to do so given his income. She began the hearing with a lengthy inquiry of Hemanto about his residential situation and his expenses, and whether he could find separate space for himself and his wife in the family home. Hemanto amiably agreed with her on her characterization of the expansive spatial dimensions of old houses, even offering to raise the interim maintenance amount slightly. She seemed sympathetic that he had been suspended from his government job and almost fired; the charges were finally dismissed because none of the neighbors finally testified, she iterated for public hearing.

In the next stage, Judge K turned to cross-examine Shibani, to ascertain whether she had cause to stay away from her husband while continuing to claim maintenance from him. Like many other litigants in this court, Shibani was silent while standing in the dock and facing a barrage of questions. Finally, in the face of the judge's growing irritation at her silence, she muttered that she left the house because she was *'nirjatito'* ('tortured,' a word brought into this discourse primarily through feminist activism). Judge K continued to scold Shibani for her silence, but was also obviously skeptical of the alleged torture, and scornful of Shibani's unwillingness to return to the marriage: 'You're not willing to live with him under any circumstances, but you still want maintenance. You tried to have it both ways by filing a 498 while the other case is going on. If he was convicted you would have lost all the money so this strategy of playing both things would not work. You're not some simple dumb woman (*sadashidhey bokashoka non*), you were able to put him through this process so I know you know what's going on and you must respond in court.' She ridiculed the maintenance lump-sum amount Shibani had asked for, saying to Hemanto, 'You would have to have a very different sort of government job than mine to have that sort of money in the bank!' She refused to adjust court dates to accommodate Shibani's brother accompanying her, saying '*You* must be there, you can't rely on your brother for the rest of your life, you need to know what's going on'; here, Shibani's disinclination to return to the marriage became grounds for insisting on a whole new package of legal and cultural subjectivity from her, including mobility and independence as an extension of her 'modern' claim.

Shibani's case exemplified the sort of legally 'enterprising' behaviour that draws suspicion from judges. The judge's comments implied that the claim of 'torture' was spurious, filed in order to get maintenance while avoiding conjugal responsibilities. The fact that Shibani had lost the S498A case she filed did not of course mean that no violence had occurred (especially given low rates of conviction for S498A), nor did it acknowledge that the civil court might have a different standard for 'cruelty' than the criminal setting. The availability of these two fora for adjudicating domestic violence, civil and criminal, thus posed double jeopardy for women in judges' eyes rather than enabling plurality. The sanctions of job suspension and possible job loss for those convicted of violence that were instituted as deterrent measures in order to signal the seriousness of the offence were depicted here as vengeful at worst, and self-defeating at best.

The two legal provisions (for maintenance and against violence) are located in separate niches of law, meant to provide very different kinds of remedies. Women are economically dependent on marriage for survival (given their lack of natal and marital property shares, labour market inequities, and ideologies of women's domestic responsibilities), and thus on alimony and child support in the event of impending divorce. Thus, the legal requirement that claims for maintenance be made to the spouse, against whom one might also be filing criminal charges, sets up a conundrum where the two provisions are posed against each other: either a potential conviction under S498A negates the very earning power that is relied upon in the maintenance claim, or the criminal charge has to be foregone in order to ensure continued maintenance. Each remedy works only if the other fails. The onus of resolving the contradiction often seems to fall upon the female litigant, meaning that either violence complaints must be held back or withdrawn in order to maintain the cash flow, or the possibility of economic support must be abandoned in order to pursue the symbolic redress of violence.

* * *

What does it mean to launch one law as opposed to another? The apparatuses for addressing marital trouble, as we see, are located in sites which generate a number of contradictions for litigants, and indeed for the governance of law. Civil law venues like the Family Court, created in substantial part in response to demands from the women's movement, focus on non-adversarial outcomes, including undoing marital discord itself if at all possible through reconciliation (Basu 2012), and on monetary negotiations which are typically resisted by husbands and desperately sought by wives. Criminal law venues for addressing domestic violence, also created in response to demands from the women's movement, focus on public punishment, such as the imprisonment of affinal family members or job suspension. Given the currency of respectability and shame, the latter (criminal provisions) carry some power as forms of leverage against the former (civil) ones. But the power is a delicate one, easily upset, where the public exposure of marital discord to organizations or worse, to police or courts, may be interpreted as a point of no return.

In this fragile and complicated choreography, the timing of registering a local complaint, of filing a S498A case, or asking for divorce or maintenance can easily thwart the outcome sought; for example, criminal prosecution of violence may be impossible if the complaint cites the wrong provision, or the divorce case is filed just in time to make the criminal complaint look suspicious. Mediators, lawyers, police, and judges, not to mention litigants, are often unclear or ambivalent about how these provisions will work with respect to each other. And yet, these mediating sites play the primary role in shaping strategy, in traffic flows that are cognizant of each other's' roles but sometimes in contradiction with each other when interests or hierarchies are in conflict.

Redress of domestic violence, whether economic or criminal, is thus orchestrated as a matter of legal strategy, of a fit between the litigant's prioritized needs and the resources or sites available to help formulate those needs into legal categories. Criminal remedies may be sought in order to leverage civil monetary settlements, on the one hand, or suppressed despite incontrovertible violence in order to enable economic negotiations, on the other. Civil remedies such as alimony may be affected by the timing or results of criminal charges. But when civil and criminal remedies are simultaneously sought, the fear is that the use of plural venues may lead to an unfavourable outcome at both, that is, to a total failure of potential leverage. In effect, one remedy closes off the other. In this calculation, given the critical urgency of subsistence, criminal prosecution is usually the favoured casualty.

In the scenarios profiled in this chapter, the repertoire of criminal laws against family violence that are a direct legacy of the staunch anti-violence drive of the women's movement appear most useful when applied in conjunction with the (gender-neutral) protectionism of civil alimony laws. Ironically, when criminal provisions provide the most effective leverage, they result in violence being effaced out of narratives in favour of economic settlements. Prevailing cultural suspicions against S498A fuel the enthusiasm for such erasure among police, judges, and mediation boards. Notably, litigants themselves are loath to foreground claims of violence in venues designed to adjudicate it (whether for shame, mockery, or perjury is impossible to tell); alternatively, they narrate physical violence as part of a chain of economic deprivations and failures of kinship obligation, rather than foregrounding it for special sanction. Thus, the presence of domestic violence, in a world of global initiatives for gender justice, is a successful tool of negotiation; but its success lies mainly in its own erasure, in the interest of material needs.

Every space profiled in this chapter, even the court and the police station, depicts itself as being part of new landscapes of alternate dispute resolution, of working with context and settlement rather than the narrow strictures of law. Remarkable, then, is the profound shadow of law, or of specific legal sanctions, in shaping the forms of negotiation: judges work though evidentiary and testimonial procedures to mold litigants' alleged direct access to law; police use the non-cognizability of S498A to pressure men's families to attend counseling sessions (while deliberately holding off arrest); the mediation Board holds the imminent threat of police custody to draw up a property settlement; a feminist group's advice is necessarily shaped through categories of legal remedy. That is, while the specter of law is seemingly exorcized in venues which claim to work strategically, this exorcism is achieved through deploying the possibilities and sanctions of law.

Notes

1. The Family Court is staffed by a number of officials commonly called 'counselors', who help mediate cases, draw up petitions, and represent cases to judges.

2. The third mistake/punishment, by implication, refers to the child custody case.

3. Shibaji evoked a passionate narrative of rescue and protection: his wife came to him at 16, running away from her adoptive mother and the (mother's) paramour who tried to sell the girl. The mother had Shibaji arrested on kidnapping charges for two weeks but later publicly declared it not to be a kidnapping. Even now, he claimed, her family wanted them to split up because they wanted her to continue as a professional model, and make money off her. In response, his offers too were outrageous and manipulative: he had suggested that they live in the same house to raise their son but lead separate lives, and that he would give up custody for visitation if she were present during the length of each visitation. He reduced her to sobs by offering three times the maintenance as she asked, Rs. 6000 rather than Rs. 2000, in a reversal of the customary behaviour of men at this point. In his own defense, he claimed to have cross-examined her and demonstrated contradictions in her court statements about violence to the judge, and to have been exonerated on 'domestic torture' charges. Given his wife's repeated absences and lack of response, the counselor recommended that he back off and give her more time.

4. This data is drawn from an extended ethnographic project on Family Law and Family Violence in Kolkata, India for which I have conducted research since 2001, in two extended periods of fieldwork in 2001 and 2004–5 with ongoing annual investigations since then. I have observed a variety of family law,

domestic violence, and marriage mediation related settings in Kolkata, including participant observation of the Family Courts, the Women's Grievance Cell and a variety of organizations that undertook marriage mediation, field visits to litigants' homes with counselors, and interviews with judges, counselors and feminist activists. My total observational and interview archive in Kolkata consisted of 234 cases. Mediations were primarily conducted in Bangla (Bengali), interspersed with occasional English and Hindi. Names of mediators and litigants are pseudonyms.

5. Clients may have some sense of this political reach, but not necessarily of the specific ideologies of gender that differentiate these organizations.

6. The move was ultimately turned down by the legislature. Among various protests about the scope and nature of authority of these units, there was a prominent concern among those not affiliated with the ruling party that the units might be overly influenced by the political connections and interests of litigants. Talwar and Shramajibee Mahila Samity (2002: 18) affirms the profound influence of political alliances in *shalishi* cases.

7. There is also a punning sense in which it could be read as 'Women Police Investigative Center', given the prominence of female police officers.

8. In the other settings, while an occasional family member was called to mediation sessions, the focus was on talking to couples individually and then jointly.

9. These limitations were also present for Talwar's study of women-centered NGOs: 'if the intention is restoration of family life which is what the women want most often, it becomes necessary to deal sympathetically with the perpetrator' (Talwar and Shramajibee Mahila Samity 2002: 20).

10. Talwar also reports that activists found the legal provisions to be useful in that fear of legal action could be used to negotiate modifications in behaviour (Talwar and Shramajibee Mahila Samity 2002: 27).

11. As previous accounts showed, configuring alimony or maintenance is one of the principal tasks of the Family Court. For Muslim women under the prevailing laws in India, this could take the form of monthly payments for sustenance before divorce and 'fair and reasonable' provisions for some amount of time after divorce, or the payment of deferred dower or settlement of property in lieu of monthly payments.

12. Since 2004, the number of S498A cases formally filed in West Bengal has gone up substantially, indicating the emergence of other strategies.

References

Agnes, Flavia. 2004. *A Study of Family Courts, West Bengal*. Kolkata: West Bengal Women's Commission.

Basu, S. 2012. 'Judges of Normality: Mediating Marriage in the Family Courts of Kolkata, India', *Signs*, 37(2): 469–92.

CSWI. 1974. *Towards Equality: Report of Committee on the Status of Women in India*. New Delhi.

Engel, D. M. 1980. 'Legal Pluralism in an American Community: Perspectives on a Civil Trial Court', *American Bar Foundation Research Journal*, 5(3): 425–54.

Gangoli, Geetanjali. 2007. *Indian Feminisms: Law, Patriarchies and Violence in India*. Hampshire: Ashgate.

Gopalan, Sandeep. 2001. *Towards Equality—The Unfinished Agenda—Status of Women in India*. New Delhi: The National Commission for Women, Government of India.

Hautzinger, Sarah. 2007. *Violence in the City of Women: Police and Batterers in Bahia, Brazil*. Berkeley: University of California Press.

Kumar, Radha 1993. *A History of Doing*. New Delhi: Kali for Women.

Lazarus-Black, Mindie. 2007. *Everyday Harm: Domestic Violence, Court Rites, and Cultures of Reconciliation*. Urbana-Champaign, Il: University of Illinois Press.

Menon, Nivedita. 2004. *Recovering Subversion: Sexual Politics Beyond the Law*. New Delhi: Permanent Black.

Merry, S.E. 1988. 'Legal Pluralism', *Law and Society Review*, 22(5): 868–96.

Moore, E.P. 1999. 'Law's Patriarchy in India', in Mindie Lazarus-Black, and Susan F. Hirsch (eds.), *Contested States: Law, Hegemony and Resistance*, pp. 88–117. New York: Routledge.

Rajan, Rajeshwari Sunder. 2003. *The Scandal of the State: Women, Law and Citizenship in Postcolonial India*. Durham: Duke University Press.

Ray, Raka. 1999. *Fields of Protest: Women's Movements in India*. Minneapolis: University of Minnesota Press.

Sharma, A. 2006. 'Crossbreeding Institutions, Breeding Struggle: Women's Empowerment, Neoliberal Governmentality and State (Re)Formation in India', *Cultural Anthropology*, 21(1): 60–95.

Shehabuddin, E. 1999. 'Contesting the Illicit: Gender and the Politics of Fatwas in Bangladesh', *Signs*, 24(4): 1011–44.

Talwar, A. and Shramajibee Mahila Samity. 2002. 'The Shalishi in West Bengal: A Community Response to Domestic Violence', Women Initiated Community Level Responses to Domestic Violence: Summary Report of Three Studies. Series: Domestic Violence in India: Exploring Strategies, Promoting Dialogue #5. Washington, DC, International Center for Research on Women, pp. 14–30.

Williams, Rina Verma. 2006. *Postcolonial Politics and Personal Laws: Colonial Legal Legacies and the Indian State*. Delhi: Oxford University Press.

2

PRATIKSHA BAXI

'Pyar Kiya to Darna Kya'*
On Criminalizing Love

Tracing the histories of 'minor jurisprudences' in European law, Goodrich (1996) contends that the history of the jurisdiction of love reveals that with the hierarchical relationships between the sovereign and subject developed rules that confined relationships of heterosexual love to their function of reproduction.[1] It is his argument that the reproduction of social order, traced through specific historically-constituted masculinist juristic genealogies, erased minor jurisprudences in Europe premised on different conceptions of justice. The courts of love established in the year 1400 by Charles VI of France dramatize this erasure (Goodrich 1996). The courts of love were constituted to hear disputes between lovers and were adjudicated by women selected by a panel of women on the basis of their recitations or written presentations of poetry. These courts were committed to a different vision of legal prose, a prose predicated upon the 'existential commitments of writing', which constituted justice as desire and not law (Goodrich 1996: 4). Today, it is the 'negation of eros and of love to a space outside of serious social speech or law' that concerns social justice (Goodrich 1996: 5).

---

* A previous version of this chapter was published as Pratiksha Baxi. 2014. 'Love Affairs and Rape Trials in India', in *Public Secrets of Law: Rape Trials in India* (New Delhi: Oxford University Press; pp. 234–282).

In this chapter, I suggest that the jurisdiction of heterosexual love is made manifest in the domain of the law on rape, where love has historically been constituted as a function of social reproduction through what Goodrich (1996) calls masculinist juristic genealogies.[2] I depart from the doctrinal view of the rape law by arguing that the analytics of heterosexual love and heterosexual marriage in the field of violence assumes critical centrality to understand the social and juridical frameworks of rape in India.[3] The blurring of love and rape or consent and lack of consent has a specific manifestation when we look at the right of women to choose their partners. I begin with a brief explication of the judicial routes the assertion of the right to marry takes in India.[4]

A criminal complaint against the partner of the daughter charging him with statutory rape, abduction, and/or kidnapping is a stabilized legal strategy to 'recover' a daughter who enters into an 'improper' alliance.[5] The resourcefulness with which the natal family, in consultation with lawyers and police, deploys the laws on rape, abduction, and kidnapping then follows a rather efficient police procedure. The police hunt the couple down. After finding the couple, they are brought to the police station for questioning. If the woman states that she was not abducted or raped, she may face custodial violence, which is normalized under the category of police remand. If she is able to withstand the pressure and violence to break off her relationship, she may be jailed on grounds of a criminal complaint brought against her usually on grounds of having stolen some valuables from her parents' home before she eloped. Or she may be detained in a state-run institution for women. Detention in state institutions of consenting adults follows a stabilized legal strategy. The woman bears the burden of proving that she was not raped, abducted, or kidnapped. She must now prove to the court that she is a consenting subject in a situation when she cannot appeal for resources for legal representation from her natal family who initiate the proceedings against her, and all the resources for the legal dispute over her must flow from her affinal family who bear the costs of legal representation for their son and his wife.

State law is also used to *counter* the criminalization of love. We encounter a bewildering number of petitions and counter-petitions filed in different courts by both the parties. The appeals to state law range from petitions to quash the FIR, challenges to illegal detention and plea for personal liberty under the writ of *habeas corpus*, and filing collusive suits for the restitution of conjugal rights (see Chowdhry 2004). Typically after the couple marries, the husband may file a case of restitution of conjugal rights *against* his wife. The case of restitution of conjugal rights is aimed to gain legal recognition of the fact that the woman was not abducted nor was she forced into marriage. This sets the stage for the woman's *consent* to be certified. The performance of women's agency in court is grounded in the anticipation of police action, that is, fear of arrest, illegal detention, and custodial violence.

The ethnography that follows shows how the power of state law stakes a hold over the life of a young woman who refuses to say she was raped, by the man she was in love with, and whom she ultimately marries. In a sense, this narrative details the situatedness of the category of rape and the meaning of victimhood. I look at how this case is articulated at different sites such as the police station, the hospital, the jail, the state-run women's shelter, the prosecutor's chamber, and the courtroom. The journey, which this case takes, helps us explicate the nature of regimes of legality and illegality that operate under the sign of the state law. The narrative of a love affair between Chetna and Roshan that follows allows us to trace how love materializes in a rape trial.

The Court

When I first visited the Sessions Court in Ahmedabad (Gujarat), the court building was still under construction in 1996. The court compound comprised a parking lot where police vans of prisoners were a common sight, and usually was crowded with typists, touts, and litigants. The signboard on the court building marked it as the *Nyaya Mandir*, which literally means the temple of justice, in Gujarati and Hindi. The building had eight floors, with the ground floor comprising spaces for lawyers to work. The lawyers worked on chairs and tables, placed close to each other and tied to each other with iron chains to secure each workstation. The court canteen was located at the other end. The first floor opened into the District and Sessions Judge's courtroom at one end, and the Additional District and Sessions Judge's courtroom on the other. The second floor housed the Assistant District and Sessions Judges' courtrooms. The public prosecutors' office was located here. The upper floors were allocated to the magistrates of various ranks, the rank decreasing in the hierarchy, from the lower floors to the upper floors. This spatialization of hierarchy, pointed towards the way in which the different powers allocated to the various judges and magistrates, were mapped by the court architecture.

On the first day in the courtroom, I remembered Peter Goodrich's words:

> The day in court is likely to be experienced in terms of confusion, ambiguity, incomprehension, panic, and frustration, and if justice is seen to be done it is so seen by outsiders to the process. Nor is justice likely to be heard to be done by the participants in the trial. The visual metaphor of justice as something that must be visible and seen enacted has a striking poignance, in that it captures the paramount symbolic presence of law as a façade, a drama played out before the eyes of those subject to it (1990:191).

The noisy, busy, and sweaty courtroom with simultaneous hearings was unfathomable to me at first. Over time I learnt that during a trial, the defence and the prosecutor stand in the well facing the judge. The witnesses take the witness box on the right side of the judge and the accused on bail stands on the left side (diametrically opposite the witness box). Whereas the accused in custody occupies the dock situated at the end of the courtroom facing the judge and the constables accompanying him or her sit on a bench next to the dock.[6] Behind the witness box, there is a row of chairs reserved for lawyers. Right behind these a few rows of chairs are placed for the litigants, public, journalists, or other witnesses. On that unforgettable first day in a courtroom, I made many mistakes. The court was yet to begin its session. I looked around and sat down on a comfortable chair reserved for lawyers and was at once chastised. Abashed, I walked to a bench, which was reserved for the accused. Yet again I was severely chided. Then I walked to the first row of chairs, to be told again that this row was reserved for witnesses. As days passed by, I managed to mark a chair with a broken armrest nearest to the witness box as my place in the court. Sometimes when I was lucky, I could secure permission from the court to sit at the lawyer's table from where I could hear the proceedings better.

Even from the first chair (towards the witness box) reserved for the public, it was difficult for me to hear what was being said. The accused, separated spatially cannot 'hear' most of what is being said, but views the proceedings from the distance. I agree from experience with the insight of Goodrich that the court is an auditory space organized on the principle of 'visibility of justice rather than its audibility' (1990:191).

I noted that the greater the audibility the closer an individual is to privilege. More often than not, depending on the viewing and listening positions of the actors in a courtroom, the courtroom is experienced as 'theatrical autism with all actors speaking past each other' (Carlen cited in Goodrich 1990:193). The ethnography that follows conveys this sense of theatrical autism each time I mark a question or a response as inaudible in the oral transcript.

The fieldwork was mainly concentrated in two spaces in the trial court—the prosecutor's chambers and the courtroom. In the courtroom, I did not follow the route set out by Matoesian (1993) who combines structuration theory with conversational analysis to study courtroom talk in rape trials, specifically the cross-examination of the survivor of rape. Matoesian is right when he says that 'the 'mere' recitation, and incantation of 'boring' details in courtroom talk, which Holmstorm and Burgess, and Largen lament, might well organise the sonorous rhythmic design found in charismatic discourse' (1993: 21). It was impossible for me to replicate the techniques of recording and transcription, which may generate 'such a density of conversational detail that literally thousands of utterances and conversational properties become available and analytically relevant' (Matoesian 1993:65). The method itself presupposes the possibility of recording trial proceedings on tape or video (see Epstein 1978).[7] In a sense, participant observation during the trial proceedings was conducted under the 'judicial stare', which is the 'dogmatic precondition of the narrative structure of the (legal) discourse and is also its normative guarantee of objectivity' (Goodrich 1987:165). Ethnographic writing under the judicial stare meant recognition of this pre-condition of judicial narrative.

The Case

When I met Chetna and Roshan in the trial court, I explained to them the nature of my research and asked them if I could interview them. Roshan laughed and said, 'oh, we don't mind if you tape or give her name, our names. She will go on T.V.'.[8] I visited their home one Sunday afternoon where I interviewed both of them and Roshan's married sister, Kumud who was visiting them. The case history is based on police documentation, court proceedings, and ethnographic interviews. The translations are from Gujarati.

Chetna was seventeen and a half years old when her mother threw her out of her home, on discovering her relationship with Roshan. Her parents opposed the love affair on the grounds that they belonged to the Patel caste and Roshan belonged to the so-called lower Prajapati caste.[9] Chetna went to Roshan's house. Roshan was not home. He worked in a shop in the clothes market in the old city. When he came back from work, she narrated the entire incident to him. Subsequently Chetna's mother went to the police and lodged a complaint stating that her daughter was missing and that Roshan had seduced her and abducted her with the intent to have illicit sex with her. She further alleged that Chetna had taken some gold jewellery from home. The same night following this complaint, the police picked up Roshan and Chetna from Roshan's home. Subsequently, the police recorded the statements of Chetna's sisters and parents. Roshan and Chetna were sent for medical examination and their bodily samples were sent to the forensic science laboratory. Roshan who was arrested on the grounds of rape, abduction, and kidnapping (under Sections 376, 366, and 363 IPC respectively), secured bail a week later. Two days after the complaint was lodged, the police arrested Chetna for abetting rape, abduction, kidnapping and theft. Chetna was sent to the Central Jail and then to a shelter for women. After nine months, the police petitioned the court to drop the charges against Chetna since there was no evidence against her. After Chetna was released, she ran way to marry Roshan when she came of age and by the time the case came to court they had borne a son. Her mother agreed to compromise and testified that Roshan had not kidnapped, abducted, and raped her daughter. Roshan was acquitted at the end of the trial.

In the Prosecutor's Chamber

I heard of this case for the first time when the Additional Public Prosecutor (APP), whom I call Hirabhai, drew my attention to the police papers that had been sent to him. Hirabhai shaking his head in disapproval said,

> Baxi, look at these papers! There is no reality in them. The medical shows hymen intact, yet the police said she was raped. Parents opposed the relationship. The girl is a Patel girl. The boy is Prajapati. She married him later. Has a child. Now the family wants to compromise. The girl is very smart. I asked her, 'did you not feel scared, all this happened?' and she said, 'why live in terror when one has loved (*pyar kiya to darna kya*)?' (He laughed).

The reference here is to a popular Hindi song[10] from a classic Hindi film *Mughal e Azam*. It spans several contexts to give meaning to Hirabhai's reading of Chetna's life in categories of popular culture that re-articulates the legal framing of that which had happened. *Mughal e Azam*, a popular film made in the 1950s is a story about King Akbar's son Salim (enacted by Dilip Kumar) who was in love with the beautiful courtesan, Anarkali (enacted by Madhubala). Akbar opposed his son's love affair with a mere courtesan. He was enraged when he learnt of the relationship. The defiant Anarkali in a performance in the princely court sings and dances to a song (composed by Naushad) to the lyrics, 'why live in fear when one has loved, one has loved; not stolen, why should one sigh in secret' (*pyar kiya to darna kya, pyar kiya hai chori to nahi ki, chup chup ke ahe bharna kya*)? This song dramatizes love as resistance to the sovereign. It signifies that sovereign power cannot dictate its will to the love that animates lovers, which defies social chasms between a prince and a courtesan. The identifying marker of true love then is one that does not know fear of the sovereign. Love is without guilt. It is posed in radical opposition to crime. Love is not theft. Love is not illicit. It is love that is all that law cannot be (see Raes 1998).

After the acquittal, Roshan said to me 'Do you know what the pros-ecutor asked Chetna? He asked her, "you married in another caste, you are Patel and he is Prajapati, what is this?" So she said, "so what? Is he not a man? Is he not a human being? That is what she said." Then he said, *"Pyar kiya to darna kya?"'* Roshan continued, 'If that is so, then where could he see caste?' Chetna added, 'Caste is always one. You are a woman. I am a woman.' The evocation of a love song then indicates that serious legal language could not communicate what Chetna sought to say about caste and love. She does so by evoking the category of human, where caste refers to the human species, while Hirabhai cites a love song, which lies outside the serious legal language (Goodrich 1996). He represented Chetna as an extraordinary woman whose sense of the social could only be framed through cinematic references.

The Spectacle of Violence

In the context of caste-based socialities, which represses love, we find the narrative of repetitive violence. It is important to detail how legal subjects represent the repression of love and the repetitive narrative of custodial violence. I suggest that Roshan frames the story through a cinematic understanding of love, violence, state, and family, raising the issue of 'the very organisation of vision and its effects' (Doane cited in Pinney 1992:47). Here, I am less concerned with the question about scopophilia or 'the pleasure of looking which causes libidinal excitation', and more with how cinematic language provides a genre for organising elements of love and violence, separation and re-union of lovers, familial opposition and state's compliance—a melodrama with a happy ending (Pinney 1992:28). The re-telling of what happened in Roshan's words is a striking example of how the narrative is organized as if it were a story of a film.

Hence, the cinematic mode is not about the 'ordinary'. Roshan and Chetna told me that there had been many inter-caste marriages in the neighbourhood, including the marriage of a Brahmin woman with a lower caste man. In none of these instances, had anything like this ever happened. Chetna's mother opposed their relationship since as Chetna put it, 'he was not from our caste'. The following excerpts are from a long interview in Chetna and Roshan's home. Chetna was nursing a young baby at the time. The excerpt given below, which I have translated from Gujarati, is in Roshan's words. Roshan's sister, Kumud also recounted what had happened.

> R: Chetna's mother threw her out of the house. She threatened to go to the police, to the court. This 'story' started at 9:30 p.m. like a 'picture' and ended at 11:30 p.m. I came back at 9 p.m. then I came to know that her mother has thrown her out of the house. Her mother had come to know, her mummy said, 'go to his house'. I explained to her (Chetna) that 'we are not married and this will become a long *lafara*[11] (public brawl)'. So her mother did a long *lafara*. Then her mother phoned Chetna's maternal uncle (*mama*).
>
> K: He (Chetna's maternal uncle) is a goon.
>
> R: No, he is not a goon. But he goes to clubs so he has contacts. He is quite old; he is 45 years old. So, her mummy called the maternal uncle. Her (Chetna's) uncle's sons have a kite shop and there were many young men hanging out there. They all came here to beat me up. They told the neighbours, if anyone interfered then we would beat you up also. Everyone locked their houses and sat inside. Only one man—do you see that man who is wearing a white cap (points in the street, I see a man pass by through the door)? He took my father to the police station later.

Anyway, then they really beat us up, beat me. There were approximately 10–15 people. All the people they came to beat me up. Then her mother said, 'Come home' and she (Chetna) said, 'I will not come. You are getting someone's son beaten up. Like you, he is also someone's only son'. Then she (Chetna) was also slapped a few times. She (Chetna) began to say, 'It is my wish'. Then everyone started beating me again. Then she said, 'Why are you beating him up? Don't touch anyone'.

K: He (Roshan) kept his cycle and her mother came with Chetna and shoved her and said, '*challa bharwa*,[12] keep the girl'. Her mummy called her uncle and everyone else. Her mother did this—did a *danga*[13] with us. I was unmarried then. I got married later. They said, 'let us abduct their daughter'. I hid behind a gas cylinder for one hour.

R: They said, 'they did this to our girl, so let us abduct theirs'. When Chetna refused to go with them, she was beaten up too.

Chetna's maternal uncle had three sons and no daughters, so looked upon his sister's daughters as his own. Roshan explained, 'that's why he came after us, like a villain her uncle (*mama*) came after us. That's why his name does not appear in the court. He escaped'. Chetna's father went along with the police complaint since, Chetna explained, 'Papa was scared that what if in future my uncle gets him in trouble?' The villain in a Hindi film is one who typically escapes the gaze of the police and law. The cinematic mode of representing the role of the maternal uncle offers a counter frame as if the cinematic can 'constrain the meaning through narrative chains of signification' to situate 'otherwise undecidable images within sequences that produce an argument and express intention' (Pinney 1992:27). The alliance between the police and Chetna's family to discipline and punish is experienced as excess that could not be represented in the category of the legal. The incommensurality between experience and the accusation narrates the spectacle of custodial violence as phantasmal. It is phantasmal for Roshan insisted that 'love marriages are not suggestive of modernity; as if a deviation from traditional Indian society rather it is an ancient practice, as traditional as tradition can be'.

The *Fariyad* as Custodial Violence

Usually custodial violence has been used to refer to police in detention or in judicial custody. The struggle to retain a hold over an unmarried daughter's sexuality is equally a description of custodial power. When guardianship or the right of the father wears the terrifying face of custodial power, the father's home is often a site of custodial violence. A daughter who escapes the hold over her sexuality by crafting a choice marriage encounters a double articulation of custodial power—at her father's home and in the police station, also a site that regulates the politics of honour. This face of criminal law allies with the task of restoring the honour of the father with backing. Chetna's assertion of her right to choice and refusal to renounce love provoked further custodial violence.

Let us follow what happened next. Chetna told her mother that she would live in Roshan's house. When her family realized that she was on Roshan's 'side', they left without taking Chetna with them. Roshan and Chetna thought that they must have reconciled and the matter would end there. Hence, they decided not to lodge a police complaint against the men who beat them up. Besides as Chetna said, 'if we had gone to get a complaint written then there may have been a problem'. They were afraid that the police could hand over her custody to her parents. Roshan continued to narrate what happened thereafter. I cite Roshan and Kumud below:

The *Fariyad*

On learning that Roshanbhai Pannachand living in our society bungalow [number] and my daughter Chetna have illicit relationship I scolded them both.

On [date] I and my daughter and my son Sameer were present at home. My husband had gone to work and on scolding my daughter there was exchange of words. That night at 8:30 p.m. my daughter Chetna left without saying a word to anyone. When she did not come home we searched for her at our relative's home. On searching at Roshan Pannachand's house there

---

R: Then we did not come to know. We were watching TV. We were sitting here (in the living room where we were sitting). She (*pointing to his sister*, Kumud) was in that room. Parents were also inside. We were sitting here and we had locked the door.

K: No, it was like this. When he was eating the food then everywhere there was blood even in the plate, there was blood and blood.

R: They beat me up so badly. There was blood.

K: They beat him up a lot, with a stick. The plate had cooked rice; soon it was full of blood. The police came in a big van.

too they weren't found. When daughter Chetna left home at that time she took from the locker the gold chain and earrings kept there. Roshanbhai made my daughter run away with him with the intent of marrying her by enticing, bribing and seducing her for the purpose of illicit sexual intercourse and that's why I give this *fariyad*.

On [date] at 8:30 p.m. from [place] Roshanbhai kidnapped my daughter with the intent of illicit sexual intercourse that is why I am getting this *fariyad* written down.

R: Then they said, 'Who is Roshan Pannachand and Chetna Patel?' So she (Chetna) only opened the door. She said: 'you will not open the door, what if someone comes and beats you up?' So she opened the door and she said, 'come, I will go with you', then they caught both of us and took us.

The police complaint lodged by Chetna's mother was in effect a way of securing guardianship rights. It marks a socio-legal route of compelling women to withdraw from relationships of love, at the pain of a criminal charge against the man and violence against the self. In Chetna's case, the law was used to coerce her to say that she was a victim of rape, abduction, and kidnapping. Chetna refused to say that Roshan abducted and raped her. It was at this point that the *fariyad* was written. Roshan was now positioned as a criminal who abducted and raped and Chetna positioned as his victim.

The effect of the police complaint was to initiate criminal charges against Chetna. She was accused of stealing jewellery from her parents' house. We see that Chetna's disobedience and defiance of parental authority bring together the law of the family with the law of the state, categories of discipline with categories of punishment. As a transgressor of familial normativity when categories of impropriety are translated into categories of illegalities there is a shift towards locating Chetna as a criminal. The complaint of theft is constituted as a punitive action for disobedience. As Roshan recounted:

This story happened in [month] 1994. The policemen said, 'the girl is on his side so get a *fariyad* written'. Her mummy said that she has brought jewellery and all. Then they asked her (Chetna about the jewellery), she said that 'I am wearing a jersey, I did not even wear slippers in my feet'. The policewalas locked me in. Then told her to go home. They did not want to write her complaint (*fariyad*). She said, 'I won't go home, you take him out (release him)'.

The policemen said to her mummy, 'your plan is not going to work(*apki daal galne wali nahi hai*). The girl is on his side. So write a *fariyad* against the girl'.

They applied penal sections (*kalam*) against her and against me, too.[14]

K: They (Chetna's family) bribed the police.

The narrative of custodial violence was erased from the police documents.

R: Then they took me in custody. Pappa was there. Mummy was crying. Then in the morning (they) took our remand—a lot. You know they have women constable. They told her to take her (Chetna's) remand. She said, 'she is a small girl. I will not take her remand'. The PI (Police Inspector) took us to the senior inspector and told him, 'He (Roshan) took the girl and raped her'. He said, 'beat him' and so, they beat me up really badly. Then she (Chetna) felt that he is suffering so much beating for me.

K: The police took stick (*danda*) to beat.

PB to Chetna: Did they take your 'remand' also?

C: Yes. They beat both of us.

Custodial violence is normalized by the category of remand and remand substitutes the category of custodial violence.[15] After the medico–legal examination, Roshan and Chetna were brought back to the police station from the hospital. Roshan was kept in the custody room overnight while Chetna sat outside the room in the police station. Until then Chetna's statement was not taken. In Roshan's words:

Then they took me back. They kept me inside for one night and she was made to sit outside. The next morning, I was taken to Gaekwad Haveli[16] (Crime Branch) there they took my photograph and applied god knows what sections.[17] They took me to the Magistrate's house. He was not there. It was a Saturday. All this happened on Thursday, Friday night. They took me to the Mirzapur court. I thought being Saturday[18] it would be a holiday. There they asked me if I had anything to say, I said, 'I don't want to say anything'. That Police Inspector—he put pressure on me that 'if you speak then I will call you from the Central Jail to take your remand'. That's why I felt fear, that's why I said.

C: He said he would make him lie on a slab of ice.

R: He said like this. That policeman—these people—say the incorrect things that we will take your remand like this or like that make you lie on a slab of ice. That's why I did not say anything in court. I thought they would take remand and get me from the Central Jail.[19]

Roshan was then taken to the Central Jail. On the same day, Chetna's statement was taken and she too was arrested. In the meantime, Roshan's brother contacted a lawyer who lived in front of his house in the city. This lawyer[20] helped Roshan get bail. On 13 January 1994, Roshan was released on bail for Rs. 15,000. Chetna remained in jail, as Roshan could not bail her. The *fariyad* is a form of custodial violence enacted by the family in conjunction with the police in the police station. The experience and threat of police violence remains erased from the legal documents but is constitutive in the framing of the legal event.

Hospital Narratives

The hospital narratives presented herein suggest that the averted gaze of the medical practitioner operates in a differential distribution of 'scandal and the light' (Foucault 1977:9). The medico-legal gaze is arrested by specific body parts, which correspond to the evidentiary sources for the purported crime. The medico-legal case is 'the individual as he may be described, judged, measured, compared with others, in his very individuality; and it is also the individual who has to be trained, corrected, normalized, excluded, etc' (Foucault 1977:191). The averted medico-legal gaze normalizing remand turns 'real lives into writing', as Foucault says, 'functions as a procedure of objectification and subjection' (1977:192). The scandal of remand, as narrated by Roshan below, does not meet publicity. The injured body in the aftermath of remand is not made visible by the medical gaze.

After the remand, Roshan was admitted to the Civil Hospital by the police and released from the hospital the following day. In Roshan's words,

Then in the morning of 7th after taking our remand, the police put both of us in a *rickshaw* to take us to Civil (hospital). Then my mummy told my brother and they were trying to get us released. But, it took approximately 8–9 days. On 6th and 7th, I stayed in the custody room and on 8th and 9th, I was sent to the Central Jail. So, in the morning, they took us to

Civil (Hospital). They did tests for both of us. Took the saliva and other stuff. They did this for her also. They brought me back from there'.

PB: Did they not record the marks of the beating?

R: They did not really examine me. They did the saliva–valiva *(sic)* test and did the test of below (genitals). If they had examined my back then I would have told them. They did a very wrong thing by taking remand. I told them I was sick. In the hospital, I vomited. She (Chetna) came there with a bowl. I could not even walk. She had to hold me.

The doctor did not record marks of injury apart from the abrasions on Roshan's cheek and neck. The medico-legal report does not offer any explanation as to why Roshan was vomiting when he had jaundice 25 days earlier. The symbolism of the word *patient* to describe Roshan brings forth an entirely different sketch of the hospital and the doctor-patient relationship when subsumed under a medico-jural sign. The examination of Roshan's back is not a medical concern here; in fact, it is not a surface that arrests the doctor's gaze. The MLC released a month after Roshan had been examined at the Civil Hospital is cited below:

Doctor's Remarks: History given by the patient himself

Pt (patient): well built, well nourished.

No external mark of any stain on the body.

Triple linear abrasion on right cheek and right side neck.

Secondary sex characters including external genitalia are well developed.

Patient is having vomit. Jaundice 25 days back.

Glans wash for epithelial shows no vaginal epithelium.

Smegma negative.

Sealed samples of blood and saliva handed over to the police. block quote ends

The medical practitioner was concerned with injuries, stains, the presence or absence of smegma or epithelial cells on specific parts of the body under suspicion of deviance. It is deviance that is the object of scientific enquiry rather than a therapeutic understanding of an injured body. This constitution of a deviant body has the effect of making invisible the evidence of violence incurred during the police remand. Chetna was admitted to the hospital overnight and released on the following day. The MLC in her case read as follows:

> Doctor's Remarks: History given by the patient herself
>
> Pt well built, well nourished
>
> No external mark of injury on the body
>
> No external mark of any stain on the body
>
> Pubic, axillary (*sic*) hair black, not matted
>
> Ext genitalia breast well developed
>
> LMP four days back
>
> Sealed sample of blood and saliva handed over to the [G] police station
>
> Vaginal stains show no spermatozoa
>
> Indoor findings (vaginal examination): P/S not possible, hymen intact, P/V even one finger P/V difficult.
>
> Comment: Clinical impression: Not habituated with sexual intercourse, probable she never had any intercourse.

Chetna further told me that the several medical students who had accompanied the doctor while he was making the examination later reassured her that medically the police could not prove that she had been raped. The medico-legal certificate would later act to certify through what was phrased as 'indoor' findings that Roshan had not raped her. It is only when the matter came for hearing in the trial court that the certification of the doctor that she was not 'habituated to sex', acted to verify Chetna's statements. In a sense, the grounds of the failure of the case in terms of a conviction were generated within one month of the legal event. However, by this time, Roshan was released on bail and Chetna was jailed. The charges against Chetna are detailed below.

From Victim to Criminal

The normativity of the family lies in bringing together categories of love with power, and rights with obedience. In the absence of this normativity, no future could be imagined for the disobedient daughter within the family but such an imagination condemned her to inhabit the punitive institutions of the state. In this instance, the public complaint of rape or seduction is not considered stigmatic for the identity of the family is traced through the capacity of the family to bring punitive measures against her. Failure to do so would be more threatening to normativity. The transformation of a victim (*bhogbannar*) to a criminal must be understood in the context of the family's decision to condemn Chetna to life lived in state institutions. This condemnation finds itself in the writing of police records. When Chetna refused to change her testimony following the remand, on the same day we find in the police records a statement by Chetna's father. I cite the statement below, originally in Gujarati.

> Today I myself the bearer of the signature below, M.R. Patel give the statement that my daughter Chetna Kumari Patel is in the possession (*kabja*) of and after today all the responsibilities of my daughter shall be borne by Roshanbhai Pannachand. She is in the possession of Roshanbhai Pannachand at this moment of time at present.
>
> Since this incident happened, despite our telling her, she did not stay with us and this Roshan Pannachand seduced her and took her and that is why she is with him.

The description of what happened is summarized by the use of the word 'possession'. Chetna's defiance of familial persuasion is seen as enough reason for her father to give up all his responsibilities towards her. Furthermore, it is the father who is seen as the natural guardian in law who has the authority to transfer the responsibility. The family for Chetna is the kin who betrays her to a future that is lived in the institutions of law by abandoning her because of her refusal to obey their command to leave Roshan. The police station then is the site of betrayal for Chetna where her father instead of gifting her in marriage to the man of her choice chooses to sign away his responsibilities as her guardian to Roshan by way of a police statement. It is poignant since now the consequences of the criminal charge brought against her by her own family had to be borne by her alone. The law then is the site where the family articulates its power to discipline and punish Chetna. While Roshan was taken to jail, Chetna was questioned at the police station. She did not change her stance and the police recorded the following statement.

Roshan's Statement

On being asked in person I am getting written that I live with my mother-father and sister and work in a clothes shop and earn approximately Rs 1000 per month. My job timings are from 1 am to 8 pm. My date of birth is [date] 1969. On last [date] 1994 at eight thirty Chetna came to me and said to me, 'I was thrown out of my house and (told) go stay with Roshan'. Hearing this I said, 'you go back, don't come to my house'. Despite this, she did not go back to her house. During this time her family members came and after beating me up went away. After 10-15 minutes, the girl came back to my house with the desire to live in the house and her family members said 'you only keep her, we don't want to keep her with us'. I kept the girl in my house and at the time, she was in my house. I did not have any bodily pleasure *(sharirik sukh)*with her. During this time, her mother and father lodged a complaint with the police and took Chetna and me with them to the police station. After Chetna and I were introduced, we used to meet each other here and there, now and then. One year ago, I was married to Aruna who was from my caste. I terminated my relationship with Chetna. My in-laws said that Aruna wouldn't go anywhere. I got a divorce. A week ago, I got a cover (letter)

Chetna's Statement

On being questioned in person I am getting written that I live at the aforesaid address. I live at home with my mother and father and study in standard 12th.

On this day you sir *(saheb)* have called me to the [name] police station in connection with ICR [number] registered under IPC sections 363, 366, 376, 380, and 164. I am getting written that in response to the questioning of the crime that Roshan and I both live in the same society near each other. Roshan and I are in a relationship since the last four years and from then under some pretext or the other I used to go to Roshan's house. And since the last nine months this came to be known to my mother and father and we are four sisters and one brother.

On the day of [date] 1994, in the evening, a letter written by me to Roshan Pannachand found its way to my mother's hands and with mummy, words were exchanged and she scolded me and told me to get out of the house. You don't have any right *(adhikar)* to live in this house and go manage Roshan's house and go now to Roshan's house. Saying this she pushed me out of the house and did not even allow me to wear my slippers *(chappals)* in my feet. At this at that moment I went to Roshan's house and went and told from Chetna. I apologise for the trouble you have faced because of me and I want to live with you. She sent one photo and proposed to marry in the court. When she came to my house then she was not carrying any jewellery and she was bare foot [*sic*].

what happened, hearing which Roshan advised me to go back but I stayed at Roshan's house because mummy had asked me not to come back.

Chetna's statement continues as follows:

In the meantime my cousins (maternal uncle's sons) came and took me forcibly from Roshan's house but I came (back) to Roshan's house.

At that time, I stayed at Roshan's house. Roshan has not had any body pleasure (*sharir such*) with me. After that the police came and arrested Roshan and took him to the [name] police station.

A few days ago, I wrote to him asking him to marry me and sent him some photographs. Because of which my mummy threw me out of the house and did not even let me wear slippers on my feet, and I have not taken any jewellery from the house. The fact of my having stolen jewellery is completely false and I don't know anything about the jewellery. This is my reality. It is true and factual and as I have got it written.

On the same day when Chetna's statement was recorded, the PSI wrote to the Chief Judicial Magistrate petitioning the court to take Chetna into judicial custody. Chetna was charged with Sections 363, 366, 376, 380, 114 IPC. The chargesheet was not filed for nine months. During this period, the police received the age-determination test report, which held that Chetna's age was over 18 and under 20. While the medico-legal report had been received; the police had not filed the chargesheet, since they waited for the FSL report, to bring the investigation to a close. The police received the FSL report nine months after the complaint had been filed. The forensic analysis did not reveal any evidence of what is referred to above as 'body pleasure'.

Nine months later, Roshan was chargesheeted on the following grounds:

The accused on [date] 1994 at 20:30 hours made the daughter of the woman complainant (*fariyadibai*) named Chetna age 17½ run away with him from lawful guardianship with the intent of illicit sex (*jharkam*) by enticing or seducing her did illicit sex with her. He was caught on [date] 1994 at 1700 hours.

While Roshan was chargesheeted, the PSI wrote a petition to the Chief Judicial Magistrate asking the court to release Chetna on the basis of lack of evidence. I reproduce the document, translated from Gujarati below:

> Subject: G Police Station under Sections 363, 366, 376, 380, 114 the accused named Chetna d/o M.R. Patel under CrPC 169[21] is being released.
>
> With Hail India (*Jai Bharat*) the [G] police station's Police Sub-Inspector Shri. Patel petitions in this honourable Court this report that during the course of investigation no evidence was found against the accused in the matter in G police station under ICR no. [number] under Sections 366, 363, 376, 380 and 114. The accused girl Chetna who is M.R. Patel's daughter by caste Patel, by age 17 ½ by occupation student, resident of [place] was arrested on [date] 1994 at 19:00 hours, charged with the above mentioned crimes. Under Section 169 CrPC, it is our petition to free the above-mentioned Chetna.

Chetna was charged with the theft of jewellery under Section 380 IPC.[22] There was no evidence that she had stolen the said jewellery.

This is a story of entitlements. By going against the wishes of her parents, Chetna lost all entitlements in her family to anything that she may have otherwise been gifted. The loss of entitlement in family property translates into a charge of theft, whereby nothing truly belongs to her, such that over and over again we are told that Chetna left with nothing, not even a pair of slippers on her feet. The accusation against Chetna repudiates the possibility of any kind of gift giving, inheriting self–acquired property, or later as a bride receiving any form of material or symbolic gifts. The alliance with Roshan symbolized a severance of all social relations with Chetna such that no gifts would flow from the Patel family to the Prajapati family. It is not jewellery that is the object of contestation so much as her right (*adhikar*) to the resources of the family, which cannot be devolved on her on marriage to a lower caste man and hence, a daughter becomes a thief.

The chargesheet also applied Sections 376, 366, 363, and 114 of the IPC against Chetna. Section 114 IPC states that when an abettor to a crime is present at the scene of crime then she or he will be charged with the offence as if she or he had committed the crime herself or himself like the principal offender.[23] This section when applied to Chetna is confounding for it describes Chetna not only as guilty of abetting the crime but in being present at the scene of crime as an abettor she is charged with the offence 'as if' she committed it.

This simultaneous positioning of the woman as abettor, victim, scene of crime, and accused is not a contradiction in law for we are being told that the interpretation of the law makes it possible to constitute a woman as abetting and committing rape, abduction, and kidnapping against herself. She is a victim since the offence is against the guardian. As the scene of crime, her body is constituted as 'evidence' devoid of subjectivity. As an abettor she instigates, plans and influences someone to execute the offence against the guardian and on her body. She is present at the site of crime since the crime is constituted on her body and she is found in the company of the accused. In other words, her decision to live with Roshan, despite the fact that she was a minor and could not legally marry him yet, when translated in these categories equals the charge that she abetted her own rape, abduction, and kidnapping and should be treated as if she were a principal offender since she was present at the scene of crime.

Chetna is a split subject for her body itself is constituted as the scene of crime and she, party to its violation. The fetishized female body exists as evidence of the crime, and injury against society is that which is incurred on this scene of crime. Crime against society refers to both the crime against the legal guardian and the crime against caste politics of honour. As the worst form of transgression in caste sociality, the minor upper caste woman's body enters the law as 'a scene of crime' where love can only be named as rape. Here, the social imagination of a lower caste man's love for an upper caste woman can only exist in a mimetic relationship with upper caste imagination to substitute love by rape (see Rao 1999).

The consequences of this 'mistake in law' were severe for Chetna. She was taken to the Central Jail in Ahmedabad, two days after Roshan and she had been brought to the police station. She was to spend two months there. Roshan recollected:

> I was in the Central Jail for 8–10 days. On 14th, at 12 in the afternoon, I entered my house. They brought her on the second day to the Central Jail. I did not know this. And inside the Central Jail, a PI said to me, 'one girl has come, Chetna Patel, she is your *lover* isn't she?' I said 'yes, sir'.

I did not know that they had brought her in. Then she stayed there for two months.

The English word 'lover' as the police inspector is reported to have said, reflects an everyday understanding of the use of the rape law to legislate love affairs, while positioning Chetna rather derogatorily as a 'lover'—a category, which is not used to describe a wife. Chetna is characterized as Roshan's 'lover' to signal an illicit relation, and hence, increasing her vulnerability to the possibilities of violence, which accrues to women when they are classified as 'lovers' or 'bad' women, as we will see below.

PB: Chetna was in the Central Jail for two months?

R: Yes, for two months. I stayed there for 8–9–10 days but she stayed for two months. Her mummy–pappa gave her up (*chhoot gaye*). 'We don't want the girl'. That's why no one went to release her. Her mother two months later sent her message, 'change your stance and we will get you released'. Her mother had got lesser age written, so I could not get her released. I had come out but I could not get her released. Our lawyer got her transferred to a state run home for women (*nari gruh*). There she stayed for four months. She wanted to take her twelfth exams (final year at high school) from there (the women's home). The police arranged that ... then they would take her in the police van so that she could take her exams everyday.

PB: How could you study?

R: There were all girls living there in the state run home for women (*nari gruh*). Then she wrote a letter to her uncle that it is not too good here—with the girls and all.

C: Those inspectors (police inspectors) used to come at night for the girls. They would knock at the door. I wrote saying: 'come and get me released from here'.

R: People make wrong use, don't they? She wrote to her uncle: 'Come and get me released'.

R: After three months, her uncle—her father's sister's husband—came to take her. After which for two to three months, she lived with her father's brother.

The circulation of the story could have put Chetna at risk of sexual violence following incarceration. Chetna told me that it was fortuitous that she met a woman warden who protected her and allowed her to study. The warden exempted Chetna from having her meals with the other inmates and protected her from those who knocked at the shelter's doors at night. As Chetna put it, 'the environment was not good. People make wrong use.' Chetna's parents had ignored the threat of sexual violence and the pressure of the final examinations at school. Her uncle ultimately helped her escape institutionalization. The story of custodial violence is then dispersed at various sites; the family, police station, the hospital, the jail, and the state run home for women. Chetna's story provokes us to re-think the category of custodial violence as the domain that straddles the familial and the legal simultaneously. With the exception of two women, a woman constable who refused to take her remand and the woman warden who protected her from custodial rape, the narrative of custodial violence that represses love is repetitive.

'Happy Ending'

I describe here the narration of the 'happy ending', which brings a certain closure to the narrative. The closure describes the beginning of the compromise for after the marriage the parents are forced to accept that there is no point in pursuing legal proceedings against Roshan. Let us hear what happened after Chetna's uncle came to fetch her. She spent a few months at her paternal uncle and aunt's home. Then she went back to her parent's house for two months.

> R: We needed the school leaving (certificate) to get married. When she was staying with her mummy, she did not speak to her. She only used to talk to her two sisters.
>
> PB: Papa?
>
> C: Papa said later that if you want to marry, then marry that boy (*referring to* Roshan).
>
> R: He said that later, but in the beginning...
>
> PB: Then how did you spend those two months?
>
> C: My sister does beauty parlour work. I used to help her.

Chetna secured the documents that could get her married.[24] Roshan, in the meantime consulted the defence lawyer who fought their case till the very day of the judgment.

R: Near the collector's office. There is a temple near the court; at that temple Chetna came wearing a dress, like yours.[25] That temple's priest gave a dress. He said that one girl had come to get married—wear those clothes. Then she wore the other dress. Many marriages take place there. This is the photo of the priest who married us. (They showed me photographs.)

PB: You look very happy in these photographs.

C: This is of the engagement, this is of the marriage, and the temple priest is sitting in this one. This one is of the court (*laughs*).

R: We got married under the Hindu Marriage Act (HMA); otherwise, we have to get our name written and everyone else comes to know. That's why we got married under the HMA. When her maternal uncle's son died, then there was no one at her house. Her elder sister knew that she was going to get married. She (Chetna) reached before us (*laughs*). I reached there with the lawyer. She got the ration card, school leaving (certificate) because I had told her everything.

C: We had to do this (*laughs*). Otherwise, if at home any problem cropped up again then I would become old just like this (as a single woman).

Chetna laughed mischievously.

R: Then she took a direct bus and came to the court. It took the entire day. We came back at six in the evening. Then when she went home no one knew. The lawyer had said, 'don't tell anyone anything; tell after one month that I have got married'. After one month, she woke up in the morning and told her mother. Mummy said, 'go'. On Saturday the registry came. We had made Xerox of all the papers, three bunches, I said, 'give the registry in your mother's hand'. Mummy started saying, 'this has happened and now, I can't do anything'.

C: It was a Saturday. Saturday is lucky. We got married on a Saturday. I was born on a Saturday. I was arrested on a Saturday (*laughs*).

Lucky on Saturdays is how Chetna constructs all the critical events in her life—her birth, marriage, arrest, and declaration of her marriage to her mother. In constructing her arrest as a twist of luck, she speaks ironically of the helplessness of the family and law to discipline love and her prolonged laughter celebrated her luck to be with Roshan after all. I joined her infectious laughter, as I looked at their honeymoon photographs in the album.

A sombre note replaced the laughter. Chetna's sister Deepika (whose statement we find in the police records) was not alive to witness the compromise. Chetna's marriage was followed by the marriage of her older sister Deepika. She was 23-years-old when her parents married her to a man in their own caste. Chetna recounted her memories of her sister with a deep sense of loss in her voice.

K: Her sister, no. 3—Deepika. She was like you—her sister.

R: She was murdered. For dowry.

K: Her mother gave a lot of dowry.

C: She was married for two months, and then the neighbours told my mother that Deepika has put a noose around her neck.

R: She was going to do a PhD; she was going to go to Delhi.

K: She would have gone very far, wouldn't she?

C: Yes, she was not the one to sit idle, she would embroider, she wrote.

PB: Where was she married?

R: In Patel. Not in another caste. Now if we sit with her mummy she never tells what the problem was. She lived with him for two months. Not much.

The loss then was magnified—having been punished for opposing familial normativity as well as experiencing grief on the murder of a sister. 'She was going to do a PhD; she was going to go to Delhi. She would have gone very far, wouldn't she? She would embroider, she wrote.' If we look at Chetna and Deepika's stories together, we find a sense of mourning about how parents imagine their daughters' future within caste based patriarchal normativity. In Chetna's case, there could be no anticipation of future within the folds of convention unless she agreed to the wishes of her parents. In the absence of her obedience, her future could only be imagined as one that lived in other disciplinary spaces of the state. The anticipation of future in Deepika's case was one, which was controlled, planned, and projected within convention.

We know that everyday violence of dowry folds into normativity of the heterosexist family. The idea that daughters are a burden till they are married, in the case of Chetna and Deepika constituted the present lived in the spectre of dowry violence in the future. The control over the daughter's sexuality so that she is fit to be exchanged in marriage as a 'good' woman constitutes her present. The category of the 'good' woman is unstable, constantly in need of reiteration. It has to be continually proven that a woman is a 'good' wife. Part of the process of such social proof is being able to meet dowry demands; failing which torture and murder may be an outcome. Caste normativity and the family in this case authored two kinds of biographies for Chetna and Deepika. For both kinship ties were enacted differently within and outside the fold of convention. Both were expected to conform to ordinary notions of parenting. The dowry murder unlike the love affair then did not bring stigma to her parents. Stigma accrues to that which disrupts normativity. It is only when a daughter is a 'bad' wife that issues of honour and stigma may emerge. For, the possibility of rape, torture, or even murder is folded in heterosexist normativity, it is its disruption that is alterity or the asocial.

Compromise: The Structure of Testimony in the Courtroom

We may recall that the case against Roshan continued after the marriage. It had dragged in the trial court till Roshan appeared before the Additional Sessions Judge. The APP at this time had decided that there was no truth in the charges of rape, abduction, and kidnapping. How then did the compromise come about? When I asked Roshan about this he replied,

> We got a date (for hearing). We went in front of the magistrate (he named the Additional Sessions Judge who heard his case). He (Judge) said, 'Why don't you do a compromise (*samadhan*) with them? Call her (Chetna's mother) and go to their house.' I said, 'I cannot go, if I go then if they beat me up and you lock me up then?' He started laughing and said I will send summons. Then those people sent the summons.

Chetna's uncle who had got her released then phoned her mother. Then he said, 'you are going to be called to the court and what are you going to do?' They replied, 'we are going to do nothing, now marriage has taken place and has a child as well, now what will we do?'

One and half years have passed since then and we have been getting dates.

Roshan communicated to the court the irony in the idea that he should initiate the compromise. He shifted the onus onto the judge to send the summons. Compromise then appears as the shared vocabulary between the legal experts. Chetna's mother agreed to the compromise. Chetna's family did not tell her maternal uncle about the compromise or about the hearing. On the day of the hearing, Chetna and Roshan were present with Roshan's sister's husband. Chetna's parents were there as well. When I approached them for an interview, they refused to speak to me. I waited in the courtroom for the hearing to begin. It was nearly fifteen minutes to one in the afternoon. The courtroom was packed. The court was very busy that day. There were several cases to be heard and each with witnesses. Finally at five past one the hearing in this case began. This case was not held *in camera*. Hence, other lawyers waiting for their case to commence were present, and there was a steady stream of movement in and out of the courtroom. The proceedings cited below were conducted in Gujarati. Hirabhai said to the judge, 'in this case, compromise has taken place. There is only one certificate on evidence.'

J: What is the case about?

APP: This case ... [G] police station

APP: Come on. Come on. Call them (to Chetna). You are the accused (to Roshan)? Chetna called out: Mummy, oh mummy (She stood near the witness box).

Chetna's mother walked in.

APP to the mother: Come.

APP (to J): There are bundles of cases. There are witnesses in each case.

Komalben took the stand. Chetna stood next to the lawyers' table. Hirabhai asked Chetna to sit in the row of chairs reserved for witnesses.

While the testimonies of the complainant and the prosecutrix were heard, all other expert witnesses including the *panch* were dropped. Komalben, Chetna's mother as the complainant was the first to testify. While Komalben stood in the witness box, the typist was sent for.[26]

APP to Typist: Write name.

Typist: I am waiting for the bench clerk.

The bench clerk told her the Sessions Case No., Citation, Name.

J: Keeping God as my witness I state that I will speak the truth and nothing but the truth.

K: Repeats

Typist types: Given oath.

J: It is not *in camera?*

APP: No, Sir (*xerox*).

Chetna was sent out.[27]

APP: You have one son and four daughters?

K: Yes (nods).

J: Of my children I have four daughters[28] and one son.

APP: Third ... (*inaudible*)

K: Yes (*nods*).

J: My third daughter's name is Chetna.

APP: The incident happened approximately three years and three months ago.

K: Yes (*nods*).

Typist types: the incident happened approximately three years and three months ago.

APP (d): during this incident Chetna was studying in High School.

APP: The name of the accused is Roshan?

K: Yes (*nods*).

J (d): I recognize Roshan Pannachand. He lives in our society.

APP continued to question as the judge dictated: Look ... (*inaudible*)

K: (*inaudible*).

J (d): After Chetna left then she and the accused have been married and at present Chetna has

APP: Four months.

J (d): Has a baby of four months also.

Komalben did not deny that she went to the police.

APP: Did the police do a *panchnamma* of your house?

K: Yes.

J (d): Police did a *panchnamma* of our house.

PP: Did you give the police Chetna's school leaving certificate?

K: Yes.

J (d): I gave the police Chetna's birth registration xerox copy.

APP: When you found Chetna did you take her to the dispensary for medical examination?

K: laughs

DL: You don't know.

K: Yes (*nods*).

J (d): When Chetna was found then after that the medical examination was done.

APP: Got the medical examination done.

The judge signals the end of the chief-examination and turns to ask the defence lawyer if he had any questions to ask.

J to DL: Do you want to ask?

J: Do you have a *vakalatnamma*? Check it.

A *vakalatnamma* is the official record that shows that the lawyer is officially enlisted on the bar as well as hired by the accused. The judge remembered the presence of the defence lawyer after the chief-examination was over and asked the bench clerk to check the record. Subsequently, Hirabhai cross-examined Komalben instead of the defence lawyer. Hirabhai asked the judge whether he should question the witness about Chetna's age.

In the meantime, the typist typed: From the accused's side Shri Bharwad, cross-examination.

APP: When this incident happened had the accused come to your house?

K: No

J (d): It is true that when the incident happened on that day during that time that the accused had come to our house that did not happen.

APP: Chetna went out on her own?

K: Yes (*nods*)

J (d): It is true that Chetna went out of the house on her own.

APP: And she used to meet him again and again?

K: Yes (*nods*)

J (d): It is true that we used to tell Chetna constantly not to meet the accused but she would not listen

APP: Enough. Go sit down.

APP (to J): The entire case depends on the girl; otherwise, we will have to take evidence on injury. Drop the husband (Chetna's father). We do not need too many witnesses.

The Prosecutor did not ask Komalben if she threw Chetna out of the house, nor did he ask if her family members beat Roshan up subsequently. The aim of the cross-examination was to prove that Roshan did not coerce Chetna. It was Chetna who initiated the relationship and not Roshan who coerced her. Chetna was called to the stand subsequently.

APP: (*inaudible*)

C: (*inaudible*)

APP (d): The incident happened approximately three years ago.

APP: (*inaudible*)

C: (*inaudible*)

APP (d): During the incident the accused used to live in our society in front of our house.

Chetna's response in the transcript of the testimony is framed in the past tense, as if Roshan were the 'accused' for her and does not refer to him as Roshan or her husband. Although the translation of her response is in the first person, it indexes a legal moment corresponding to the legal narrative when Roshan was named as the accused.

APP: Which standard did you study in then?

C: In 12th standard.

APP (d): during the incident I used to study in the 12th standard.

APP: (*inaudible*)

C: (*inaudible*)

APP (d): At that time, my age was 18 years.

Chetna testifies that she was eighteen years old at the time the incident happened. It is important that the evidence of her mother on the question of age is not taken except that she is asked if she submitted the school-leaving certificate, which gives the officially recorded age as proof.[29]

APP: You had a relationship of love (*prem sambandh*)?

C: No, we used to meet in the society (society here means residential neighbourhood).

APP: You had love only ... not bad love (*kharab prem*)?

C: Yes.

APP (d): I had only a love (*prem sambandh*) with the accused. There was no bad love *(kharab prem)* between us.

Chetna construed the first question regarding the love affair to imply that Roshan and she were in an illicit sexual relationship. She denied the suggestion that they were in a sexual relationship. 'No, we used to meet in the society'. Thus evoking the idea that they used to meet in public space of the neighbourhood and were therefore not in a clandestine sexual relationship. Hirabhai understood Chetna's meaning and rephrased his question. 'You had love only'. Bad love (*kharab prem*) was deployed as euphemistic allusion to pre-marital sex. The shared discourse here is one, which does not name sex in an open courtroom. She was not asked very explicit questions for now she is a married woman with a child, and the compromise altered the structure of the testimony such that sexually explicit questions were not posed to her in open courtroom. The objective here was not to challenge her testimony by attacking her character.

We see here that the object of crime has altered. Chetna was no longer required to say whether or not she had consented to sex or not. The medical evidence already available to the prosecutor made it clear that clinically she was not 'habituated with sexual intercourse, probable she never had any intercourse'. Hence, Chetna was not asked whether she was raped. Chetna testified to a relationship of love, which was then translated as love distinct from 'bad love', suggesting thereby that virginity purifies the experience of love placing it in the moral realm that differentiates between the *good* versus the *bad*. This classification is produced within the legal framework of ascertaining whether she had sex with Roshan or not on which could pin further questions of rape and seduction, or force and consent. It is produced under the specific context of the hearing, which is articulated in the shadow of compromise that had already taken place. In order to consolidate the legal narrative indicating what happened, Hirabhai, then asked her questions relating to the conditions under which she left home. These questions were not posed to her mother since this distinction between good and bad love was not one shared by Chetna's mother. I reproduce these below:

APP: On the day of the incident mummy gave you a scolding, right?

C: Yes (*nods*)

APP (d): And my mummy gave me a scolding.

APP: And mummy said, get out of my house

C: Yes (*nods*)

APP (d): and mummy said that you get out of my house

APP: Mummy said, get out of the house, go to Roshan's house (this will make it short) saying this she pushed me.

C: Yes (*nods*)

APP (d): You don't have any right (*adhikar*) to live with me. And you go to Roshan's house. And go to Roshan's house. Saying this she pushed me out.

After dictating APP asked, 'Ok is this all right?' Chetna nods an affirmative.

APP (d):And didn't even let me wear slippers on my feet. That's how I went to Roshan's house. At that time Roshan was not at home. His mother–father (*ma–bap*) were there. I told them the above-mentioned incident.

Hirabhai referred Chetna's police statement while framing his questions and dictating the testimony. He established through this line of questioning that Chetna was forced to leave her house without even being allowed to wear her slippers, indicating the abjectness of her condition. Next, Hirabhai turned to the reason behind the quarrel between the mother and daughter.

APP: Did Roshan write you any letter?

C: No.

APP (d): And he did not propose to marry me.

APP (d): reads out from a statement the part on the letter.

J to C: Did you write him a letter? You marry me, sent him a photograph also?

C: (*inaudible*)

J (d): Some days ago, I posted Roshan a letter saying that I want to marry you and with it sent a photograph.

APP: Then the police investigation began

C: (*inaudible*).

APP: Police arrested Roshan and me.

Having established that Roshan did not write a letter, rather it was Chetna who not only wrote a letter but proposed marriage, the onus shifts; it foregrounded Chetna's desire to be with Roshan. We must remember that the case against her, which was finally dropped by the police, was not relevant here. We do not find references to the theft or the charges brought against Chetna. It is not her story that is being represented by the prosecution in its entirety. It is those parts of the story that address the charge of rape and seduction against Roshan that is the issue here.

APP: And then the medical examination ... blood ... right?

C: Yes (*nods*).

APP (d): Then I was sent for medical examination to the hospital and my clothes were confiscated. A *panchnamma* was done.

APP: (*inaudible*)

C: (*laughs*)

APP: She has a child.

APP (d): I have been married to Roshan and we have a four–month–old baby also.

We may note that while referring to the present moment, Hirabhai did not refer to Roshan any longer as the accused. He was now positioned as Chetna's husband, and referred to as Roshan. Subsequently, Hirabhai asked Roshan's lawyer if he wanted to ask anything. When Roshan's lawyer did not speak, the judge upon the prosecutor's persuasion decided not to take evidence on the issue of age. Chetna was asked to leave. The police officer who had arrested Chetna and Roshan, taken their remand, and was in charge of the investigation did not show up for the next hearing either. He was finally dropped from the list of witnesses to be examined. A fortnight later Roshan was acquitted.

I wish to derive two observations from the proceedings cited above. First, here the testimony to love is not effaced. Throughout this narrative we find that the burden of proving Roshan's innocence lies on Chetna. It was Chetna's testimony that is critical to proving Roshan's innocence. The testimony situated Chetna as an agent of seduction and had the effect of situating Chetna as a protector. Second, the structure of the rape trial was altered here. In the instance of compromise, when the woman is re-integrated within structures of alliance, the line of questioning is not against her honour. Categories such as 'bad' or 'good' love, which preserve gendered discourses of honour of men and modesty of women, inflect courtroom talk. This is in contrast to the routine sexualization of the testimony to rape, which sets out to defame the survivor of rape.

★ ★ ★

In constructing Chetna as a victim or witness, or accused, she is called to bear witness to something other than the experience of her subjectivity, and denied the possibility of testifying to custodial violence. The story of custodial violence narrated in this chapter is a revelation of the incommensurality between the legal subject's experience and the way she is named in law as a victim, witness, and accused in the crime of and for planning to kidnap, abduct, and rape her own body. This is a stunning illustration of what Lyotard has called 'differend'. As Davies (1996:41) argues, a differend arises when 'the parties are not speaking the same language—either literally or in effect or if there is no rule which can be applied to them in common' . While the law always 'artificially sets up a differend between itself and both parties to a dispute, because it requires them to submit to its set of norms and speak to its language', in this instance the experience of the woman does not exist (Davies 1996: 41). The police interpret the law to suggest that women can be constructed as abetting and committing rape on their bodies, which does not exist in women's experience. It is this incommensurality that has been the object of ethnographic exploration in this chapter.

The competing accounts of rape show how over time the object of criminalization alters. Roshan and Chetna's marriage transforms that which was initially criminalized. Chetna was now reinserted in another kind of normativity. With the acquittal, it is this normativity that the judgment restored. Love, then is considered asocial because it has the capacity to disrupt rather than nurture given imaginations of social reproduction. In the ultimate analysis, the testimony to love succeeds after the compromise is effectuated, and only when Chetna is fully assimilated in another normative structure as a wife and the mother of a son, putting law beyond the threat of love. When love and law are pitted in such a radical opposition, public secrecy is not the socio-legal route to imagine a future. Rather ethnographies of rape trials in India narrate how law fears love, how love finds justice, and how love mourns its loss. Reminiscent of Auden who says 'law... like love we don't know where or why, like love we can't compel or fly, like love we often weep, like love we seldom keep'.

Notes

1. Goodrich maintains that 'faith, fidelity and desire were alike to be directed to the goal of reproducing the church, the ecclesial commonwealth and the male line' (1996:48).

2. We know that the laws of abduction in late nineteenth century Canada, for instance, were used by parents to punish a daughter and her boyfriend for marrying against their wishes. Dubinsky (1993) suggests that the English

laws on abduction, which were applied in Canada in the 1840s, expanded the criminalization of the abduction of propertied daughters to include all women under the age of 16. She argues that the prosecutions against consenting adults were scripted around those 'improper' alliances between Canadian women and 'foreigners' from East or South Europe.

3. Whilst I refer to the law on rape prior to its amendment in 2013, the arguments forwarded in this chapter become even more pertinent now. In 2013, the age of consent was increased from 16 to 18 years. No amendments in law or reform measures have been instituted to prevent the criminalisation of love.

4. The recent literature on the right of women to choose marriage, if and when they want to, has inaugurated feminist critiques of the techniques by which a range of laws are used to criminalize love in plural legal contexts in South Asia (see Baxi 2006; Chakravarti 2005; Chowdhry 2004; Mody 2008; Welchman and Hossain 2005). While I do not wish to detail the many painful instances where consensual marriages forged on love have resulted in extra judicial killing, in what has now come to be named as 'honour killings', I wish to make a few brief points on this issue. First, state law exists in the field of legal pluralism with plural structures of power (Baxi 1985). Second, state law is often withdrawn when non–state law forces reconciliation on an unwilling wife, violently recovers a consenting bride or mandates a spectacular death to lovers. Third, state law mimes non–state law by absorbing notions of transgression that are mobilized by the apparatus normally seen as the 'other' of state law. Fourth, state law allows the performance of different kinds of discourses (for instance, rehabilitation and rescue), which address the rationalities of state law and non–state law simultaneously through a complicated circulation of categories, sites and certifications.

5. This may be accompanied with a *habeas corpus* petition that alleges that the daughter is held in private detention.

6. The Criminal manual issued by the Gujarat High Court specifies that 'the accused person should be informed by the Court at the beginning of every trial that he may sit, if he desires to do so, and chairs or benches should, whenever available, be provided for this purpose. …The accused must, however stand up, whenever he is addressed by the Court. At the time of hearing of the criminal case against the accused who are on bail the accused, instead of being made to sit in the dock, be allowed to sit at a convenient place set apart in the Court room, a distance from the dias where the judge or magistrate sits' (1977:59).

7. Moreover, it assumes an order of proceeding where one case is heard at a particular point of time, and a virtual absence of background conversation.

8. Even so, the names have been changed. Likewise, the names of the police officer and police station have been changed.

9. Prajapati traditionally a potter caste is listed as an OBC caste.

10. The lyrics translated from Hindi are: A human being loves someone in this world once, lives with this pain, dies with this pain. If one has loved, why fear? One has loved; it is not theft. Why sigh in secrecy, in hiding? The desire for him will remain in the heart; the flame of the light will live in the celebration. To live in love, to die in love; now what else can I do? Our love cannot stay hidden; everywhere is his presence. When there is no veil from God, why draw a veil from fellow humans?

11. *Lafara* has several connotations to it. It means affair, fight, brawl, trouble and event.

12. *Bharwa* literally is used for a pimp. Here it is used as an abuse, indicating that Roshan was not capable of being an appropriate partner in a marriage alliance and hence, he was insulted by being called a man in the business of selling and buying women in prostitution.

13. *Danga* is a word used to imply collective violence. It takes on a specific trajectory in relation to communal riots in India. In other contexts, it is used to refer to mob violence.

14. *Kalam* means a clause or a section in law as well as a pen or means by which writing is inscribed.

15. Remand means the act of sending back a prisoner into custody, especially in order to obtain further evidence on the charge. Here, taking remand (or its threat) encodes violence in police custody.

16. The Crime Branch was located in a place known as the Gaekwad Haveli in the old city. The Crime Branch was first established in 1931. Now it is infamous for torture.

17. According to the police papers, Roshan had been charged with abduction, kidnapping and rape under Sections 366, 363 and 376 IPC. At that time, Roshan said, he did not know which sections of the penal code were being applied against him.

18. The trial court is closed on two alternate Saturdays in a month.

19. From a police officer whom I asked about techniques of interrogation, I learnt that such interrogation contains within it a range of violent practices such as beating on the soles, making a person lie on a slab of ice, beating with tyres, and other forms of violence.

20. The lawyer who helped Roshan get the bail introduced Roshan to Mr Bharward who took up their case for the years to follow. We may note that both the lawyer and the client belong to the OBC castes.

21. Section 169 of the Cr PC holds that 'if, upon an investigation under this Chapter, it appears to the officer-in-charge of the police station that there is no sufficient evidence or reasonable ground of suspicion to justify the forwarding of the accused to a Magistrate, such officer shall, if such person is, in custody,

release him on his executing a bond with or without sureties, as such officer may direct, to appear, if and when so required, before a Magistrate empowered to take cognisance of the offence on a police report, and to try the accused or commit him for the trial' (Ratanlal and Dhirajlal 2002:266). This law allows the police officer concerned to petition for the release of the accused on the grounds that there is no evidence against her.

22. Section 380 of the IPC holds that whoever commits to theft in any building, tent or vessel which building, tent or vessel is used as a human dwelling, or used for the custody of property, shall be punished with imprisonment of either description for a term that may extend to seven years, and shall also be liable to fine (see Ratanlal and Dhirajlal 2001).

23. Section 114 holds that wherever any person who is absent would be liable to be punished as an abettor, is present when the act or offence for which he would be punishable in consequence of the abetment is committed, he shall be deemed to have committed such an act or offence. This section is stringed along with the other offences and does not specify if it is applicable to the theft charge alone. If this had been the case the charge of theft would have been read along with the law on abetting.

24. In her study on love marriages in Delhi, Mody (2002) says that the easiest way for couples, who marry against the wishes of their families, is to undertake what is commonly dubbed as the 'Hindu marriage'. This entails marriage in Arya Samaj temples. The accompanying documentation produced includes photographic evidence of the ceremony, and an affidavit signed by the couple. The affidavit signed by the couple specifies that the marriage is in accordance with Hindu customs, and that they are both Hindus or converted to Hinduism. The affidavit certifies that the woman is above eighteen years old and the man above twenty–one years of age. Mody is right in pointing out that the most important statement in the affidavit is the declaration that 'they have left home of their own free will, and that they have taken nothing from their homes except the clothes they are wearing' (Mody 2002: 245). She argues that this declaration is critical since families file 'false' cases of kidnapping and theft against their children or their spouses so that the police can recover them, and they can pressurise them to break up (Mody 2002: 245). This marriage is then registered in the court. This route is preferred to civil marriage under the Special Marriage Act, since it prescribes a different procedure of putting up a notice of the impending marriage for a period of one month and if after that period no one raises any lawful objection to the marriage a civil marriage is permitted. Mody's ethnography provides a remarkable account of the way such marriages are negotiated in courts of law and within the domain of the familial. In this case Roshan and Chetna relied on their lawyer to ensure that they were legally married and this marriage was kept a secret until the time

the marriage was registered. Chetna's mother accepted the registration of the marriage in the court of law.

25. Roshan meant that Chetna was wearing a cotton *salwar kameez*; similar to the one I was wearing at that time.

26. In the transcript provided below, we will see that Hirabhai (referred to as APP) also questions the witnesses, although the case was with the prosecution (Mr Desai, referred to as D). I have indicated where the responses were inaudible and specified where the witness nodded an affirmative by adding 'nods' in parenthesis.

27. Chetna could not have remained in the court to hear her mother's testimony since she was to take the stand next. Judicial objectivity demands that witnesses are not influenced by what is said in the Court and therefore they are not allowed to sit in the court until they have testified on the day of the hearing.

28. Komalben does not mention that of her four daughters, one of her daughters Deepika was murdered by her in laws at the time the case was on trial. The question posed to her was based on the *fariyad*.

29. The age recorded on school leaving certificates, which is considered, as evidence may be different from natural date of birth for a number of reasons.

References

Baxi, Pratiksha. 2006. '*Habeas Corpus* in the Realm of Love: Litigating Marriages of Choice in India'. *Australian Feminist Law Journal*, 25: 59–78.

———. 2014. *Public Secrets of Law: Rape Trials in India*. New Delhi: Oxford University Press.

Baxi, Upendra. 1985. 'Discipline, Repression and Legal Pluralism', in Peter Sack and Elizabeth Minchin (eds), *Legal Pluralism Proceedings of the Canberra Law Workshop VII*. Australia, Pink Panther: Law Department, ANU.

Chakravarti, Uma. 2005. 'From Fathers to Husbands: Of Love, Death and Marriage in North India', in Lynn Welchman and Sara Hossain (eds). *'Honour': Crimes, Paradigms and Violence against Women*, pp. 308–31. London: Zed Books.

Chowdhry, Prem. 2004. 'Private Lives, State Intervention: Cases of Runaway Marriage in Rural North India', *Modern Asian Studies*, 38(1): 55.

Davies, Margaret. 1996. *Delimiting the Law: 'Postmodernism' and the Politics of Law*. London: Pluto Press.

Dubinsky, Karen. 1996. *Improper Advances Rape and Heterosexual Conflict in Ontario 1880–1929*. Chicago & London: University of Chicago Press.

Epstein, A.L. 1978. 'The Case Method in the Field of Law', in A.L. Epstein (ed.), *The Craft of Social Anthropology*, pp. 205–30. Delhi: Hindustan Publishing Corporation.

Foucault, Michel. 1977. *Discipline and Punish: The Birth of the Prison*. New York: Vintage Books.

Goodrich, Peter. 1987. *Legal Discourse: Studies in Linguistics, Rhetoric and Legal Analysis*. London: Macmillan.

————. 1990. *Languages of Law: From Logics of Memory to Nomadic Masks*. London: Weidenfeld and Nicolson.

————. 1996. *Law in the Courts of Love: Literature and Other Minor Jurisprudence*. London and New York: Routledge.

Gujarat High Court (GHC). 1977. *Criminal Manual*. Ahmedabad: Gujarat High Court.

Matoesian, Gregory M. 1993. *Reproducing Rape: Domination through Talk in the Courtroom*. Cambridge: Polity Press.

Mody, Perveez. 2002. Love and the Law: Love-Marriage in Delhi. *Modern Asia Studies* 36, 1: 223–56.

————. 2008. *The Intimate State: Love–Marriage and the Law in Delhi*. Delhi: Routledge.

Pinney, Christopher. 1992. 'The Lexical Spaces of Eye-Spy', in Peter Ian Crawford and David Turton (eds). *Films as Ethnography*, pp. 26–49. Manchester: Manchester University Press.

Raes, Koen. 1998. 'On Love and Other Injustices: Love and Law as Improbable Communications', in Hanne Petersen (ed.) *Love and Law in Europe*, pp. 27–51. England: Ashgate and Dashmouth Publishing Company.

Rao, Anupama. 1999. 'Understanding Sirasgaon: Notes Towards Conceptualising the Role of Law, Caste and Gender in a case of "Atrocity"', in Rajeswari Sunder Rajan, ed. *Signposts: Gender Issues in Post- Independence India*, pp. 204–47. Delhi: Kali for Women.

Ratanlal and Dhirajlal. 2001. *The Indian Penal Code*. Nagpur: Wadhwa and Company.

————. 2002. *The Code of Criminal Procedure*. Nagpur: Wadhwa and Company.

Welchman Lynn and Sara Hossain (eds). 2005. *'Honour': Crimes, Paradigms and Violence against Women*. London: Zed Books.

3

DANIELA BERTI

Binding Fictions

Contradicting Facts and Judicial Constraints in a Narcotics Case in Himachal Pradesh[*]

A noop Chitkara is considered by the High Court judges in Himachal Pradesh to be one of the top lawyers specializing in narcotics cases. I first met Chitkara in the corridor of the High Court building after the judges of the court I was attending had decided to take a break. I was told by a judge that this lawyer had been invited to take part in a two-day conference on the Narcotic Drugs and Psychotropic Substances Act, or NDPS Act, which was about to take place in Shimla in March 2010 on the initiative of the Judicial Academy. Apparently, this was the first time that a lawyer had been invited to give a paper at a meeting of this kind, where speakers were usually chosen from high-ranking judges or advocate generals along with various experts on the topic in question. As I was still unsure whether the Chief Justice, the head of the Academy, would allow me to attend the event, I was

[*] Research leading to this chapter was funded by the French National Research Agency's programme, 'Justice and Governance in India and South Asia' (ANR-08-GOUV-064). I would like to thank Véronique Bouillier, Gilles Tarabout, and Anthony Good for their comments on the first draft of this text.

curious to glean something about the paper that Chitkara was going to present at the conference.

Smiling at my question, the lawyer told me that he was still work-ing on his paper, although he was rather sceptical about achieving a positive outcome from the conference, which, as the Chief Justice had announced, was intended 'to improve the quality of investigations of NDPS cases'.[1] He pointed out that in India, despite the extremely stringent nature of narcotic legislation, those accused were usually acquitted. These acquittals, he said, were mainly due to procedural mistakes made by the police during investigations as well as to con-tradictions that emerged during the trial between the way the police replied to the questions about how investigations had been conducted and what had previously been written in the police report. The paper he planned to present at the conference would thus throw light on the essential steps that the police had to follow so that prosecutors would be able to prove their cases. 'As a lawyer,' he told me, 'I defend all these people who become involved in a narcotics case. Who better than me to tell the judges about the way to improve the quality of investigations in such cases?'

However strange the idea of a defence lawyer helping the police to improve their investigation might appear, Chitkara did not seem wor-ried about this. 'I am going to place all my cards on the table, and then we'll see if they get me, but they won't', he said confidently. Indeed, he was fully convinced that regardless of the clues passed on to the other side, he would continue to win cases. The reason for his self-assurance went hand in hand with his complete mistrust of the police, whom he considered to be incompetent, sometimes corrupt, and constantly com-ing up with 'fabricated stories'. 'They present these stories as the truth, but they never tell the truth', he concluded.

Although Chitkara accused the police of not telling the truth, he did not mean that people in the area, including his clients, were not involved in narcotic trafficking and that the police always incriminated innocent people. Though this is the official version that lawyers always present before a judge, his discourse implies something else. It refers to the notion of the police's concern about providing the court with an 'ideal' report that does not exactly correspond to how investigations are carried out in the field. According to this discourse, which is commonly upheld in court circles, an element of fiction is introduced by the police in their report which is due to police efforts to show that they have duly followed the relevant procedures, even in cases where they have not done so. This element of fiction would inevitably lead police officers to lie or to contradict one another when cross-examined during the trial, and would consequently undermine their credibility before the court. The tendency of police officers to provide an idealized and thus untrue report of the investigations was also often put forward by judges, which is probably the reason why they decided to invite a defence lawyer—hence someone used to finding contradictions in police reports—to take part in the NDPS workshop.

The problem of truth is ever present in criminal cases not only in relation to the version of events written by the police at the time of the investigations, but also in reference to the testimony provided by witnesses during the trial. Judges and prosecutors alike always complain that most witnesses called to the bar by the prosecutor to support the accusation will eventually lie for the benefit of the accused, denying what they said in their previous statements.

In this chapter, I will base my findings on a case study I followed at a Session Court in a district of Himachal Pradesh to examine the notions of truth and untruth that were put forward by its protagonists. The analyses of court dialogues in both oral and written forms show how the lawyer's defence strategy consists in demolishing the police's credibility and in presenting another fictional version of the story, which is suggested during the trial itself through cross-examination techniques. Unlike the way in which the police compile the investigative report, the lawyer's story does not have to follow procedural rules or legal provisions. Instead, it relies on a more intuitive scenario that was commonly used in the court cases I observed in Himachal Pradesh, according to which the accused is falsely implicated in a case by a family member or by someone from his or her village. In the case presented here, the plausibility of this counter-story was not immediately evident to the court but came across at the end of a long process during which the defence lawyer challenged the veracity of every detail of the police account. I will show how the version strategically proposed by the defence lawyer became legally plausible when the police version of the case had gradually lost its credibility in the eyes of the judge. The defence's story, though constantly reduced to strategic fiction by both the prosecutor and the judge in the initial stages of the trial, eventually prevailed at the end of the trial and was used in part by the judge to back his decision to acquit the accused.

The analyses of the interactions that took place during the hearings will be discussed here with reference to the notion of 'binding', which in court studies denotes a legal procedure according to which a statement 'must confront past statements, generating inconsistency and contradiction' (Scheffer 2007: 5). The notion of binding regularly emerges in Indian trials when a witness's statement is considered to have more or less evidentiary value according to specific procedural rules. Furthermore, the case discussed here shows how the issue of binding is related to a constant shift between writing and orality in an Indian judicial setting and, more specifically, to the extent to which an oral testimony and its written equivalents are likely to be considered admissible evidence by the court. In this chapter, I examine how the court manages to deal with contradictory oral and written versions of a story and how greater evidentiary value is attributed to one of these versions. I also address the fictional aspects of the trial proceedings by considering the ways in which the judge, the police, and the prosecutor discuss the case out of court.

However, before introducing the case study, and in order to contextualize the court dialogues, I provide a more general view of the ways in which narcotic issues are discussed and perceived in government and judiciary milieus as well as by society at large.

Formal Meetings and Local Discourse

After my conversation with Anoop Chitkara, it turned out that the Chief Justice had no objections to my attending the conference at the Judiciary Academy; he even came to welcome me personally during the coffee break. The style of the conference was rather formal; though the speakers were all from the Higher Judiciary, the audience was made up of district judges and prosecutors, young trainee judges, high-ranking police officers, and forestry officials, as well as a few journalists seated in the middle of the room.[2]

During the workshop, narcotic cases were assessed from an international perspective. Judges reminded attendees that the actual source of narcotic trafficking in Himachal Pradesh comes from outside the country itself, evoking 'narco-tourism' from Israel and European countries or 'narco-terrorists'. Drug-trafficking experts had been invited to heighten junior judges' awareness of the dangers of drug use and of the means by which drugs produced in India circulate on the international market. Discussions were mostly geared towards improving the performance of the police and prosecution services by providing advice on technical issues or suggesting strategies to avoid errors that commonly prevent judges from taking the decision to convict the accused.

One of the first speakers at the workshop was Justice Deepak Gupta who at that time was appointed to Himachal Pradesh High Court after having spent part of his career as a High Court lawyer. Deepak Gupta is a very modern, efficient judge and well aware of the need to speed up court proceedings and to computerize the court system. He regularly updated the court website himself and posted his own judgments online. His favourite expressions were 'constitution', 'human rights', and 'the rule of law'. At the workshop, he began his speech by analyzing what he considered to be the commonest reason why prosecutors lose narcotic cases in India, stating his viewpoint that 'if you follow the system, the prosecution cannot fail'. One of his major criticisms was addressed to the 'investigative agency', that is to the police; as Chitkara had done, he remarked that police officers were mistaken in believing that they were required to proceed according to the Act, which resulted in their falsifying their reports. By way of an example, he cited an occasion when the police had claimed that a case was registered on the spot at night in the glow of a scooter's headlamp, yet the defence lawyer had shown that the documents were so neatly written that they had obviously been drafted at the police station. 'Why can't you say that there was not enough space there, that it was dark and so we moved to an office?' he bust out with, addressing the few senior police officers sitting in the room.

Justice Gupta put forward another common mistake where police officers who make 'a search' in a private house systemically include the name of a senior officer who allegedly took part in a raid merely in order to respect the requirement defined in the Narcotic Act. He noted that he had encountered this problem a number of times in the past two weeks, explaining,

> When the constable gets the information, the senior says, 'Go and take my name!' [as if he had been with him]. Now what happens is that when the senior becomes linked to the operation, the search is already over, and when he is cross-examined in court, he cannot give even the slightest

description of the building where the search took place or of the people involved in the search, clearly showing that he had never been there.

Turning to the prosecutors, the judge blamed them for withdrawing all too quickly a case when they see witnesses turn hostile or for not taking the time to cross-examine them. He also held the magistrates and session judges responsible for frequently omitting in their transcription of the evidence many important facts that emerge during hearings and which need to be recorded in the court report as they may be relevant to revision of the case by the appeal judge.

Gupta's paper, like the others scheduled for that day, reflected the superior position from which High Court judges address both members of the lower judiciary and the police. By contrast, in his concluding words the judge congratulated Anoop Chitkara, the aforementioned High Court lawyer, for the paper he was about to present, which Gupta had already had the opportunity to read. He described the paper as a wonderful checklist for police officers and worthy of being printed and distributed to every policeman to ensure that they are in a position to prove a case. Chitkara was visibly flattered by the judge's comments about his paper, the preparation of which had occupied his junior assistants for several days. The lawyer then embarked on a point-by-point discussion on the many technical procedures the police were required to follow in order to provide prosecutors with the chance to prove their cases. He associated the 'technicality' of the Narcotic Act with 'the need to protect innocent citizens from being falsely implicated in a narcotic case' (Chitkara 2010). He also referred to the possibility that a false case could be made against a villager not only by one of his or her enemies, but also by police officers themselves in order to enter into negotiations with the accused.

The discourse of a 'possible misuse of the Narcotic Act' is quite commonly made in the court milieu, not only by lawyers but also by judges. This is demonstrated in a speech delivered by Justice A. R. Lakshmanan at another workshop of the Narcotic Act organized by the Judiciary Academy in 2008. In his paper, Lakshmanan highlighted the contrast between the severity of the Narcotic Act and the fact that during some festivals, such as Holi, a cannabis-based preparation (*bhang*) is used freely before the eyes of police officers, because it is considered to be a traditional local beverage. According to the judge, however, 'nothing could prevent the police from making arrests and throwing everyone at a Holi party into jail' (Lakshmanan 2008:55). Indeed, this appeared to him to be a good way for politicians and others to get rid of their enemies. The judge concluded by noting how many innocent people 'languish in jail indefinitely [...] after ganja [cannabis] has been deliberately planted in their household or belongings [by connivers in the police force].' (Lakshmanan 2008: 55.)

Lakshmanan's reference to the cultural aspects of cannabis in the area is something of an exception, as these Academy workshops usually focus on legal procedures and penal sections. By contrast, villagers involved in the cultivation of cannabis strongly emphasize the cultural value attributed to cannabis, the cultivation of which, they say, is a traditional practice that has been maintained exclusively for domestic and religious purposes (Berti 2011). Local newspapers give a great deal of visibility to this discourse, often reporting that villagers consider cannabis cultivation to have been approved by their village deities. For example, an article appeared in *The Tribune* in 2004, entitled 'Where devta tells them [villagers] to grow cannabis' includes statements from a number of villagers, who claimed that 'unless Jamlu god tells us to grow other crops, we will grow only cannabis'. Furthermore, the vice-president of Malana village, a place in the region famous for growing cannabis, is quoted as saying, 'Cannabis has been grown here since time immemorial'.[3]

Other newspapers report on villagers' discourses that criticize the criminalization of cannabis activities. The article *Hardships Multiply for Cannabis Growers* is representative of the kind of discourse reported in the press. The same journalist, Kuldeep Chauhan, refers to the way villagers consider the anti-cannabis Act as 'city-centric anti-villager law'. He writes about young girls who were asked by their parents 'to give up their studies as the anti-cannabis team has destroyed their only source of income.' He refers to Mand Das, a ward member of the panchayat complaining that 'we can't grow cannabis, the traditional source of handicrafts and staple food [though] our ancestors have survived on these two sources of livelihood down the centuries'(*The Tribune*, 6 October 2005).[4] The problem villagers have with the Narcotic Act is often presented as being linked to the policy regarding forest protection. The article reports, for example, how villagers belonging to the Great Himalayan National Parks area complain that their traditional practice of collecting herbs from the forest is now banned. The journalist explicitly takes the defence of the 'poor villagers' against the implementation of the law, reproaching forestry and police officials for not providing 'convincing answers.' (*The Tribune*, 6 October 2005)

Nevertheless, this local discourse has to be regarded as only part of the picture. As Molly (2001) underlines, for the last forty years cannabis cultivation has been under the control of national and international dealers whose only concern is to sell the product on foreign drug markets. The discourse on the 'traditional' use of cannabis also appears to contradict the fact that, in some cases, fields previously reserved for ordinary crops have recently been turned into cannabis fields—and in most cases, this has been requested by outsiders. The domestic and religious use of cannabis may well persist, but a villager cultivating cannabis today does it, first and foremost, to reply to a market demand (Berti 2011). The economic interest behind cannabis cultivation has even led villagers to develop some strategies in order to escape police control, such as sowing cannabis on woodland instead of private land so that nobody can be punished (*The Tribune*, 12 December 2005).

Though supported by the press and sometimes referred to by lawyers in informal conversations, the ongoing discourse about the cultural and religious importance of cannabis, is never used as a 'defence argument' inside the courtroom where narcotic cases are considered to be extremely serious and are punishable by very harsh sentences. However, these social and cultural dynamics inevitably impact the proceedings of a trial, often leading all village-based witnesses to side with the accused. This is especially true in cases where cannabis has been discovered on the property of the accused, whether cultivated in a field or hidden in his or her house. The judicial process may also ultimately be hampered by recurrent procedural errors made by the police during the investigation, which often results in the total collapse of the prosecutor's case. In order to analyze the interactions that took place during the trial I observed, I first examine various police documents included in the case file, which will help to introduce the case and to give some insight into the way investigations are reported before the court.

Writing up the Story

Though never invoked before the judge, the discourse on the cultural and religious value of cannabis may be part of a preliminary version given by the accused before the case is taken up by the defence lawyer.

This was what happened in the case presented here, which was registered against Kishan Ram and his son Hari Chand[5] under Section 20b of the Narcotic Act, which asserts that 'whoever produces, manufactures, possesses, sells, purchases, transports, or uses cannabis shall be punishable by rigourous imprisonment for a term which may extend to ten years, and with a fine which may extend to one lakh [one hundred thousand] rupees'.

In the FIR (First Information Report) for the case, the inspector noted the following:

> On [date], along with [seven police officers' names], I went in the day squad, and at six o'clock I received secret information that the accused, Kishan Ram, and his son, of Rajput caste and of [village], were involved in cannabis trading at their residential house and the report was reliable. At this time, the village president Devi Varma was informed [about the raid that the police wanted to make] on her mobile. On her arrival, the report about the search warrant was prepared and the copy of this authorization was sent to Constable Puran Chand of the criminal branch. Then, along with other officials, I went to the village of the accused and Kishan Ram was found at his house (Police diary).

The opening passage of a FIR such as this provides information which is of legal relevance. During the trial, each police officer who appears before the judge as a prosecutor witness is asked to repeat, orally, all the details written in the document, which may include the number and names of the officers who took part in the operation, place names, procedures followed, their exact timetable, and so on. Based on these details, the defence lawyer looks for contradictions in the police officers' replies. In fact, police records not only 'look backward at the events they describe, but they are also drawn up in anticipation of their prospective use by criminal law professionals' (Komter 2006:202).

In the case analysed here, the investigation reports were intended to fulfil the provisions indicated in the NDPS Act. Section 42 of the Act allows a police officer, superior in rank to a peon or constable, to possess the power 'of entry, search, seizure, and arrest without warrant or authorization [from a magistrate]'. An officer is also given the right to keep the identity of his informant secret, even though he is obligated to write the so-called grounds of belief—a document explaining why he should be allowed to proceed with the search without applying to the court for a warrant—and send it to his superior officer within seventy-two hours of the search. To be more precise, an officer must justify why he believes that waiting for a warrant would provide 'the opportunity for the concealment of evidence or facility for the escape of an offender' (Section 42, NDPS Act). Despite the importance of this procedure in proving a case before the court, there are a number of instances in which police officers do not send the document in time or else draft it incorrectly, and defence lawyers regularly cite such mistakes as evidence that a false case has been invented against a client.

After official registration of the case, the facts are recorded by the police in the so-called police diary, which covers the period of the investigations.[6] The police diary for the case I witnessed included results from the questioning of the accused, which was carried out to obtain further information about the other people involved in the case. The inspector wrote that the two accused '[were] not saying anything related to the case'; they were 'clever' (*chalaka*) and 'of a criminal nature' (*apradhikism ke*). The report also described how, after twenty-four hours in police custody, the men were brought before the magistrate for the police to apply for permission to detain the accused in jail for three more days:

> The accused have been brought before the judge, and the judge has heard both parties' points of view and given his consent for three days in police custody. This time, the inspector and his colleagues have reached the jail with the accused. Food has been given to them and the guard is doing his duty. I, the inspector, am talking on the telephone to DSP Brijesh Sood of the crime branch.

A summary was provided at the end of the diary which concluded by assuring the reader that 'investigations into the case are underway, the file is being kept safe, and the report is being sent to the officers'.

Total transparency is guaranteed through the existence of a written record. Although no reference was made in the diary to the way the questioning was conducted, the accused reportedly said that the cannabis found in their house 'had been rubbed from the plants by their own hands, and [that] it had been kept in their house in order to be distributed as *prasad* (offerings) to *baba* and *sadhu* (ascetics) who were to come during the Shiva *puja* (worship)'. The version of events reported in the diary echoes the aforementioned cultural discourse about cannabis; the accused explained the presence of cannabis in their house using a religious/cultural argument, which implicitly led them to admit that cannabis was actually found in their house. This cultural argument also appears in the first documents presented before the court that were produced while the two men were being held in police custody and which describe how the inspector of police presented them both to a judicial magistrate to prolong the custody order on the grounds that the men refused to speak.[7]

Despite featuring in the version of events given to the police by the accused, this was the last time that this cultural/religious discourse appeared in the official documents. No reference was made to it during the session trial, either in oral interactions or in written records. It did not therefore prejudice or contradict the defence's successive juridical strategies; neither was it binding for the accused, nor did it influence arguments during the trial. As we will see, not only did the defence lawyer attempt to show that no cannabis had been found in the house but also that no police officers had ever been there.

The Trial: The Orality Stage

The ethnographic observations regarding the case presented here began at the time of the trial itself, which was held at the Session Court in 2010, almost one and a half years after the case had been registered. During this period, after spending three weeks in police custody, the father and son had been released on bail and had returned to their village.

The first time I saw the two men was at the entrance to the court-room while they waited for their case to be called. When their turn came, they were asked to enter and stand at the back of the courtroom. They looked very nervous, heads bent, staring at the floor. For their defence, they had hired a lawyer specialized in narcotic cases, a some-what self-assured man who was always keen to tell stories about how he had succeeded in unsettling police officers during cross-examinations.

The prosecutor for the case was the district attorney, the highest authority at the Prosecutor Bureau, a rather elegant, sophisticated man in his sixties, whose main passion in life was not so much talking about law or criminal cases but about spirituality, meditation, and philosophy; whenever I called on him to ask about a case,it seemed that he would have happily talked for hours about these topics.

The session judge was a very jovial man, fond of English litera-ture and always keen to receive me in his *chambra* to discuss the cases of the day. He liked to recount humorous anecdotes about previous cases, which he used to illustrate the dysfunctionality of the Indian judicial system. Although he sometimes described sitting in court all day as 'boring', he was a conscientious, hard-working judge. During the trial, he took an active part in the proceedings, calling upon his former experience as a lawyer to question witnesses directly, especially those who turned hostile. The trial began with the presentation of evidence, during which the prosecutor's witnesses were called to the bar to affirm before the judge what they had stated during the investigation.[8]

Analysis of the subsequent court interactions shows the fluctuating value attributed to oral and written testimonies. While witnesses' written statements, as reported by the police in the file, need to be confirmed orally before the judge, the verbal interactions that take place in Hindi during the trial are simultaneously translated into English by the judge and written in the form of a first-person narrative from the point of view of the witnesses. In his re-transcription of the oral interactions, the defence lawyer's primary concern is that contradictions emerge in the police's version of events and that an alternative version be provided;[9] it is essential for the lawyer to ensure that this document is on record in order to undermine the story established by the police in their investigation accounts. As we shall see, the defence lawyer achieves his ends by asking police witnesses for very detailed, trivial information which he puts on record in the hope that this may contradict the police's previous written statements or provide accounts that are inconsistent with those of other police witnesses during cross-examination.

At the time of the trial therefore, the evidentiary value of the 'oral' statement eventually becomes less important than its written re-transcription. The most significant *oral* part of the trial—witnesses' testimonies before the judge—paradoxically focuses on recording, i.e., writing the evidence. This shift in value between orality and writing will emerge in the analysis of courtroom interactions presented hereafter.

The Beginning of the Defence's Subtext

The first witness to be called to the bar was the *patwari*, a local land officer. *Patwaris* are commonly summoned to testify in narcotic cases, as they need to certify the identity of the person on whose property, i.e., land or house cannabis has been found. By questioning the witness, the lawyer put on record that the house of one of the accused was joined to his brother's house and that, because his brother was now dead, he and his sister-in-law had both inherited his brother's property. The lawyer also put on record that this house was joined to the house of the widow's brother and that the two houses had not been partitioned. Although this information may appear insignificant, it was in fact crucial evidence to support the lawyer's version of the facts, which was that the case had been completely invented by the police at the instigation of the widow's brother.

The next witness to appear before the court was a man who owned a shop in the village where the accused lived. At the time of the search, one of the police officers involved in the raid had asked the shopkeeper to lend him weights and a set of scales to weigh the cannabis found in the house of the accused. When the shopkeeper reached the bar, the prosecutor told him, 'You tell the truth and do not worry. No mountain will fall upon you. Why are you hiding something, and why are you carrying this burden on your back?'

These words were particularly revealing; the prosecutor had evidently realized that this witness was now on the side of the accused. The judge looked at the prosecutor quizzically, which prompted the prosecutor to explain his words—'This man is hiding and he is not telling the truth'—which clearly referred to the brief interaction that the prosecutor had had with him before entering the court.[10] The following is an extract from the oral interactions that took place in the courtroom in Hindi and in which the witness was expected to say that the police had taken the scales and weights to weigh the cannabis:

Judge: When did it happen [that the police came]? Can you tell us?

Man: I don't know.

Judge: Rack your brains and try to picture when it happened.

Man: Some men came at eight o'clock and took some weights and scales.

Judge: How many men were they?

Man: There were two.

Judge: Did they give them back to you?

Man: Yes, they returned them after a while.

Prosecutor: Do you know why they took them?

Man: I don't know.

Prosecutor: (*angrily*) Why did you come here then? If you do not want to say anything, then why come to court?

The prosecutor had presumed that the shopkeeper would say that the police officer had told him that the weights and scales he had asked to borrow were needed to measure the cannabis found in the house. However, the man did not give this information when questioned, and the prosecutor did not ask to cross-examine him. The tension between the witness and the prosecutor was palpable during this part of the hearing, but this did not come across in the record.

The next witness was a taxi driver who had been hired by the police on the day of the search to take them to the village where the accused lived, which was situated in the mountains a fair distance from the main road. When the prosecutor asked this man to recount what had happened that day, the latter stated spontaneously that a CID (Criminal Investigation Department) officer, whom he referred to as Shiva Lal, had hired him to drive them to the village of the accused. However, this name—Shiva Lal—had not been given by the driver at the time of the investigation one and a half years earlier. In the police report, the driver had simply affirmed that the CID had hired his taxi, without mentioning a name.

At that stage in the trial, the name Shiva Lal did not rouse any particular interest in the prosecutor or the judge. No mention of it had ever been made in their presence, nor was there any record of it in the case file. Moreover, since the name had been given spontaneously by the prosecutor's witness, it appeared to be a completely 'neutral' piece of information. The judge therefore proceeded to translate into English what the witness had said, dictating to the stenographer, '[On the day of the search], a certain Shiva Lal of the CID had taken my taxi to a village named Haripur.' The defence lawyer asked the driver if Shiva Lal was the 'widow's brother' (the brother of the sister-in-law of one of the accused), which the driver confirmed.

The role that Shiva Lal played in the defence's version of the events would be clearly revealed by the lawyer later in the trial, when the police officers were called to the bar. Yet even at this early stage, the defence lawyer—as he hinted to me later—was trying to discreetly construct the 'subtext' of his defence by having a prosecutor witness introduce a 'seemingly' irrelevant piece of information (the name Shiva Lal) for the record, information that would ultimately be a crucial part of his defence. Such a strategy is sometimes developed beforehand by a lawyer who may encourage the accused, as the lawyer seemed to infer in this case, to persuade a prosecutor's witness to say something during the trial that can later be used to lend weight to the lawyer's story.[11]

Witnesses Turning Hostile: The Woman *Pradhan*

Up until that point in the trial, no witness had been explicitly declared hostile. The first real moments of tension occurred during the testimony given by the *pradhan*(president) of the village where the cannabis had been found. Before carrying out any search, police officers are obliged—according to a provision in the NDPS Act—to contact the village pradhan and to involve him or her in the search. Aside from serving as a guarantee for the accused, this provision reflects the responsibility that a pradhan has assumed within the village in which he or she has been elected.[12] Despite the major role that pradhans are called upon to play during investigations, they are often considered to be unreliable witnesses since they come from the same village as the accused. It is often thought that, as an elected member from the locality of the accused, the pradhan is likely to take sides with the accused and therefore to become a 'hostile witness' (cf. Berti 2010, 2011).

The pradhan in the case I attended, a peasant woman in her forties, was asked to repeat an oath after the judge: 'Whatever I say, I will speak the truth in all honesty and in accordance with *dharma*.' She was then told to recount the events that took place on the day of the search, one and a half years earlier. In her statement recorded by the police, the pradhan had said that she took part in the search and saw that cannabis had been found in the house of the accused. Although the statement had been written on her behalf by a police officer, she had signed some parts of the paper (memo) as required by law. However, the following passages, taken from the court dialogues, demonstrate how the pradhan denied each and every point in the statement. They also illustrate how the judge assumed an active role during the hearing, almost completely taking over from the prosecutor.

Judge: What happened on that day?

Pradhan: The police came to our place.

Judge: Did the police ask you anything [when they asked you to go with them]?

Pradhan: They did not ask me anything.

Judge: Where did [the police officers] go then?

Pradhan: They went to Kishan Ram's house [of the accused].

Judge: Were you outside?

Pradhan: Yes, I was outside.

Prosecutor: Did they tell you anything [about] why they had to go inside?

Pradhan: They didn't tell me anything.

Judge: So why didn't you stop them? A pradhan can stop the police from doing certain things if they don't inform you of the illegal acts going on there. That is the law.

Pradhan: They [the police] did not tell me anything, though I asked them. They just told me that they had to go there [to the house of the accused] because they had some work to do.

The pradhan thus denied before the judge what had been written in the police statement, namely, that she had been told the reason they wanted to search the house of the accused. Her replies were given in a rather pitiful tone of voice as if to convey the popular idea that police officers acted rudely and abused their positions of power vis-à-vis villagers. Although she was questioned many times, she insisted that she had not been told anything. The judge then dictated directly in English: 'At this stage, the learned public prosecutor has put forth a request that he be allowed to cross-examine the witness, as the witness has resiled from her previous statement. Allowed.' He then began to cross-examine the pradhan, since she was now clearly on the side of the accused.[13]

Judge: The police showed you some papers that you had to read and understand before signing.[14]

Pradhan: I did not read them because I was in a hurry, as I had to go to a wedding.

The judge stared at her incredulously while the prosecutor shook his head, baffled. With this reply, the woman completely lost any credibility she had had before the court.

Prosecutor: You are a pradhan, and you sign without reading what you are signing? How can you do that? Why did you write your signature without reading the papers?

Pradhan: (*after some hesitation*) We trust the police, and we believe that whatever they write is correct. So I signed [the *memo*].

By trying to provide a plausible answer, the pradhan in fact contradicted what she had alluded to only a few minutes before, that is, to the idea that police officers abused their power.

Prosecutor: How much time did you spend there with the police?

Pradhan: I don't know.

Judge: Try to give some idea.

Pradhan: I am not sure; almost an hour.

Judge: You are a pradhan—you are sharp-witted, so you must know.

The judge proceeded to test the pradhan with a series of questions that had no relation to the case, with the aim of unsettling her.

Judge: Whose marriage was it?

Pradhan: My aunt's son's.

Judge: What's his name?

Pradhan: I've forgotten.

Judge: Was it the girl's or the boy's marriage?

Pradhan: It's my paternal aunt's son.

Judge: What is your aunt's name?

The woman was quiet for some time; then she quietly uttered a name, leading the prosecutor to think that she was lying.

Prosecutor: It took a long time to reply, and after a lot of thought... I would be able to give my auntie's name without any hesitation!

The prosecutor's comment provoked some laughter in the audience. Convinced that the pradhan was lying, the judge continued to ask her for details of the wedding. He then started questioning her about the cannabis that had been found in the house and about the fact that she was supposed to have followed all the police operations. The pradhan denied witnessing any such discovery and replied to each question that she did not know anything.

By denying that the police had found cannabis in the house, the woman effectively admitted that an unjust arrest had occurred and she had done nothing about it.

> Prosecutor: Did you file a written complaint that people from your area had been taken away by the police for no reason?
>
> Pradhan: No, I didn't.
>
> Prosecutor: Is it not your duty to protect the people of your area?
>
> Pradhan: Yes—I told them [the police] not to arrest them, but they didn't listen to me.

Although the judge and the prosecutor were visibly convinced that the witness was lying, they questioned her as if they believed she were telling the truth. This sort of dialogue is very common during cross-examinations; the person asking the questions follows the logic of the respondent in order to expose gaps in his/her arguments, even though the questioner thinks that the witness is lying.

Referring to the police report, the judge and the prosecutor proceeded by asking the pradhan to confirm her version of events as recorded in the statement she gave to the police when the cannabis was discovered in the house of the accused.

> Judge: When the search took place inside the house, a packet was found on the first floor, hidden in a cupboard on the veranda.
>
> Pradhan: No, nothing was found there.
>
> Judge: While checking that packet, cannabis was found there in the form of long sticks.
>
> Pradhan: I did not see it.

The judge dictated 'It is incorrect that on searching the house of the accused, the police found a packet kept concealed in a cupboard on the first floor, and on taking the said packet, cannabis in the shape of sticks was found; nor did I state this to the police' (Court record, 2010). Then, still in English, he dictated various passages from the pradhan's statement that had previously been recorded by the police in order to highlight contradictions with her present assertions. These passages were added as an aside after each reply from the pradhan before the court under the heading '(Confronted with statement [police reference] in which it is recorded)'.[15]

This way of recording the evidence produces a narrative in which, paradoxically, the person speaking repeatedly denies what she says. In fact, the main aim of the questions is not to elicit a reply from the witness, but rather to orally 'reconstruct' and rewrite in English what has been recorded in the police report. Thus, when the judge decided that the pradhan needed to be cross-examined, he in a sense implicitly re-established the police report's authority.[16]

Compared to the aforementioned police diary, the police report is seemingly more binding. Its contents can be used during the trial as a starting point when questioning a witness, and can also serve as a mirror to make the witness contradict themselves. In principle, the 'oral' version of events provided by the witness and subsequently written in the court record is considered to be more valuable in terms of legal evidence than what is written in the police report. However, as we have seen, in the case where the reply given by the witness to the court contradicts what they supposedly said to the police during the investigation, this contradictory statement will be added in brackets to the recording of the oral reply preceded by the formula 'Confronted with...'

At the end of the cross-examination, the judge finally said to the pradhan, 'Look, you are protecting them because they are your supporters and you are doing this to win their votes.' The pradhan then replied: 'No, they are not my supporters. They are from the other party.'

The judge dictated for the record in English: 'It is correct that the accused are of my *panchayat*. It is incorrect that they are my supporters. Self-stated that they are supporters of the other party. It is incorrect that I have received consideration from the accused and that for that reason I am telling a lie.' (Court record, 2010).

Referring to the electoral link between the accused and the witness is a typical way of concluding a hearing with a village pradhan. It is a standard formula added at the end of the court interaction to intimate that the witness is telling a lie and to provide a motive for this. In the case discussed here, both the judge and the prosecutor were convinced that in addition to winning the vote of the accused, the pradhan had received money from them. Yet, the electoral reference was a conventional form of recording the fact that the pradhan had turned hostile. Moreover, although there was no direct reference during the hearing to any money that the pradhan may have received, the term 'consideration' used by the judge in recording the evidence tacitly suggested such a deal.

While the judge and the prosecutor used the cross-examination to 'rewrite' the police report entirely (using the formula Confronted with...), the defence lawyer based his argument on it. He again referred to Shiva Lal, the CID (Criminal Investigation Department) officer whom the taxi driver had identified as the man who had hired him on the day of the search. He asked the pradhan to confirm the taxi driver's assertion that this Shiva Lal was the brother of the sister-in-law of one of the accused, which the pradhan confirmed. She was also asked to confirm that this woman, now a widow, continued to live in her husband's house, which she shared with the family of the accused. After the pradhan had verified these statements, the cross-examination was transcribed in the court record as follows: 'It is correct that Shiva Lal, a CID official, is the brother of the widow of Hira Singh. It is correct that the relations of the family of the accused and the family of Hira Singh are strained. Self-stated that they are living separately but in the same house. Inside the house, there is no partition' (Court record).

According to the subtext to which the lawyer was alluding before the court, Shiva Lal had instigated his sister, who shared a house with the accused, to lodge a false case against them. The lawyer prompted the pradhan to state that all the signatures on the police report were false. He also showed the judge one of her signatures that had apparently been added between two lines by the police, with no serial number. All these replies were translated into English and put on record as the judge dictated them.

At the end of the pradhan's hearing, the judge stared at the woman and addressed her in Hindi in a grave tone of voice: 'Look, it is your first time as village president. If you have told the truth before the court, you will get good results [*tera udhar ho jayega*]. Otherwise, if you have told a lie, you have ruined your *karma*.[...] The police have done their work, and if you have made a false statement, then you have done yourself wrong.'

The judge's reference to a moral or religious order brought the hearing to a close. This kind of assertion does not have the same judicial value as the standard forms of accusation delivered in English at the end of a cross-examination so that they might be put on record. Although the latter are not usually intended for the witnesses themselves (most of whom cannot understand English), but rather for those reading the file at a later stage (e.g., appeal judges), the moral judgements are addressed exclusively to the witnesses and are not put on record.

On the Look-out for Police Contradictions

The issue of truth that emerged in the pradhan's testimony cropped up again at the beginning of the police hearings. At this stage, the defence lawyer used the cross-examination to undermine the police officers' credibility and to show that they had entirely invented the case. He asked for extremely detailed information that was aimed not so much at explaining the reasons why the case had been fabricated than at increasing his chances of finding contradictions.[17] Here, the 'proof of truth' lay in a systematic search for minor elements of divergence between what had previously been written in the report and how the officers replied to the lawyer and the judge, as well as between the replies each of these officers gave before the court.

The lawyer's attack on the credibility of the police began during the cross-examination of the first police witness who had taken part in the raid. During the cross-examination, he fired a long list of detailed questions at the witness in order to fit each event into an exact timetable: What time did you leave there? Were you all together from the very beginning, or did you pick up people on the way? At what time did you reach the place? How many villages did you stop in and at what time? Where did you stop to take tea? At what time did the inspector write the grounds of belief, and where did he write it? Who brought the grounds of belief to CID headquarters? Did they come back afterwards? At what time did you get back to headquarters, how, and with whom?

To be most effective, the lawyer asked these questions very quickly, using a tone of voice to suggest that the officer had invented the whole story. This strategy has a cumulative effect: the more the lawyer succeeded in undermining the policeman's credibility, the easier it was for him to discredit the other officers. During the long question-and-reply sequences, each of which is routinely translated and dictated by the judge to the stenographer, the lawyer managed to slip an important detail into the dictation or to frame a sentence to his liking, since his expertise lies in memorizing any minor detail that is likely to contradict the police officer's replies.[18]

Doubt was cast on the truthfulness of the police version when the first officer called to the bar was asked to recall the time at which the inspector had received the information that the witness had cannabis in his house. Significantly, the officer's answer did not match the timing written in the report. After asking which of the two times was correct, the lawyer, in an accusatory tone of voice, promptly dictated on his behalf in English: 'My today's testimony is correct, whereas the time of receipt of secret information written in seizure *memo* is incorrect.' Many other replies contradicted the report and therefore, on many occasions, the lawyer was able to put on record that the report made at the time of the investigation was incorrect.[19]

At the end of the cross-examination, the lawyer dictated to the stenographer some concluding sentences in English without having asked the witness any questions:

> It is incorrect that all the papers were prepared later on in the police station just to comply with the provisions of the Narcotic Drugs and Psychotropic Substance Act. It is wrong to suggest that the case has been planted upon the accused by the police in connivance with Shiva Lal. It is wrong to suggest that the taxi was hired by Shiva Lal. It is incorrect that I am deposing falsely. (Court record, 2010)

This kind of declaration serves to summarize the lawyer's version of events through the witness's denial of what the lawyer appeared to be stating. This is common practice in court; it allows the lawyer to put forward his account without giving the accused any opportunity to respond.

Once the police's credibility had been questioned, the judge himself seemed to be in a dubitative frame of mind. When the second police officer came to the bar to be cross-examined, the judge asked him a series of questions: Where were you patrolling that day? Who was with you? When did you arrive at the house? What did you and the other officers find, and where did you find it? Who took the cannabis, and what did they do with it? How many seals did they put on the samples?

The atmosphere in the court had started to change: it was clear that the judge now mistrusted the police officers, and was disappointed in their work. Meanwhile, the accused, though unable to follow the English part of the dialogue, appeared to be a little more relaxed, and had moved slightly nearer to the bar to follow the interactions more closely. They now dared to show their faces to the judge, although nobody addressed them directly. The situation definitely shifted in their favour with the introduction of the next police witness, after whose testimony the whole case collapsed. The young man (another CID officer) looked terrified. By the time he entered the courtroom, the judge was already visibly annoyed by the turn of events, which served to unsettle him even more. The judge began by asking the officer to give precise information, such as the names of the other officers involved and the registration plate of the taxi hired by the police, to which the young man, panicking, responded by trying discreetly to read some notes he had written on the palm of his hand. As people around him began to laugh, making him more nervous, the judge changed his attitude and addressed the man calmly: 'You have written on your hand, so read it and look at the words properly.' The witness told the judge that the officers had stopped at some places on the way to the house of the accused, but when the judge asked for the names of the places, he looked confused and kept quiet. 'This is useless! He never went there', commented the defence lawyer.

Sensing that he was getting embarrassed, the judge addressed the young man in a sympathetic tone of voice

Judge: Do you feel sick?

Man: Yes, I do.

Judge: What's the problem?

Man: I've got high blood pressure.

Judge: Since when? Don't be scared and don't get embarrassed. Make yourself at home. Be happy. Why are you scared? It is a good thing that you seized the cannabis. Just tell us what happened there.

The judge was now convinced that the case was hopeless, but he did not want to stress the young man any further. The officer continued to give contradictory replies. 'All my witnesses are now working for the lawyer!' the prosecutor exclaimed scornfully.

When the defence lawyer's turn came to cross-examine the witness, he began by stating for the record that the man had written something on his hand: 'It is correct that the name of the officers, the vehicle number, and the timing have been written by me on my hand for remembrance.' He then attempted to elicit from the officer every single detail about the way the investigations had been conducted and completed the cross-examination by dictating a few sentences in English, still from the point of view of the witness but this time without even asking him any relevant questions.

However, these sentences are preceded by 'It is correct that' or 'It is incorrect that', depending on whether the person asking the question thinks that the witness would deny or confirm his statement.[20] Thus, the dictation for the young officer's cross-examination reads as follows: 'It is incorrect that no contraband was recovered from the house of the accused. It is also incorrect that I was not with the police party on that day. It is incorrect that Shiva Lal, the CID official, was with us on that day. It is incorrect that I am deposing falsely, being an official. It is incorrect that a false case has been set up against the accused' (Court record, 2012). By putting these set phrases on record, the lawyer's aim was to suggest that the exact opposite was true: no contraband was recovered from the house of the accused, and the police officer who was testifying was not with the team of policemen on that day (and was thus lying). He also wanted to put on record that Shiva Lal, the CID officer, was with these policemen on the day of the search, which would have supported his theory that orders for the raid had been given by him.[21] The police officer who was testifying was most probably unaware of the lawyer's strategy to build the 'widow's brother complot' theory. This explains why he denied what the lawyer asked him—that Shiv Lal was with the team of policemen on the day of the search. Instead of weakening the lawyer's theory, his denial seemed to reinforce the general perception that the police were lying because the officer was contradicting what the taxi driver had previously stated.

After this last cross-examination, and even though there were more witnesses waiting to testify, the judge proceeded with the resolution of

· the case. He suggested that the prosecutor close the evidence and fix the date for the arguments; clearly, he had already reached a decision and was intent on not wasting any more time. 'Now it's time for arguments, not for witnesses', he said bitterly.

The analysis of the interactions, therefore, shows how contrary to the pradhan's testimony discussed previously, the police's loss of credibility did not lead to these officers being declared hostile. This reveals a major difference in the way the officers' statements, on the one hand, and the pradhan's, on the other, were perceived as untrue by the court. The police officers did not present a completely new version of events, as the *pradhan* had done by saying, for example, that nothing had been recovered from the house of the accused. The difference between the officers' oral testimonies and the previous report, which they had produced themselves, concerned the details of the investigative procedure. Yet without actually being declared hostile, the police officers contradicted their own report and therefore invalidated the accusation even more than the pradhan had done by turning hostile.

The preceding discussion reveals how the position of power that police officers enjoy during the investigations may be completely overturned at the time of the trial, when their words—both written and oral—may be challenged and even ridiculed. In addition, this case study exemplifies how the courtroom may become a hostile environment for police officers in instances where the judge begins to side with the defence lawyer rather than the prosecutor. While some police officers appear to be somewhat used to the kind of pressure one experiences when interacting with legal specialists, others, like the young man described above, feel very uneasy in court and can end up completely destroying the police's credibility.

Out-of-Court Discussion On the Case

The lawyer for the accused did not provide any defence witnesses. Instead, he strengthened his counter-story for the case using the questions he had put to prosecution witnesses and the techniques he had used during cross-examination. In his version of the events, Shiva Lal appeared to be a crucial figure. On the one hand, he was presented as an accomplice in a plot organized by Kishan Ram's widowed sister-in-law, who wanted to stop sharing her husband's property. On the other hand, he was presented as a CID officer, which could explain why he had been able to convince the CID inspector to order a raid on the property of the accused.

As a matter of fact, since the defence lawyer's version of the story had not been taken seriously by anyone, no one had taken the trouble to check whether Shiva Lal was really a CID officer or even whether he really existed. While the case was pending, I had a particularly interesting conversation with the judge in his *chambra*. 'Shiva Lal?' he exclaimed. 'That's just the defence's story! This name does not appear anywhere in the statements. The taxi driver made up the name of this man during the hearing because he had sided with the accused.' The judge explained to me that the lawyer had to provide a story in order to 'problematize his case', and that the tale about Shiva Lal most probably filled this role. He did not seem particularly bothered about this. 'We are concerned with the main witnesses,' he explained, 'which in this case are police officers, and the police officers have contradicted themselves a lot. Two of them have said that one of the officers was not present; others have said that he was. This contradiction has cast doubt on the presence of some police officers at the scene.' What he, as a judge, was required to consider, he told me, was whether the accused was fully aware that there was cannabis at his property. 'You must have noticed that the defence has laid out the case based on the fact that the house is joined to another house and that the widow of the brother of one of the accused also resides there', he remarked. 'The prosecution was bound to prove that the house was not the joint property of the other family members. If this is not proved, the possibility that some other persons residing in the house could have kept the cannabis there cannot be ruled out'.

The prosecutor, who was very disappointed in the police officers, did not seem to lend much importance to Shiva Lal either. When I went to see him in his office, he was waiting for a visit from the state inspector who had investigated the case and whom he had invited for a meeting. The inspector, who had recently retired, was required to appear in court as a witness the following day, and the prosecutor wanted to bring him up to date regarding the situation. Upon the inspector's arrival, the prosecutor handed him the investigative report and started listing the many errors that the inspector had committed. The inspector looked puzzled and muttered some vague excuses, but he put forward no real argument.

The prosecutor's first reproach concerned the 'search warrant' that the officer had sent to the deputy police superintendent via a constable in order to proceed with the search without waiting for the warrant issued by the magistrate. Instead of using Section 42 of the NDPS Act (about searching property), the inspector had used Section 50, which deals with questions and answers. Moreover, although he had written the 'grounds of belief' and had sent it to his superior officer, the inspector had forgotten to add the disclaimer that there was 'no time to wait for court authorization, as there is the risk that the cannabis might be hidden or thrown away' (section 42d NDPS Act). 'I don't know whether it's out of ignorance or what,' remarked the prosecutor rather disappointedly, addressing the inspector, 'but this is mandatory procedure. Otherwise, this document [the grounds of belief] is just wastepaper. For three days, I have been ridiculed in court because of you.'

Trying to reassure the inspector, the prosecutor added, 'Okay, what's done is done. Now it's too late, but I tell you that I am incapable of proving the offence.' However, the prosecutor continued to admonish the inspector, listing other failings; for instance, the name of the pradhan had been added to the list of witnesses with no serial number. 'You put her name there without a number', he began 'That looks as if you added her name later, and in the court she denied that this signature is hers. There is no sign under the carbon and no number anywhere. Now, you see, we can neither explain these things nor can we withdraw it all because this is the original document.'

The prosecutor's third criticism of the investigation concerned the alleged timing of events. In the police report, the time at which the police had received the tipoff was listed as 7:30 a.m., but the time at which they had sent the 'grounds of belief' was 6:35 a.m.—nearly an hour earlier! 'What's the meaning of all this?' the prosecutor cried. 'Why do you put the time then? It is not necessary to put it.' Finally, he mentioned the raiding party: 'Let me say that bringing ten men for a raid is not an intelligent thing to do. They will make a lot of contradictions before the court. Two or three men are enough.' The prosecutor again mitigated his censure by adding, 'Okay, it's too late now'. He reminded the inspector that the following day he would have to explain all of these issues to the judge and, even more distressingly, to the defence lawyer. He told the inspector to take the file with him and to read it at home at his leisure.

The inspector left the office with the file under his arm, and after a time another officer entered. He was the deputy police superintendent, the inspector's superior officer, a more self-confident, well-educated man. The following day, he too would have to appear before the judge to be questioned about why he had not stopped the investigations once he realized that the document the inspector sent him was not accurate. Speaking in Hindi mixed in with a number of English expressions, he apologized many times to the prosecutor, saying that he had given full instructions to his 'men'—the inspector and others—and had told them to draft the documents in a certain way, yet despite his instructions they had done it all wrongly. 'I was so shocked on seeing that report', he said. 'I thought about going to beat them up! Actually, I really reprimanded him [the inspector], but what was to be done? In fact, I never punished him.' 'I know', said the prosecutor. 'I'm also like that.'

'I was really very upset, really very upset', continued the deputy superintendent. 'I didn't know what action I could take without completely destroying the inspector's career. I didn't do anything because he was about to retire. Actually, sir, you know this. We don't have a good investigating officer. Those who investigate are not there all the time, so you can't always give full instructions.'

The interactions I have just described need to be contextualized within the institutional relationship between prosecutors and police officers. Since 1973, Indian police have operated separately from the prosecutor agency and have had complete control over investigations. Although some high-ranking police officers have offices inside the district court complex and even, in some district courts, just next door to the prosecutor's office, the prosecution is not supposed to intervene in investigations until the *challan* (chargesheet) has been prepared. In most cases, investigations are carried out in the field by lower-ranking officers (so-called non-gazetted officers) who are monitored by their superiors (gazetted officers). In the case study presented here, we have seen how operations were led in the field by the inspector; he had sent the grounds of belief to his superior officer, and, as was stated in court, the operation was already over when this superior officer reached the house of the accused. He also left the scene of the crime before the raid party had completed its task. As he explained to the prosecutor, by the time he realized that there were mistakes in the document it was too late: 'I could neither change the document nor explain the mistakes'.[22]

Police officers do not usually have solid excuses for their mistakes when they are face to face with a prosecutor. I had the opportunity to converse with some CID officers at their headquarters and it was obvious that they had far more to say in their defence there and then than in court. They particularly criticized a defence lawyer's habit of systematically declaring that all cases are fictitious. As one officer explained in Hindi, 'They always say that we arrested the accused for no reason, that we didn't draw the map straightaway, and that all the documents were in fact prepared at the police station. This is a total waste of time.' The officers also complained about the delay between the investigations and the trial and about the conditions under which they had to testify before the court:

> When I'm called to give my testimony, I arrive at the court one hour before and I have only one hour to read the file. I am asked before the court—but I can't remember the small details of the case—what time I was present and what I was doing there and things like that. I can't remember all that. The defence lawyer'll asks how far it is from that place, and how many houses there are in that village, and how far it is from another place, and he'll proceed with a cross-examination. I'll tell him everything because I drew the map, so I'll tell him everything, and after that he'll want more information on very minor questions that I cannot give, especially when the case is two or three years old or even more.

The Defence Version Prevails

After all the evidence had been presented, both the inspector and the superintendent of police were cross-examined at length by the defence lawyer, but this had no further impact on the prosecutor's case. By this point everyone was convinced that the prosecutor had lost the case and that the accused were going to be acquitted. Subsequently, the accused were examined under Section 313 of the Code of the Criminal Procedure. This is the only moment in a trial, when the accused has the opportunity to express themselves before the bench. However, in most cases this part of the trial does not lead to any great surprises. The questions for the witnesses are prepared beforehand, and begin with 'It has come in the prosecution evidence led against you that [...the charges are listed]. What have you to say about [...]?' The replies are usually very standard, with the accused systematically stating, 'It is incorrect',

'It is wrong', or 'I don't know'. It is only at the end of the series of questions that the replies may include some supplementary information to sum up the defence's general theory. In weak cases, where the prosecutor has failed to prove the case, the statement of the accused is a mere formality. In the case discussed here, for example, the statement was even taken in the stenographer's office with only the lawyer, the prosecutor, and the accused present.

Apart from denying all the points raised in the questions, the accused stated that no cannabis had been found in their house and that they had been framed by the police at the request of Shiva Lal, who was working in the Criminal Investigation Department' (Court record 2010). We have seen how this version of the events was overlooked during the trial; even when the defence lawyer, by questioning the pradhan, explicitly disclosed how Shiva Lal was crucial to his counter-narrative of events, the role of this man and even his very existence had not been challenged by the prosecutor. The attorney's team even considered my efforts to look into the matter to be a total 'waste of time'.

Yet the 'Shiva Lal story' was to be unexpectedly put forward as a fully legitimate account by the judge who ruled to acquit the accused. In his twenty-five-page judgment, after recalling in detail the main logic behind the defence's 'complot theory', the judge wrote,

> By whom the taxi was hired remained a mystery. One police witness said under oath that the taxi had been hired by the inspector, but this version has been contradicted by the taxi driver, who said that his taxi was hired by a man called Shiva Lal, of the C.I.D.

The judge then continued as follows:

> The said contradiction apparently does not appear of much significance, but if read in conjunction with the defence set up on behalf of the accused [the 'complot's theory'], it has become most significant. (Court record, 2010)

At the beginning of his judgment, the judge had merely referred to the 'Shiva Lal story' as a possible reason why the accused 'may have been falsely implicated in the case.' Nevertheless, this story ultimately proved to be crucial for him in providing the case with a narrative logic.

It should be noted that the 'complot theory' is constantly used by the defence lawyer in criminal cases. The potential impact of such a theory on a judicial decision increases if the case is referred to an appeal court. After all, it is in the interest of the defence lawyer at the trial to make reference to an 'enemy', whether real or invented. In fact, should a case go to appeal, this type of issue may raise doubts in the judge's mind, but only if it had been put on record during the trial.[23]

During the trial discussed above, not only had the defence lawyer but also the judge cross-examined the police witnesses at length in order to discern contradictions between their testimonies. In his ruling, the judge underlined every detail of the incongruities in the accounts provided by the police officers when they were questioned at the bar. 'The said contradictions,' he wrote many times in his text, 'have rendered doubtful the presence, manner, and mode of the [police] proceedings from the headquarters [to the house of the accused] in the manner set up by the prosecution'. He also emphasized the problem of the joint ownership of the house where the cannabis had been found, which prevented the prosecutor from proving 'that the charas [cannabis] in question had been found in the possession of the accused and no one else [...] as a result of which the prosecution has miserably failed to prove that the accused were found in exclusive and conscious possession of the contraband in question' (Court report, 2010).

Technical arguments over, for example, procedural errors or contradictions in police stories emerge systematically in narcotic cases which lead to many similarities between different investigations. Similarly, the 'social' argument—that there was a conspiracy against the accused—is part of a repertoire that is regularly proposed by the defence lawyer. Both are forged through cross-examination, although the relevance they may acquire varies considerably according to which judge conducts the trial.

A judge's personality and the style he adopts in court are important variables in determining the direction a trial may take, and both have a sizeable influence on the way the evidence is assessed.[24] During the case in question, the judge and the defence lawyer ultimately appeared to be of one mind in doubting the police's version of the story, but other judges may have turned the evidence around to suit the prosecution.[25] The impact of a judge's attitude on a trial's outcome is a topic frequently raised by defence lawyers, some of whom try to adjust their styles of cross-examination to curry favour with the judge. In situations where the odds are 50-50, the judge does not generally have a clear idea of the verdict when the trial draws to a close, while in the case presented here, no one seemed to doubt that the police officers had lost all credibility and that the accused would be acquitted.

Although the police officers had clearly made many mistakes, the final verdict was in all likelihood elicited by aspects of the trial that were difficult to convey in writing; it relied on a certain court dynamic, on the performance of the various protagonists in the trial, and on the power relations enacted both inside and outside the courtroom. These aspects, which were highly perceptible in the trial setting, are barely traceable in the way trial interactions have been put on record.

* * *

My concern in this chapter has not been so much to understand how true the defence or the police story is but rather, by relying on a case-study, how the notions of 'truth' and 'untruth' are used and managed in a court of law. Kolsky (2010) has shown how the issue of truth was a constant concern for the British in India, especially when it came to administering justice. Colonial administrators often characterized Indians as people who could not 'distinguish fact from fiction' or who had a 'notorious disregard for truth' (Kolsky 2010:108–9; see also Lal 1999). The case presented here shows how the culturalist discourse on truth is reproduced by many Indian judges and prosecutors who cannot help stating that Indian people, especially villagers, tell lies before the court.

The notions of 'truth' and 'fiction' were constantly evoked in the court both by the prosecutor (or the judge) in cross-examining witnesses from the village of the accused and by the defence lawyer in cross-examining police officers. In order to understand what these notions mean in this context we must draw upon what emerged from the details of trial interactions as well as from how people involved in the trial understand the case outside the court.

By suggesting that the pradhan was lying, the judge was implicitly endorsing the police's version of events. However, this presumption proved to be incorrect; in the follow-up to the hearings, the judge began to doubt the credibility of the police story. In fact, due to the police officers' contradictory replies, the very 'fact' of their presence in the house of the accused was increasingly challenged by the judge, even though this in turn contradicted the part of the pradhan's statement that was thought to be true by the judge, that is, that the police had actually gone to search the house of the accused.

As it transpires from the court interactions, the relationship between telling the truth and lying was not, as Lynch and Bogen note in reference to a different case, 'a simple binary opposition between making true and false statements' (Lynch and Bogel, 1996). The judge was convinced in this case that both the pradhan and the police were lying but not about the same point: the pradhan was considered to be lying when she said that cannabis had not been discovered, and the police officers were considered to be lying when they said that they had all taken part in the raid. We may note that there is a discrepancy here between what was written in the court record and what emerged from the informal discussions. The judge dictated in the record that the pradhan was lying for political reasons, though he was of the opinion that the woman had received money from the accused. On the other hand, the judge did not record the fact that the police officers were also telling lies despite his conviction that contrary to what they had claimed, some police officers had not taken part in the raid. During our informal conversations, the judge told me that the police's lies were due to their desire to make the case appear stronger for the prosecution, whereas in his written judgment he supported the defence's version of the story, that the police officers had invented the case on Shiva Lal's request.

As we have seen, the perception of truth and lies in such contexts relies partly on the performative skills of the legal professionals in challenging the other party's version of events, as well as on the witnesses' guile when replying while giving evidence—which particularly appeared to work against the police in this case.

Finally, the definition of truth appears to be related to the question of whether a previous statement is considered to be legally binding. For example, the accused initially admitted that the cannabis in their house was for use during religious ceremonies, although this statement was not binding—even if reported in the police diary—as far as the outcome of the case was concerned. Despite showing implicitly that the police had gone to their house and had discovered cannabis, neither the prosecutor nor the judge referred to this version of events during the trial. The fact that this information was overlooked during the trial may be due in part to the somewhat unconventional nature of the so-called 'police diary'which is often a neglected aspect of the police investigation report. Court hearings focus on the report of the witnesses' statements collected by the police during the investigation. Although these statements are said to be non-binding for the witnesses, as they have to be confirmed orally, they are used as a gauge to evaluate the truthfulness of their replies in court. Indeed, the case presented here has revealed the ambiguous value of the 'principle of orality' in Indian criminal procedure. Though a witness's statement must be confirmed orally during the trial, what is taken into account by the judge when making his decision—and by higher-level courts in the event of an appeal—is only what has been put on record in writing during the trial.

Finally, the case analysed here raises the issue of the importance of fiction in the judicial process. By comparing court documents with informal discussions, at least three kinds of fictions can be identified. The first, commonly attributed to police officers, is interpreted as a way of ensuring conformity between investigative practices and the so-called technicality of legal provisions. A second fiction is created by villagers who, having negotiated with the family of the accused, deny whatever the police have written on their behalf in the report. The final fiction is that of the defence lawyer, who tries to challenge the police's version of the story not only by undermining the officers' credibility vis-à-vis the court, but also by proposing a conventional social scenario—that of a family conspiracy—which has ultimately been accepted by judges as the possible truth.

Notes

1. Tribune News Service 'Chief Justice for steps to check drug menace', *The Tribune* (Himachal Pradesh edition), Shimla, March 27, 2010. http://www.tribuneindia.com/2010/20100328/himachal.htm#6, 26/06/2014.

2. This kind of official meeting is an occasion for people dealing with criminal cases in their everyday work to discuss issues in a more analytical way. The Narcotic Drugs Act is a topic frequently chosen by the Academy, which shows that judges are aware of the problems involved in the Act's implementation.

3. Chauhan, Kuldeep 'Where devta tells them to grow cannabis.' The Tribune (Himachal Pradesh edition), 27 July 2004.

4. Chauhan, Kuldeep,'Hardships multiply for cannabis growers', The Tribune (Himachal Pradesh edition), Shimla, 6 October 2005. http://www.tribuneindia.com/2005/20051006/himachal.htm#1 (accessed 29 May 2014)

5. Most of the names used here have been changed.

6. The diary also contains a step-by-step account of the actions undertaken by the accused while they were in custody: when they ate, dates of medical examinations, whether a guard was present, and so on. The person who made the report, who identifies himself by his role ('I, the inspector, am talking'), recorded the names of all the people within the police force who were involved in the investigation. Additionally, he provided information on how the file concerning the accused was circulated within the police department.

7. At this stage, the magistrate was authorized to set bail even though he himself would not be trying the case; it was to be tried by a higher court because it was punishable by more than ten years' imprisonment.

8. The prosecutor must select witnesses amongst those put forward by the police.

9. Most of the time, this alternative story is constructed entirely by the lawyer on the basis of his own questions, which are translated and reformulated in English in the first person from the point of view of the witness by simply adding the words 'It is correct that...' at the beginning if the witness confirms what the lawyer asks, or 'It is incorrect that...' in the case where he or she denies it.

10. The prosecutor meets the witnesses before they enter the courtroom to refresh their memories about the information they provided in previous statements.

11. Negotiations with the prosecutor's witnesses are carried out not by the lawyer but by the accused or his/her family members, who come to the lawyer's office to receive instructions.

12. According to Section 47 of the NDPS Act, it is the 'duty of certain officers to provide information to any police officer when it may come to his knowledge that any land has been illegally cultivated with opium poppies, cannabis plants, or coca plants, and every such officer of the government who neglects to give such information shall be liable to punishment'. Evidence shows that during the colonial period, a similar procedure existed in which a headman from the area where the accused lived was brought in to witness the investigation during the investigation process (cf. Singha 1998:16).

13. Although a request to cross-examine a witness is always recorded by the judge as coming from the prosecutor, most of the time it is the judge himself who decides when to make this request and who actually begins the cross-examination.

14. Here the judge is referring to a part of the police record called memo, which is made whenever the police take something from the scene of the crime during the investigation. Contrary to the oral statement that witnesses give to the police, the memo must be signed by an independent witness.

15. During the cross-examination, the witness was systematically confronted with his/her previous statement, which was referred to after every question as a way of casting doubt on his/her reply.

16. This technique recalls what Conley and O' Barr observed (2005:26) in reference to an American context where he noted that 'Because each of the tag questions is preceded by a statement that is damaging to the witness the answers are almost irrelevant. Even if the witness answers in the negative the denial may be lost in the flow of the lawyer's polemic. By controlling question form, the lawyer is thus able to transform the cross-examination from dialogue into self-serving monologue.'

17. For the use of this cross-examination technique in a UK context, see Good (2004).

18. As a judge explained to me, a good lawyer has to 'master the file'. However, a prosecutor rarely does so because, unlike the defence lawyer, he does not have a team of junior lawyers working for him.

19. One wonders how the officers could actually remember all these details, including the exact timing of each operation some eighteen months after the report had been written. According to the procedure established by the Indian Evidence Act, witnesses (including police officers) are asked to reply without the report in front of them, but they may 'refresh their memories' by reading the file again just before entering the courtroom. What is required of them, therefore, is not to accomplish the impossible task of remembering every detail, but to succeed in replying to the questions put to them during the trial without contradicting what they wrote in their previous report. It is more a performance based on the witness's capacity to reproduce orally what has been written in the file than an actual recollection of facts.

20. Any legal professional in India who reads these sentences, including the appeal judge, recognizes that this is the method a lawyer uses to suggest the exact opposite of what a witness appears to confirm or deny in the report.

21. It should be noted that the use of a double negative such as 'It is incorrect that I was not...' is sometimes confusing even for judges, and some lawyers seem to play on this double negative to frame the statement to their advantage.

22. Although the prosecutor now showed his disappointment in the police, it seems that he himself had not noticed all the technical mistakes before approving the *challan* that needed to be filled in at the session court. As reported in Chapter 4 of the prosecutor manual, one of the prosecutor's tasks is to 'scrutinize the final investigation report': 'In the case where there is non-compliance or where the investigation is still incomplete regarding a crucial aspect, the prosecutor will bring the matter to the notice of the police superintendent who may order action to bridge the gap in investigations' (Prosecution Manual 2008).

23. A High Court judgment can only be based on information from the trial, which means that a recording of the evidence is crucial for reaching an eventual resolution of the case. When attending High Court hearings, I noted that the judge always asked the lawyer if any enmity between the victim and the accused had been mentioned (and recorded) in the trial evidence.

24. Compare with Conley and O'Barr (1990:108-12).

25. An extreme example of this comes courtesy of a case conducted by another session judge, which was held in the same court as the case presented here. This judge had very strict rules for recording evidence during the trial: when witnesses came to the bar, instead of letting the prosecutor question them, the judge immediately began to dictate to the stenographer what the police officers had recorded for the witness statement at the time of the investigation. This was done in order to reduce the likelihood of a witness turning hostile. His way of conducting the trial provoked discontent among the lawyers, who complained that they were no longer allowed to cross-examine the witnesses in the manner to which they were accustomed. With this new judge, there was barely room for a lawyer to propose a conspiracy theory like the 'Shiva Lal version'. When one looks at the decisions taken by this judge on narcotic cases similar to the one described here, one finds sentences such as 'There was not even a suggestion of previous hostility of the witnesses of the prosecution with the accused person. As such, the possibility of false implication was ruled out' (State of HP v. [xx], 2009).

References

Berti, Daniela. 2011. 'Trials, Witnesses and Local Stakes in a District Court of Himachal Pradesh (North India)', in Johanna Pfaff and Gérard Toffin (eds.) *Citizenship, Democracy, and Belonging in the Himalayas*, pp. 290–313. New Delhi: Sage.

———. 2010 'Hostile Witnesses, Judicial Interactions and Out-of-Court Narratives in a North Indian District Court', *Contributions to Indian Sociology*, 44 (3): 235–63.

Chitkara, Anoop. 2010. 'Common Lacunae in Investigation of the NDPS Cases: A Lawyer's Perspective', conference paper, Krishi Vishav Vidhyalaya (Palampur, HP): Workshop on NDPS Act, 27 March 2010.

Conley, John M., and William M. O'Barr. 1990. *Rules versus Relationships. The Ethnography of Legal Discourse*. Chicago: University of Chicago Press.

———. 2005 [1998]. *Just Words: Law, Language, and Power*. Chicago: University of Chicago Press.

Good, Anthony. 2004. 'Expert Evidence in Asylum and Human Rights Appeals: An Expert's View', *International Journal of Refugee Law*, 16: 358–80.

Gupta, Justice Deepak. 2010. Conference paper. Krishi Vishav Vidhyalaya (Palampur, HP): Workshop on NDPS Act, 27 March 2010.

Kolsky, Elizabeth. 2010. *Colonial Justice in British India: White Violence and the Rule of Law*. Cambridge: Cambridge University Press.

Komter, Martha L. 2006. 'From Talk to Text: The Interactional Construction of a Police Record', *Research on Language and Social Interaction* 39, no. 3: 201–28.

Lakshmanan, Justice A.R. 2008. Conference paper. Krishi Vishav Vidhyalaya (Palampur, HP): Workshop on NDPS Act & Related Issues.

Lynch, Michael E. and Bogen, David. 2006. *The Spectacle of History, Speech, Text, and Memory at the Iran-Contra Hearings*. Durham, NC: Duke University Press Book.

Molly, C. 2001. 'Drug Trade in Himachal Pradesh: Role of Socio-economic Changes', *Economic and Political Weekly*, 36(26): 2433–2439.

Prosecutor Manual. 2008, *Government of Himachal Pradesh*. Department of Home, Directorate of Prosecutor: Himachal Pradesh, Shimla.

Singha, Radhika. 1998. *A Despotism of Law: Crime and Justice in Early Colonial India*. New Delhi: Oxford University Press.

Scheffer, Thomas, Hannken-Illies, Kati and Kozin, Alex. 2008. 'Bound to One's Own Words? Early Defenses and Their Binding Effects in Different Criminal Cases', *Law & Social Inquiry*, 32(1): 5–39.

4

CHIARA LETIZIA

The 'Secularism Case'

Prosecution of a Hindu Activist before a
Quasi-judicial Authority in the Nepal Tarai*

In December 2009, I entered the office of the vice-president of the
District Bar Association in the city of C., located in the southern
plains of Nepal (the region known as the Tarai), to hear her thoughts
on the legal implementation of Nepal's recently declared secularism.

* This essay is based on fieldwork conducted between November 2009 and
January 2010 and November 2010 and January 2011, while holding a Newton
Fellowship at the University of Oxford for work on religious change in Nepal.
This fieldwork was made possible by the support of the Newton International
Fellowship and the Project ANR 'JUST-INDIA: A Joint Programme on Justice
and Governance in India and South Asia', directed by Daniela Berti and Gilles
Tarabout, to whom I owe my heartfelt gratitude. I wish to thank David
Gellner for his precious comments on an earlier version of this chapter. I
would also like to thank my husband, Philippe Gagnon, for his assistance with
legal matters during fieldwork, Sange Lama for his help and his precious social
skills, and all of my informants, who so patiently tolerated my presence and
questions as they went about their work. For the most part, I have chosen not
to mention their true names in this chapter to protect their privacy. I also wish
to thank for their advice and kindness: Dr Ananda Mohan Bhattarai, Judge at
the Court of Appeal, Patan; Rajit Bhakta Pradhananga, Professor of Criminal

During our interview, she shared her understanding of secularism as an opportunity for inclusiveness and equality, the recognition by the Hindu majority of the rights of religious minorities: 'In Nepal, 80 per cent of people are Hindus, but we have many other religions, so secularism is good as it protects other religions and gives them equality and freedom; secularism means no domination of one religion.' Then she mentioned that 'Manoj', the leader of an anti-secular criminal group similar to the Defence Army,[1] had recently been arrested on suspicion of having masterminded many criminal assaults.

Later that day, I also met one of her colleagues, a lawyer and activist fighting against dowry practices. I had assumed that this woman's activism was a secular endeavour against a religiously sanctioned discriminatory tradition and expected her to be in favour of secularism, but it soon emerged that she was not motivated by any secularist conviction. Instead she attributed dowry to a lack of education and a degeneration of the original Hindu practice. She was actually fervently anti-secular; for her, secularism was an attack on Hinduism: everything should be done in order to preserve Hinduism, otherwise 'a researcher coming to Nepal in the future might no longer find any traces of it'. She then suggested that I speak to Manoj, an 'expert in this matter', who could give me all the good reasons why secularism was detrimental to Nepal. She recommended that I visit him in jail, and added: 'if you ask for 'the secularism case', everybody will know'. According to her,

---

Law at the Nepal Law Campus, Tribhuvan University; Nripadhwoj Niroula, Registrar of the Appellate Court of Patan and member of the National Judicial Academy; Bidur Koirala, Under Secretary to the Hon. Chief Justice, Supreme Court; Rewati Raj Tripathee, Deputy Government Attorney; Madhav Kumar Basnet, Lawyer at Triune Legal Service; and Om Prakash Aryal, Lawyer at Rights.

As a researcher, I solicited the personal views of many actors involved in this case, who, for research purposes, shared with me personally held beliefs, without any pretence of expressing any opinion as to the actual guilt or personal responsibilities according to the law of any of the persons involved.

The date of the court papers and of the laws related to the case are given according to both the official calendar of Nepal, Bikram Samvat, and the Gregorian system. Unless otherwise indicated, translations from Nepali are my own.

Manoj had been arrested for illegal possession of weapons, but in reality he had done nothing wrong, and he had certainly 'never attacked any Muslim or Christian'. He had been caught because of the highly visible nature of his anti-secularist protests.

Thus, two lawyers of the same age, sex, caste, religion, and education, who shared the same office in the same city, linked Manoj's case to my enquiries into secularism and gave two very different viewpoints: for the former, Manoj was an anti-secular fundamentalist jailed for criminal activities, while for the latter, he had been framed for his anti-secular activism. Their interpretations of the case were at odds with one another, mirroring the divergence in their views on secularism.

I eventually paid a visit to the jail where Manoj was being held and managed to arrange an interview (discussed below), which revealed a charismatic Hindu activist who seemed obsessed and tortured by the harm secularism was doing in Nepal.

A few days later, I was interviewing the Superintendent of Police (hereafter the SP) about the way the police dealt with crimes of cow slaughter (*gobadh*) and proselytization (*dharma parivartan garaune*)[2] since Nepal had become a secular country. The SP explained that even though these laws were still in force, Nepal's secular status had created some uncertainty about their application, for the Maoists now dominating politics did not abstain from eating cow meat. He told me that some Hindu associations protested because cows were being slaughtered with impunity, and again the name of Manoj was brought up: I was told that he was suspected of being the president of a Hindu underground association called Ranvir Sena,[3] and of having orchestrated several bombings in the city in protest against secularism. Thus, within a few days, the name of Manoj had come up several times in connection with secularism. Intrigued by the personality of the accused, who perceived and presented himself as a sort of anti-secular Hindu hero, I ended up following these serendipitous signs[4] and decided to make this case the focus of my research.

This chapter is a first attempt to interpret the data collected during fieldwork in 2009–2010 in the city of C., where the accused was imprisoned in September 2009. My work is not an ethnography of the court hearings; all data are derived from interviews and court papers. During fieldwork, I conducted repeated interviews with the main people linked to his case (i.e., the accused and his family, notably his father and sister, who were two of his main defence lawyers; the administrator of the prison; the superintendent of police who arrested him; and the District Prosecutor who first received his deposition); I also paid daily visits to the police station, the District Court, and the District Office, thanks to which I was able to collect (and translate from Nepali) documents concerning the investigation, the proceedings, the defence, the prosecution, and the adjudicating authority, and thereby to reconstruct the way the case had unfolded.

Manoj was accused and convicted of illegal possession of arms and ammunition under the Arms and Ammunition Act 2019 (1962). He was not tried and judged in a district court; section 24 of this Act gives the Chief District Officer (the CDO) the original jurisdiction to hear and decide such cases.

The CDO is accountable to the Ministry of Home Affairs and is the highest-ranking administrative officer in a district. One of his main responsibilities is to maintain peace, order, and security in the district, for which he has authority over the District Police Office. The CDO is also mandated under several laws to preside over one of the many 'quasi-judicial bodies' (*ardhanyayik nikaya*) in Nepal. In his quasi-judicial role, the CDO adjudicates disputes and under more than twenty separate statutes can summarily sentence individuals to terms of imprisonment for offences such as making a public nuisance or illegal possession of firearms.

The fact that Manoj's case was heard by a CDO prompted me to consult judges and lawyers both locally and in Kathmandu to better understand how the quasi-judicial system worked.

My general aim was to understand whether social and religious factors influenced legal procedures and if so, in what way. More precisely, my hypothesis was that the views, actions, and status of the accused— when considered in the particular context of the newly declared secular Nepal and of justice administered by the CDO—may have played a significant part in the procedures and the outcome of this case.

This chapter starts with a few considerations on secularism in Nepal. It then introduces the accused through his first interview, before moving on to examine the way the case unfolded from the investigation to the decision and its appeal, focusing on peculiarities concerning the court hearing. In the final section, I look at the more general subject of criminal justice administered by quasi-judicial bodies in Nepal, which appear to operate outside many legal norms and to provide an opportunity for extra-judicial factors to play a role in the procedures and results of a case.

The Context: Secularism in Tarai

The Hindu religion (*dharma*) is a recurrent theme in the case discussed here, not only because religious and anti-secular fervour was the main motivation behind the actions of the accused (which earned him respect and sympathy), but also because the fact that his activism took place in a political scene dominated by 'secularists' was used as part of his defence.

In May 2006, the House of Representatives declared Nepal a secular state, putting an end to the symbiotic relationship between Hinduism and the state that had existed for almost two centuries,[5] during which Nepali rulers had made Hinduism an essential component of national identity and the cement that united their culturally and ethnically diverse subjects. The establishment of a secular federal republic was brought about by numerous factors that can only be listed here, including: the rise of ethnic claims in the 1990s; the profound political and social impact of the Maoist People's War (1996–2006); the People's Movement of 2006, which united people and all main parties against the King; and finally the political weight of the UCPN-Maoist party following the elections of 2008. For the minorities—who in the 1990s started to be collectively referred to as Janajati[6]—'secularism' (*dharmanirapeksata*, 'autonomous from/indifferent, impartial to *dharma*') meant that all religions practised in the country would enjoy equal rights and recognition, and that the state-sponsored primacy granted to Hinduism would be abolished.

The impact of secularism was felt particularly keenly in the Tarai due to the simultaneous presence of deeply religious Hindu communities, a significant proportion of Muslims (15 per cent), an increasing number of Christians, and groups linked to the Bihar- and Uttar Pradesh-based Hindu Right. The Tarai also saw the sudden emergence of the violent Madheshi movement in 2007. The term Madheshi ('plains-dwellers') encompasses many different ethnic, linguistic, and religious groups inhabiting the Tarai region who have always lacked representation in the government and are generally acknowledged to have experienced discrimination from both the state and other Nepali people. Madheshi discontent crystallized in 2007, leading to clashes between Madheshis and 'hills-dwellers' (Pahadis) (ICG 2007), and resentment against the declaration of secularism is believed to have been used as a rallying call for the Madheshi movement (ICG 2007: 11; Mathema 2011: 67–8). Some leaders of Madheshi parties initially associated with activists from the Indian Hindu Right, who were interested in their potential role as a defence against Maoist penetration in the Tarai region (ICG 2007: 28, 33).

My interviews in the Tarai showed that *dharmanirapeksata* is a sensitive term whose meaning varies depending of the user. Welcomed by ethnic and religious minorities as a sign of recognition in a country dominated by high-caste Hindus, by Muslims as an opportunity for *shari'a* law to be recognized for their community, and by Christians as an implicit authorization to proselytize (despite the letter of the law), secularism appeared to evoke strong feelings from the Hindu side, and I came across many anti-secular voices. Secularism was associated with a language of violence and competition between communities, and its declaration gave rise to a number of violent attacks on Christians and Muslims involving underground Hindu associations (see note 2).

The Interim Constitution of Nepal 2007 did not provide any clear model of secularism, and no information campaign was launched after its declaration; thus, the task of explaining secularism to the masses in the Tarai was taken up by pro-Hindu Kingdom parties and right-wing Hindu organizations.[7] These activists capitalized on widespread fear among the Hindu majority that secularism would empower other communities and weaken Hindus. Those who tried to define secularism were mostly its opponents, for whom secularism was at once a despicable measure attacking the identity of the country and leading to communal violence, a Christian or Muslim conspiracy, and a stepping stone towards mass conversion and the indiscriminate killing of cows (Letizia 2011). The Tarai also played host to the erstwhile king Gyanendra on several occasions between 2009 and 2011, when he took part in a considerable number of religious rituals and festivals, surrounded by supporters chanting slogans for the reinstatement of the monarchy. Anti-secular voices were heard more and more loudly as the constitution-drafting process stalled. My interview with Manoj revealed that he was one of those voices.

The Accused in Jail: Charisma, Obsession, and the Secularist Westerner

Before authorizing my visit, the prison administrator talked to me at length in his office. He told me that Manoj was admired by the other prisoners for his strong Hindu devotion; he spent eight hours a day performing *puja* ('worship') in the prison's Shiva temple. According to the leader of the prisoners, whom I met afterwards, Manoj read the Mahabharata and Ramayana fourteen hours a day, and had obtained special prison privileges due to his religious zeal.

The administrator also shared with my assistant Sange and me his opinions on religion, invoking discourses with which I was becoming increasingly familiar through my interviews with Hindu activists. In his view, Hindu religion precedes, encompasses, and tolerates all other religions: 'The Hindu religion being the oldest religion of the world, in ancient times all people were Hindus: Muslims came after, and so did other religions. They are all secondary religions that split from the Hindu religion. The Hindu religion is liberal and never rigid, and allows people to practise freely their secondary religions, and in Hinduism itself there is a large diversity.'

The administrator was eager to get me to understand that the prisoner I was about to meet was no fundamentalist, but a person admired for his devotion, since there was no place in Hinduism for intolerance and violence.

Finally, we were allowed into the jail to carry out the interview, which was held in the visitors' room.[8] Manoj, a high-caste (Bahun) engineer who spoke English (the interview was conducted in both Nepali and English), had an aura of authority afforded by his professional status and Hindu piety and was treated with some deference by the guards: the visit of a foreign anthropologist no doubt contributed to this.

From the outset, it was clear in his eyes that I represented all 'Western Christian countries imposing secularism in Nepal and conspiring against the Hindu religion under the cover of human rights and secularism'. For thirty minutes, Manoj passionately expressed an impressive mix of complaints, contempt, and suffering on the subject of secularism in Nepal, taking me as his rhetorical enemy. He affirmed that state and religion cannot be separated, that secularism does not exist in any country, and that the Western countries that want to impose secularism on Nepal have not achieved it at home (the President of the United States has to be Christian, he explained, while the British Prime Minister must be a Baptist). He argued that secularism came to Nepal as part of a foreign Christian conspiracy: it will take away the last land of the Hindus, create division in the country, provoke the mass slaughter of cows, and bring about indiscriminate conversions through the use of economic incentives, leading to the death of Hinduism, to which the only response can be Hindu terrorism. He did not condone violence, however; he told me that his Hindu association organized programmes to help people, and that he spent his time in prison engaging in worship, meditation, and yoga. He explained that he was in prison due to a political conspiracy.

Policemen and prisoners alike listened to our interview in respectful silence. There was strength and stamina in this discourse, which invoked nationalism, devotion, pride, and the feelings of a persecuted Hindu majority. As I will show, Manoj's views (but not the reference to 'Hindu terrorism') were widespread, and this appeared clearly in my interview with the aforementioned Superintendent of Police who had arrested him.

Interview with the Superintendent of Police

The SP told us that when Manoj was first caught, he confessed to having carried out several bombings in the city to call attention to his demands. The SP added that Manoj had been part of the Hindu extremist group Nepal Defence Army ('NDA'), led by R. P. Mainali (see note 2), but that he had later left and founded a 'more peaceful organization, the Ranvir Sena, which was not willing to kill, but to raise people's awareness'. In the SP's words, 'Mainali took the path of violence, while Manoj the path of non-violence'. Mainali had not forgiven Manoj's 'betrayal', and when the former was arrested, he had been carrying a letter asking his aides to kill Manoj. Apparently, it was Mainali who had told the police how to find Manoj. This information about the links between Manoj and Mainali was not brought up at any subsequent stage of the case.[9]

The SP concluded by telling us how Manoj had become a popular figure in the city:

> There are many people who are in favour of his activism and knowledge; his anti-Maoist and pro-Hindu activities are appreciated. People cannot say it openly, but they agree with him, and accept his vision. I myself es-

teem his intelligence and knowledge, but not his choice of expressing his criticism in an illegal way. I told him that if he could use his knowledge in favour of the nation, it would be better.

The SP told us that Manoj criticized the police for providing security at mosques during Friday prayers, or for not doing enough to prevent cow slaughter in the city. Manoj would ask them angrily why, in a country with a Hindu majority, they wasted time protecting the minorities, and why they did not go and arrest these minorities when they were eating cows. He would say that Islam is a 'strangers' religion' (*agantuk dharma*), and that the police should give priority to the 'indigenous religion' (*adivasi dharma*). Convinced as the SP was of Manoj's links with the infamous NDA and of his use of terrorist tactics to publicize his cause, he nevertheless showed consideration for Manoj's ideas and criticisms, agreeing with some elements of his discourse (though not his ways), which he recognized as being widespread in the city.

The District Police Officer under the command of the SP is the first important actor because, through the investigation process, he brings cases for prosecution. Let us now see how Manoj's case passed from his office to those of the public prosecutor and the CDO.

The Case (Chronology and Procedures)

Generally speaking, trials are conducted at the District Court. However, there are various laws entitling many administrative offices, such as the Chief District Office, the District Forest Office, the Customs Office, the Immigration Office, and the Land office, to exercise quasi-judicial powers to conduct criminal trials.[10]

As previously mentioned, Manoj was tried and judged before the CDO, whose quasi-judicial authority was bestowed by the Arms and Ammunition Act 2019 BS (1962) (hereafter the AAA), under which Manoj was accused. Such cases are subject to the *same* laws of procedure as the cases presented before the District Courts,[11] which are governed by the Government Cases Act 2049 (1992),[12] the section on Court Management of the new Civil Code (Muluki Ain), and the Administration of Justice Act, 2048 (1991).[13] As for rules of evidence, The Evidence Act, 2031 (1974)[14] applies to all courts and quasi-judicial bodies.

First Information Report, Investigation, and Custody

On 6 September 2009, police officers entered Manoj's apartment, arrested Manoj himself and sealed off the place. A police inspector filed the First Information Report, which stated that Manoj was suspected of illegally possessing arms and ammunition.[15] The investigating officer obtained a permit for search and seizure; in Manoj's room, officers found guns, bullets, and all the necessary materials for making explosives,[16] along with personal items (a computer, a printer, a camera, a mobile phone, and a computer processor). The police officer prepared a detailed list of the evidence collected, which was signed by the suspect and several witnesses. An arrest warrant was issued on the grounds that Manoj was suspected of illegal possession of arms and ammunition. A week later, a further search uncovered several other items, including seven pistols, ammunition, and six bombs.

Statement of the Accused

According to the Evidence Act Section 9 (2), the statement of the accused amounts to a confession and forms good evidence for a conviction, provided that it was obtained without coercion or the use of torture. As per the Government Cases Act Section 9 (1), the interrogation of a suspect should be carried out in the presence of a Government Attorney; this provision was introduced to prevent torture, but apparently it is rarely followed (CeLRRd 2002: 17).

From what I could gather, the police interrogated Manoj once, after which a formal deposition was taken before the District Prosecutor. The following synopsis is drawn from this formal statement, which was written in the first person, signed by Manoj, and dated 15 September 2009. In the document Manoj refuses a lawyer and declares himself to be the leader of the GFP Ranvir Sena, an underground organization involved in the Hindu ideological revolution.[17] He acknowledges that weapons and explosive materials were found in his room and confirms the report of the police inspector; he bought guns and bullets in India, while he made the bombs himself. He declares that, as he has been involved in the Hindu ideological revolution for a long time, he has often received death threats from his opponents and so bought the weapons for his own protection. He affirms that he once organized a mass gathering of

Hindu activists and that they were attacked; thinking that such attacks could reoccur, he kept the weapons as a precautionary measure. Manoj admits that he was keeping them illegally and confesses to having used the explosive materials to carry out bombings at different sites in the city. He affirms that these bombs were not put there to harm anyone, and they never did, but just to publicize his cause.

Manoj's statement to the District Prosecutor then assumes the form of an apology and an ideological statement:

> Hinduness [*hindutva*] is the identity [*paichan*] of Nepal. It is the identity of 90% of the people's culture [*samskriti*] and beliefs [*astha*]. Trying to protect it, as I am doing, is not an act of disturbance to religious harmony [*dharmik sahisnuta*], but a means to bring about religious unity [*dharmik ekata*]. (....) I never attacked any Mosque or Church; but I think that the followers of all the religions in the country should recognize the need to protect Hindu religion as the State religion. I did not do anything with criminal intent, nor did I intend to make any disturbance to peace and security, or to national unity. This is clearly mentioned in our pamphlets.

When the District Prosecutor asks Manoj how he can say that by using bombs he was not intending to harm anyone, Manoj replies that his bombs were made of low-grade explosives and there was, therefore, a minimal chance of their causing any serious damage. The document ends with Manoj's signature, confirming the truthfulness of his account.

Manoj's line of defence seems clear: he presents himself as a Hindu anti-secular activist (invoking certain sentiments that he knows are shared by the people questioning him) who uses arms to defend himself against opponents and carries out bombings to increase public awareness, itself construed as a form of self-defence for the threatened Hindu community.

To complete the investigation, on 1 October 2009, the police asked three witnesses to sign a statement about what they saw at the search site. In this document, two of the witnesses, the neighbours GR and PR, declare that the accused was caught in his room with weapons and explosive materials and confirm the validity of the list presented in the search and seizure document. They affirm that Manoj had collected these arms only for his self-defence and security, and that he had formed an association called Ranvir Sena to protect and preserve 'Hinduness', through non-violent protest ('only for peace'). The third witness, KCC, does not really confirm the police findings. He affirms that he has known Manoj for a long time and that Manoj is a good person who has always worked to preserve the Hindu religion and is a firm believer in religious harmony. The witness states that he came to know *from newspapers* that Manoj is the leader of GFP Ranvir Sena and that weapons were found in his room.

Prosecution

The prosecution of crimes is the Attorney General's constitutional responsibility[18] and the final decision as to whether or not to prosecute is made by him, a power that he can delegate to his subordinates.[19] In the case discussed here, once the police officers finalized the report of their findings, they submitted it to the District Prosecutor, who decided to prosecute Manoj for illegal possession of weapons (*hathatyar kharkhajana*) under Section 20(2) of the AAA for violating the following Sections: 3(2), which prohibits the manufacture, repair, and possession of arms or ammunition without a licence; 4(2), which prohibits anyone without a licence from bringing arms and ammunitions into or out of Nepal; and 5(1), which prohibits anyone from carrying arms without a licence. The said Section 20(2) determines the punishment for violation of the Sections mentioned above and provides for imprisonment ranging from three to five years or a fine ranging from NPR 60,000 to 100,000. Surprisingly, the District Prosecutor chose not to prosecute Manoj for the bombings he had confessed to. Moreover, the police did not conduct any further investigations into these explosions, despite having found homemade bombs, bomb-making paraphernalia, and instruction manuals in Manoj's room. When I enquired about this, the Superintendent of Police replied that they would have charged Manoj on this count only if he had succeeded in refuting the first accusation. On 2 October 2009, the District Prosecutor submitted the chargesheet to the CDO.

According to the Nepali criminal procedure, cases proceed in three stages: a) the bail hearing, when the suspect is produced, his or her deposition is recorded, and the court decides whether to keep him or her in custody or release him/her on bail; b) the post-bail hearing, where the judge evaluates the investigation findings, the chargesheet, and the statement of accused, and where witnesses for the prosecution and the defence are brought before the court to testify and be cross-examined; and c) the final hearing, where the verdict is delivered and sentence is passed at the same time.

Bail Hearing (tunchek)

On 4 October 2009, Manoj, this time accompanied by an armada of no less than fifteen lawyers, was brought before the CDO. He proceeded to give an entirely new statement that contradicted the previous one.[20] The following synopsis is drawn from the document of this new statement, which was written in the first person. Manoj denies having been caught in his room and claims that the police had found him in the street. He also denies being the leader of the Ranvir Sena or having any contact with this organization. He affirms that his previous signed statement did not contain his words and that it was a pre-prepared confession that the police had forced him to sign under mental and physical torture (e.g., death threats, waterboarding, and beatings). He denies that bombs and weapons were found in his room and states that at the time of the search and seizure, he was made to sign a blank sheet of paper, on which the police subsequently added the list of weapons. He also provided the names of different people who could act as witnesses (sakshi).

The statement concludes with the following claim: 'Since 2052 I have been performing many peaceful public programmes for the protection [sanrakshan], preservation [sambardhan], and development [bikas] of my Hindu religion. To this effect I have been organizing so many conferences, pressure, and peaceful programmes; for this reason my opponents, the supporters of secularism [dharamanirapeksavadi] trapped me [malai phasaune kam garieko ho]'.

The CDO recorded that the suspect denied the accusations and, invoking Section 24/a of the AAA, ordered that he be put in jail pending trial. Manoj waited in jail until the next hearing, which did not take place for another six months. By the time the sentence was delivered in June 2010, he had already spent nine months in jail.[21]

Witness Testimony (sakshi bakpatra)

According to the case records, the CDO held the second hearing on 25 April 2010, and called for the witnesses for the prosecution and the defence to testify. The fifteen defence lawyers attended again, but neither the District Prosecutor nor the CDO were present, the latter having delegated this task to his junior staff. In order to discredit the police and portray the whole case as a frame-up, the defence produced two witnesses (DM and RCY) who confirmed Manoj's account, saying that they saw Manoj being arrested in the city and not in his room, and that they went to his house and saw the police recover a computer, a camera, a mobile phone, and a printer, but no weapons or ammunition. They affirmed that the search and seizure of documents produced by the police were false (*jhutha*). Furthermore, they said that Manoj was the national president of Hindu Jagaran Mahasangh (Federation for Hindu Awareness).There was no public prosecutor to cross-examine them.

Then the two witnesses for the prosecution (MO and GR) were heard. MO had signed the search and seizure warrant. A member of the CDO staff asked if the signature was his, and he confirmed it. The witness was then turned over to the defence for cross-examination.

Asked by the defence lawyer which objects were actually found in Manoj's room, MO replied that he saw the police recover a computer, a printer, a camera, and a mobile phone. When confronted with the document of search and seizure, MO said that the arms and ammunition were not recovered in front of him. Asked why he had signed the document, MO explained that the police had instructed him to sign an empty form, claiming that they would add the list of recovered items subsequently. He declared that the hearing was the first time he had heard about the arms and ammunitions. The defence lawyer asked MO if he had entered Manoj's room with the police officers, to which he replied that he had not been allowed in the room.

The second witness, GR, who had also signed a statement concerning the police's findings, confirmed that the signature on the document was his but stated that the description was not, venturing that the police must have added this themselves. As there was no public prosecutor to examine these witnesses, they could not be confronted with their previous statements nor be asked leading questions, as provided for in the Evidence Act Section 50(4–5).

According to the rules of court procedure, the testimony of the witnesses should have been given in front of the CDO, and the Government Attorney should have been present to examine the prosecution witnesses and cross-examine the defence's witnesses. Therefore, the procedure followed in this case did not comply with the rules prescribed under the applicable Acts. Indeed, my fieldwork revealed that in cases involving CDO jurisdiction, it is common for the rules of court procedure to be ignored. If we compare what happened in Manoj's case not with the rules but with standard practice, we can observe that the delegation of CDO duties and the absence of lawyers (on both sides) is *normal*, whereas what was really unique about this case was the presence of defence lawyers and the fact that they actually conducted an examination of the witnesses according to the rules. To sum up, it appears that in this case there was an extraordinary compliance with the rules.

Indeed, my interviews in the Tarai and in Kathmandu's legal circles confirmed that in general neither public prosecutors nor defence lawyers attend hearings before the CDO and quasi-judicial authorities.[22] To help me understand how rare it was for the prosecutors to attend CDO hearings, the Danusha District Prosecutor told me that in the last fifteen years, he had attended only one hearing at his district CDO office. Likewise, the Under Secretary to the Chief Justice of the Supreme Court told me that CDOs rarely give advance notice of the hearings, so that the accused cannot be defended by a lawyer. In the case of Manoj, however, the defence lawyers were both aware of and prepared for the hearing, and their number at the hearing was something unheard of.

As a result of the defence lawyers' presence at this hearing, some aspects of the prescribed court procedure were strictly adhered to (i.e., the production of witnesses, their examination, and cross examination by the defence), which was striking when one considers the usual practices in CDO offices. However, other aspects (i.e., the absence of the CDO and the public prosecutor) were more consistent with usual practices. In my view, rather than an effort to adhere to legal norms, the significant show of strength by the defence team was an attempt to ensure success in an adverse setting and to counterbalance the strength of the chargesheet.

Final Hearing: Decision (*phaisala*)

The final hearing, where the CDO rendered the decision, took place on 24 June 2010. In articulating his decision, the CDO quoted the statement that Manoj had given in his office to the effect that he had been tortured and forced to sign false statements, that he denied being in possession of arms and ammunitions or being involved in Ranvir Sena, and that he had pleaded not guilty. However, the CDO affirmed that the statements of the accused could not be independently verified, except by the statement given by his own witnesses, and that there was no evidence of torture.

In the absence of any 'independent evidence' contradicting the evidence of the prosecution, and considering the first statement of the accused to the public prosecutor and the police reports, Manoj was found guilty for possession of arms and/or ammunition without a licence, for bringing arms or ammunition into Nepal without a licence, and for carrying arms without a licence (AAA Sections 3(2), 4(2) and 5(1)). Manoj was given a fine of NPR 60,000 and sentenced to one year's imprisonment according to Subsections 20(2) and 20 (3) of the same Act, which was the very minimum for both offences.[23]

Release

On 6 September 2010, after completing the year of detention ordered by the CDO, Manoj was finally released.[24] As soon as I returned to the city several months later, I met with a member of his family (and one of my principal informants about the case) who immediately gave me the 'good news' that Manoj had been released: 'He has been released as he had not done anything. They kept him in custody for observation; as they could not find any evidence against him, it was decided that he did not commit any crime. It was recognized that whatever he did, he did it just for religion; it was just a religious activity. Seeing Manoj's fairness, the CDO has said, 'You do not seem guilty; you can go for appeal'.'

This version of Manoj's release is an example—by no means unique—of the type of information I was usually given by the parties to the case. Accessing the documents, finding out the facts, and establishing the chronology of the events were themselves problematic issues. At the beginning of my research I was given a great deal of incorrect information, as each party remained quiet about some details and underscored others, as if I were a judge who had to be convinced. In the example given above, my informant, who was involved in the defence of the case, was clearly aware that Manoj had been found guilty and punished accordingly, but she glossed over this. If her account were to be believed, it would seem that the CDO did not trust his own verdict!

Although this meant that I was forced to continually double-check everything I was told, there was a positive aspect to this process in that it allowed me to apprehend the different versions of the facts and the arguments of both the accusation and its defence. I soon realized the danger of being seen as a sort of judge (or international witness) rather than as an anthropologist doing research. I thus made it clear that I had no prejudice or personal interest in the case; my intention, I explained to all of my informants, was not to enquire or decide, but only to better understand their experience of the criminal procedures applied in this case. The actors involved, aware of my growing knowledge of the case but also of my detachment, eventually appeared to relax and offered their time and assistance more willingly.

The Appeal (*punaravedan patra*)

On 23 September 2010, the accused lodged an appeal against his conviction before the appellate court (AAA Section 24 (2)). In the writ of appeal, written in the first person, Manoj affirms that the decision is 'full of mistakes'. Claiming once again that he did not know who wrote the statement that was attributed to him or how the weapons were recovered, he states that he had been tortured, accuses the police of having fabricated evidence, and affirms that he has been trapped (*phasaunu*) in a 'false case' (*jhutha mudda*). He explains what was behind this false case as follows:

> I believe that Nepal should be a Hindu state, that some parties guided by foreign countries have declared secularism [*dharmanirapekshata*] instead of a Hindu state, showing contempt [*tiraskar*] for the sentiments [*bhavana*] of Hindu majority; Hindu Jagaran Mahasangh, an organization registered in Nepal and uniting different religious institutions, affirms that Nepal should be a Hindu state. I am convinced that both the State and the Constituent Assembly should be given ideological pressure to this effect. For these reasons, on the indication of some administrators and some specific parties, I was arrested and framed, even though I had not committed any offence. ... The Hindu Jagaran Mahasangh is a social institution working for the preservation [*suraksha*] and implementation of Hindu religion, regularly registered in the district administration office of Saptari District, and I am the central president of this association. Even though I have declared that I am not involved in the Ranvir Sena, and even though my witnesses have stated that I am involved in the

Hindu Jagaran Mahasangh, the decision found me guilty; I request the
appellate court to reconsider this.

The appellant protests that the decision was based on forged evidence
presented by the police, which was subsequently contradicted by every
witness, including the prosecution's own witnesses. He argues that the
police frequently trap persons for political/social/financial reasons by
planting a weapon in a person's house during an investigation and subsequently accusing him or her of illegal arms possession; the appellant
says it is also common for them to threaten and torture a detainee to
make him or her sign confessions that he or she did not make. Therefore,
the statement of the police alone should not have been taken as reliable
evidence, whereas the statements of the witnesses should.[25]

To counteract these evil police practices, says the appellant, the
legislature has fixed a procedure for the investigation and collection of
evidence involving, among other things, the presence of municipal/vil-
lage development committee representatives (Government Cases Act,
Section 8), the prior search of police and witnesses entering the search
and seizure area, and the drawing up of a list of the objects seized and
its delivery to the owner of the house, none of which were followed
here. Manoj concludes that the police evidence is unreliable; documents
were made illegally and arms were surreptitiously mixed with objects
found in his house. He offers the following summation:

> I am a literate person, a scholar, a civil engineer working in D [...] Con-
> struction Company. Due to the situation of the country, I am involved
> in a Hindu organization, which is not illegal; since it is my strong belief
> that Nepal should be a Hindu state, as 90 per cent of the population is
> Hindu, the government has trapped me—an innocent person—with a
> conspiracy [*shadyantra*] under a political plan of security, and the District
> Officer has found me guilty; my domestic objects were called 'arms' and
> the case has been filed in an illegal manner. I ask therefore that the deci-
> sion be quashed.

The appeal document reveals a strategy of highlighting problems that
in some legal cases prove to be true (e.g., the CDOs' lack of technical
competence in the legal procedure, the use of torture, the orchestration of false cases to imprison political opponents) to point to technical
failings in the investigation, cast doubt on the evidence brought by the
police, and deny any offence on the part of the accused.

In the end, the Appellate Court refused to invalidate the CDO's decision and rejected Manoj's appeal. Manoj did not launch an appeal before the Supreme Court.

Comments on the Case

The Strategies of the Defence

The first strategy of the defence was to come to the hearing with fifteen lawyers (which my informants agreed was an unprecedented show of force) and to stick firmly to the court procedures, thereby maximizing the opportunity to make the case for the defence in a context where the absence of the prosecutor was assured and therefore the prosecution's witnesses could retract their testimony without risk of cross-examination. Yet such was the discretion of the CDO that this effort was only partially successful, to the extent that the CDO simply decided that the statements of the witnesses lacked corroboration, a roundabout way of saying that he did not believe them. However, the fact that all of the witnesses confirmed Manoj's version of events was undoubtedly perceived as a plus for him, and he used this argument before the Appellate Court.

Another strategy of the defence was to invoke torture to nullify the first confession and the police evidence. It has been confirmed by many of my legal informants that torture is widely used by police during interrogations, and that making allegations to this effect is a common way of seeking to invalidate a damning statement. As an informant at the Supreme Court told me, 'police personnel can use "third degree" methods to obtain a confession easily. But afterwards before the court, the accused tends to deny it. This is a major problem of our justice system.' When I asked the District Prosecutor or the police officers I interviewed whether they were worried—or even offended to be accused of torture by people they knew well, they played down the allegations, saying that Manoj was not accusing them but only trying to extricate himself from this situation, and that they had nothing to worry about.

In seeking to put Manoj's allegations and the postulated 'torturers' lack of worry in their wider context, it is important to note that even though Nepal acceded to the United Nations Convention against Torture in 1991,[26] torture is still not a crime under Nepali law. While the 1990 Constitution declared torture to be unconstitutional,[27] the government failed to criminalize torture per se despite intense lobbying from human rights activists for many years. Instead, a Compensation Relating to Torture Act was passed in Parliament in 1996, giving victims the right to seek compensation.[28](Manoj did not pursue a claim through this Act, even though his numerous legal advisors would have readily offered their assistance had he chosen to do so.) The current Interim Constitution, promulgated in 2007, is the first proposing to criminalize torture that occurs during official detention (see article 26), but a bill to criminalize torture had not yet made it into law (Human Rights Watch 2008).[29]

Lenient Treatment

The decision of the CDO seemed particularly lenient given the charge-sheet, the material evidence, and the range of possible sentences.[30] The sentence appeared all the more lenient given the accused's alleged links with the Nepal Defence Army, and the same could be said of the process as a whole.[31] Not only was the sentence minimal, but also the charge was limited to the offence of illegal possession of arms and any evidence relating to the actual bombings was ignored completely. The CDO mentioned only part of Manoj's first statement (where he admitted to having bought arms in India), eliding the section where Manoj confessed to having set off bombs in the city, and none seemed concerned about this. Moreover, the public prosecutor was not present at the hearings to press for a more severe sentence.

'I Cannot Ask for the Documents—They will Think I Want to Appeal'

When I learned that Manoj had filed an appeal, I returned to meet the District Prosecutor so I could find out what his next move would be. I was surprised to find myself being the one informing the other of both the decision and the appeal. He told me that he had not yet received the copy of the decision so he had not been able to appeal himself, even though the defence had already done so. At that moment, I was seriously concerned that my presence might condition the development of the case itself, since my questions seemed inevitably to alter the 'natural' course of the case.

Concerning his absence from the hearings, the District Prosecutor told me that he had not been given notice and that the hearing might have taken place while he was training overseas. He had nevertheless heard about the sentence. While he did not agree with the lenient punishment, he did not seem especially eager to obtain the decision document in order to file an appeal. This appeared clearly when I asked for his help to obtain a copy of the CDO's judgement.

Attempting to get hold of the case papers in fact comprised a large part of my fieldwork in terms of energy, time, and diplomatic skills. The lawyers for the defence were sometimes reluctant in this regard (although I did get some documents from the accused's father), while the CDO refused to meet with me, and it proved difficult for me to get the documents directly from his office. Thus, I obtained the majority of my documentary evidence through the prosecutor's office. The prosecutor would never go to the CDO's office in my company, as he would to the Court; instead he would send a boy with money for the photocopies. The process of getting my hands on the documents required a mixture of courtesy, name-dropping, and patience; it was also revealing of the mechanisms of power between the various parties and offices.

When I asked the District Prosecutor to help me obtain a copy of the decision, he seemed determined to send me to the CDO office alone (which was bound to result in failure). He was not willing to ask for the document himself, he told me, even though it was high time he obtained it. 'If I send you with my boy,' he explained, 'Manoj's family will think that I am pressurizing them and getting the decision for *me*, in order to appeal; you see, we know each other well [*chinchau*]. If I go and ask directly for the document, they will think badly of me.'[32] For this reason, he could not be too proactive in the prosecution, despite his feeling that the decision was too lenient and should be appealed. Similarly, he found it particularly uncomfortable to ask something 'from the big people, arrogant and bossy, who hold big posts and do not want interference', by which he was referring—not so subtly—to the CDO. As mentioned previously, the District Prosecutor does not usually take part in CDO hearings, and he is expected to wait for the decision to arrive on his desk, which can take many months.

Dogged negotiations ensued with the District Prosecutor, during which I invoked his own kindness and help on previous occasions, as well as the scant authority that I could muster with a letter from my advisor in Oxford, and a verbal promise from the Registrar of the Supreme Court that he would come to my aid should I encounter problems accessing court documents.

In the end, the prosecutor, on the pretext that he did have a citizenship issue to resolve at the CDO office, proposed to take with him my friend and assistant, Sange Lama.

When he reached the office, the prosecutor asked the deputy officer how my assistant could get some documents he was interested in. The officer replied that only the persons concerned and private lawyers could obtain a copy of the files, whereupon the prosecutor and Sange thanked him and left.

My assistant told me that as they exited the office, the prosecutor said with a satisfied expression, 'as you see, Mr Lama, we did a good thing to ask the CDO how to request a copy of the documents. Now we can call a lawyer and ask him to do this.' The prosecutor's *mise en scène* was a skilful way of helping me without asking anything for himself. By asking (rhetorically, as he already knew the answer full well) how one could access the documents, he was showing that he was following the procedures exactly and was not doing anything 'privately' (i.e., that he had no intention of filing an appeal or giving me documents surreptitiously). Moreover, he had found a way of letting the CDO office know that he knew that the document was ready and that it was time for him to have it.

The Social and Religious Dimensions of the Case

The concerns of the public prosecutor to not act in a way that might offend Manoj's family prompted further considerations of the hypothesis that the social position of the accused played a role in both the procedure and the outcome of the case. It is not easy to say for certain why Manoj was treated so leniently, as the CDO did not explain his reasons for the light sentence. However, Manoj's powerful family of lawyers, his respected profession, and his Hindu activism seem to have influenced the people involved at different stages of the case.

Manoj comes from a well-connected family of Brahmans. His father is a prominent member of the legal profession who has been both practising and teaching law for several decades. As the latter told me during a long interview in his hometown in the Tarai, his students work all over Nepal as lawyers, judges, and court officers at Supreme, Appellate, and District Courts (a ubiquity confirmed by enquires I made in Kathmandu). This partly explains why as many as fifteen lawyers agreed to attend Manoj's hearings and were able by sticking to court procedure, to give the defence a much louder voice.

Manoj's father organized a movement of support outside of the CDO proceedings in the hope of securing his son's release from jail. He was particularly eager to show me two letters of support on behalf of Manoj, signed by local party leaders from the district where Manoj's family resides. The letters, which were dated February 2010, were addressed to the Ministry of Peace and Reconstruction and asked for the release of Manoj and the dismissal of the case. The first letter was signed by a district peace committee, the second by a significant number of local leaders from every political party, including the Maoists, the UML-Communists and Madheshi parties. Both letters present Manoj as a 'follower of the Hindu religion who wants to make Nepal a Hindu state, who established the Hindu Jagaran Mahasangh, who has always demonstrated equal respect to Hindu ascetics, to all parties and to different religions and sects, and who never committed any crime'. They affirm that Manoj's detention is 'related to the state' (*rajya samma sambandhit*, i.e., it is a political issue) and to his political and religious beliefs, and therefore ask that the case be dismissed.

The Ministry of Peace and Reconstruction forwarded the letters to the Ministry of Home Affairs (which oversees the CDOs), requesting that the latter let the CDO know about them. Obviously, the letters sought to bring about an executive intervention in the case, and this was being done openly. (The judicial independence of the CDO will be discussed further in section 6.)

For some actors in the case, the legal sway of Manoj's family seemed to count for more than other aspects of the accused's status. The District Prosecutor was one such individual. As a lawyer, he knew Manoj's family well and showed deference to them, to Manoj himself, and to his lawyers. However, he did not seem impressed by the efforts of Manoj's lawyers to justify their client's actions as 'religiously motivated'. To put it in his laconic terms, 'the accused has the right to speak about secularism and Hinduism, but he has no right to have weapons at home'. The documents show that the case was prosecuted in a strictly technical way. Although the prosecutor took pains not to appear overzealous in his actions, being particularly careful to remain on good terms with Manoj's family, he nevertheless asked for the maximum punishment under the AAA.

The police officers and members of legal circles I spoke with shared Manoj's views. The Superintendent of Police told us how many people agreed with Manoj's pro-Hindu activism even though they did not declare it openly themselves; he himself respected Manoj's criticism of the police and appeared to truly believe that Ranvir Sena had chosen the 'peaceful way' despite carrying out bombings. The choice of the SP and the prosecutor not to pursue a conviction for the actual bombings showed that while there was no desire to set the accused free, there was certainly no interest in making a stronger case against him.

Manoj's treatment in jail was also marked by respect. I became acutely aware of this after visiting the offices of District Prosecutor and police from other districts and witnessing first-hand how prisoners were treated, the intimidation they were subjected to, and their bodily postures of fear. In one almost surreal instance, I observed three prisoners' shock at being invited to sit on a couch facing the one I was occupying in the prosecutor's office. No words were spoken, but the exchange of looks between the prisoners, the prosecutor, and the police officers made it clear that, had I not been there, those men would have been made to sit on the ground. The questions put to them were patronizing and brusque, which reinforced in my mind the privileged position occupied by Manoj, who had been able to have polite exchanges with the police officers and the prosecutor and even to discuss his ideas.

The fact that Manoj was an engineer known for his construction work in the city was probably another favourable factor in the sentencing, as it had clearly earned him a measure of respect among his accusers. According to the public prosecutor, it was easy for a man of his standing to convince the prosecution witnesses that they should retract their statements.

For the general public, fellow prisoners, and friends and neighbours, Manoj's worship and recitation of the Hindu scriptures in the prison temple, his 'guru appearance' showing his devotion to the cause were all worthy of respect and consideration. All the witnesses, even those for the prosecution, agreed that he was a devout Hindu and a good person.

My visit to Manoj in prison and my interviews with the police and prosecutor (from the way they spoke of him) clearly demonstrated that the very fact that Manoj was passionate about the Hindu cause and expressed opinions that were pro-monarchy and pro-Hindu state in the context of the Tarai (a region where such views were widespread) ensured that he was met with a certain deference and respect wherever he went. It cannot be affirmed whether such views had a direct influence on the procedures or their outcome, but Manoj's religious considerations[33] and his devotion to the Hindu cause were certainly a main strategic component of the defence's rhetoric. The threat of religious terrorism was completely obfuscated, even though the police had linked the accused to the terrorist group NDA.

The above-mentioned social factors were used to 'colour' the file in favour of the accused. Needless to say, it is not my intention here to prove which factors were foremost in the CDO's mind when he passed his sentence (not least because I was never allowed to meet him). But in the last part of this paper, I want to reflect on the particular position of the CDO as one of several quasi-judicial bodies in Nepal, which are structurally open to allowing such extrajudicial factors to play a role.

Justice Administered by Quasi-judicial Bodies

The case of Manoj prompts many questions regarding the informal procedures followed in the criminal cases tried before CDOs. From what I could see in this case, the legally prescribed procedure was either not followed or else followed in a partial, one-sided way so as to favour the accused, which cast doubts on the possibility of conducting a fair trial. Another issue that emerged from this example was that cases tried by CDOs often failed to meet the standards of an independent judicial system. This was demonstrated when letters were sent to the Ministry of Peace and Reconstruction by Manoj's father in order to exert pressure on the CDO. Such attempts at influencing the CDO's decision from above were indicative of major issues, namely the overlap of the executive and judicial function of government in the person of the CDO (or other government officials), and also the lack of independence of quasi-judicial bodies vis-à-vis the governmental hierarchy and political will.

A recent research report on the criminal justice system administered by quasi-judicial bodies in Nepal (Niroula 2010), published by the

National Judicial Academy(NJA),[34] confirms the findings of the present study and raises many of the same questions. In what follows, I will briefly discuss some of the critical themes that emerge from the NJA report and my interviews with its authors and other legal experts.

The first theme concerns the quasi-judicial authorities' insufficient compliance with the prescribed procedure due to a lack of skill and manpower. Since such authorities and their staff mostly have little or no legal training or knowledge, they fail to follow strict court procedures and cannot ensure a fair trial. Moreover, the main duty of CDOs is to administer their district, and therefore presiding over criminal cases is not their priority. To give an example of simple procedures being over-looked, the NJA report found that quasi-judicial bodies generally do not comply with their obligation to notify the defendant's lawyer and the public prosecutor of the hearing, which was something I had observed in my fieldwork in connection with the CDO. As a result of this lack of compliance, defence lawyers do not attend CDO proceedings and their clients' interests cannot be effectively safeguarded (which makes the multipronged support enjoyed by Manoj all the more exceptional). Public prosecutors are also generally absent, so the task of examining witnesses and handling the case procedure rests with the undertrained staff of the very same quasi-judicial body charged with reaching a decision. As mentioned above (section 4.5), many defence lawyers and public prosecutors say that they have no inclination to go and plead at the CDO's office, since CDOs do not apply the court rules. The solution proposed by the NJA to the problem of non-compliance is for the government to depute some judicial personnel and provide training to quasi-judicial bodies.

A second problem pointed out in the NJA report is the lack of independence of quasi-judicial bodies, which is further complicated by the fact that, as administrators, they are potentially subject to political interference. For example, the CDO is an official under the jurisdiction of the Home Ministry and does not have a fixed tenure as judges do. Thus, if the Home Ministry is not pleased with a CDO, it can transfer him to another position (e.g., moving him to a remote district or to a district near Kathmandu as a form of demotion and promotion respectively). This structural condition limits the autonomy of these officers, and this is found to affect not only their final decisions but also the procedures themselves. An Appellate Court judge told me that if a CDO found himself presiding over a high-profile case, he would generally refer the matter to the Home Minister.

Related to the issue of autonomy is the problem of political interference. According to all my sources (including judges), it is common practice for political leaders to pressurize CDOs into arresting political opponents and into having them charged under the Some Public (Crimes and Punishment) Act 2027 (1970) (which includes offences such as public nuisance, trespassing, and uttering threats) or the AAA itself, in order that they might be kept in custody for many months without trial.

Adjudicating cases like illegal arms possession technically requires answers to simple questions: did the accused have such arms or ammunition in his or her possession and did he or she have the requisite license? Nothing else really matters in passing a guilty verdict. The CDOs do enjoy a degree of discretion in reaching decisions, but given their lax procedural practices and their lack of structural independence, the limits of this discretion have been expanded to the extent that a grey area has developed between legal standards and the point beyond which the CDO's decision might be overturned on appeal. The possibility of a successful appeal structurally limits the CDO's discretion, but it is also true that not all of those convicted have the means to appeal, and that by the time a bad decision is reversed, the accused may have already spent many months or even years in prison.

A last critical theme mentioned in the NJA report is that some quasi-judicial bodies have the power to imprison defendants for up to fifteen years.[35] This is why members of the NJA and other legal circles have recommended that the government institute a reform whereby quasi-judicial bodies should not be entitled to handle cases for which the sentence exceeds six months of imprisonment. The need for reform was subsequently confirmed by a 2011 Supreme Court decision in a Public Interest Litigation that had been filed by the Nepali NGO Advocacy Forum in 2009 to challenge the quasi-judicial power to hear criminal cases that various Acts accorded to CDOs. A three-judge bench went further by declaring that the quasi-judicial bodies—a vestige of the past, according to them—lacked the independence and competence to render fair judgements in criminal cases (Government of Nepal v. Ambar Bahadur Raut in ILF-Nepal 2011).[36] Finally, a UN assessment report on citizens' access to security and justice and the strength of the rule of law in Nepal, based on qualitative interviews of 299 informants conducted by six national consultants over two months in 2011, affirmed that quasi-judicial bodies 'have low capacity and are lacking in fairness, promptness and procedural compliance' (Donnelly et al. 2011:19).

***

My perspective on the case discussed in this chapter is not so much concerned with the discrepancy between the practices of quasi-judicial bodies and the legal standards that they are supposed to follow. While I agree that this discrepancy presents an important challenge in the pursuit of justice and legality, I find it interesting to examine another aspect of these practices, namely, the opposition between 'normal practice' (i.e., the 'norm', even if this does not comply with the prescribed rules) and what can be read as an exception to this 'norm'.

According to this perspective, a procedure adhering to the court rules (e.g., having a proper hearing in the CDO office with the lawyers present), which should constitute normal practice, appears 'abnormal' and part of a possible strategy of taking control of the hearing. In this sense, the fact that Manoj was the son of a famous law professor who could assemble a team of fifteen lawyers played an important role in changing the 'normal' practices. Given that rules of procedure are not normally adhered to, to the point that individual lawyers do not normally attend the hearing, it seems likely that the defence needed to present such a show of strength to ensure that court procedures, rather than the 'normal' (yet legally deviant) practice, would be followed.

Another interesting way of approaching this case is to look beyond the judicial truth (proven beyond reasonable doubt) or the truth in a broad sense and to make use of what one might call the concept of 'plausibility'. As mentioned above, cases under the AAA rely on simple and technical questions, where establishing precise facts (i.e., whether one possessed arms and/or a licence) determines the verdict and *mens rea* is not a significant factor (unless, of course, related to the notion of 'possession').

However, this case was adjudicated in a context where torture, frame-ups, political intervention, lack of judicial independence, arbitrary exercise of power, and weak prosecution are all recognized, if not as the norm, then at least as *plausible* events or facts in the justice system. The plausibility of allegations of injustice rides on the plausibility that the system is marred by such widespread practices. For example, it is common practice among the accused to question police evidence, to deny their statements, or to affirm that they were made to sign a blank 'statement', because it is plausible that the person has been tortured. Similarly, it is plausible that a person has been falsely accused for political reasons or persecuted through a criminal justice system that lacks independence and strict procedures. However, it is equally plausible that the same 'flexible' procedure observed in quasi-judicial offices can also be used in the accused's favour. In our case, for example, the prosecution witnesses who became hostile were not cross-examined. This was counteracted by the CDO's discretionary power to disregard unanimous testimonies, and yet he also was lenient in his sentence. Given the general context described above, both versions (that the accused suffered from or took advantage of the process) appear to be plausible, and the CDO's 'Solomonic' judgement in issuing the minimum punishment seems in this respect a middle-way decision that does not risk seeing either a guilty man walk free or an innocent one receive a severe sentence.

Ensuring that a theory comes across as 'plausible' is how criminal lawyers raise 'reasonable doubt'. However, the plausibility factors in the case discussed in this chapter are of a different order: plausibility here does not arise as a reading of specifically adduced evidence, but already permeates the system on multiple levels (e.g,. the plausibility of false evidence and false retraction). The actors navigate and negotiate the plausible doubts generated by common practices and develop strategies to deal with them: the defence secures unchallenged testimonies in its favour, while the CDO, knowing that the practice of denial is widespread, shows that he is not impressed by the witnesses' retractions. The justice system is affected: unwritten, undocumented possibilities enter into the realm of the plausible and become real in the public imaginary, further weakening the justice system, such that it cannot be said whether the case was dealt with on the basis of the simple legal questions set out in the AAA or if other considerations played a part.

On this stage, the accused plays the role of a Hindu hero, invoking his part in political and religious Hindu-nationalist activism against the secular state. During the case, depending on the observer's perspective the traits of this Hindu hero are transformed from those of a) an alleged fundamentalist terrorist, to b) a religious activist reliant on violence to protect himself and publicize his ideas, to c) a religious, peaceful, anti-secular activist trapped by secularists in a false case. Let me elaborate on these three transformations:

a) On the day of his arrest (8 September 2009), the police and news-papers presented Manoj as the leader of the religious terrorist group Ranvir Sena, an underground association linked to the infamous NDA. Newspapers reported the arrest of 'an armed group "kingpin"'[37] and a now defunct website called him the Nepali Bin Laden.[38] Manoj's vigorous rhetoric fit this image of an aggressive leader, and in his organization's propaganda, he did recognize the urgency of forming a violent movement in Hinduism comparable in strength to al-Qaeda.

b) In his first statement to police, Manoj presented himself as a religious activist dependent on violence to protect himself and his movement and to incite public awareness. The police now presented Ranvir Sena as a splinter group that had distanced itself from the NDA's violent means and that followed a more 'peaceful way' (or 'a more pure Hinduism', to quote Manoj's lawyer). While both the police and the prosecutor acknowledged Manoj's right to express his ideas, with which they sympathized, they distinguished between their shared ideals (and deference for his position) and their condemnation of the criminal deeds of which he stood accused.

c) Lastly, Manoj assumed the role of the religious, peaceful, anti-secular activist trapped by secularists (i.e., the Maoists). The appeal, the letters to the Peace Ministry, and the rhetoric of his main lawyer—his famous father—combined to lend credence to this characterization. The name of Ranvir Sena disappeared from his discourse and the case papers, to be replaced by the peaceful and ecumenical designation Hindu Jagaran Mahasangh. Manoj played the part of the Hindu hero, a quasi-ascetic figure who, according to his lawyer, left his wife and children to dedicate himself completely to his cause. With his devotion both to the political idea of a Hindu state and to Hinduism, he portrayed himself as representative of the Hindu majority persecuted by the political leaders of the secular state, and thus took on a political dimension. In our interview in 2010, Manoj's father traced the recent history of Nepal as a war between secular forces and Hindus. According to him, the various political parties and the Maoist insurgents united and dethroned 'the king of the sole Hindu kingdom in the world', and imposed a secular state. The new constitution was not yet written, however, and anti-secular forces were fighting to restore the Hindu state. In 2008, Manoj organized a major mass meeting to promote a Hindu Constitution. As the power of his Hindu movement was threatening the Constitution-drafting process, the Maoist Government brought a false case against him to suppress him and his movement. Manoj's father made it clear that if a CDO could condemn his son, it was only because Nepal had a Maoist Home Minister. The detention itself was a stroke of luck, as Manoj's political opponents were so numerous that had he not been jailed he surely would have been killed.

The justice applied in this case is ostensibly secular: the decision does not make any reference to religion, and neither the police nor the public prosecutor accept that religious ideas and activism justify criminal deeds. However, religious considerations had a bearing on many aspects of this case, and it is possible to read the case through the three portrayals outlined above. This chapter has attempted to describe and make sense of the political, social, legal, and religious environments that make all three interpretations plausible.

Appendix

Letter from Ranvir Sena

(Original in Nepali, believed by the police to have been drafted by Manoj)

GFP (Gun of Peace) Ranvir Sena.
Letter to all Ministers, the Constituent Assembly, the Parliament, the Prime Minster, the Parties and the President.

Subject: Recommendations for the state's cultural policy
Since Nepal has been, from immemorial time, the place of origin of *sanatan* Hindu culture, the government should adopt a policy to preserve and develop this culture and make it prosper. The government should give this culture high recognition, and it should step forward to

support Nepal's historical unity; to this effect, the GFP offers here some recommendations:

1. All high-ranking state officers (ministers, secretaries, etc.) should be Hindu, just as one must be a Christian in America or in England in order to become a prime minister or a president.

2. All members of the Nepali army and the judiciary should be Hindu (just as in Irak, Iran, Afghanistan and Saudi Arabia, they are Muslims).

3. Persons involved in the commerce of sex, prostitutes (such an inhuman crime) *and* persons making the commerce of religion and persons committing awful crimes like religious conversion should be deprived of all rights by the state, which should seize their properties and confine them to life imprisonment (while those who cause conversion should be sentenced to death by hanging).

4. In the entire world, it has been proven that Madrasas are nurturing and producing Muslim terrorists, [*follows a long list of different 'terrorist' Muslim organizations, in different countries, like Afghanistan, India, Bangladesh, Turkey, and Palestine*] and it has been seen in this country that schools organized by missionaries become also places of religious conversion. Opening such non-Hindu religious schools should thus be prohibited.

5. For non-Hindus, there should be a different type of citizenship. In order to obtain citizenship, non-Hindus should be recommended by at least ten Hindus or should receive the permission of at least two Hindu organizations.

6. Keeping in mind the increasing population of Nepal, its physical configuration and the issue of state sovereignty, the state should cancel all types of citizenships other than citizenship based on descent. Without official permission, non-Hindu foreign citizens should not be allowed to stay more than one month.

7. The state should give all religious followers the freedom to believe in their religion, provided that they keep in mind that Nepal is historically recognized worldwide as a Hindu country. The construction of permanent non-Hindu temples like Churches and Masjids should be prohibited. There should be a rule prohibiting the reconstruction and renovation of old and destroyed non-Hindu temples.

8. There should be a rule making it compulsory for non-Hindu entrepreneurs who want to do business in Nepal to establish a partnership with a Hindu person.

9. It has been seen that women working abroad are being sexually harassed, for example in Saudi countries, or are being involved in prostitution. The majority of these women stay in Arab countries like labour prisoners. Therefore, a ban against sending Hindu women abroad should be established, and those who send Hindu women working abroad should be given the same punishment as murderers.

10. Non-Hindu men who give lascivious and vulgar looks to Hindu women should be hanged, like in Arab countries. There should be a restriction against allowing non–Hindu men to work with Hindu women.

11. Non-Hindus should be restricted from making propaganda and holding religious programs publicly, in open spaces. Non-Hindus should be prohibited from publicizing their religious activities with microphones.

12. The government should cease all forms of assistance for Hajj management. The government should organize special assistance packages to allow Hindus aged over 60 to go on a pilgrimage.

13. There should be many ministries taking care of the preservation, protection and development of Hindu religion. A minimum of five percent of the state's budget should be invested in the preservation, protection and development of Hindu religion. This money should be used nationally or to help the international Hindu community.

14. If the name given to any institution (schools, factories, roads, places) does not reflect Hindu culture, it should be changed into a name belonging to Hindu culture.

15. Temples of related goddess and gods should be established in each government office, government school, etc.

16. The State should give a half-day holiday on Tuesdays instead of Fridays, so that on this half-day, civil servants can gather together in nearby selected temples and participate in collective prayer.

17. For the protection of cows, the government should manage cowsheds in different locations. The sale and purchase of old cows should be prohibited. The state should strongly preserve and protect cows.

18. A national educational system using a single syllabus should be implemented, which should describe the historical and proud *sanatan* Hindu culture.

19. At least twenty five percent of the Constituent Assembly should be composed of people connected to temples, holy shrines and religious organizations.

20. Institutions degrading Hindu culture or publishing articles expressing aversion against respected gods and goddesses, religion or religious epics should be banned, and the publisher involved should be hanged.

21. Women are very powerful and they should enjoy equality in the Constitution and in the society; their right to dignity should be recognized.

22. Citizen ownership of the temples, *guthis* [land endowed for religious purposes] monasteries and religious places should be established and government interference should cease. Temples, *guthis*, monasteries and religious places should all be free from the Guthi sansthan.[39]

23. In education, the study of *dharmashstra* and religious books should be compulsory.

24. A free entry visa should be provided to all international pilgrims coming to Nepal for pilgrimage, and the state should also provide them security.

25. In all sectors (minerals, water resources, mines, industry, trade), priority should be given to Hindu investors.

26. Poor people should be given residence management and subjected to compulsory family planning.

27. To enhance the *sanatan* culture, the state should construct temples and shrines in various locations at crossroads.

28. In order to be nominated to Parliament one should have knowledge of yoga and have received a spiritual, moral and intellectual education.

29. To ensure the continued existence of social customs and culture, the state should provide special training in ritual performances and astrology to Janajati and Dalits. The state should provide them with economic facilities [*so that Christians cannot convert them*].

30. Villages with strong faith and cultural identity should be preserved, renovated and developed, so as to be used as religious touristic places.

Sent to the Prime minister, the President and the Parties
Signature: Chakradar Singh, secretary of Ranvir Sena
Department for the re-establishment of Hindu national religious culture

Notes

1. The Hindu extremist group Nepal Defence Army became known to the general public when it claimed responsibility for bombing the Assumption Catholic Church in Kathmandu in May 2009. Its leader, Ram Prasad Mainali, also claimed responsibility for a bombing carried out during evening prayers at a Mosque in Sarauchiya, Morang District, in March 2008, killing three people. While in prison, Mainali declared that the group 'will continue such attacks until Nepal is reinstated as a Hindu nation'. The extremist group was also suspected of the murder of Fr. John Prakash, a Salesian priest in Sirsiya, Morang District, in July 2008. The group orchestrated two other bombings in Kathmandu (November 2011 and January 2012).

2. Despite its secular framework, the Interim Constitution of Nepal 2007 still bans conversion through proselytizing, and the Muluki Ain—the National Code—still continues to view cow slaughter as a criminal act (a law dating back to 1854, and currently justified on the grounds that the Nepal Constitution declares the cow the 'national animal'). However, few people are actually prosecuted for the crime of slaughtering a cow while no prosecutions for the crime of conversion have been documented since 2002 (although occasional reports of arrests and subsequent release do appear in the media). By contrast, my fieldwork revealed that these issues have been the two bones of contention around which opposition to and support of secularism have been articulated.

3. Ranvir Sena is an illegal and extremely violent caste army of the Bhumihars (landlords) in contemporary Bihar, known for its infamous massacres of lower castes and Naxalites (Kumar 2008: chapter 5). However, no association was made between Manoj's Ranvir Sena in Nepal and the Bihari Ranvir Sena during the case.

4. Regarding serendipity in ethnography, see Fabietti (2012).

5. Nepal's secular status was reiterated in the Interim Constitution of Nepal 2007, before the Constituent Assembly (CA) finally declared Nepal a secular, federal, democratic, republic on 28 May 2008.

6. On Janajati, see among others Gellner (1997), Pfaff-Czarnecka (1999), and Hangen (2010). Founded in 1990, their umbrella organization, the *Nepal Janajati Mahasangh* ('Nepal Federation of Nationalities', NEFEN), has played a major role in the political events of the last twenty years. In 2003, to include the term *adivasi* ('indigenous'), the name was changed to *Nepal Adivasi Janajati Mahasangh* ('Nepal Federation of Indigenous Nationalities', NEFIN).

7. I use the term 'Hindu Right' to denote those Nepali organizations and political parties associated directly or indirectly with Indian Rashtriya Swayamsevak Sangh, Shiva Sena, BJP, or Vishwa Hindu Parishad. Among others, I interviewed the Nepali members of the Vishwa Hindu Mahasangh (World Hindu Federation), the Shiv Sena Nepal, the Janata Party (a branch of the Indian BJP), and the Hindu Swayamsevak Sangh (affiliated with the RSS).

8. The prisoners were gathered in a small room about 1.5 metres away from the visitors who were standing behind a 1-metre-high wall. To catch the prisoner's words, we had to lean over the wall separating us. At one point, this wall was used as a table to serve us milk tea, a surreal break that set us apart from other visitors.

9. This is all the more surprising when one considers that Manoj's father confirmed in our interviews that Mainali intended to kill his son.

10. Such powers form part of the specialized administrative duties of these authorities. In the case of Manoj, the CDO's quasi-judicial authority to adjudicate upon illegal possession of arms comes from the jurisdiction of the CDO to administer the licensing of firearms and ammunition.

11. Not all quasi-judicial bodies are bound to the same procedures as the Courts; some of the laws governing these institutions prescribe their power to investigate, prosecute, and adjudicate, as is the case for the District Forest Office, Tax Office, Customs Office, and Immigration Office (which deal with offences not listed in Schedule 1 of the Government Cases Act 2049). They follow an inquisitorial system of justice, which existed in Nepal prior to the 1990 Constitution and the promulgation of the Government Cases Act 2049 (1992) (CeLRRd 2002). In the case described here, the trial continues to be the responsibility of a member of the executive branch. In this sense, this case is situated midway between the aforementioned inquisitorial system and the adversarial system with an independent judiciary, which now prevails in District Courts.

12. The Government Cases Act provides for the role of the police and government attorneys in the investigation, the gathering of evidence, the arrest and release of suspects, their interrogation and statements, the decision to file or withdraw a case, and the contents of the chargesheet. It also prescribes the role of the government attorney in examining witnesses in court and pleading the case, as well as the procedure for appeals once the verdict has been reached.

13. The Administration of Justice Act establishes the jurisdiction of the District and Appeal Courts, describes the procedure for appealing to the Supreme Court, and deals with other matters relating to the administration of courts.

14. The Evidence Act establishes the rules of evidence before the Courts (Section 2 specifies that 'Court' includes any other authority that hears a case).

It deals with matters of admissible evidence, the burden of proof, documentary and oral evidence, the examination of witnesses, and so on.

15. The Government Cases Act Section 3 (2) requires that the First Information Report contain the venue and date of the crime, the names of the culprits, and details of the alleged violation.

16. The police seized 1.5 kilograms of gunpowder, 2 kilograms of sulphur, 1 kilogram of soda, one packet of boric acid, 500 grams of sodium sulphate, 500 grams each of potassium permanganate, potassium nitrate, and potassium magnate, one packet of aluminium metal powder, 500 grams of ammonium nitrate, and iron rods and pipes.

17. GFP stands for 'Guns for Peace' (*shantiko laghi hatyar*) (See Appendix).

18. See Article 135(2) of the Interim Constitution of Nepal 2007.

19. Under the Office of the Attorney General in Kathmandu, there are 16 Appellate Prosecutor's Offices that correspond to the Appellate Courts, and 75 District Prosecutor Offices (one for each district, working alongside the district courts). The District Prosecutors are subordinates of the Attorney General.

20. The public prosecutor later told us that Manoj might have been advised by his lawyers to do this.

21. Some of my interviewees speculated that Manoj's prolonged detention pending his trial was due to the fact that the CDO was busy with the administration of the district, and that it was difficult for the prosecution to produce its witnesses; a defence lawyer blamed the 'present environment in Nepal', with its continuous strikes; another explained that the police were looking for the accomplices; on a different note, some members of the Muslim community opined that he was kept in jail more for his own protection than for punishment.

22. Nripadhwoj Niroula, Registrar of the Appellate Court of Patan, told me that defence lawyers do not go to the CDO's office, because they cannot effectively plead before him or any other quasi-judicial body. By way of an example, he related his own experience of trying this (for the last time) as a lawyer in 1993: defending a client in a land dispute case, he went to the Land Office to plead, but the officer was sleeping and sent his personnel to let him know that he had already decided the case and that his presence was not necessary.

23. Section 20 sets out various sentences depending on what items were possessed without a license. Subsection 2 applies to arms, the sentence for which is three to five years' imprisonment and/or a fine of NPR 60,000-100,000, while Subsection 3 applies to ammunition, which carries a sentence of one to three years' imprisonment and/or a fine of NPR 20,000-60,000. The CDO imposed only one year of detention for the ammunition plus a NPR 60,000 fine for the arms, settling for the minimum fine for arms possession and the minimum prison term for the possession of ammunition.

24. When I met him as a free man for the first time, Manoj had changed his 'tormented-guru' appearance for a more intellectual one (wearing stylish glasses and western clothes, his hair neatly cut). He was writing a book to prove the inconsistencies of Christianity, and he appeared as motivated and obsessed by his ideology as before.

25. There have been several decisions made by the Supreme Court establishing that in the absence of other corroborating evidence, the statement of the accused recorded by the police can be the sole basis for conviction. See Government v Bijaya Gachchadar NKP 2044 p. 1224, Decision no. 3286, cited in CeLRRd (2002: 18).

26. See Convention against Torture and Other Cruel, Inhuman or Degrading Treatment or Punishment (1984).

27. See The Constitution of the Kingdom of Nepal 1990, Article 14 (4).

28. The Act has numerous shortcomings: it fails to criminalize torture, provides victims of torture with a civil remedy limited to seeking monetary compensation, and includes a very short (35-day) statute of limitation. District Courts can award nominal amounts of compensation, but they cannot order authorities to initiate criminal investigations against the perpetrators. Instead, the latter may be subject to 'departmental action', such as demotions, suspensions, and delayed promotions. For an up-to-date research on torture in Nepal, see the report of Advocacy Forum-Nepal (2014).

29. According to Advocacy Forum Nepal (2007), other pieces of legislation fail to prevent and criminalize torture; the Evidence Act, for example, lacks provisions on witness protection, while the Nepal Police Act 2012 (1955) does not explicitly state that police personnel must refrain from torture.

30. That the punishment was far too lenient was affirmed by all the members of the legal circles I happened to speak with about the general outline of the case.

31. One of my informants, who adhered to the conspiracy theory against Manoj, added that in this type of case people usually remained in jail for years, and the fact that Manoj was released with only a minor punishment was proof of his innocence.

32. Apparently, this good relationship was not undermined by the allegation of torture, to which the prosecutor referred in an amused way: 'Manoj says I tortured him!' Since the deposition of the accused is taken in the presence of the prosecutor, the latter was also implicated in the alleged torture committed by the police.

33. With 'religious considerations' I mean Manoj's devotion and will to affirm in all spheres of social and political life in Nepal the prominence of Hindu religion.

34. The NJA was established in 2004 to serve the training and research needs of judges, government attorneys, and other persons involved in the administration of justice in Nepal.

35. For example, Section 26 (1) of the National Parks and Wildlife Conservation Act 2029 (1973) entitles the Wildlife Conservation Officer to sentence killers of rhinoceros and other protected animals to jail terms of fifteen years. The quasi-judicial authority of government officers to impose jail sentences based on a statute has no equivalent in India.

36. The Court refrained from invalidating the laws that give the CDOs their quasi-judicial jurisdiction since this would create a legal vacuum, but it ordered the government to form a research committee to recommend changes and to submit a report within six months. As an interim measure, the Court ordered the appointment of a legal expert to implement changes to the infrastructure of the quasi-judicial proceedings within one year. The government eventually formed the committee in July 2012, but still in April 2014 the UN Human Rights Committee reiterated 'its previous concern regarding the quasi-judicial authority of Chief District Officers (CDOs), whose dual capacity as members of the executive and judiciary in criminal cases contravenes article 14 of the Covenant.' (UN HRC 2014: 6).

37. These newspapers are not cited so as to preserve the accused's identity.

38. On this website, it was said that Manoj's aspiration was to build an extremist Hindu group modelled on the Taliban, a Nepali al-Qaeda.

39. The Guthi Corporation Act 1964 was enacted to nationalize all land regulated under *guthi* tenure to a centrally organized corporation, the Guthi Sansthan.

References

Advocacy Forum-Nepal. 2007. 'Torture Still Continues: A Brief Report on the Practice of Torture in Nepal'. Accessed at http://advocacyforum.org/downloads/pdf/publications/26-June-publication.pdf11/08/2012.

———. 2014. 'Promising Developments, Persistent Problems: Trends and Patterns in Torture in Nepal during 2013'. Accessed at http://advocacyforum.org/downloads/pdf/publications/torture/promising-development-persistent-problems.pdf on 22/06/2014.

Donnelly, Paul, Bipin Adhikari, Hari Phuyal, Indu Tuladhar, Rabindra Bhattarai, Satish K. Kharel. 2011. *Access to Security, Justice & Rule of Law in Nepal*. Accessed at http://www.un.org.np/reports/access-security-justice-rule-law-nepal on 12/12/2012.

Fabietti, U. 2012. 'Errancy in Ethnography and Theory: On the Meaning and Role of 'Discovery' in Anthropological Research', in H. Hazan and

E. Hertzog (eds), *Serendipity in Anthropological Research: The Nomadic Turn*, pp. 15–30, Farnham UK, Burlington USA: Ashgate.

Center for Legal Research and Resource Development (CeLRRd). 2002. 'Research Report on Trial Court System in Nepal (part 1): General Background of Criminal Justice System and Research'. Accessed at http://www.childtrafficking.com/Content/Library/?CID=45fbc6d3e05ebd93369 ce542e8f2322d|51595a. 15/10/2012.

Convention against Torture and Other Cruel, Inhuman or Degrading Treatment or Punishment. 1984. Accessed at http://www.ohchr.org/Documents/ ProfessionalInterest/cat.pdf. On 13/11/ 2012.

Gellner, D. N. 1997. 'Ethnicity and Nationalism in the World's only Hindu State', in D. Gellner, J. Pfaff-Czarnecka and J. Whelpton (eds), *Nationalism and Ethnicity in a Hindu Kingdom: The Politics of Culture in Contemporary Nepal*, pp. 3–31, Amsterdam: Harwood Academic Publishers.

Hangen, Susan. 2010. *The Rise of Ethnic Politics in Nepal: Democracy in the Margins*. London and New York: Routledge.

Human Rights Watch. 2008. Chapter 5 '*De jure* Impunity', *Waiting for Justice: Unpunished Crimes from Nepal's Armed Conflict*. Accessed at http://www.hrw. org/reports/2008/nepal0908/index.htm. on 3/06/2012.

International Crisis Group (ICG). 2007 'Nepal's Troubled Tarai Region', *Asia Report*, 136.

ILF-Nepal (International Legal Foundation-Nepal) (2011), 'Cases Notes, Fall 2011'. Accessed at http://theilf.org/news/case-notes on 1/10/2012.

Kumar, Ashwani. 2008. *Community Warriors: State, Peasants and Caste Armies in Bihar*. Delhi: Anthem Press India.

Letizia. C. 2011. 'Shaping Secularism in Nepal'. *European Bulletin of Himalayan Research*, 39: 66–104.

Mathema, Kalyan B. 2011. *Madheshi Uprising: The Resurgence of Ethnicity*. Kathmandu: Mandala Book Point.

Niraula, Nripadhwoj (ed.). 2010. *Ardhanyayik nikayabata hune faujdari nyaya sampadanko bartaman abastha. Anusandhanmulak adhyayan pratibedan* (The present condition of performance of criminal justice from the quasi-judicial bodies. Research report). National Judicial Academy Nepal: Lalitpur, 2067.

Pant, Shastra D. 2007. *Comparative Constitutions of Nepal*. Kathmandu: Pairavi Prakashan.

Pfaff-Czarnecka, J. 1999. 'Debating the State of the Nation: Ethnicization of Politics in Nepal—A Position Paper', in J. Pfaff-Czarnecka, N. A. Rajasingham, and T. Gomez (eds), *Ethnic Futures: State and Identity in Four Asian Countries*, pp. 41–98, New Delhi: Sage Publications.

Pradhananga, Rajitbhakta, Meghraj, Pokhrel, and Yugraj Pandey. 2005 (2062), *Faujdari Kanunko Parichaya* (Introduction to Criminal Law), Kathmandu: Bhrikuti Academic Publications.

Shrestha, Shanker Kumar. 2004. *Kanun tatha nyayasambandhi shabdakosh angreji-nepali* (Dictionary of Law and Justice English-Nepali). Kathmandu: Pairavi Prakashan.

The Constitution of the Kingdom of Nepal 2047. 1990. Accessed at http://www.ncf.org.np/upload/const/1990_Constitution_English.pdf. on 1/10/2012.

The Interim Constitution of Nepal 2063. 2007. http://www.ncf.org.np/upload/const/2010-10-13-NEPAL_Interim_Constitution_8amd.pdf. 1/10/2012.

United Nations Human Rights Committee [UN HRC]. 2014. *Concluding observations on the second periodic report of Nepal*, with respect to the International Covenant on Civil and Political Rights, CCPR/C/NPL/CO/2, 15/04/2014.

Table of Acts

The English text of the acts listed below can be found on the website of the Nepal Law Commission http://www.lawcommission.gov.np/index.php?option=com_remository&Itemid=53&func=select&id=34&lang=en

Arms and Ammunition Act 2019 (1962)
Administration of Justice Act 2048 (1991)
Compensation Relating to Torture Act 2053 (1996)
Evidence Act 2031 (1974)
Government Cases Act 2049 (1992)
National Parks and Wildlife Conservation Act 2029 (1973)
Police Act 2012 (1955)
Some Public (Crime and Punishment) Act 2027 (1970)

Case Documents (in Chronological Order)

21/5/2066 (6 September 2009).
Notice of search/order for search and seizure (*khan talasi janau purji*). Letter signed by the police inspector authorizing a search of the suspect's room according to Muluki Ain A-ba 172.

21/5/2066 (6 September 2009).
Search and seizure: collection of evidence (*khan talasi baramadi muculka*). List of objects found in the room: bullets, petrol bombs, etc.

21/5/2066 (6 September 2009).
Arrest warrant (*pakrao purji*) by police inspector finding the accused guilty of illegal detention of arms and ammunition (*hathatya karkhajana*).

21/5/2066 (6 September 2009).
Arrest (*tunuwaka purji*). Letter authorizing the police to take the accused into custody, according to Muluki Ain A-ba 121.

30/5/2066 (15 September 2009).
Statement (*bayan*) of the accused taken by the District Prosecutor.

15/6/2066 (1 October 2009).
Statement collected from witnesses at the search site (*bastu sthiti muculka*) (it was collected from three witnesses/neighbours and signed by the Superintendent of Police).

16/6/2066 (2 October 2009).
Chargesheet/indictment against the accused for illegal possession of weapons (*hathatyar kharkhajana*), signed by the District Prosecutor and submitted to the CDO's office.

18/6/2066 (4 October 2009).
Statement (*bayan*) made by the accused at the bail hearing presided by the Chief District Officer. He denies the affirmation made previously in front of the District Prosecutor and affirms that he has been tortured. He is represented by fifteen lawyers.

18/6/2066 (4 October 2009).
Bail hearing/order of custody (*tunchekadesh parcha*) in which the CDO writes that the accused denied the accusation, but that he is to be put in jail pending trial.

12/1/2067 (25 April 2010).
Witness statement (*sakshi bakpatra*) at the CDO's office. Only defence lawyers and witnesses are present. Government witnesses become hostile and there is no Public Prosecutor to cross-examine them.

10/3/2067 (24 June 2010).
Decision (*phaisala*) of the CDO.

7/6/2067 (23 September 2010).
Letter of appeal (*punaravedan patra*) on the defendant's side. Signed by the accused and made against the police inspector and the Nepal Government.

5

NICOLAS JAOUL

A Strong Law for the Weak

Dalit Activism in a District Court of Uttar Pradesh*

The Law's Self-defeating Stringency?

In application of Article 17 of the Indian Constitution, an anti-untouch-ability law was adopted in 1955 and subsequently revised in 1976 and 1989. This legislation assured Dalits that the judiciary would stand by them in cases of caste discrimination and violence. Moreover, as noted by Marc Galanter in his pioneering study of this legislation, it was conceived as a pedagogical tool to promote democratic behaviour and standards of equality (Galanter 1989).

However, the law's symbolic efficacy proved severely limited due to the combined absence of political will and compelling mechanisms regarding its implementation. In the late 1970s, this was made evident by unprecedented massacres in retaliation against new assertive behav-iour and claims by Dalit villagers (Mendelsohn and Vicziani 1999). Marc

* Research leading to this chapter was funded by the French National Research Agency's programme, 'Justice and Governance in India and South Asia'. (ANR-08-GOUV-064). Certain names have been changed. I would like to thank Pratiksha Baxi for her generous comments and suggestions.

Galanter notes that 'The rate of convictions during the two years 1978 and 1979 fell to a mere 18 percent—very low indeed for any offence in India' (Galanter 1989: 220). Galanter thus criticizes the method of addressing the untouchability issue through legalistic means for generating a counterproductive process. On the one hand, he argues, judges display cultural tolerance toward the practice of untouchability by hesitating to apply severe punishment to upper-caste perpetrators, who are treated complacently for 'merely following' their social and religious customs. On the other hand, the law's strong punitive measures make it imperative for the accused to fight cases actively and to avoid punishment by hiring competent lawyers, even relying on illegal judicial strategies 'by marshalling witnesses, intimidating or suborning prosecution witnesses, and all those familiar tricks'. Therefore, according to Galanter, 'by raising the stakes the new act has created more determined and resourceful opponents, but it has done nothing to upgrade the performance of the law' (Galanter 1989: 220–1).

In response to the wave of massacres in the late 1970s, the Scheduled Caste and Scheduled Tribe (Prevention of Atrocities) Act (POA Act), which was enacted in 1989, comprised an institutional implementation mechanism, including judicial measures such as the setting up of special courts and prosecutors. Other administrative measures to coordinate and supervise this implementation as well as preventive measures against 'atrocities' (the new official term adopted by this law to designate untouchability-related offences) in identified sensitive areas, were later listed in the Scheduled Caste and Scheduled Tribe (Prevention of Atrocities) Rules.[1]

The POA Act is essentially a pragmatic law that seeks to remedy institutional blindness or insensitivity to caste, thus requiring a high level of precision in the designation of untouchability practices. Set against the prevalent idea that untouchability belongs to the realm of 'tradition' versus an ongoing secular process of development by the state, the law identifies twenty-two contemporary ways of practising untouchability. Its most innovative aspect is to target the institutionalization of caste prejudice within the administration itself as a way to harass, dispossess, and victimize Dalits (for instance, use of the judiciary and police to falsely accuse or of the tax administration to appropriate one's land and property). The Act contains provisions to imprison biased representatives of the State who wilfully neglect their duties, thus framing the judiciary as the ally of Dalit emancipation and reminding it of its constitutional role to guarantee that the administration fulfils its duties.

Despite this high degree of legal commitment, the institutional arrangements and preventive measures of the Act have remained largely ignored by the quasi-totality of States, which treat them as optional recommendations. *Frontline* magazine thus noted that 'to date, not a single official in India had been punished despite serious violations of the Act all over the country', and characterized the act as 'a clear instance of wonderful legislation but useless implementation'.[2] Even in Uttar Pradesh (UP), where the rules of the Act became effective under the reign of a Dalit chief minister (Mayawati), its implementation is comparatively better than in other States but nevertheless highly problematical. Interestingly, this State, whose Scheduled Caste (Dalit) population constitutes 21 per cent of India's total SC population (2001 census), recorded 53 per cent of all court cases according to an official report by the Human Rights Commission based on figures from the year 2000. This not only shows that UP has a high level of anti-Dalit violence, but moreover that Dalits are inclined to make use of the law, which reflected their political awareness and expectations from the State under the Mayawati regime. The same sources also show that, under the POA Act, while the conviction rate for the whole of India was 11 per cent, cases of conviction in UP were slightly higher (16.8 per cent) but still very low compared to other crimes (NHRC Report on SC Act 2004).[3]

Writing about the previous law (the Untouchability Offences Act, 1976, UOA), Galanter noted the astonishing fact that '[p]olice are often uninformed of the provisions of UOA r even of its existence' (Galanter 1989: 212). Although the current POA Act can no longer be ignored due to the level of Dalit awareness and activism, it has been met with opposition both from society and from within the state. Highlighting the judiciary's own resistance, Pratiksha Baxi brings to our attention several cases that were filed to contest the constitutionality of the Act, which was nevertheless systematically defended by appellate courts (Baxi 2014).

Anupama Rao argues that this law could be self-defeating by stressing that 'laws to protect Dalit victims could impart a spurious legitimacy to treating stigmatized existence as the status quo' (Rao 2009: 223).

Adding a performative dimension to this semiological observation, she contends that the law not only enforces a social stereotype of Dalits as victims and members of upper castes as perpetrators, but also engenders its own transgression by dominant castes whose public claims to power and status can take the form of 'performance and spectacle' (Rao 2009: 179) by massacring Dalits. This disturbing argument thus furthers Galanter's point of view that the judiciary itself has become a site for dominant castes to enact their supremacy by making public statements about their capacity to be above the law and to neutralize it.[4]

Such pessimistic and negative views of the implementation of the law fail to convey the positive symbolic value of the POA Act for the Dalit movement. Providing us with a more positive semiotic understanding of the law, P. Baxi thus recalls that 'protectionist laws, such as the POA Act aim to infuse criminal law with constitutional ideals of substantive equality, by re-signifying previously stigmatized bodies as bearers of rights' (Baxi 2011: 284). However, one still needs to understand how Dalit expectations regarding this law translate into practice. In order to do so, I propose to examine the everyday Dalit experience of the judiciary in a district and sessions court. I will thus provide an ethnographic account of the Dalit experience in a local district court in Uttar Pradesh, highlighting Dalit networks of social activists and professionals and their savoir-faire as well as their views regarding the implementation of the Act.

With the rise to power of BSP in the 1990s,[5] UP witnessed two complementary but sometimes contradictory processes of Dalit social assertion from below, on the one hand, and political empowerment from above, on the other hand (Jaoul, 2007). Intensive BSP mobilization in UP rural areas starting in the mid-1980s and the party's subsequent rise to power in the 1990s generated a historical movement of Dalits asserting their rights that heightened the rural caste and class conflicts. Jaffrelot (1998) thus noted that between 1989–90 and 1995 (before and after BSP reached power), the number of First Information Reports (FIR) filed by Dalits at UP police stations increased fifteen fold. This was simultaneously due to a rise in the number of conflicts and to local administrations' newly receptive attitudes to Dalit complaints under the first BSP government. Although Dalit chief minister Mayawati initially issued public warnings to administrations, urging them to register Dalit FIRs properly and thus indirectly encouraging her constituency to make use of the judiciary, the rapid transformation of the BSP into a government party led to it distancing itself from grassroots Dalit activism. In seeking acceptability among upper castes, BSP implemented a new strategy whereby the use of the controversial POA Act was discouraged. Mayawati thus passed a government order in 2002 against the alleged 'misuse' of the Act by Dalits. Although her unconstitutional order was later cancelled by the Supreme Court, it nevertheless sent a signal to the local police administration and was met with resentment by local Dalit activists, whose main preoccupation under her regime has been to make use of this newfound support from the State. Despite BSP's eventual estrangement from the Dalit movement, the first BSP governments of the 1990s had a profound impact on the Dalit's relationship with the law. An informal culture of legal activism was initiated whereby local activists encouraged fellow villagers to lodge complaints, offering assistance to ensure that police would record them and that oppressors would be challenged in court.

Each case fought under the POA Act represents a struggle that requires skill, commitment, and determination. A savoir-faire has thus emerged in the course of these efforts, thanks to informal networks of Dalit activists and professionals such as judges, prosecutors, and lawyers. The aim of this ethnographic essay is to describe this popular engagement with the law, which represents an important but unacknowledged feature of Dalit assertion.

An Ethnography of Kanpur *Kachehri*

Besides Agra, Kanpur is one of the two major urban strongholds of Dalit emancipation in UP. Dalit organizations have maintained a historical presence since the 1920s. A sizable Dalit middle class, dominated by government employees and officials, has developed whose support is actively sought by Dalit organizations in terms of finances, activism, and interventions from within the administrations on behalf of activists and their clients. The activists maintain a presence near the court premises and are keen to provide assistance to victims of caste oppression, the majority of who are poor villagers. Kanpur is therefore a place where Dalits are organized, vigilant and therefore relatively less vulnerable to caste oppression compared to several other areas of UP. Hence, this study of a local court does not claim to be representative of the state as a whole, but it shows that even in such a position of relative strength, the Dalit movement experiences great difficulties in court matters.

The Dalit Panthers is the most prominent local Dalit organization (it claimed 50,000 members in the early 2000s) and the only one to maintain a regular presence near the court. In December 1980, the UP section of the Bharatiya Dalit Panthers was founded in Lucknow with the aim of elaborating a strategy against caste violence (Jaoul 2013). Although officially fused with the Republican Party of India in 1990, the local branch of Kanpur refused to dissolve. Their resolve to remain independent from political parties was based on the observation that political parties and politicians could not be trusted in the fight against atrocities due to their own electoral compulsions. The Dalit Panthers' influence remained strong in the countryside of Kanpur and Kanpur Dehat districts. As the BSP started to distance itself from the Ambedkarite committees that it had originally founded in villages, the Panthers enrolled their activists and took over leadership of the grass-roots Dalit movement in the region (Jaoul 2007). Thanks to their daily presence in the kachehri, today the Dalit Panthers help Dalit victims to navigate their way through complicated administrative and court procedures.

Although it means literally 'the court', the word *Kachehri* designates the entire professional neighbourhood in the former colonial area behind civil lines. At the time of the fieldwork in March 2010, it comprised local courts as well as the civil administration of two districts of Kanpur Nagar and Kanpur Dehat, the latter being the adjoining rural district that was renamed Ramabai Nagar in July 2010. Its civil headquarters and courts of justice were therefore shifted to Akbarpur since then. However, during my fieldwork (March 2010), Kanpur Dehat district's main court was still situated in the city. Reflecting on this arrangement, the president of the Kanpur Bar Association pointed out to me that with its 8,671 registered lawyers, Kanpur Kachehri was Asia's biggest district court. With a population of approximately 1.8 million and 4.6 million in Kanpur Dehat and Kanpur Nagar respectively according to the 2011 census, Kanpur Kacheri was thus the judicial centre for a population of nearly 6.4 million, although subdistrict (*tehsil*) courts were scattered throughout the rural district.

I will start by describing the *kachehri*, whose human density and saturated space have their own relevance in our understanding of how things work there. The old colonial buildings used by the civil and police administration, as well as the multi-storey buildings more recently built that are used by the courts, were surrounded by rows of lawyers' offices. Although the Kanpur Bar Association did not possess any data regarding the number of lawyers from each caste, its president gave me an idea by estimating that roughly 50 per cent were from upper castes (of which two-thirds were Brahmins), 30 per cent OBCs, 5–10 per cent Muslims, and only 5 per cent Dalits.

The large space occupied by lawyers on all sides of the official buildings was impressively congested. Space was organized hierarchically: there were two compounds with large lanes where cabinets of established lawyers (around eight hundred, according to the president of the Kanpur Bar Association that controlled the allocation of these offices) had their offices inside the old colonial buildings. Those larger lanes were surrounded by narrow lanes of lawyers' offices squatting in surroundings that looked like shanty towns. In the lanes, many typists occupied small wooden tables or sat on the floor with old typewriters and handwritten boards indicating either 'Hindi' or 'English'. Computers had not yet found their way into the Kachehri, perhaps due to the frequent power cuts in Kanpur. Space was overcrowded, and the whole area looked like a busy slum of tertiary-sector professionals: there was a constant clatter of typewriters and a steady stream of lawyers hurrying back and forth, dressed in ragged black and white clothing, carrying brown paper files and followed by their clients. It was a public space, overwhelmingly masculine, where urban and rural worlds met, where the poor and illiterate encountered bureaucracy with the help of all sorts of brokers and facilitators with different aims.

There was a regular traffic of convicts who were brought to the court in blue police trucks and surrounded by wives, children, and relatives who used this occasion as an opportunity for meeting, passing cigarettes, packets of chewable *masala*, and bank notes through the truck's wire grills. I witnessed painful scenes like that of a young Muslim woman wearing a burqa holding the hand of a young child and an infant in her arms who seemed to be paralysed by her emotions when the truck left, with a vacant expression, tears rolling down her face. Along with tragedy, there was also an element of archaism, like the frequent spectacle of individual prisoners being led through the lanes by policemen, their wrists bound with thick rope. Local *netas* (politicians) were another common sight, accompanied by a cohort of followers on their way to meet officials and have work done for their clients. The canteens were crowded with established and aspiring *netas*, lawyers, and journalists, for whom frequenting these places was the best way to obtain fresh news about crime, gossip, and local happenings that fill the local papers. Beyond its main official function as the administrative centre, the Kachehri was thus the heart of public life, where local representatives of the state, political parties, and the media could be contacted. Hence, it represented a natural breeding ground for local politics and all kinds of manoeuvres: it was the materialization par excellence of what Partha Chatterjee (2004) describes as India's chaotic 'political society'.

While hanging out in the Kachehri, I frequently encountered people already familiar to me, mostly Dalits whom I knew from the late 1990s to early 2000s, when I was living in Kanpur to study the local Dalit movement. Pramod, a Dalit Panther activist in his forties who earned a reputation in activist circles for being the most emphatic slogan shouter, had not lost his exuberance, but he seemed totally distressed. He was spending his days in the Kachehri trying to rescue his eighteen-year-old nephew (*bhatija*) along with three friends from his locality in old Kanpur. He explained that they had been falsely charged with robbery and murder. The real culprits had walked away scot-free after bribing the police inspector with four lacs (400,000 rupees), leaving some poor innocent fellows to face the music. His nephew was made to forcibly confess to the crime by the investigating officer, whose report contradicted the FIR.

I met another old friend of mine, a bank clerk in his early fifties. Usually a reserved yet cheerful person, I could sense that he was preoccupied and anxious. Whispering in my ear—apparently out of shame—he explained to me that he had been falsely implicated in a case of speculation (*satta*) using his clients' money, a form of fraud that has become a notorious practice among bank staff. He alleged that he was being harassed by upper-caste colleagues who resented his professional achievements as a Dalit. Ten years ago, when I visited him at his workplace, he and his Dalit colleagues were indeed talking about harassment and all kinds of professional injustices that they encountered on the grounds of caste discrimination.

Although it is not my purpose to ascertain whether he was innocent or not, what is certain is that false cases (*falzi mukatma*) have become a source of harassment and stress for many and are now part of popular everyday life. The casual meetings I have just described, as well as others not mentioned here, show how central the Kachehri is to the lives of common folks as a place where individual and social conflicts are played out through legal means. The double-dealing and misuse of the courts were on everyone's lips and minds. My Dalit respondents argued that there was a caste angle to injustice, since Dalits were considered helpless and vulnerable to legal harassment. Although Dalits cannot be regarded as mere victims, their stories reveal the extent to which they can be harassed in court cases. As we will see in the following section, my encounters with Dalits in the Kachehri nevertheless show determination to get strategies to evolve and to develop legal strength and awareness. Enabling Dalits to fight back by legal means implies a proactive, fighting-spirit attitude, which is a radical departure from an attitude of passive dependence on state protection. Therefore, the activists' presence at the Kachehri has special relevance as far as the Dalit struggle for emancipation is concerned.

Dalit Panther Activism at the Court Doors

Although Dalit politicians were seen visiting the Kachehri with their clients, they suffered a bad reputation as corrupt and self-seeking, and who could not be relied upon in the event of conflict. A decade earlier, during my previous fieldwork, I was witness to several incidents involving anti-Dalit violence in villages, including murders that demonstrated the unreliability of the BSP MLAs (members of legislative/provincial assembly) and MPs (members of the national parliament). In several instances, when contacted by victims who asked for help in having complaints registered by the police—they asked for bribes that the victims could not afford. It was more profitable and less troublesome for them to accept bribes from the other side since this prevented them from entering into conflict with the dominant castes. They had purchased their investitures ('tickets') from the BSP at high rates and financed their campaigns with help from certain factions of the dominant castes. Moreover, despite having been elected mostly thanks to Dalit votes, these representatives had no commitment to the local Dalit movement.

One such instance of a conflict where the BSP representative failed Dalits is the Sabalpur village murder case in 2001, in which an old Dalit man was shot during the night while he was asleep. Having secured the support of the BSP MP the accused Thakurs summoned him to the police station to validate their truncated story. This was despite the fact that the PM was from the same sub-caste as the victim. The victim's son, who was involved in petty criminal activities, was a personal rival of the Thakur gang. The Dalit party alleged that the murderers had intended to kill the son but had mistakenly killed his father instead, who was sleeping outside his house with his face covered by a blanket. Owing to the intervention of the BSP MP, the Thakurs obtained a false written report from the police. The son of the victim, Vinod Sankhvar, was accused of parricide, on the alleged motive of inheriting a tiny plot of land. Therefore, he and his Dalit friend were accused of acting as his accomplice and jailed. The Dalit Panthers took up the matter and a long battle ensued, including several *dharna* (protest meetings) at Kanpur, a symbolic *gherao* (sequestration) of the Kanpur Dehat District Magistrate, and trips to the Scheduled Castes Commissions of Delhi and Lucknow.

The Dalit Panthers are regular organizers of such *dharna*, where shocking incidents of caste violence and administrative biases are publicly denounced.

In contrast to the BSP representatives' unreliability, the Panthers' commitment to upholding the POA Act, as well as their official connections and practical knowledge regarding court and administrative procedures, has cemented their popularity among Dalit villagers. Since they do not have a proper office in the Kachehri, the organization's activists can be found every day in Kaushik Park, a public garden adjoining the (*thana*) police station). Dalit victims are received by activists and brought to meet lawyers and officers of the police and civil administration. Several activists are law students or junior lawyers who are in constant contact with the organization and work for it whenever their schedules permit. Given the number of individual demands, activists are usually surrounded by a small crowd of people waiting for their cases to be heard or dealt with.

Although people approach the organization with individual demands, the Dalit Panther leader, Dhanirao Bauddh conceives of his mediation as a service to the Dalit community (*samaj seva*). Commercial brokers also portray themselves as *samaj sevak*, and Dhanirao distinguishes himself by associating his brokerage with collective action. One of the striking features of his presence in the Kachehri is the crowd that constantly surrounds him. When entering an officer's room he is always accompanied by a small crowd of Dalits who are waiting for him to hear their cases. The crowd materializes the democratic pressure that he puts on the administration, thus replicating inside official premises the role that the organization performs in local public life when staging protests outside. In order to keep the crowd mobilized around him, individual solicitors are sometimes kept waiting for days, which is a way of testing their commitment to the cause as well as to show his ability to draw crowds. As a non-elected street leader in constant need of proving his popular mandate and his capacity to bother the local authorities, his skills in crowd management is part of his street politics. This illustrates perfectly what Thomas Hansen (2005) has labelled the 'politics of permanent performance'.

The economy of the Dalit Panther brokerage also differs from ordinary brokers' immediate cash expectations. Dalit Panther services entail commitment to the organization, thus meaning future presence in public events and protests as well as cash donation (if the client's financial position permits), and/or other, non-monetary services in terms of labour and so on, which are fixed by the leader. Although it is based on the reality of brokerage, this economy differs from commercial forms of brokerage that prevail by denoting a longer temporal regime of moral indebtedness and commitment to the organization. Indeed, moral debts contracted by individuals who have been rescued and comforted in times of trouble create long-term commitments to the organization, as I will illustrate with two examples.

The first is that of the previously mentioned Vinod Sankhvar, the young Dalit villager who was falsely accused of parricide in the Sabalpur case. After he was eventually granted bail and released from jail, Vinod remained at the Dalit Panthers' headquarters, both to monitor the case and out of fear of retaliation in his village. On eventually returning to his village, Vinod disappeared after becoming involved in a fake currency business—his brother, who continued to visit the Panthers headquarters regularly, thought that he was murdered. During my stays at the headquarters, I met several youngsters seeking refuge either from the police or from criminals. Not all of them were innocent victims, and like Vinod some did have criminal records, but the leader nevertheless considered them victims of casteism. Such youngsters with criminal backgrounds were welcomed by the organization as long as they did not participate in any criminal activity during their stay and helped with activities. The organization sought to politicize them by winning them over to the cause of the movement. Despite their emphasis on constitutional means of struggle, local Ambedkarite activists addressing the realities on the ground recognized the importance of developing 'muscle power' through such connections. Rather than focusing on moral reformation, what the organization proposed them was a form of political redemption by serving the movement. It was expected however, that moral reformation would follow.

The second example of the way the organization recruits individuals after helping them in times of legal problems concerns Anil. Now a lawyer in the Kachehri, he became a Dalit Panther activist in his student days after obtaining Dhanirao's support in times of trouble. Anil came from a village 50 km from Kanpur to study law and stayed in a Scheduled Caste (Dalit) student hostel upon his arrival. At that time, he regularly attended Dalit Panther events but had no personal connection to the organization. He became implicated in a conflict in his home village with a neighbour whose leg he fractured during a fight. He resented his neighbour's drug trafficking, which caused nuisance in the lane. After being arrested by the police, Anil called upon Dhanirao Bauddh, who negotiated a compromise at the police station and managed to cancel the First Information Report. Later, Dhanirao offered him free accommodation at the Dalit Panthers headquarters. In return, Anil became one of Dhanirao's personal secretaries and the latter also found him a job as an assistant to a Dalit civil lawyer in the Kachehri. Furthermore, Anil became a regular Dalit Panther correspondent for Dalits in the Ghatampur area, where his village is situated. He distributed pamphlets and motivated people to attend public protests and functions. In the same manner, the Dalits of Sabalpur became regular participants in such events once Vinod had become a regular activist. Helping individuals not only creates individual commitment, but also enhances the Panthers' credibility in villages and fosters long-term loyalties to the organization. As a result of such individual commitments, entire rural and urban Dalit *bastis* (segregated Dalit neighbourhoods) have become strongholds of the Dalit Panther.

The headquarters of the organization, situated on the edge of a labour colony, about 1 km from the Kachehri, has become a community centre for local Dalit people. Dalit villagers who visit Kanpur for administrative and court purposes come there to find support, discuss their strategies, and as a place to stay. In exchange, these villagers are expected to become members of the organization and to support it according to their individual capacities. Their contributions range from cash and food, grain, oil, and vegetables brought from the village to different services rendered to the organization (such as secretariat work, stitching flags, painting banners, or maintaining the building), depending on one's skills and resources. Let us now go back to the Kachehri lanes once again to meet the Dalit lawyers.

Dalit Lawyers in the Kanpur Kachehri

The 'juniors'

The first step for a young lawyer seeking to establish himself is to accept the rather unrewarding position of a 'junior' (assistant) in a lawyers' practice. These positions are accepted in the hope of finding an office through contacts or when the 'senior' retires. The shortage of space for setting up offices is therefore a major issue for young lawyers, whose careers are thus blocked without much hope to see some change. In this section, I introduce two young Dalit lawyers who are both part of the Dalit Panther organization: Sundeep, who is a junior, and Anil whose story I have already mentioned. Refusing to abide by this condition, he 'established' himself by the roadside without a proper office.

Anil, a Dalit in his mid-thirties was my closest contact in the Kachehri, as well as a dear friend. Our friendship began at the time of my PhD fieldwork when we both stayed at the Dalit Panthers headquarters. He used to take me to visit his village, where his father was a primary school teacher. After his marriage, Anil set up his 'office' on the sidewalk of the Kachehri's main road. Being married to a woman who was still a student and having a young child to look after, he had no choice other than to start earning and could not afford to remain a junior. This step enabled him to earn around 6,000 rupees a month, a modest salary that was nevertheless about four times more than what juniors usually received (around 1,500 rupees, which was equivalent to what casual labourers earned in Kanpur at the time of fieldwork).

Anil's sidewalk 'cabinet' consisted of a table, two benches, and a metal box. At night, he brought all of his valuable items and important documents back home with him on his bicycle and locked the furniture with a chain to the fence of the court. His presence at the gate of the rural district court, among shoe shiners and vendors of tea, snacks, and fruit, brought him all kinds of visitors, mostly poor villagers involved in justice cases that sat there randomly, asked for directions, and chatted about their cases. Some of them knew him because of his old association with the Dalit Panthers and sought his advice regarding their court proceedings. He was thus available as a free legal adviser, although some people eventually ended up hiring him. However, he often preferred to give free advice rather than to work for people who would not be able to pay him or tried to bargain on fees. He enjoyed chatting with villagers as it helped him to stay in touch with his rural district's local politics, where he had his own ambitions.

People also sought his legal advice back in the village, which gave him some standing and helped him build his influence in his village. There were four advocates in his village, two of whom were from Dalit castes and two of whom were from OBCs; one of them settled in the sub-district (Tehsil) court of Ghatampur, while the three others were based in Kanpur. Thanks to the regular visits of such lawyers, villagers have easy and free access to legal advice, and launching a court case becomes an accessible option in the event of conflict with fellow villagers.

Sundeep was another young Dalit lawyer and an activist in the Dalit Panthers. He studied law together with Anil at the time of my PhD fieldwork. Sunil's family has been historically associated with the Ambedkarite movement (his uncle was a local Ambedkarite leader in the 1960s and 1970s). Sundeep himself has been a victim of legal harassment. In 1999, a Brahmin murdered his brother in a property dispute in their ancestral village. The police FIR accused Sunil of shooting at the Brahmin first, which he denies, claiming that the murderer shot himself in the leg in order to make this allegation and to prove that he shot the victim in self-defence. Sundeep was convicted in 2007 by what he claims was 'a purely Brahmin court'. He was able to obtain bail after three days spent in jail, but his case was still going on at the time of fieldwork, which caused him a great deal of stress.

Sundeep was now working as the junior of an upper-caste lawyer in one of the small lanes. He earned between 1,000 and 1,500 and in rare cases up to 3,000 rupees, depending on the work, and lived with his wife at his parents' house in Kanpur. He was resentful of the exploitation of the junior lawyers, which he interpreted as casteist exploitation, since many of them were Dalits or from lower-caste and minority backgrounds. Along with Anil and other friends from such backgrounds, he formed the Lawyer Friends' Association in 2009. Interestingly, the organization's name did not make reference to caste or community, although Sundeep described it as a non-Brahmin organization (in reference to the same ideology) which accepted non-upper-caste members only. It was created by five lawyers from Dalit, Muslim, and OBC backgrounds, all of whom come from lower-class or lower-middle-class families. At the time of my fieldwork, Anil was the city president, while Sundeep was the 'national' general secretary (in spite of these ambitious titles, the organization only operates in Kanpur). In spite of its small size, its purpose was to contest the leadership of the two established lawyer associations, whose leadership was monopolized by upper caste lawyers. According to its charter, four to six years of government help are required to help young lawyers set up their practice. It also demands the introduction of rehabilitation measures for convicts instead of a merely punitive approach and an increase in financial support for victims to provide them with the option of hiring a lawyer instead of depending on the public defence. Sundeep explained, with regard to the latter point, that when fighting cases under the POA Act, victims rely on prosecutors who represent their cases on behalf of the state. He argued that the venality of prosecutors makes them unreliable, hence the need for an independent lawyer. In order to finance the organization, Sundeep sought donations from the Dalit community. In this sense, the organization replicated the Dalit movement's economy based on donations and adhered to its goals. However embryonic this initiative it was nevertheless indicative of young Dalit lawyers' attempts to organize themselves professionally in keeping with their ideology and to reinforce their position in the Kachehri. It thus represented a spontaneous step toward legal activism within the traditional Ambedkarite movement.

A Dalit Criminal Lawyer at Work

R. B. Vidyarthi is a senior criminal lawyer whose excellent reputation was readily attested to by the most established lawyers of the Kachehri with whom I spoke. I had already met him several years ago to discuss a major atrocity case that he fought in 1993, in which several Dalit Panther supporters were massacred in a barbaric manner (their bodies were cut into pieces) in Indrukh, a Kanpur Dehat village. The case ended due to the fact that the victims' relatives accepted a compromise with the accused: this was a major setback for Vidyarthi as a lawyer specializing in the POA Act, as well as for the Dalit Panthers. Visiting him for the first time in a long while, I found him sitting at his desk surrounded by some fifteen people who remained silent as they followed the dialogue he had with each of them. His office was still in the same unofficial lane as before; a large room of about twenty square metres, painted pink salmon, with only basic furniture. His desk, a small wooden table covered with a bright colour sheet in the middle of the room, was surrounded by many chairs and benches for his clients. Several juniors, who were coming and going either to plead in court or to do some administrative work with clients, shared two desks at the back of the room. A large number of court files and books were neatly stored on the shelves behind them amidst a big portrait of Ambedkar, whose presence sanctifies the Dalit struggle and recalls its constitutionality.

On several occasions, men entered the room merely to greet the lawyer and then left after a short while, indicating his notoriety and status. There was a constant turnover; newcomers entered and touched his knees, a gesture of respect that he received with apparent disapproval as well as nonchalance. The sigh he made seemed to convey that he did not have the energy required to fight such Brahminical gestures of deference, even while disapproving of them ideologically. After being invited to sit down, I told him about my research into the implementation of the POA, and he silently conveyed his approval by slowly moving his head from side to side. He responded after a pause: 'Everybody fears this Act. But implementation is in the hands of the upper castes. If they did their work honestly, within a year, casteism could be a thing of the past in India' (in Hindi). He continued to discuss the importance of caste as a factor in its own right in Indian society, something that he visibly wanted to impress on me as a foreign researcher who might not be able to understand this particularity of Indian society.

As I could tell that the time he could give me was counted, I rapidly shifted our discussion from his lecture on the specificity of caste that Ambedkarite activists generally wish to highlight for a foreign scholar, to his biography. Now fifty-five years old, he was born and raised in a village in eastern UP, where untouchability was vigorously enforced. However, his family was relatively wealthy and independent from landlords, which gave them the economic foundation to assert their dignity. They were members of the Communist Party (CPI), and 'we used to face others' (although speaking in Hindi, he said this sentence in English). When he joined the 9th class he was sent to Kanpur, where he lived with his elder brother, a clerk at the Elgin textile mills. In 1979, after studying law, he started practising as a lawyer. In addition, he became politically active in the Ambedkarite movement and edited a magazine that sought to fuse Marxism with anti-caste ideology. However, he rarely took part in rallies organised by the local Ambedkarite movement, and his main commitment as a professional lawyer was to provide a legal service to Dalits.

Vidyarthi suddenly interrupted our discussion. He remained mysteriously silent for a couple of minutes, before shifting his attention to one of his clients whom he asked to explain his case. The victim, a middle-aged villager dressed in rags, answered in a seemingly exaggerated beseeching tone of voice, probably with the intention of persuading the lawyer of the authenticity of his case as a victim. Ignoring him, the lawyer started to dictate a letter to his assistant regarding a different case, his tone assured and lyrical. The public around him listened religiously. Having carefully transcribed his senior's statement, the assistant started reading out the letter; Vidyarthi then dictated some minor amendments before sending the assistant to have it typed. He then turned to two children girls sitting on the bench. Adopting a childish tone, he asked them if a particular person had given them 100 rupees to buy sweets. They nodded timidly. He then instructed his assistant to accompany them to the investigating police officer and to have their statements written. He told the assistant to reply in the negative if the officer asked him whether he himself had suggested the statement. In constrast with the secrecy required, he said this openly in front of other people crowded into his office. He then asked his assistant to take another client somewhere—he did not specify where.

Some people seemed to have been waiting forever in his office for their turn to come. One of them, a retired government employee whom I had met previously at an Ambedkarite function in the outskirts of Kanpur, looked depressed. He explained to me that his daughter had been physically beaten by her in-laws, who had asked for more dowry, and that he had been kept waiting by the lawyer for days, even though Vidyarthi summoned him by phone. This manner of keeping people waiting and deciding in an unpredictable manner whose turn seemed to have something to do with his manner of wielding his authority. He was the master of time and space, the brains, the unpredictable organizer who kept the people around him in a state of dependence, while making things work based on his own experience and understanding of what to do and when. The necessity for him to impress this authority on his clients will be better understood in the next section, where I describe how Dalit victims' determination to fight their cases is watered down in courtrooms. Some of the skills required by this lawyer to win his cases were therefore psychological: imposing his own authority over his clients was a way of compelling them to resist the judges' insistence on offering a compromise and on closing the case.

Courtroom Ethnography

In accordance with POA rules, there was a total of four SC/ST special courts in Kanpur, at the time of my fieldwork, which dealt specifically with untouchability related crimes: one each for both districts, plus two fast-track courts specially assigned to reduce the former's level of pendency. At Kanpur Dehat SC/ST special court, there was a pendency of about 700 cases. The fast-track courts were in charge somewhat ironically of the 550 oldest pending cases. Each court had a fixed quota of fourteen cases that had to be settled each month, at the rate of thirty to forty hearings per day. A case generally took six months to two years to be judged and required multiple summons (*tariq*) of the witnesses and the accused.

Upon my arrival at the beginning of a session, I introduced myself to the judge of the fast-track court of Kanpur Dehat. The judge told me that since the courts were open to the public, I was allowed to follow the proceedings. However, he asked me to sit at the back of the room next to a policeman, which made things difficult to follow. A large portrait of Gandhi dominated the room: his presence in official buildings is common, but it seemed to me to be out of place in this special court, considering Gandhi's historical opposition to judiciary means of struggle against untouchability.[6] One could also see popular Hindu iconography, such as calendars and stickers of Hindu gods, on the desks of judges and personnel. The hearings, thus, commonly took place in the presence of political and cultural signifiers that Dalit activists consider part of a hostile caste order.

Sitting there with the policeman, I was only able to hear fragments of cases that had been going on for months or year and therefore grasped little in the way of contextual understanding. On the right side of the room, there was a covered terrace where the accused—at least those on bail (hence free)—and the witnesses were waiting their turn. The prosecutor stood in front of the judge, from whom he was separated by a wooden barrier. On the left-hand side, a young woman with a baby and an old woman in a sari were squatting on the floor with their arms on their knees, a typical posture taken up by villagers. I asked the policeman if they were the victims. He confirmed this and then tried to engage me in a conversation, asking me a number of casual questions about France's political system and agriculture.

At this point, the witnesses—approximately fifteen in number—were brought to the bar, suddenly crowding the scene. The judge called them by their names. An old lady who seemed to panic said that her accused son, currently in jail, had not been brought to court. The witnesses signed a paper while those who could not write applied their inked thumbprints to it, and the peon took small bank notes from them. The judge announced that the session was adjourned because of the absence of the accused. He then summoned the victim to the bar and called me over to explain that the victim was receiving 150 rupees from the court for her travelling expenses. I asked him what the nature of the case was, and he replied that she had been raped in 1995. I did not dare to ask any further questions.

The judge then advised me to go to the next building to see bail being granted to individuals. Although I would have liked to follow more hearings, I had no choice but to follow his injunction to leave the room. Outside the building, I met a Dalit activist. Shortly afterwards a villager whose hearing began when I left the court joined us. Looking disgusted, he said that the judge had asked him to compromise with the accused in order to close the case. He said that he did not dare refuse. The activist smiled at me and rubbed his thumb and index finger together. The activist explained that the judge was probably aware that an out of court settlement (*'samjhauta'*) had been reached. His gesture indicated that this particular compromise between the two parties involved an exchange of money.[7] The activist tried to persuade the victim to get the case transferred to a different court and a different judge in order to contest the closure of the case, and to find a competent lawyer familiar with the procedures. The victim agreed but he did not turn up to the meeting that was arranged with a lawyer for later that afternoon.

Obviously, the activists' strict conception of justice called for determined victims who could be willing to challenge the judge's authority. Most of the time, however, the victims abide by the decisions of the judiciary; seeking justice therefore usually leads to compromise. One is often reminded that villagers will have to return to their villages and face the consequences of challeging fellow dominant caste villagers in the court. Whereas a court sentence will generate resentment and more conflict, a compromise will be conducive to a peaceful settlement. Therefore, the use of the judiciary system seems to be favoured by Dalit activists only—and, initially at least, by the victims—while the judiciary itself seems committed to extra-judicial means of conflict resolution. In view of this paradox, the contrast between Ambedkar's portrait in Vidyarthi's room and Gandhi's in the courtroom becomes particularly meaningful. It underlines the fact that the judiciary abides by Gandhi's unofficial conception, while it is the Dalits who are left to struggle for Ambedkar's conception of the legal struggle against untouchability, which was rendered official by the Constitution. Thus, the judiciary itself is the site of resistance against the anti-untouchability legislation it is supposed to implement.

Entering the rural SC/ST regular court, I sat at the back of the room next to the Dalit prosecutor, whom I had been introduced to earlier by Prabhu Dayal, a retired Dalit judge and Ambedkarite activist. The judge summoned the accused villager, a Thakur (upper-caste) man, by using the derogatory word *tum*. He shouted at the man telling him that he needed to bring his lawyer immediately. The villager, who seemed to be in his thirties, was thin and poorly dressed, despite being from an upper caste. The prosecutor explained to me that this case had been going on for eleven years. The victim was a Dalit whose house had burnt down and who had subsequently had to flee the village. He was attacked for protesting against two Thakur youngsters who had made sexual remarks to his sister as she bathed in the village pond. Fearful of being molested, she had shouted for help; her brother had come to her rescue and had chased away the accused that came back with their fellow caste men and beat him up.

The two accused and the victim squatted together on the ground outside the courtroom. In this setting, they looked like poor fellow villagers in an equal position of subalternity, and there was no trace of animosity between them. But in spite of this apparent camaraderie, the accused's defence was based on what is currently known as a cross case: a counter-accusation against the victim recorded by a separate police First Information Report. In this instance, the accused upper caste men complained that the Dalit man had started beating them first. Since their lawyer was busy pleading in another court, the hearing was adjourned, but they were asked to produce a written note from him. Outside, I met the victim and his father, who told me, 'We do not want a compromise [*samjhotta*]; we want justice [*nyay*]'. He explained that their family had to flee from the village because of the threats. He then asked me to follow him behind the court building, saying that he had something to tell me in private.

He said that although his brothers still lived in the village, he could not afford to return there. If he was killed or injured, who would look after his children? He claimed that the investigating police officer had 'purposely weakened his case' (*jabardasti mamla kamzor kar dya*) by failing to register the eyewitness's evidence properly. The police officer, a Thakur, was a close relative of the accused. While we talked, his son called him over to sign the adjournment form. Interestingly, the accused from an upper caste applied a thumbprint to the form, while the Dalit victim actually signed it. When I asked the victim if he knew how to write, he replied that he could not but that he nevertheless knew how to write his name. He said that he made a point of signing, since thumbprints create a negative impression. Apparently, he believed that being seen as an educated citizen would help him to obtain justice.

The date of the next summons was written on a small piece of paper and given by the staff to the accused and victims. They were instructed to return to the court three weeks later. The victims complained that it represented a considerable inconvenience for them, since they wouldn't earn any money on that particular day and would have to cover their own travel expenses. They confessed that they had been duly given 6,000 rupees to fight the case, in keeping with the rules of the POA Act, but that was a long time ago and the money had since run out. Of these funds, they paid 2,000 rupees just to hire a lawyer to help them with the paperwork. Although they were supposed to be given money for travel expenses with each summons, the father and son complained that they had never seen this money: 'The lawyers and court employees eat the money. We're illiterate'. Even for exemplary victims like them who were determined to obtain justice and not to compromise, routine faced in the lower ranks of the court administration proved to be disheartening.

Dalit Judges' Testimonies: From Contestation to Judicial Activism

I witnessed a large amount of resentment for judges among lawyers, who alleged that their so-called 'corruption' was the greatest hindrance to their work. One upper-caste lawyer pretended that in the past, lawyers would mediate bribery between the accused and the judge. However, according to him, judges nowadays took the money directly, 'and bargaining takes place also. They're bloody so corrupt; they've just opened a grocery shop. They don't feel the dignity of being judge and magistrate' (in English). A Dalit lawyer estimated that 90 per cent of judges were corrupt, just like the rest of government officials—which facilitated the fact that witnesses turned hostile. According to a prosecutor and several Dalit lawyers, if judges wished, they had the legal means to take action against such hostile witnesses for making false depositions in the first place. But my informants argued that instead of discouraging this practice, the judges preferred to accept bribes and close their eyes. Closing the cases helped them meet their professional targets.

Although their version would have been necessary to mitigate these pure allegations, the judges whom I contacted at their workplaces in the four SC/ST special courts in Kanpur refused to speak to me on account of legal restrictions. Looking at the names, it appeared that they were all from upper caste backgrounds. The fact that I was able to find Dalit judges, whether retired or from other courts in UP (not in Kanpur), who were willing to speak to me, possibly reflects the fact that I was able to meet them outside the workplace thanks to prior introduction. Another factor that facilitated this contact was that two out of those three Dalit judges were retired and were thus not subject to any professional agreements. Furthermore, these judges may have felt compelled to speak to me because of their personal inclination towards the Dalit cause. It is also important to mention here that I was able to meet these judges through Dalit activist networks.

The first judge (hereafter J1), who was retired, was contacted on my behalf by a prominent Ambedkarite activist from Lucknow. The second judge (J2) and I were put in touch by one of the young Dalit lawyers in Kanpur, and the third judge (J3), also retired, was already known to me as a prominent activist in the Ambedkarite movement in Kanpur. Speaking to them led me to realize that Dalit networks of solidarity inside the administration are not just ideological, but also depend on professional hierarchies and patronage. For example, J3, the retired Ambedkarite judge, gave me the contact details of a Dalit public prosecutor in Kanpur. J3 explained that the prosecutor, who was from a simple lawyer background, owed his new position to him, and I was given to understand that the prosecutor would cooperate with me since he was morally bound to oblige anyone sent by him.

J2, although neither an activist nor an Ambedkarite, nevertheless felt sympathetic toward the community as a Dalit himself. Interestingly, the organization of young Dalit lawyers in Kanpur had arranged a farewell party for him on the day of his transfer from the Kanpur court as gratitude for his support on many occasions. By showing their appreciation, the young Dalit lawyers thus sought to create an emotional bond with Dalit judges. These attempts to create informal professional networks of Dalit solidarity between different actors (such as activists, lawyers, prosecutors, and judges) were a way to counter the institutionalized caste biases that hindered the implementation of the POA Act. J1, who practised at different levels of the judiciary in UP before retiring, conveyed his sense of disillusion with the mandate to deliver equitable justice, which he saw as being thwarted by police reluctance and pressure on victims from the accused:

Police personnel are managed by these persons who do not want the act to be applied [...] For fifteen days, the victims have to run here and there to get the their complaint lodged, and in the meantime the witnesses are made to feel that the accused are so powerful that there is no use of giving evidence, and they are won over by them. Even when the FIR is lodged, in the most heinous cases, the police does not arrest the accused; instead they give him long rope, like getting bail by means of surrender, etc . If some big person is arrested in the village, it has its own effect on the people: he will be handcuffed, abused by the police, and sent to jail. But when the matter goes to the court, then the evidence is that most cases end in acquittal. One of the reasons is that the witnesses turn hostile; they are won over by the accused and they don't support

the prosecution. Winning over means through intimidation, threatening. Poor people are not able to resist, since they are dependent on them.
(Interview in English.)

J2, whom I met in his appointed district, argued that judges were
not free from subtle forms of caste prejudice against their Dalit colleagues, even though this hardly translated into open discrimination.
He explained that if the judges themselves had this mindset, there were
reasons to think that their professional decisions could be affected too.
Although he did not define himself as an Ambedkarite, he felt inclined
to help Dalits in a discreet manner, such as by receiving people at his
residence on evenings and Sundays in order to give them professional
advice on their cases; these people came to him after being introduced
by activists.

J3 was more openly engaged in the Ambedkarite movement, even
before his retirement. In addition to this, he argued, he had shown his
dedication to Dalits through his professional commitment to guarantee
justice in SC/ST special courts. It was by working overtime and being as
efficient as possible in his job that he had helped the maximum number
of Dalits to obtain justice. Hence, in the special court where he ended
his career, he oversaw a significant reduction in the number of pending cases: while his predecessor achieved just 20 per cent of the official
target of settling one case per day, his own performance reached 1,300
per cent! His rate of conviction was also higher than that of his colleagues. He was of the opinion that almost 100 per cent of cases judged
under the SC Act were genuine, since the police had already filtered
the cases to a considerable extent. Hence, according to him, committed
people were all that was needed to apply the law. His protégé, the Dalit
prosecutor of Kanpur, also argued for the need to nominate more Dalit
prosecutors and judges in order for the law to be applied effectively;
extending the SC quota to the judiciary would thus be a positive measure in favour of justice. The prosecutor argued from his experience
that since the government itself neglected the POA Act, the responsibility to implement it fell on the shoulders of Dalits themselves.

'Misuses' and Beyond

Interestingly, when Dalits insist on using the law as others do, the
dominant discourse talks about misuse. Resistance to the POA Act was

palpable inside the Kachehri itself, as I discerned from my talks with upper-caste lawyers. Discussing the Act with them invariably led to allegations that it was misused by Dalits, a common statement which seemed to have reached the status of an established truth. One day as I entered the special court of Kanpur Nagar, a young lawyer walked towards me in a hostile manner, asking me what my purpose was. I realized from his name that he was a Brahmin, and from his speech that he was a caste conservative who criticized the POA Act in the name of equality before justice: when I told him about my attempt to study the special court, he replied that 60 to 70 per cent of cases under the POA Act were false and that there should be no special court if justice is to be the same for everyone.

Another young conservative Brahmin lawyer, who met with me in his office thanks to the introduction of his Dalit assistant, also became aggressive when I told him about my research and immediately raised the subject of misuse. He accused Dalits of taking advantage of the political conditions brought about by the BSP and using them to instil fear in the villages:

> Even the SC/ST [i.e. Dalits] try to misuse it, particularly in view of the present government, because a Harijan [old fashioned Gandhian word for Dalit] lady is Chief Minister of UP. Police officers don't have courage to just negate lodging an FIR, even when they know that the information given to them is false. But since they apprehend that they may be put into trouble, they don't carry out the independent investigation. It is a very mechanical investigation; they never bother to discover the truth. Police fear that if they make a final report [i.e., refuse to write the FIR], the SC people will approach some leaders. Therefore, the chargesheet is produced by the police under pressure to avoid trouble. [Translated from Hindi.]

Beyond this dominant stereotype regarding Dalit misuse, I heard other allegations that complicated the discourse on misuse. Progressive non-Dalit lawyers, as well as Dalit lawyers, argued that although misuse did exist, it was not necessarily attributed to Dalits.

Saeed Naqvi, one of the most illustrious criminal lawyers in Kanpur and a Communist, argued that Dalit misuse would not be possible without support from dominant castes: 'Even under the BSP, Dalits can't stand before the Brahmins and Thakurs without the support of the Brahmins and Thakurs. There is always some backing' (in English). He explained that a false case under the POA Act rarely stemmed from the initiative of Dalits themselves, who were not in a position to face the consequences of enmity in their villages. Conflict with the dominant castes had too many negative implications (in terms of issues such as employment, access to the village commons, and harassment) to be initiated without a valid reason. Misuse existed, but this was mostly instigated by members of the upper castes, who enrolled their Dalit labourers in order to harass their own upper-caste enemies. A common technique was to ask a Dalit to accuse one's enemy of using violence or casteist language, etc. According to Saeed Naqvi, some Dalits agreed to play this game for their own gain, providing that they felt adequately protected by powerful patrons. By engaging in such practices, they could pocket the government's immediate compensation for small offences, which was 6,250 rupees after lodging the FIR, with a further 18,750 rupees if a case ended in conviction. Compared to genuine cases, in which the police were usually reluctant to register Dalit complaints against influential individuals, such FIRs were easily registered as a result of bribes and connections. The lawyer who headed the Kanpur Bar Association, a Communist Brahmin, made the same observation, adding that these practices were extremely nefarious since they added to the level of pendency in courts and drew a veil of suspicion over authentic cases.

This type of misuse, which involves inter-caste cooperation, discredits the stereotypical image of vulnerable Dalit victims struggling against upper-caste oppressors while conversely enforcing another stereotype, that of villagers' general dishonesty and manipulativeness, whether for factional reasons or in order to abuse public funds. Interestingly, even my friend Anil, the young Dalit lawyer, insisted that many Dalits were involved in dirty business in villages and he refuted the image of Dalits as mere victims. This reflected his experience as a village-level Dalit activist who constantly faced internal opposition from Dalits bought off by anti-Dalit factions in the villages.

As Dalit lawyer R. B. Vidyarthi rightly pointed out, the general association of the POA Act with misuse was in itself indicative of the fact that a casteist society could not abide by this particular law. He argued that other laws were subject to greater abuse, especially gender-related ones governing dowry disputes and rape cases. Hence, discrediting the POA Act—the misuse of which, he claimed, was comparatively much less—was simply another manner of defaming the Dalits. The way he identified Dalits with the law is revealing. Not only has its implementation come to depend on efforts *by* the Dalits to overcome the hurdles of institutionalized casteism: due to these very struggles, the POA Act has also become a major device in the process of Dalit emancipation on which the conservative society focuses its resentment. In short, although conceived *for* the Dalits and their protection by the Indian government on behalf of the whole society, it has become the law *of* the Dalits, i.e., Dalits against society's established interests, as much needed by them as it is hated by those whose traditional privileges are threatened by it.

From Informal to Organized Dalit Legal Activism?

Espousing the Dalit cause, the professed purpose of the POA Act was to assure Dalits that the state would stand by them along their path to emancipation. Yet Marc Galanter argues that the contrast between a stringent law and the incapacity to ensure its implementation on the part of beneficiaries only reinforces the notion of Dalit vulnerability and dependence. In encouraging its opponents to mobilize their economic and social assets to fight back legally, inequality before the court is on the increase. The law's stringency thus becomes self-defeating. Though not explicitly, Galanter's critique thus ultimately converges with Gandhi's opposition to the legalistic method of addressing untouchability. In short, such arguments deduce that a strong law only creates more animosity toward the weak and that it therefore falls short of its target as a legal incentive for social change.

However, this pessimistic statement on anti-untouchability legislation contrasts with the POA Act's current popularity with the Dalit movement in spite of the difficulties that its implementation creates. Encouraged by the BSP governments' reaches to power, the vibrant Ambedkarite movement in UP has taken up the challenge of implementing pro-Dalit measures from below, thus engaging with the Indian Constitution's professed aim of building a casteless and classless society. Among grassroots activists like the Dalit Panthers of Kanpur, there is a practical understanding that the local court requires a vigilant presence precisely to disallow it from being a site of disenfranchisement and dismemberment of the law. While impunity has become a means for dominant castes to advertise their power to stand above the law, this article has highlighted the Dalit activists' efforts to reactivate the law through their struggles and ability to manoeuvre. The constant vigilance, efforts and skills that are deployed testify to a strong determination on the part of Dalit activists to show others their capacity to defend their rights in the present institutional setup.

The stakes involved are indeed broader than the practical ability to fight and win particular cases. My point here is that the stakes are deeply political, from two points of view. First, they testify to the ability to resist a process of disenfranchisement, which is engineered by the dominant castes with the complicity of the local administrations. In a way, because of the vigilance and struggles involved by Dalit activists, every court victory can be advertised in a certain locality as the concrete victory of an emerging Dalit power. Second, from the internal point of view of the Dalit community, fighting cases registered under the POA Act also has an importance in terms of politicization which is to monitor, energize, and infuse with broader ideological meanings people's individual struggles against untouchability. Keeping this political aim in mind, the stakes of legal activism for an organization like the Dalit Panthers of Kanpur are equally practical. Considering that court matters have become an integral—and painful—part of people's lives, their daily activity at the Kachehri represents a strategic attempt to occupy a crucial place. Their presence is indeed required in order to establish their leadership in the Dalit community. The legal assistance and administrative brokerage they offer on a voluntary basis enables them to recruit members, gain popularity, and finance the organization through an informal economy of donations. The informality of this economy thus reflects the functioning of the Dalit movement and of what Chaterjee describes as India's 'political society' more broadly. This spontaneous adaptation of political praxis to the field of justice thus does not represent legal activism in the conventional sense, which requires a higher degree of specialization.

In contrast to the activism that is witnessed outside the courtrooms, once the court and the lawyers take over cases, the militant energy and hectic mobilizations give way to a routine of summons, adjournments, and paperwork in a discouraging atmosphere of alleged venality and intrigue. By definition, court decisions are supposedly hermetic to democratic pressures, and Dalit activists cannot help being confined spatially and temporally to a sphere outside and prior to the court proceedings.

While such pressures can be felt keenly at the police level, once the complaint is registered, there is little to be done other than motivating the victims to pursue the case and not to accept compromise.

The informality of this legal activism however implies certain inefficiencies that will only be overcome by increased specialization. The current attempts by the National Campaign for Dalit Human Rights—and more specifically its legal branch, the National Dalit Movement for Justice (NDMJ)[8]—to rationalize and professionalize the Dalit movement, thus point to a new era of full-fledged Dalit legal activism. Its aim is to increase legalistic skills in the Dalit movement through professional training programmes. Labelled as 'recapacitation' (a term that somehow betrays the pretention of technocratic norms to humble traditional political praxis), these professional trainings are based on the critical study and technocratic reformulation by NGO experts of the existing savoir-faire of local activists. Although the NDMJ has established itself in a small office on the outskirts of Lucknow, its presence was too young and its scope too limited to be felt in Kanpur in 2010 when my fieldwork was conducted. While its professional dynamism offers new possibilities for overcoming the biases against the implementation of the POA Act, one must bear in mind that the current NGO-ization of the Dalit movement departs from the existing grassroots organizations' informal economy as a legal and aid provider. These local Dalit organizations' ability to maintain their financial autonomy and impose their authority within their constituency is largely based on such mediatory services. The success of this new endeavour by the NDMJ will therefore depend on its ability to connect with local Dalit organizations without being perceived as a competitor.

Notes

1. The Scheduled Caste and Scheduled Tribe (Prevention of Atrocities) Rules were adopted only in 1995 to implement the Act by providing detailed guidelines and methods of implementation such as the appointment of state-level nodal officers to coordinate implementation, vigilance committees and special officers to monitor cases at district level, and state-level vigilance and monitoring committees, as well as a number of preventive measures such as the identification of atrocity-prone areas, the distribution of arms licenses to Dalits, the confiscation of arms to non-Dalits, and the establishment of NGO-

led awareness centres. In addition, these rules fix the amount of compensation to victims according to the offences and provide victims with travel and maintenance allowances to go to court, etc.

2. Venkitesh Ramakrishnan and Ajoy Ashirwad Mahaprastha, 'Victims Always.' *Frontline*, Vol. 26 No. 24, 21 November–4 December 2009, pp. 7–8.

3. The provincial states can amend criminal laws. POA Act was amended in UP to make some offences such as the hate speech ones cognizable. These cases went up, while many atrocities weren't registered in UP ten years after the enactment of the law (Saksena 2010).

4. An example of such public demonstrations by dominant castes is the 2006 Khairlanji massacre, which took place in full public view in Maharashtra (Jaoul 2008).

5. BSP, a Dalit led party, first took part in a coalition government in December 1993. It formed two other short-lived governments with the support of BJP in 1995 (four months) and 1997 (six months), and eventually took power independently in 2002 (seventeen months) and 2007 (five years).

6. This is an allusion to Gandhi's creation of the Harijan Sewak Sangh in 1932. Ambedkar resigned because his recommendation of providing legal aid to Dalits was ignored by Gandhi in favour of anti-untouchability propaganda and social work, which he called 'constructive work'.

7. There are complex reasons which may leave judges with no option but having to accept out of court settlements. Further, we may surmise that considering the problem of pendency in the courts, judges have their own professional incentives to close cases in order to fulfil their work targets.

8. http://ncdhr.org.in/ndmj/ndmj

References

Baxi, Pratiksha. 2014. *Public Secrets of Law: Rape Trials in India*. New Delhi: Oxford University Press.

Chatterjee, Partha. 2004. *The Politics of the Governed*. New Delhi: Permanent Black.

Mendelsohn, Oliver and Vicziany, Marika. 1998. *The Untouchables: Subordination, Poverty and the State in Modern India*. Cambridge: Cambridge University Press.

Galanter, Marc. 1989. 'Missed Opportunities: The Use and Non-use of Law Favourable to Untouchables and Other Specially Vulnerable Groups', in *Law and Society in Modern India*, pp. 208–233. New Delhi: Oxford University Press.

Hansen, Thomas. 2004. 'The Politics of Permanent Performance: The Production of Authority in the Locality', in Zavos, John et al. (eds.), *Politics of Cultural Mobilization in India*, pp. 19–36. New Delhi: Oxford University Press.

Jaffrelot, Christophe. 1998. 'The Bahujan Samaj Party in North India: No Longer Just a Dalit Party?', *Comparative Studies of South Asia, Africa, and the Middle East*, 18 (1): 35–51.

Jaoul, Nicolas. 2007. 'Political and 'Non Political' Means in the Dalit Movement', in Pai, Sudha (ed.), *Political Process in UP: Identity, Economic Reform and Governance*, pp. 142–68. New Delhi: Pearson.

———. 2013. 'Politicizing Victimhood: The Dalit Panthers' Response to Caste Violence In Uttar Pradesh in the Early 1980s', *South Asian Popular Culture*, 11 (2) Special Issue: Terror and Media: 169–79.

Rao, Anupama. 2009. *The Caste Question: Dalits and the Politics of Modern India*. Berkeley: University of California Press.

Saksena, H.S. 2010. *Atrocities on Scheduled Castes: The Law and the Realities*. New Delhi: Serials Publications.

Saxena, K.B. 2004. 'Report on Atrocities against Scheduled Castes', *National Commission on Human Rights (NHRC)*. http://www.ambedkar.org/NHRC Report/prelim.pdf (last accessed on 11 June 2014)

6

DEVIKA BORDIA

Cultures of Policing

Panchayat-Police Practices and the
Making of a Criminal Case

In different parts of India, police and court practices point to a discrepancy between legal procedures outlined in the Code of Criminal Procedure and the way legal institutions work on the ground. Contributions to this volume by Pratiksha Baxi, Daniela Berti, and Nicolas Jaoul demonstrate how legal practices consist of non-official compromises, the fabrication of evidence, negotiations with police officers, lawyers, and local leaders, and the marshalling of false witnesses. These practices are an outcome of regional, pre-colonial, and colonial histories of state formation; the intersection between state practices, local community-based institutions, and ideas of custom; local-level and state-level politics; the background and training of legal practitioners, including police officers, lawyers, and magistrates; and the presence and impact of social and political movements and other state institutions in shaping community-based leaders.

In this chapter, I draw on fieldwork conducted at the police station and during panchayat meetings in Kotra bloc in the Bhil and Girassia 'tribal'[1] regions of southern Rajasthan. I present the case of a woman who was accused of murdering her husband, the son of an influential Girassia leader. The incident was initially recorded as an accidental death but was later reclassified as murder. My fieldwork reveals that rather than fact-finding and gathering substantial evidence by the police, the making of this criminal case depended on decisions taken during panchayat meetings, the negotiations between police officers and panchayat leaders, and the various configurations of local politics. I demonstrate that by mustering public opinion around the character of a Girassia woman and employing political contacts, tribal leaders were able to influence the police to change how the case was initially recorded. Therefore, I analyse this case in terms of the historically constituted practices of panchayat and police institutions, the emergence of new forms of tribal leadership over the last thirty years, and the popular public perception that both non-tribals and Girassia men hold about Girassia women.

The case that I describe here points to the intersection between panchayat and police practices, and the way in which local politics shape institutional practices. In the following section, I locate the historical co-emergence of different institutions in southern Rajasthan in terms of the broader anthropological literature on law and panchayats in villages in India. I then examine the emergence of new forms of tribal leadership and participation in dispute resolution and panchayat meetings, and show how associations and connections with state officers is crucial for tribal leaders to gain authority and political power.

Panchayat-Police Practices

Anthropologists and political scientists working within the context of 'village studies' scholarship in the 1950s, 1960s, and 1970s have sought to understand how and why people access legal institutions for reasons that don't always pertain to seeking justice. According to these scholars, the value systems of legal institutions established during British rule are incommensurable with those of panchayat governance. Panchayats have been described as institutions responsible for dispute resolution and arbitration and adjudication (Cohn 1987; Galanter 1984). Based on his fieldwork in a village in Uttar Pradesh in the 1950s, Bernard Cohn emphasizes the process-based aspect of dispute resolution, where there is a focus on discussion among panchayat leaders rather than formally or informally selected bodies. For instance, the role of the panchayat leader is to direct public opinion with respect to the people and events surrounding a dispute and among the villagers who attend a panchayat meeting. Furthermore, since panchayat leaders belong to the same village as the disputants, there is a focus on arriving at a compromise, and usually a decision is reached only after several meetings have been held. Finally, individual personalities and character traits are central to the adjudicative process.

According to village studies scholars court practices are built on the assumption that each individual is as equal in the eyes of the law, that the court gives a verdict rather than working toward a compromise, and that courts adjudicate one dispute at a time (Cohn 1987). The value systems of 'Western' legal institutions are interpreted differently by villagers (Cohn 1987; Marriot 1955; Srinivas 1960), who use the courts to harass or punish their opponents but seldom to seek justice. As Cohn (1987:610) recalls, 'To the villager, the rights and wrongs of a case were secondary to his ability to manipulate the court through access to minor court officials, the hiring of clever lawyers, the fabrication of evidence, and the marshalling of false witnesses'. In this vein, village studies scholars have shown that people access state institutions like courts in order to demonstrate their authority and their ability to influence other villagers, and to flaunt their connections with legal practitioners and state officers.

The everyday practices of panchayat institutions in southern Rajasthan involve similar processes to those outlined by village studies scholars, though they differ in focus and emphasis. Tribal leaders are personally acquainted with many of the disputants as well as with other panchayat leaders, and they present themselves as embedded in their community and knowing and understanding their community. Furthermore, they use legal institutions to demonstrate their legal and political competencies and to gain authority and political power. However, while Cohn and other village studies scholars view the value systems of legal institutions established by the British as different from those of panchayat institutions, my fieldwork experiences and archival research reveal the co-production and co-emergence of institutions that have otherwise been described as incommensurable in this academic field. Furthermore, as I demonstrate in subsequent sections, police officers draw on historical and cultural ideas about law and tribal life in order to justify police practices by stating that tribals, for instance, are incapable of understanding state law and can most effectively be governed by panchayats. This suggests that the values underlying various legal systems are not necessarily inherently different but are constructed as incommensurable by state officials and legal practitioners. The politics of incommensurability (Clarke 2009) focuses on how relationships of power emerge through individual, state, regional, and international legal practices, which co-exist uneasily with other culturally and historically constituted conceptions of justice.

The intersection between panchayat and police practices can be traced to colonial forms of state-making. In the pre-colonial and colonial periods, the district of Udaipur fell under the jurisdiction of the Kingdom of Mewar. The regions inhabited by the Bhil and Girassia people which are today located in southern Udaipur could not be effectively controlled by the ruler of Mewar. Therefore, in 1856, British officers posted in the region formed the Mewar Bhil Corps (MBC) in collaboration with the ruler of the princely state in order to bring the hilly tracts under the control of the Mewar State. The MBC functioned as a counter-insurgency unit and forcefully brought the Bhil and Girassia regions under the control of the Mewar State.

The British enjoyed military control over these regions while civil and criminal jurisdiction was exercised by native chiefs and rulers. Criminal cases considered 'heinous' or cases connected to other princely states were referred to authorities who represented the ruler of Mewar. In practice, however, this led to competing and overlapping forms of governance between the native chiefs, the ruler of Mewar, and the British officers of the MBC. The British officers believed that the native chiefs and the Maharana's agents were absent, apathetic, and oppressive, and that they were incapable of adequately governing these regions. The British believed that a 'competent panchayat' could effectively preside over cases that were not being properly addressed by the Maharana's agents and they therefore sought to convene and preside over panchayat meetings despite this being outside their jurisdiction. These panchayats adjudicated in cases that included murders, often passing the sentence of 'the transportation of life'. By inscribing panchayat proceedings as resembling procedures of a court of law, the British legitimized and justified a particular practice of panchayat governance. This intervention enabled colonial officers to expand their sphere of authority and regularized and routinized a particular form of panchayat meeting. After India's independence legal practitioners continue to rely on panchayats for everyday governance.

State-making and particular forms of panchayat governance emerged in the context of the emergency rule of the Mewar Bhil Corps. The British commander of the MBC had the troops behind him and was the highest local authority in the district. The MBC was formed along the lines of the Khandesh Bhil Corps in the Bombay Presidency, where British officers burned villages, pursued Bhils and even recruited Bhils into the army to police the other Bhils who they called 'wild Bhils'. The British violently suppressed the Bhil anti-colonial movement in Mewar, and in one incident they fired on a gathering and killed hundreds of Bhils.[2] Along with these episodes of violence and massacre, everyday governance under the MBC consisted of firing at and killing Bhils at any hint of perceived unrest.

The civilizing mission of the colonial state—the project of disciplining supposedly recalcitrant Bhils—enabled the British to justify employing violence on a daily basis and also intervening in cases that were outside their sphere of jurisdiction. Correspondence between colonial officials depicts Bhils as desirous of the discipline and punishment that would instill in them a sense of being human. The British believed that Bhils could adopt the manners and habits of civilized beings once 'their wrongs are carefully inquired into and redressed and their rights are maintained', and 'when they are treated like other villagers in the neighbourhood'.[3] Disciplining Bhils involved not only the use of force but also intervening in criminal cases in order to ensure adequate punishment for crimes committed by Bhils, even if these cases were outside the jurisdiction of the British. As mentioned above, the British officers of the MBC also intervened in cases by governing through panchayats. They were able to expand their sphere of jurisdiction because they had the backing of a military force. For example, the colonial state convened International Panchayats involving representatives from several princely states, which were always held in Mewar so that colonial officers had military support during the proceedings with which to enforce their decision.

In the everyday practices of governance during the colonial period, the commander of the Mewar Bhil Corps had control over police, military, and panchayat functions. The lack of a clear distinction between political, military, and judicial authority persisted after independence in 1947. Before the establishment of the Rajasthan Police Service in 1951, Muslims and high-caste Hindus who served on the higher rungs of the MBC came to occupy the positions that were left vacant by the British officers. These individuals performed policing functions and also adjudicated disputes at the panchayat. For example, Faujdar Sahib, now in his nineties, lives in Kotra bazaar, and told me about his experiences as a faujdar or an army officer of the MBC during the colonial period, the policing roles he performed after independence, and how he was called to be sarpanch of panchayat meetings regarding disputes among tribals. Faujdar Sahib pointed to how there was very little difference between his work and duties as the faujdar during the colonial period and the decades after independence and as a sarpanch during panchayat meetings. He said that he was involved in panchayat meetings, that he listened to both sides and gave his opinion, and that it was his responsibility to ensure that both parties adhered to the resolution of the panchayat. During panchayat meetings disputants were aware that the faujdar was present and the authority that he commanded usually steered the direction that the case took, and ensured that the parties involved adhered to the decision of the panchayat. Therefore, a specific form of emergency rule in the colonial period led to a lack of separation of military, political and judicial power that continued in the decades after independence. As I describe below today panchayat and police practices continue to shape each other.

The ideas, terminology, and languages that people in Rajasthan use to describe panchayat-police practices can also be traced to particular forms of statecraft that were found in the princely states. In Rajasthan today, the role that the police play in panchayat meetings and dispute resolution is called rathori, a term that people trace etymologically to the Rathore jati of the Rajput caste. The Rathores have historically been rulers at various social and political levels, whether as revenue collectors and landowners in villages or as the rulers of princely states and kingdoms. In the pre-colonial and colonial periods, panchayat leaders of different castes would take disputes to the ruler or chief of their village, who in turn would assist in dispute resolution or pressurize people to come to a compromise. People of the Rathore jati have also historically been police officers and soldiers. Rajputs were classified as "martial races" by the colonial state and were recruited in large numbers to the army. Today the police force consists of people from different castes and Rajputs occupy the highest ranks.

In Kotra tribal leaders, police officers, and lawyers referred to rathori to explain contemporary police practices of intimidation and bullying in order to ensure that those engaged in a dispute come to a compromise and agreement. This involves police officers threatening disputants by saying that they will lock them up or inflict violence on them, and also indiscriminately incarcerating people and using force. Police officers will also inform people about the legal consequences if a case goes to court, including, at times exaggerating the lawyer's fees, inflating the duration of a court case, or exaggerating the fine or prison sentence that will be meted out in the event that they are found guilty. The colonial forms of emergency rule and cultures of rathori historically associated with statecraft have led to a situation where the role of the police is to use violence, force, intimidation, and bullying rather than to enforce the law according to criminal codes.

While the literature on village studies argues that the values and practices underlying state law and panchayats are incommensurable, in southern Rajasthan historically formed practices of panchayat, police, and court institutions shape each other in crucial ways. Specific forms of panchayat practices emerged during the colonial period that enabled the colonial state to gain power and authority by convening and presiding over panchayats. After India's independence, panchayats became institutions through which community-based leaders could claim to represent and therefore gain authority over their community. Furthermore, panchayat and police practices overlapped in the cultural practices and idioms of the princely states and the colonial state used their control over the military to convene panchayat meetings and ensure that panchayat decisions were implemented. These historically formed institutional practices have led to a situation in the last thirty years, where tribal leaders gain authority through their association with panchayats and their interaction with police officers and lawyers, and all cases are addressed through the negotiations between tribal leaders, police officers, and lawyers.

The Changing Forms of Tribal Leadership and Authority

Participating in dispute resolution and attending panchayat meetings is crucial for Bhil and Girassia leaders seeking to gain authority and political power. During panchayat meetings, political loyalties are tested and made visible and tribal leaders demonstrate legal and political competencies and their ability to influence and shape police and court practices. The form of interaction between police officers and tribal panchayat leaders has changed over time. In the decades following independence a few older male leaders would interact with state officers. Since the mid-1990s, tribal leaders have been associated with state-recognized Panchayati Raj Institutions, political parties, social and political movements, and non-government organizations. A large number of younger tribal leaders gain political authority by addressing cases at the police station, in the courts as well as through the panchayat.

Panchayats were not legally recognized when the Indian constitution came into effect in 1952.[4] However, in the mid-1950s, the Indian government began taking steps to rectify this. Officers in the central and state governments, and political leaders inspired by Gandhian ideas believed that panchayats could connect villages to the administrative apparatus of state- and national-level governments. During the panchayati raj movement, panchayats were viewed as channels for development funding and the elevation of the rural poor. Early efforts to recognize panchayats led to the emergence of two major institutions of local governance in post-independence rural India: non-state panchayats responsible for dispute resolution and state-recognized panchayats with a more administrative role.

As a result of the ideas and the advocacy work that emerged during the panchayati raj movement, in 1992 parliament passed the 73rd and 74th amendments to the Indian constitution. With the implementation of these amendments, all states in India were legally bound to establish a three-tier system of Panchayati Raj Institutions (PRIs) at the district, intermediate, and village levels. Under the PRI system, elections are now held every five years for leaders at different levels of the system. Seats are reserved on a rotational basis for women and for people categorized by the Indian constitution as 'Scheduled Caste' and 'Scheduled Tribe'. As a consequence of the implementation of these amendments, a large number of tribal leaders are involved in electoral politics, particularly in relation to seats in the PRI. State-recognized PRI, and non-state panchayats intersect in crucial ways. Meetings of the latter have always been central to political life in villages, as these are occasions when political loyalties and affiliations are made visible and tested. In recent years, candidates contesting PRI elections or people supporting these candidates have had to engage with non-state panchayats and dispute resolution so that they can develop a large network of contacts and associations with other tribal leaders and gain influence among villagers.

India has also witnessed the proliferation of NGOs, indigenous rights movements, and Hindu Nationalist organizations since the 1980s. People now represent themselves with reference to new forms of identification. Non-tribal fieldworkers of the Hindu Nationalist organization Vanvasi Kalyan Parishad propagate a *vanvasi* or forest dweller identity; they believe that tribals can find their proper place in society once they are reinstated into the larger Hindu fold to which they originally belonged. In a similar vein, indigenous rights groups mobilize an *adivasi* identity, with Bhils and Girassias presented as the original inhabitants of the land. These groups are also associated with and draw on transnational discourses of indigeneity.[5] Adivasi groups mobilize people to address a range of contemporary issues that include claiming land rights, focusing on government apathy and corruption, and standing up to the inexorably high rates of interest and false debt charges applied by local money lenders. Both adivasi groups and local NGOs organize a range of workshops, training programs, and rallies on law, governance, health, education, gender, and other related issues. As tribal leaders participate in these activities they develop legal and political competencies that enable them to interact directly with state officers and manoeuvre through spaces that they did not previously have access to. The last thirty years have seen the emergence of a new form of identity politics among tribal leaders in which the culture and traditions of a particular community are publicly displayed and valorized.

As I have mentioned above, in the 1950s and 1960s village studies scholars held that mobilizing public opinion around a particular case was central to the panchayat process. This holds true even today; tribal leaders must gain popular support and mobilize public opinion for any decision they take regarding a case, which they do by drawing on ideas prevailing in the public sphere. For example, for cases related to land disputes, they have begun to draw on ideas propagated by adivasi groups about how adivasis were the original inhabitants of a given region and are inextricably tied to their land. Tribal leaders will attempt to demonstrate how a particular family has ancestral claims to a plot of disputed land.

In the case I describe below, a Girassia leader was able to frame his daughter-in-law, Merki Bai, for the murder of his son by mobilizing public opinion about her character. These ideas about Merki Bai's character reflected high caste assumptions about the sexuality of Bhil and Girassia women that are reinforced by the discourses of the Vanvasi Kalyan Parishad. These examples show how tribal leaders gain authority by relating to, among other things, identity politics, indigeneity, Hindu nationalism, and gender that have emerged from social and political movements in order to shape the direction of a case.

Tribal leaders also demonstrate familiarity with state law, such as writing affidavits at the end of panchayat meetings and invoking sections of the Indian Penal Code with recourse to the legal implications of a case. During panchayat meetings, when tribal leaders cite, for instance, sections 341 and 323 of the Code, which cover wrongful restraint and voluntarily causing hurt respectively, they evidently do not have any authority to implement the law. And yet each time tribal leaders cite sections of the Indian Penal Code or demonstrate their familiarity with the law, they point to the connections that they have with police officers and index histories of panchayat-police practices in this region. Cases are frequently addressed through underhand deals, negotiations, and bribes between police officers and tribal leaders. Police officers are often present during panchayat meetings and tribal leaders draw on political contacts to influence police practices. These processes have produced a particular form of political authority where Bhils and Girassias address cases by relying on connections with the police and specialized knowledge of the law. However, such practices eclipse potential forms of solidarity through which cases might otherwise have been addressed by political leaders. I will now look more closely at some of these processes by examining the events around how a particular criminal case—that of a woman accused of murdering her husband—was registered.

The Making of a Criminal Case

There was a stir in Kotra bazaar on 5 June 2006 as the son of Kanshi Lal, the Sarpanch of Bilwan was found dead in his home. People in the bazaar reported that his wife, Merki Bai,[6] woke up in the morning to find that her husband, Naka Lal, was not sleeping next to her. She found him lying dead on the roof of the cattle shed. By the time I got to Bilwan, from Kotra bazaar, twenty kilometres away, the police had already left. Neighbors and other villagers were still gathered around the house where both Kanshi Lal and Naka Lal lived. I learnt from them that the police had conducted a post-mortem examination inside a hut in the village. The officers had then registered the case under section 174 of the Indian Penal Code as accidental death. On the same day, Merki Bai was mercilessly sent away to her father's house in Sulav village by her father-in-law, Kanshi Lal.

Kanshi Lal was a powerful man. He was elected Sarpanch (the head of the Panchayati Raj Institution) of Bilwan with the support of the Bhartiya Janata Party, the Hindu nationalist group that has gained prominence in the tribal regions of Western India in the last fifteen years. His son Naka Lal organized manual labour for a road construction project in Bilwan, financed by the recently introduced National Rural Employment Guarantee Act (NREGA). The NREGA ensures one hundred days of employment on public works for each adult member of any rural household.[7] Many workers on the road construction project had not been paid for months and were extremely dissatisfied. People blamed Naka Lal and Kanshi Lal for siphoning money that was allotted to labourers. During discussions at tea stalls in the bazaar in the days following Naka Lal's death, villagers speculated about who might have murdered the young man by enumerating the rivals his father made in the course of his political career.

A week after Naka Lal was found dead, I attended a panchayat meeting that was convened by Merki Bai's family and Kanshi Lal. Merki Bai had the support of Shamboo Singh, the elected Sarpanch of the state-recognized Panchayati Raj Institution of Sulav. Shamboo Singh was Merki Bai's parents' neighbour. The panchayat meeting was held in Bilwan, the deceased man's village, and was presided over by important panchayat leaders and the Assistant Sub-Inspector of Police. Tribal leaders representing both sides had discussed this case during a series of closed-door meetings in their villages prior to the panchayat meeting. During the panchayat, two or three tribal leaders would take small walks in order to arrive at a consensus about the case, Merki Bai and her family and Naka Lal's family members did not directly participate in the negotiations; rather, the case was mediated by local leaders and police officers. After a series of discussions, the panchayat leaders decided that Kanshi Lal would not accuse Merki Bai of murdering Naka Lal. This settlement also entailed that Merki Bai's family should recompense Kanshi Lal for the sum of money they received when Merki Bai married

Naka Lal. Merki Bai, her family members, and Kanshi Lal signed an affi-davit that stated the decision of the panchayat. Later, Shamboo Singh told me that he was able to come to an agreement with Kanshi Lal as both of them were the Sarpanch of Panchayati Raj Institutions in their respective villages and both were fieldworkers of the Bhartiya Janata Party.

A little over three weeks after the panchayat meeting, tribal leaders talked at the tea stall about how the police were under pressure from Kanshi Lal and other BJP leaders who had contacts with the local Member of the Legislative Assembly, Babu Lal Kharadia, to change the case from accidental death to murder, and to accuse Merki Bai, of murder. Ten days later, Paghna, a panch (or a leader of the non-state panchayat) from Bilwan, told me that the post-mortem report had been sent to Udaipur for further analysis.

During those weeks, I would frequently see Kanshi Lal at the police station in Kotra holding private meetings with police officers and consta-bles and speaking with influential political leaders. One July afternoon, I walked in on a heated discussion in which Kanshi Lal, accompanied by several young men from Bilwan, were questioning the inspector of police about a report in the Rajasthan Patrika, a local newspaper, about the sudden death of the Sarpanch of Bilwan's son. These five men sur-rounded the *thanedar*, or the inspector of police's, desk. Amidst a flurry of accusations, they said that the post-mortem report had been sent to Udaipur city and that further analysis would confirm that the death was a murder. Kanshi Lal and the other men with him stated that the news-paper report would undermine the consensus that they were trying to build in the bazaar, namely, that Naka Lal was murdered. The *thanedar* assured them that the newspaper article would not affect the outcome of the post-mortem report.

Around this time, tribal leaders and other people in the bazaar began speculating about Merki Bai's intent to murder. There was widespread gossip about Merki Bai's character and about how she had previously been married to another man. It is common for Girassia men and women to re-marry two or even more times. Merki Bai entered into a relationship with Naka Lal through a custom that resembles *nata*, which is practiced by people of different castes and tribes in Rajasthan and enables a woman to cohabit with a man other than her husband. The man with whom the woman goes on *nata* provides a sum of money to either her husband or her father. This practice gives a woman the choice to leave her husband and enter into a relationship with another man. In recent years, however, it has become common for a woman's first husband or father and the local panchayat leaders to try to extort money from the second husband, and often the woman has very little choice about who she goes on nata with. Furthermore, the status of a woman who goes on nata is not equal to that of a married woman, and increasingly a woman who goes on nata is considered to be of bad character. Merki Bai told me that she *chose* to enter into a relationship with Naka Lal, and she always referred to him as her husband. However, the changing perceptions of women who go on nata enabled Kanshi Lal to steer public opinion towards the notion of Merki Bai's culpability. Around the time that Kanshi Lal and other leaders were pressurizing the police to charge Merki Bai with murder, legal practitioners began making references to Merki Bai's nature. Hanuvant Singh, the Inspector of Police, claimed that Merki Bai was a woman of bad character and the kind of person who would murder her husband. The female magistrate at the Court of Judicial Magistrate of Second Class reasoned that Merki Bai was the last person who was with Naka Lal before he died. Perhaps aware that this was not sufficient evidence to accuse Merki Bai of murder, she added, 'anyway, Merki Bai is *that* kind of woman', implying that because Merki Bai had entered into a second relationship, she was a woman of bad character and was thus capable of murdering her husband.

Over time the discourse about Merki Bai's relationship with Naka Lal and the references to her character became more important in steering the direction of the case than the evidence itself. This was a corollary of the shifting status of Girassia women in the region, which is itself connected to several social and political processes that include concerns about prestige and status among Girassias of different lineages as well as the associations and distinctions that Girassias seek to forge with other tribal and non-tribal groups, namely, Rajputs and Bhils. Girassias trace their ancestral lineage to Rajput clans. In the wake of a loss of political power in post-colonial India, Rajputs have sought to forge a homogenous identity and therefore refute any association with Girassias and other tribes and lower-caste people. In this context, women become markers of status, with Rajput ideas of tradition articulated by protecting the professed honour of Rajput women, monitoring their actions, and curtailing their mobility and visibility. Girassia women, meanwhile, are considered by Rajputs and other high-caste people to have more sexual freedom because of Girassia marriage and divorce practices. They are also seen as sexually available because there are fewer restrictions on their mobility owing to the fact that they work in the fields and go to the bazaar.

The Hindu Nationalist organization the Vanvasi Kalyan Parishad seeks to reform the high caste perception that tribal women are sexually unrestrained. This organization describes tribals as vanvasi and rejects the use of the term indigenous. High-caste fieldworkers from this organization believe that tribals were originally Hindu but lost their faith due to colonial intervention or the secular policies of the post-colonial state. They initiate programmes on 'religious awakening' among tribals, which include organizing talks and celebrating Hindu festivals where tribal women are encouraged to emulate the practices of high-caste women. VKP workers encourage tribal women to dress in a 'decent' and 'modest' manner, and advise them to refrain from travelling alone. Most of the Girassia leaders whom I knew were Vanvasi Kalyan Parishad fieldworkers and many of them, including Kanshi Lal and Shamboo Singh, contested panchayat elections with the support of the Bhartiya Janata Party. In the case of Merki Bai, Kanshi Lal was able to draw on a discourse about Girassia women that has been incorporated into the mobilization strategies of Hindu Nationalist groups and party politics.

The status of Girassia women has become particularly vulnerable in the context of changing marriage practices. While non-tribals believe that Girassia women have greater freedom to choose their partners, leave their husbands, and enter into other relationships, Maya Unnithan-Kumar has shown how, unlike middle-caste and high-caste women, who get incorporated into their husband's family, Girassia women are seldom integrated into their natal homes and have a precarious position in their conjugal homes as a consequence of having previously changed partners or of potentially doing so in the future (1997: 22). As I demonstrate below, Unnithan-Kumar's observation of Girassia marriage and divorce practices and the vulnerable and insecure status of Girassia women explains Merki Bai's lack of community support, which in turn impacted the outcome of the case. Furthermore, various Girassia leaders reproduced high-caste ideas about Girassia women by invoking

Merki Bai's character and conduct in order to justify turning against her and in their wilful and arbitrary involvement in the case.

Merki Bai's Narrative of Betrayal

Merki Bai was at her father's house when I first went to visit her a few weeks after Naka Lal' death. She told me about many different aspects of her life: her first husband; her inability to conceive; how initially she had been happy with Naka Lal, but how this had changed when he got involved in the road construction project and became the target of the workers' anger. Then she spoke slowly and steadily of the night Naka Lal died:

> That evening he was unable to sleep and he said he was going outside. I woke up in the middle of the night and found he was not sleeping beside me. I went outside and saw him lying on the roof of the cattle shed. I climbed onto the roof and found him. …I screamed and stood up and then fell as the thatched roof collapsed. I was unconscious and when I gained consciousness many people had come and the police were there.

Merki Bai explained that she was then dragged away from her home and sent to her father's house. Here she was able to go to the doctor to seek treatment for her injured back. A few days after she got to her father's house the police took her and her father into custody in Kotra for one night. A policewoman was brought in, as it is mandatory that a woman can only be arrested after dark if a female police officer is present. Merki Bai recounted how the policewoman harassed her and attempted to extract a confession of murder. She explained that she had denied all accusations. The next morning, Merki Bai saw her father-in-law outside the police station:

> I was relieved to see him after being in the police station all night. On his instruction, I accompanied him to Punjab National Bank, located next to the police station. With my husband, we had a joint bank account of 50,000 rupees. My father-in-law wanted my fingerprint on a form. He said that a small amount of money needed to be withdrawn for the *lokai* [feast marking death] of Naka Lal. If I hadn't been in the police station all night, I would have been more cautious before putting my fingerprint on the form. But I had been in the jail through the night and I didn't think so much. I didn't know what all this would mean and I didn't think my father-in-law would do all this.

Merki Bai's feelings about her incarceration and harassment at the police station appeared to be overshadowed by a sense of incredulity that her father-in-law would take money from her bank account. She spoke about her marriage to Naka Lal with a great deal of fondness, and while she was visibly grieving the loss of her husband, it also appeared that she was upset that her links with Naka Lal's family had been severed. Merki Bai was in effect thrown out of her conjugal home and was forced to return to her natal family. As discussed above, this is indicative of the vulnerable position of Girassia women, who are never fully integrated in their conjugal home and in many cases receive little support of their natal families. However, Merki Bai's family did provide her a place to stay as well as treatment for her back injury, and they drew on their connections to leaders in their village to address Merki Bai's case through both the panchayat and the court.

The Politics of Tribal Leadership

Merki Bai was arrested on the charge of murdering her husband a few weeks after I visited her. In contesting their daughter's murder charge, Merki Bai's parents had the support of Shamboo Singh, their neighbour in Sulav village. Shamboo Singh was the Sarpanch of Sulav and a field-worker of the Bhartiya Janata Party and the Vanvasi Kalyan Parishad. He was also a government schoolteacher. Most villagers in this region are commonly associated with political leaders, who may be one's relatives, neighbors, friends, or work associates. As I have described, these leaders typically belong to a political party; they may be PRI leaders or know people elected to PRIs, and they may also have connections with higher-level political leaders. Tribal leaders often have some kind of government employment and are able to influence government officers and legal practitioners; they may also be associated with social movements or NGOs. Through these connections and associations, tribal leaders are able to help villagers to avail of government schemes and benefits, assist them in their interaction with police and state officers, and represent them if they are involved in a case that comes before the panchayat.

As mentioned above, soon after Naka Lal's death there was a big panchayat meeting in the village of Bilwan; the key participants were Kanshi Lal and Merki Bai's family, and the discussion was presided over by important community leaders. Shamboo Singh told me that prior to this meeting he had come to an agreement with Kanshi Lal to ensure that the latter would not accuse Merki Bai of murdering her husband. Reflecting on the events that followed the panchayat meeting, Shamboo Singh expressed his extreme disappointment that the Sarpanch Kanshi Lal had gone back on his word by mobilizing support among influential BJP leaders and negotiating with the police in order to accuse Merki Bai of murder.

After Merki Bai was arrested I would run into Shamboo Singh in the bazaar and we would talk about the case. Shamboo Singh often spoke of his close associations with Merki Bai's family. He explained that he had known Merki Bai all her life and that she was like a sister to him—it was his duty to help her. Shamboo Singh described Merki Bai as a *bechari* or a helpless girl and spoke about how she was incapacitated from her fall, her husband had died, and her father-in-law had thrown her out of her conjugal home. By referring to Merki Bai as a victim and her family as downtrodden and poor, Shamboo Singh clearly sought to assume the role of the powerful village leader who was the only person capable of finding justice for Merki Bai.

Shamboo Singh fashioned himself as an educated leader who was concerned about the welfare of his community. He depicted his fellow villagers as uneducated, poor, and incapable of negotiating with state officers and manoeuvring their way among corrupt political leaders. While Shamboo Singh represented himself as being responsible for helping villagers to navigate local politics and the state institutions, he portrayed Kanshi Lal as a leader who had gained power almost over-night and had been corrupted by suddenly gaining access to money and resources. Shamboo Singh told me that Kanshi Lal had paid the police to take Merki Bai into custody so that she would become frightened and he would be able to access her money. He went on to assert that Kanshi Lal had violated the decision of the panchayat to frame Merki Bai just so that he could gain access to the paltry sum in her bank account.

Shamboo Singh was able to arrange for a defence lawyer for Merki Bai's case. Through his involvement in previous cases, Shamboo Singh had contacts with a defence lawyer, Suresh Trivedi. Having briefed Suresh Trivedi about the case, Shamboo Singh put Merki Bai's family in touch with him. The lawyer told me that this case would be addressed in a similar way to all other cases in the region, with panchayat meetings and through negotiations between local leaders and police officers. He explained that a court case puts pressure on the leaders of a panchayat to arrive at a decision. If the negotiations are successful, the witnesses will change their testimony, leading to the acquittal of the accused. It was evident that the outcome of Merki Bai's hearing at the Sessions Court in Udaipur city would depend to a large extent on negotiations between political leaders.

Police Practices

Most of the police officers and constables, who were otherwise quite informative and open about their work, were particularly secretive about Merki Bai's case. While discussing this case with two constables at a tea stall in the bazaar one of them, Rajendra Meena, claimed that Merki Bai had a motive for murdering her husband and that she was the last person with him when he passed away. When I asked him whether this was sufficient evidence for a charge, he asserted, 'People like you who come from the city, NGO-wallas, always think that the police are wrong and the police harass women'. 'How would we get our work done if we were soft on everyone? How would we maintain order here?' Rajendra Meena's statement points to how constructions about the mental, social, and physical life of tribals, lower castes, and women generates the idea that certain groups of people must be policed in ways that are an exception to popular imaginings of normative legal procedure. In the making of the criminal case over Naka Lal's death, these practices that were supposedly an exception to the norm included the ways in which police officers colluded with panchayat leaders and followed the directives of panchayat leaders, and the threats and violence that Merki Bai claimed to have faced while she was incarcerated overnight.

Over the course of my fieldwork police officers frequently referred to ideas that point to the incommensurability of different legal systems in order to justify their close interaction with panchayat leaders and to explain why they had to resort to the use of force. Meethu Singh, the Assistant Sub-Inspector of Police, said that in the Raja-Maharaja times, or rule by native kings and princes during the pre-colonial and colonial period, the princes and the British could control caste groups that lived together in villages, but tribals were isolated from other communities and therefore developed their own forms of governance and leadership. He elaborated as follows:

> Slowly they started interacting with others and getting an education, and after independence police and court institutions came up. Now you have a system of the middle path. The police are needed to ensure that people have some fear in their minds, but ultimately the panch [leader of the panchayat] understands the people the best, so the law works in association with the police and the panch.

Meethu Singh proceeded to talk about how the profile of tribal leaders had changed over the last thirty years. He said that now tribal leaders are neither completely educated, nor are they simple farmers. Meethu Singh referred to these leaders as halfway men who enjoyed the support of government schemes and scheduled tribe reservation policies, but who, owing to their incomplete education and integration into the 'mainstream', were vulnerable to all kinds of corruption. Other legal practitioners in Kotra stated a similar point, namely that tribals were no longer primitives living in isolation with their own customary practices and ways of life, nor were they adequately modern citizens fully integrated into a large network of judicial and bureaucratic apparatus.[8] Given this situation, many police officers believed that tribals were most effectively governed by panchayat leaders and customary practices. They viewed their role as being less about enforcing the law than about instilling fear, which involves the use of violence.

Police officers justify their exceptional practices with reference to the fact that they are under pressure from tribal leaders whose demands they are expected to accommodate. Several officers cited the case of a police inspector who committed suicide over a murder investigation involving a man belonging to the Pargi lineage. The accused were boys who were related to Babu Lal Kharadia, the local Member of Legislative Assembly. The victim had been returning home from a manual labour job in Gujarat in order to give money to his sick wife when he was killed. It was believed that the Kharadia boys had given him alcohol and later robbed and murdered him. The Inspector General of Police declared the case a murder investigation and the Kharadia boys were arrested. However, several police officers and constables told me that Babu Lal Kharadia colluded with the Deputy General of Police, who in turn put immense pressure on his subordinate, the Inspector of Police, to reclassify the case as an accidental death and to cover up any evidence to the contrary. Shortly after this, the Inspector of Police was found hanging from the ceiling fan of his office. The police frequently referred to this case and the Inspector's suicide in order to show how they came under pressure from political leaders. The subsequent Inspector of Police, Hanuvant Singh, would tell me that his predecessor committed suicide because of the pressures of being posted among Bhils and Girassias. Yet police officers experience pressure from political leaders throughout the country, not only in the tribal regions. However, by claiming that the Inspector of Police who committed suicide because he came under the pressure of tribal leaders, police officers draw on wider stereotypes that non-tribals hold about how tribals can never be adequate leaders and will always become selfish and corrupt.

Gathering substantial and impartial evidence for Merki Bai's case was low priority for the police, and legal practitioners involved in this case were unconcerned about the due process. In the first place police officers justify practices that are considered exceptional to the norm by invoking ideas about the mental, physical, and social aspects of tribal life.[9] Furthermore, with regard to this specific case they were also influenced by public perceptions that were motivated by high caste assumptions about this case's gender dynamic. Such ideas about corrupt tribal leaders and immoral tribal women are entrenched in the fabric of everyday police work and are reinforced when police officers narrate stories about previous cases. The constables dismissed my question about the nature of evidence gathered for this case by stating that I am an outsider and do not know the constraints they face in policing tribals.

Law, Kinship, and the Justifications of Betrayal

When I returned to Sulav village in 2010 to find out about the outcome of Merki Bai's case, I found out that she had been convicted of murdering her husband, Naka Lal. Over the course of my fieldwork, I had often been told that such convictions were extremely rare in these regions, as panchayat leaders usually arrived at a compromise and many witnesses turned hostile in court. I asked Shamboo Singh about why he was not able to arrive at a compromise and why the defence lawyer, Suresh Trivedi had not been successful at casting doubt on the murder charge. In response, Shamboo Singh narrated an elaborate story about how he had had to stop assisting Merki Bai. According to him, three generations ago, one of Merki Bai's family members married a Girassia woman from a lower *jati*, which, meant he was disinherited of his land and ostracized from his village. For this reason, Shamboo Singh's family did not keep 'relations' with Merki Bai's family, in the sense that they did not eat and drink or enter into relationships of marriage with them. Shamboo Singh proceeded to explain that if he were to continue to assist Merki Bai then people would cast doubt over his intentions and suspect the pair of having an affair. This would tarnish not only his own reputation but also, due to the fact that Merki Bai's family was considered to be of inferior status, that of his family.

In 2010 Shamboo Singh's niece was elected Sarpanch of the Panchayati Raj Institution for Sulav village, making it the third time running that either Shamboo Singh or someone from his family had occupied the role. In the time since my last visit Singh had constructed a large *pucca* house, made of cement and concrete rather, which would have been unaffordable for most tribal and non-tribal families in the area. He was still working as a schoolteacher and as a fieldworker for the Bhartiya Janata Party and had gained greater authority in the village and seemed more secure in his political power. Shamboo Singh informed me that he and Kanshi Lal belonged to the same political party and that they had good relations with each other since they were both Girassias. This was very different from the account he had given in 2006, when he alluded to a sense of betrayal following Kanshi Lal's failure to respect the decision of the panchayat. At that time, Shamboo Singh had referred to Merki Bai as his sister and had made no mention of the fact that her family was supposedly inferior due to a past marriage alliance. While Kanshi Lal had consistently mobilized public opinion by referring to Merki Bai's character, Shamboo Singh had been more concerned about logistics of the case, such as negotiations that took place during the panchayat meeting, the leaders' adherence to the decision of the panchayat, and his own connections with lawyers. Now, however, Shamboo Singh was drawing on Girassia kinship and marriage practices in order to justify why he disassociated himself from the murder case and abandoned Merki Bai.

In a law enforcement context in which criminal convictions are rare, it may well be the case that Shamboo Singh's arbitrary involvement in proceedings played a decisive role in Merki Bai's conviction. On my return to Sulav in 2010, I also met with Merki Bai's father, brother, and brother's wife. Merki Bai's father said that since the case began the lawyer Suresh Trivedi kept asking for more money. They had paid him almost 15,000 rupees in the course of the hearings and could not afford to give him any more. Merki Bai's father had been present during the hearings but he said he had been unable to work out what transpired. In the end, Merki Bai was convicted and sent to the Central Jail in Jodhpur, a city in central Rajasthan. I asked about Shamboo Singh about whether there had been any negotiations or panchayat meetings that took place in the village. At this question he looked particularly distressed; he explained that during Merki Bai's hearings they had relied on Shamboo Singh, but then Kanshi Lal's family had paid him money and he stopped assisting them. 'They bought him over', he said mournfully. There was little that could be done about this; Merki Bai's family was not connected to any other leaders and very few leaders in their village would seek to challenge Shamboo Singh.

Merki Bai's father explained that he felt betrayed by Shamboo Singh. There was very little discussion on this case among other villagers and in the bazaar. While most murder cases continue to be discussed for years after the panchayat and court proceedings are concluded, Merki Bai's case seemed to have been widely forgotten by 2010.

★ ★ ★

With the historical co-emergence and co-production of panchayat and police practices, panchayat meetings are influenced by the ideas and language of state law, while tribal leaders and the decisions of panchayat meetings influence police practices. The making of a criminal case, and the panchayat, police, and court proceedings, depends on how tribal leaders are able to steer negotiations in the panchayat, mobilize public opinion, and influence police practices. Participation in panchayat meetings and connections with police officers are crucial for tribal leaders to gain political power and authority. These processes have resulted in a situation where tribal leaders involve themselves in cases in an arbitrary manner and often for political gain, and it is their prerogative to decide the duration and nature of this association. As the case described in this chapter demonstrates, the support of a tribal leader like Shamboo Singh can have a tremendous bearing on both negotiations at the panchayat level and proceedings in court, and therefore also on the final judgement of a case.

The case described in this chapter demonstrates how tribal leaders must successfully mobilize public opinion in order to determine how events become a criminal case and the direction that the case takes in the panchayat and the court. Tribal leaders and police officers were able to draw on ideas of gender and kinship and the politics of Hindu Nationalism to frame Merki Bai for murdering her husband. These ideas shaped how the intricacies of the case were discussed and debated in the bazaar and also determined the support that Merki Bai and her family received from other villagers.

Karuna Mantena (2010) has shown how in the late nineteenth century British officers instrumentally drew on ideas of tradition and custom in order to justify governing through native authority. These justifications were in the form of 'moral idealism, culturalist explanations, and retroactive alibis', which enabled British officers to expand their authority and spheres of jurisdiction. Today, legal practitioners continue to draw on ideas about tribal difference in order to justify legal practices that are exceptional to the way the law works in other regions in India. Contributions to this volume demonstrate how everyday legal practices in different regions of India differ significantly from proper procedure as outlined in legal manuals and law books. However, by constantly evoking ideas of tribal difference in order to explain supposedly exceptional practices, legal practitioners reinforce ideas about the mental, physical, and social aspects of tribal life and thereby contribute to the marginalization of a particular group of people and place.

Notes

1. Tribal is used here in quotation marks to highlight how colonial forms of knowledge production and practices of state-making have categorized certain groups of people, including Bhils and Girassias, as tribal as opposed to non-tribals, who are usually people of caste society living in the plains (Guha 1999; Skaria 1999; Sundar 1997).

2. The Bhil anti-colonial movement was led by Motilal Tejawat of the baniya money-lending caste from Udaipur. The 'Eka' movement as it came to be known sought to contest British rule and critiqued the practices of local princes and rulers. The British were confronted with large 'mobs' of Bhil people, they had the option of either forcing princes to change their ways or suppressing the

peaceful movement by the use of force (p. 43, Hardiman 2006). The massacre of March 1922 occurred among a gathering of people of forty-two villages in the village of Dhadhav lying on the border between Gujarat and Rajasthan. There was no acknowledgement of the Bhils who were killed during in the Dhadhav massacre by either Congress workers in Mewar or elsewhere.

3. Captain John L. Brooke to Cool. G.L. Lawrence. No. 56 of 1866, National Archives of India.

4. In 1952 the only reference to a system of governance through panchayats was in part 4 of the Directive Principles of State Policy, which were not legally enforceable.

5. Adivasi groups draw on translational discourses of indigeneity, however in their everyday ideas and mobilization strategies, these groups employ the language of reform movements, the nationalist movement, farmers' campaigns of the 1980s, and left-leaning movements.

6. The word *Bai* means sister and is often used in Rajasthan as a sign of respect for a woman.

7. The money allotted for public works under the NREGA is sanctioned through panchayats. The Gram Panchayat is supposed to decide the public work that should be undertaken in a particular village and where it should be located.

8. This view stems from the larger idea, articulated by thinkers like Rousseau, that the primitive emerges from a state of nature and is thus susceptible to all kinds of corruption.

9. There is a parallel here with how colonial officers drew on ideas about the racial and civilizational inferiority of tribals in order to justify the arbitrary use of violence and force and tentative and unstable systems of rule.

References

Cohn, Bernard. 1987. *An Anthropologist among the Historians and Other Essays.* New Delhi and New York: Oxford University Press.

Clarke, Kamari. 2009. *Fictions of Justice: The International Criminal Court and the Challenge of Legal Pluralism in Sub-Saharan Africa,* Cambridge: Cambridge University Press.

Galanter Marc. 1984. *Competing Equalities: Law and the Backward Classes in India.* Berkeley: University of California Press.

Guha, Sumit. 1999. *Environment and Ethnicity in India, 1200–1991.* New York: Cambridge University Press.

Hardiman, David. 2007. *Histories of the Subordinated.* London: Seagull Books.

Mantena, Karuna. 2010. *Alibis of Empire: Henry Maine and the Ends of Liberal Imperialism.* Princeton: Princeton University Press.

Marriott, McKim (ed.) 1955. *Village India: Studies in the Little Community.* Chicago: University of Chicago Press.

Skaria, Ajay. 1999. *Hybrid Histories: Forests, Frontiers, and Wildness in Western India.* New Delhi: Oxford University Press.

Sundar, Nandini. 1997. *Subalterns and Sovereigns: An Anthropological History of Bastar, 1854-1996.* New Delhi and New York: Oxford University Press.

Srinivas, Mysore. 1960. *India's Villages: A Collection of Articles Originally Published in the Economic Weekly of Bombay.* 2nd ed. London: JK Publishers.

Unnithan-Kumar, Maya. 1997. *Identity, Gender and Poverty: New Perspectives on Caste and Tribe in Rajasthan.* Berghahn Books.

7

ZOÉ E. HEADLEY

'The Devil's Court!'

The Trial of 'Katta Panchayat' in Tamil Nadu

One half of the world knoweth not how the other half liveth.

Rabelais (1532)[1]

India's legal landscape presents a rich setting for an analysis of the interplay of differing modes of legal reasoning and procedure. Indeed, over time, Hindu Law, Islamic Law, British Common Law, and a myriad of 'customary' laws have been coexisting and interacting in the settlement of disputes and conflicts. The plurality of legal orders remains a common feature in post-colonial countries (Benda-Beckmann, 2006: 28) and, in India, contemporary research in the field of legal anthropology has primarily been concerned with issues regarding family law, the management of natural resources as well as the political and legal configuration of the Indian State (Eberhart and Gupta, 2005). The issue of the forum shopping strategies between caste-based village judicial assemblies (or caste panchayats) and official law, once a popular research theme, has been largely left out in recent scholarship and furthermore there are virtually no up-to-date investigations exploring the contemporary structure and procedures of local caste-panchayats, besides a few notable exceptions.[2] Hence, the latest shift in the relationship between the State and village society in matters of legal reasoning and processes has largely gone unresearched. This chapter examines the bitter encounter that is taking place between the Indian judiciary and caste panchayats. This encounter has taken the form of a trial, both literal and figurative, in the course of which the apotheosized judicial assembly of 'village India' has metamorphosed into a modern-day feudal kangaroo court: the 'katta panchayat'.

And indeed, over the last decade, a new definition of the panchayat is being constructed as several states across India have exposed, through the voice of the judiciary, the pervasive hold of caste customs on many of its rural citizens. The most widely reported caste assemblies are the ill-famed Khap Panchayats, found mainly in the Jat belt,[3] which have been known to advocate heinous murders as a sanction for same *gotra* marriages in the name of honour.[4] However, a lesser-known scenario has been unfolding beyond the Vindhyas which also displays the disjunction between State law and caste custom, though on a very different note. Indeed, in Tamil Nadu, a number of court cases, both civil and criminal, have castigated the procedures and the judgements delivered by caste panchayats, labelled 'katta panchayats'[5], as 'nauseating'[6] and 'sadistic'.[7] The media, which has characterized these judicial assemblies as the embodiment of 'the devil's court',[8] has been instrumental in sending the 'caste-ridden village' back in the docks. Though the trial of caste panchayats has taken on a national dimension, I focus mainly here on the unfolding of its Tamil scenario largely constructed, as I will show, on a constitutional void, the creation of a spurious concept and a sociologically unsound amalgam.

I will begin my inquiry by defining what I do not mean here when using the term 'panchayat' and briefly explore the main stages of the process which led caste panchayats to disappear from the public gaze in the post-colonial setting. I will then examine a matrimonial dispute, *Rajendran v. the State* (2003), whose facts in themselves were quickly forgotten but which brought the caste panchayats back into the limelight and straight into the docks. Several striking features of this case will be considered closely, such as the absence of any regulations or legislations bearing on the (extra) judicial activities of panchayats and its interesting outcome through a process of State sponsored 'mediation', which some characterised as 'judges and lawyers just doing their own panchayat!'. In the third section, I study the aftermath of Rajendran v. the State, namely the construction of a spurious label, that of 'katta panchayat' that has come to be used as a synonym for 'criminal caste panchayat'. Then by looking at the press coverage (2003 to 2011) of the trials of so-called 'katta panchayat', I examine in which way they have come to be seen as a southern variant of the infamous Khap panchayat. In the fourth and final section of this chapter, I shift my attention back to the main features of the very first Tamil case (*Rajendran v. the State*) but this time around examining them in the light of the opinion and representations voiced by villagers from south-central Tamil Nadu for whom the panchayat constitutes, still today, a valid forum of conflict resolution.

The Panchayat: Imagined, Lost, and Found?

> *Nothing in India is identifiable, the mere asking of a question causes it to disappear or to merge in something else.*
> E.M. Forster, *A Passage to India* (1924).[9]

As one of the quintessential representation of eternal India, the panchayat has drawn over the last two centuries a considerable amount of attention from colonial administrators, nationalists, politicians, and researchers, each defining the panchayat according to the specificities of the local configurations they observe(d) as well as their own personal, ideological, and political agenda. The trajectory of the 'panchayat' is deeply intertwined with those of 'caste' and 'village' which, taken together, have shaped much policy and ideology in the subcontinent since the advent of direct rule in the mid nineteenth century.

Given the many incarnations, both past and present, taken on by the 'panchayat', it is essential to clarify which 'panchayat' is being referred to. This may be somewhat cumbersome but necessary as this chapter juggles directly with three understandings of the 'panchayat' and, in passing, refers to several others while trying to unravel the making of its most recent definition. It is important to note that two post-colonial formulations of the panchayat are not being addressed here: on one hand, the state sponsored panchayats (PRI, that is Panchayatti Raj Institution) which do not legally hold any judicial function and, on the other, the Nyaya Panchayat project which had aimed to invest (limited) judicial powers at the village level.

The 'panchayats' I have studied in villages of south-central Tamil Nadu are caste-based informal judicial assemblies arbitrating conflicts at the village level. An issue arises as to how to label these judicial assemblies and by choosing to use the term caste panchayats I have not fully resolved this problem. The simple solution of translating from the vernacular is not satisfactory as Tamil villagers often use the same term 'pañcāyattu', its exact meaning revealed by the context in which they enunciate it. The compound term 'village panchayat' leads to confusion with the PRIs as well conjuring the imagery of Charles Metcalfe's little republics. Affixing the adjective 'traditional' is an option but its implications detrimental to our understanding of the contemporary features of panchayats. A more recent coinage, 'non-state panchayat', is convenient and fashionable however I am reluctant to define the 'traditional-village-caste panchayat' as negating or operating outside the influence of the State. In Tamil Nadu, caste panchayats have most certainly changed considerably over the centuries but they not only pre-exist the nation-state and the colonial administration but were periodically recognized as an autonomous judicial body as such by local authorities. Many more options are possible ('community panchayat-tribunals-assemblies, community based adjudicatory system', 'customary village councils', etc...), all of them with their drawbacks. I have chosen to use 'caste panchayat', which is also not entirely satisfactory. Indeed it to draws to mind *single* caste judicial assemblies as opposed to multi-caste village panchayats which, though scarce, *do* exist, in Tamil Nadu.

Though I will begin my enquiry here in 2003, when the caste panchayats returned to the public gaze (with the first trial against Tamil panchayattars), it is important to indicate the main stages of the process by which, shortly after the time of Independence, they disappeared from the view of the court, the media as well as, by and large, academia. The scope of issues to be addressed is too broad to be examined in detail, however a few salient points will be of value to understand how the apotheosized assembly of the village republic of the early 20th century has morphed into a demonized kangaroo court in the 21st century.

For most of the 19th century, the British colonial administration took the view of caste as a self-governing body entitled to adjudicate according to custom. As early as 1827, caste questions where expressly excluded from the cognizance of civil courts[10] after which very little efforts was made to gather any further knowledge on these issues. Caste panchayats disappeared further from the view of the colonial State at the beginning of the 20th century when the 1911 Census,[11] which took a special interest in the question of village 'government' or 'tribunals', returned that it had failed to encounter, or only too rarely 'village panchayats'. Though there were numerous reports of 'caste tribunals', they were according to the census report a poor reflection of the assemblies of (the romanticized) village self-rule[12] and therefore were largely discarded as discrete corporate institutions gangrened by factional agendas.

Carried forth by Gandhian ideology, the fantasy of the village republic gained momentum in the pre-Independence decades whilst at the same time the category of 'caste' came under increasing attack. Shortly following Independence, two significant events occurred which erased the caste panchayat from public debate as well as from the legislative and judiciary agendas. Firstly, the casteless society rhetoric was enshrined in the Constitution and by and large, as Galanter (1963) indicates, legislatively, and judicially the caste issue became largely an untouchability issue. Secondly, the fantasy of the village self-rule was given a democratic avatar in 1957 when the idea of a third tiers in government was proposed by Balwantrai Mehta to give villagers the political and financial means to take responsibility of village development through the constitution of an elected local body. As the developmental ideal of the Panchayati Raj lead an uneven career,[13] partly succeeding in some states, faltering in others, the drive to create a judicial branch (Nyaya Panchayat Project) to these local bodies almost constantly failed.[14]

Besides these different attempts to give a democratic existence to the 'panchayat' in post-colonial India, which concealed ongoing caste panchayats from the public debate, the trends that shaped South Asian anthropology during the same period also jeopardized the study of caste panchayat. Indeed, in the late 1950s, the 'village' was declared an inadequate unit of study[15] and brought to a halt the production of classic village monograph which afforded us glimpses of empirically grounded data on caste panchayats. Then, two decade or so later, the assault on orientalist modes of production of knowledge contributed to relegate the study of caste panchayat in the dustbin of social anthropology, along with other malign colonial constructs.[16]

Rajendran v. the State

The gulf between traditional values and governmental values, as embodied in the Indian Constitution is nowhere more clearly seen than in the concept of 'justice'.

Robert D. Baird (2001:338)

In Tamil Nadu, the process of criminalization of caste panchayats and the so-called customary laws they are believed to enforce sparked off when the printed press disclosed the following story in October 2003:

Govt to Ban Punishment by Panchayats

The Tamil Nadu government is contemplating a legislation banning the activities of community panchayats which sit on judgement over local disputes and hand out indiscriminate punishments, some of them cruel and humiliating.

The move comes in the wake of a suggestion from Justice M Karpagavinayagam of the Madras High Court. On Sept. 29, while hearing the bail application moved by the office-bearers of Valayapatti panchayat, the Village Administrative Officer (VAO) and others, who made a woman prostrate for a whole day in a matrimonial dispute, the judge had regretted the trend of imposing illegal and inhuman punishment by community panchayat. The Valayapatti village panchayatdars had imposed a fine of Rs.50,000 on Suganthi. She had to prostrate for a whole day till the amount was reduced to Rs.19, 085.75. For each prostration, Rs.9.75 was reduced from the fine amount. The judge had stated that sitting under the banyan tree, the panchayatdars delivered judgements giving punishments and imposing fines.

In yet another instance last week at Velanur village in Pudunaduvalur panchayat of Perambalur district, two girls–Chandra (16) and Vembu (15) – both agricultural labourers, were forcibly made to hold burning camphor on their palms to prove their innocence in a theft case. The police arrested three persons including the village priest in the incident.

New Indian Express, Madurai Edition, 10th of October 2003

I will focus here on 'Suganthi's case' (Rajendran v. the State), as it inaugurated an unprecedented trend of criminalizing village judiciary practices in Tamil Nadu. This case will reveal that it was not the individuals involved who were being charged but the institution of caste panchayats as a whole which was put on trial.

Let's begin by reviewing the facts of the case which preceded the panchayat, such as they have been understood by the Madras High Court.

Suganthi (a senior telecom officer) married her husband Rajendran (an engineering graduate) in 1991. Her widowed mother (a headmistress in an elementary school) provided as dowry 25 sovereigns of jewels, 50 000 rupees in cash as well as household articles. However, soon after the marriage, Suganthi's in-laws demanded more money which her mother could not provide. Over the next couple of years Suganthi had two male children and carried on working, handing over her entire salary to Rajendran who, she claimed, did not take good care of her and his offsprings. In 1997, Suganthi's separated from her husband. Rajendran would occasionally visit and threaten to take away the children. In 1999, she made a complaint to the police who sent a warning to Rajendran not to abuse his wife and children and not to take away the children from her. In 1999, she was transferred to Chennai where he never came to see the children nor did he support them. Finally, in March, 2002, she sent a lawyer's notice to her husband, requesting his consent for divorce. Then, the following year, Suganthi was summoned to attend a panchayat convened at the request of her husband. The description of the next sequence of events is taken from the anticipatory bail hearing of the defendants, written by a prominent High Court judge who was appointed to the case:

> This case reflects the shocking episode, wherein one Suganthi and her mother Krishnammal were directed by six persons, claiming themselves to be Kattapanchayatdars of Valayapatti village, who imposed a fine of Rs.50,000/- upon them, for not having complied with their direction to join her husband, and made to repeatedly prostrate before them, in order to reduce the quantum of fine.[...]
>
> (f) On 20.7.2003, she received a telephone call from her mother Krishnammal, stating that the Panchayatdars are convening a panchayat at the instance of her husband and they asked both the mother and daughter to appear before them on 03.08.2003, failing which her mother and herself will be ex-communicated from the village. [...] she went to the village on 03.08.2003. She along with her mother Krishnammal appeared before the Panchayatdars. [...] (h) During the panchayat, the Panchayatdars asked Suganthi why she sent legal notice to her husband for divorce. She explained the position. The Panchayatdars were not satisfied with the explanation. Ultimately, the Panchayatdars gave their verdict, directing Suganthi that she must live with her husband. When she expressed her inability to join her husband, the Panchayatdars, alternatively, directed her to pay Rs.50,000/- as fine, for not complying with their direction. When she said that she was not having that much of money, they said that she and

her mother could prostrate before them as many times as they could and, for each prostration, the fine amount would be reduced proportionately. They also threatened both Suganthi and her mother that unless they do it, they will be excommunicated and her mother, who is residing alone in the village, will not have any relationship with the other families in the village. Feeling apprehensive over the consequences, both of them agreed to prostrate before the Panchayatdars. Mother Krishnammal prostrated three times before the Panchayatdars. More than that, she, being an old lady, could not continue. Suganthi prostrated before the Panchayatdars from 10.00 a.m. to 05.00 p.m. Calculating the number of times she prostrated, the Panchayatdars reduced the fine and finalised the same at Rs.19,058.75. Suganthi was directed to pay the said amount on the same day, or else, Suganthi and her mother would be tied to the temple post. Finding no other way, Suganthi collected Rs.10,000/- from her relative Ramachandran and balance amount from one Anandan, her aunt's husband, and paid the amount of Rs.1 9,058.75 to the Panchayatdars on the same day. Even then, the Kattapanchayatdars gave a further verdict, directing Suganthi to come back to the village on 10.08.2003, along with her two children, to produce before them, in order to hand over the custody of the children to her husband.

(i) Having suffered mentally and physically at the hands of mighty people, she came to Trichy, met the Superintendent of Police and presented the complaint. The same was registered in Crime No.7/2000 of All Women Police Station, Musiri Taluk for the offences under Sections 498-A, 342, 384, 385, 406, 506(i) and 149 I.P.C. against 12 persons.

The case was registered against the seven men who took part in the panchayat, as well as Suganthi's husband, her mother-in-law, two brothers-in-law and another male relative. The nature of the seven offences registered against the defendants under the IPC reveal that there are no legislations regulating or banning caste panchayats. So, in effect, legally speaking, the judiciary could not indict the holding of a panchayat *per se*. Instead, the court had to determine specific intentions and actions having occurred during the panchayat which constitute criminal offenses in the purview of Indian law. For instance, section 498 (A) of the IPC seeks to protect women harassed by their husbands and in-laws and has been used more especially in the tragic context of dowry death.[17] In Suganthi's case, reference to section 498 (A) inculpated her husband and in-laws for alleged cruelty and harassment. The seven panchayattars were also booked under this section for coercing her and her mother to meet their demands. Section 342, which punishes 'wrongful confinement', was applied in view of the obligation imposed on Suganthi to remain an entire day in the presence of the panchayattars. The fine imposed by the panchayattars was made punishable under section 384 which considers 'extortion' as well as section 385 covering 'extortion by the threat of death or grievous injury', referring here to the threat of excommunication and the threat of being tied to the temple post. Section 406 deals with 'criminal breach of trust' which punishes offences related to 'embezzlement'. The panchayattars verdict forcing Suganthi to pay the fine the very same day was penalized under section 506 (i) for 'criminal intimidation'. Finally, the last section, section 149, punishes 'unlawful assemblies'. Despite its wording, this section does not refer to panchayats but 'presence at the scene of a crime', thereby condemning Suganthi's in-laws presence during the panchayat proceedings.

At the very first court appearance (29th of August 2003), Justice Karpagavinayagam caught hold of the legal vacuum surrounding caste panchayats.[18] He immediately appealed to the Tamil government to pass an ordinance to criminalize participation in these extra-judicial fora. However, the government's reaction was non-committal. Rather than passing a new legislation, the response was to make 'the existing provisions more effective' by giving 'specific directions' both to the police and to government servants. In a letter sent to the Director General of Police and to all District Collectors on the 25th of November of the same year, the government intimates that 'action should be swiftly taken whenever receiving complaints by the public affected by judgements awarded by local panchayat ('Katta Panchayat')' and that 'a report may be sent to the Government urgently'.[19]

A week later, a fresh set of instructions was sent off to all levels of the Tamil administration from the Chief Secretary of the Government titled 'Prohibition of Government Servants' from convening and participating in 'Katta Panchayats Instructions Issued'.[20] The *Tamil Nadu Government Servants Conduct Rules* (1973) does not explicitly contain any prohibition from taking part in any panchayat. However, rule 20 (1) states that 'every member of the service shall at all times maintain absolute integrity and devotion to duty and shall do nothing which is unbecoming of a member of service'. This rule was explicitly reinterpreted by the Tamil government as signifying that 'the involvement of Government servant in 'katta panchayats' has to be considered a violation of the above said rule [and] any violation of this instruction should be viewed seriously and necessary disciplinary action taken'.[21] Then again, two days later, a circular memorandum was sent by the Director General of Police ordering all superintendants and commissioners of police to submit a monthly report of action taken on the subject of 'katta panchayat'.

The absence of any legislation making panchayats a cognizable offense and the rather weak reaction of the government to this legal vacuum prompted the court to ask the help of the Advocate General[22] to assist in deciding the case. He, in turn, appointed an amicus curiae[23] to look deeper into the matter as well as to deal with the numerous letters ('hundreds and hundreds') which were sent to the court by the public complaining of ordeals similar to that of Suganthi. Besides the offenses listed in the F.I.R.,[24] the amicus curiae identified other existing legal provisions to corner caste panchayats from several sides. She evoked further sections of the IPC (323, 352, 341, 389, 508, and 509) as well as offenses listed under recent acts aimed at protecting the weaker sections of society, namely women and Dalits: Scheduled Castes and Scheduled Tribes–Prevention of Atrocities- Act (1989), the Tamil Nadu Prohibition of Harassment on Women Act (1998), articles 21, 23, 25 and 51 A of the Indian Constitution,[25] as well as quoting seven cases, referring more especially to 1997 (6) SCC 241 (Vishaka v. State of Rajasthan).[26]

Though Suganthi's FIR was directed at the panchayattars and her husband's family, the attention of the court rapidly shifted away from these individuals. The case made by their counsel was that her clients *did* commit the offences for which they were charged but that they *could not* be held accountable given their ignorance of the law. This line of defense was accepted by the judge both as a credible and an accurate interpretation of the facts. Therefore, despite the strong stand taken by the judge against the practice of the panchayattars which he described in the harshest terms ('shocking episode', 'unfortunate victim', 'preposterous explanation', 'seriousness of the allegations', 'the obnoxious practice of imposing punishments', etc.), he will not seek to condemn the 12 individuals 'since both the perpetrators and victims are ignorant of laws regarding Kattapanchayats'. Instead, he initiated within the court a conciliation proceeding between both parties, which he described to me in the following terms: *'I myself made a panchayat between husband and wife by joining them together to find a compromise; this is also panchayat but not katta panchayat'* (Justice Karpagavinayagam, 23rd of March 2009). He convinced Suganthi to withdraw her complaint not only against the panchayattars but also against her husband and in-laws. In return he asked them to return the sum of the fine and to individually offer formal apologies inside the court to the daughter and her mother. In the judge's opinion, this was the best possible outcome for a matrimonial dispute.

Despite harsh words and damning catchphrases describing the actions of Suganthi's panchayattars, this first ever trial of the panchayat did not land a sensational verdict and its outcome, interestingly, was not reported by the Press. Ironically, the trial of the *out-of court* panchayat was dealt with an *in-the-court* panchayat and the 12 defendants were released without further charges. However, the trial of the institution they stand for had not ended. And the judge was very clear about this: '*while considering the issue* [Suganthi's complaint] *this Court has to take up the other issue, which has become the main issue* [...] : *the mushroom growth of Kattapanchayats, which are prevalent all over Tamil Nadu, posing a challenge to the law enforcing agencies*' (Justice Karpagavinayagam, 4th of April 2004). However, as shown earlier, the court failed to elicit a strong response from the Tamil government. In his closing statements, the judge mused over the legal void which surrounds panchayats: '[...] *the existing provisions are nothing but dead laws, which have not been given life. There is no answer as to why the officials concerned have not curtailed this inhuman practice, which is prevalent all these years, in spite of the prevalent statute preventing the same. Is it due to ignorance of law or due to inability to execute the law?*' Despite letting off the defendants and being let down by the State, the judge laid the foundation for the criminalization of panchayats.

Bad Justice and the Evils of Caste: The Making of the Katta Panchayat

Une croyance est parvenue ici à constituer son objet.

Louis Dumont (1967)[27]

As I briefly evoked in the introduction of this chapter, over the last century, the 'panchayat' has come and gone from public debate taking on, each time it re-appears, different guises. Suganthi's case set the stage for a previously unknown incarnation of the 'panchayat' in Tamil Nadu, a far cry from its romantic or developmental avatars. This new definition of the panchayat, after being confined for several years to Tamil Nadu, gradually gained the attention of highest ranks of the Indian State (the Supreme Court, the Law Commission, the Lok Sabha, etc...) as a pan-Indian criminal phenomenon to be eradicated.

A key component in the production of this new definition of the panchayat and an essential feature in the process of criminalization of Tamil village judicial procedures lies, as I have already suggested, in the label they are now given as 'katta panchayat'. It is important to consider the meaning of this term as its usage is not innocuous and has served as a smoke screen concealing the day-to-day socio-legal reality of (Tamil) village judicial procedures.

To understand this, let us return to Suganthi's case. In the first weeks following her FIR against the panchayat convened at her husband's request, the terms that appear to characterize it are that of 'community panchayat' or, less frequently, 'village justice'. As often in India, the term 'community' stands here as a synonym of 'caste'.[28] However, the caste factor is absent from Suganthi's case[29] and will only emerge as a defining feature of the criminal panchayat later, as we will see further down. Within four month or so of the beginning of the case, the rather politically correct the term 'community' gives way to a new formulation, that of 'katta panchayat', an ambiguous label which the judge and more widely the Tamil government administration[30] will use to designate caste-based non-state village judicial assemblies. However, in the rural parts of Tamil Nadu, this term did not, *and still does not*, hold the same meaning and value.

A 'katta panchayat', as understood by villagers in south-central Tamil Nadu, while I was conducting my PhD fieldwork (2000–2004) and more recently during research on conflict management (2009–2012), was that of an informal and sometimes (but not always) criminal organization which has neither official recognition nor local legitimacy. Very different types of organizations are labelled 'katta panchayats', ranging from small intimidation groups operating within the framework of a legal organization (such as a caste association promoting youth activities or local customs) through to small criminal organizations involved locally in the production and/or traffic of illicit liquor, of marijuana, etc. The common denominator between them is that of interfering, generally forcefully, in conflicts thereby constituting a third forum in the arena of dispute management competing both against caste panchayats and state law. A 'katta panchayat' would therefore constitute a possible recourse for a person involved in a conflict whereby in exchange of a fee and/ or loyalty, these katta panchayattars can interfere either alone or with a group of locally recruited young men in order to intimidate the opposing party by their sheer presence and even to directly engage in physical conflict. According to my observations in central Tamil Nadu, recourse to a 'katta panchayat' as described above is done in a relatively discreet or even secretive manner as it constitutes not only a punishable offence but also it is strongly disapproved of by the local community. Also, during the first years of my PhD (1999–2003), the term 'katta panchayat' was occasionally found in the printed press loosely designating the shady politician-underworld nexuses in Chennai involved in property disputes, business rivalries and debt collection.[31]

An investigation into the literal meaning of the term 'katta panchayat' does not determine who, of the villagers or the judge, is using the term appropriately. A search in the Tamil lexicon was inconclusive as it offers seven entries for *katta* covering over 16 different meanings and many with derogatory connotations, several of which may apply: 'staged', 'filthy', 'rough', etc., and a discussion with several linguists could not resolve the issue.[32] Similarly, when I questioned villagers in south-central Tamil Nadu on the meaning of the term, they would only offer a series of derogatory adjectives ('bad', 'illegal', criminal', 'not good', etc.,) but no clues as to its literal meaning. Given these ethnographic and linguistic details, the characterization of Suganthi's panchayat in the court proceedings as being a *'classic example'* of what *'is popularly called as kattapanchayat'* (§8) or again the description of the defendants as *'claiming themselves to be Kattapanchayatdars'* (§1) reveals either a lack of awareness of rural social life or deliberate disparagement. The caste panchayat was further lost in translation when, several months later, the term 'katta panchayat' came to be used interchangeably with the equally opprobrious English term 'kangoroo court'[33] whose purpose was said to carry out 'jungle law'.

As I mentioned in the beginning of the chapter, the idea and representations of the panchayat, whichever its understanding, has always been intimately linked with two concomitant categories of thought that have shaped much scholarly and political debate in India, that of the 'village' and of 'caste'. In the press coverage dealing with the trials of caste panchayats, from Suganthi's case onwards, one gets the sense that the backward caste-ridden village has raised its ugly face again and that, much to the media' s shock, medieval justice is the stock-in-trade of panchayattars. The label 'katta panchayat' and the characterization of village judiciary practices, by the judge in Suganthi's case, as 'nauseating and barbaric' echoed through the columns of the printed press as a potent reminder of Ambedkar's famous characterization of village life as 'nothing but a sink of localism, a den of ignorance, narrow-mindedness and communalism' (November 4th, 1948). Following Sunganthi's case, the sociological content fitted under the label 'katta panchayat' was largely supplied in articles, such as these:

'Village justice system in TN shocks HC'(*Deccan Herald*, Chennai edition 25/10/03)

'Outlaw Kangaroo courts, says Madras HC' (*Deccan Herald*, Chennai edition 14/04/04)

'Devil's Court' (*New Indian Express*, Madurai edition 20/07/05)

'Officials summoned over katta panchayat' (*The Hindu* 28/10/05)

'Katta Panchayat rampant in Dharmapuri district' (*The Hindu* 08/02/06)

'Katta Panchayat excommunicates 5 fishermen's families' (*The Hindu* 10/06/06)

'Katta panchayat system prevalent in 30% of villages' (*The Hindu* 24/11/06)

'Panchayat slaps fine on activists for reporting barbaric custom' (*The Indian Express* 31/12/07)

'Spreading menace' (*Frontline* 11–24 April 2009)

'Take action against katta panchayat gang' (*Express News Service* 17/12/09)

'Medieval justice: Kangoroo courts call the shots in TN' (*Times of India*, 16/06/10)

Several features (something contradictory) are recurrent throughout the articles published from 2003 onwards and, given the lack of research in this field, these have come to constitute the sociological definition the 'katta panchayat'. These features are namely that: 'katta panchayats' are found only in villages, that they are a recent phenomenon spreading fast or, alternatively a relic of the feudal past, their very existence is a slur to democracy as they uphold caste discrimination and target the weaker section of society (i.e. women and dalits). Regarding the men who compose the 'katta panchayats', they are sometimes portrayed as bored and illiterate old men or oppositely as young opportunistic criminals.

Despite this damning definition of the 'katta panchayat' and its peri-
odical materialization in Tamil Nadu, here in a courtroom, there in an
article, no decisive move was made by the government for several years
until it was found that the 'katta panchayat' had a fearsome counterpart, the khap panchayat, in north India.[34] The landmark case which
brought the Khap Panchayats in purview of the law was the gruesome
murder of Manoj and Babli which took place in Haryana in 2007. In
these regions, where village exogamy prevails, intra gotra (exogamous
patrilineal clans) marriage is prohibited. Manoj and Babli, both Jats
from the same village (Banwala gotra) eloped to marry without their
families' consent. Babli's relatives asked for the help of their local Khap
panchayat which, allegedly, ordered the killing of the newlywed who
were brutally murdered in June 2007.[35]

Suganthi's divorce (2004) and Manoj and Babli's murder (2007) both
inaugurated, in their respective regions, the trial of caste panchayats.
For a couple of years each followed their own separate trajectories
through the courts and the columns of the printed press. In the case of
the Khap panchayats, the central issue was not, as was the case in Tamil
Nadu, that (Khap) panchayattars were taking law into their own hands
in matters relating to civil law, but that they appeared to be instrumental
actors in honour killings.

The tide changed for 'katta panchayats' when the press disclosed that
'honour killings' were not only to north India but apparently deeply
entrenched in Tamil culture. The first of such report was published in
the summer of 2009 by a seasoned journalist known for his sensitive
and well researched investigations on social issues in the rural parts of
Tamil Nadu. In his article entitled 'Demons and Gods. Honour killings
in India are not confined to the northern states: Tamil Nadu has a long
history of such violence' he begins by focusing on recent murders of
eloping (inter-caste) couples and then moves on to describe the religious practice of deification of women who encountered untimely and
violent deaths.[36] Though the author never mentions any case of (Tamil)
caste panchayats ordering or carrying honour killings, the title (giving
an implicit reference to the Khap panchayats) and structure of the
article suggest the amalgam between the acts of khaps and the 'katta
panchayats'. The article set a precedent and more articles followed:
'Seven honour killings in 12 weeks: Tamil Nadu does it too' (*Tehelka*),
'Tamil Nadu katta panchayats rival Khaps' (Deccan Chronicle), etc....

Details, such as that in the north India, the murder of eloping couples is carried out against intra-gotra couples whereas in the south it occurs against inter-caste couples are not considered and, more importantly the fact that there has not been any case registered against (Tamil) caste panchayattars in connection with honour killings has been completely overlooked. More generally, historical and sociological differences between Khap panchayats and its supposed Dravidian counterpart have not been addressed (by the media, the judiciary or academia) and neither have the norms which govern the breaching of caste custom in terms of marriage been explored in a comparative manner. However, since both khap panchayat and 'katta panchayats' are viewed as illegal caste-based institutions which thrive in villages and rural areas, the die has been cast. The new definition of the criminal panchayat is now fully accepted as we can see from an excerpt of an important judgment from the Supreme Court of India in May 2011 which was extensively reported by the press: *'We have in recent years heard of "khap panchayats" (known as katta panchayats in Tamil Nadu), [...] we are of the opinion that this is wholly illegal and has to be ruthlessly stamped out'.*[37]

Meanwhile under the Banyan Tree...

May those of our descendants who do not honour this be as guilty as for the murder of a Brahman or of the black cow.
Imprecation from the Pramalai Kallar headman's charter, 1655

The trial of Tamil village judicial assemblies, as I have examined so far, has basically taken place *in absentia*. The actual procedures and norms that govern village-based adjudication have been eluded both by the government and the press leaving room for the emergence of a spurious construct, the 'katta panchayat'. In this final section, I want to examine some empirically grounded features of village based adjudication procedures such as I have observed them or as they have been described by panchayattars (pañcāyattār) and villagers of south-central Tamil Nadu.[38] Given the space constraints of this chapter, I will restrict my remarks to a few precise points which have either drawn particular attention from the judiciary or have been significantly misrepresented by the media, namely the nature of the phenomenon, the social profile of the panchayattars and some features of the penalties (fines and social sanctions) delivered by panchayats in the light of those Suganthi was subjected to.

In many, if not most, of the articles and government correspondence covering the issue of the so-called 'katta panchayat', the reader is given the impression that the practice of village and/or caste based adjudication is a recent phenomenon which is rapidly spreading through the countryside. Some articles suggest that this 'village court', a relic from the past, was until recently a defunct institution that was recently revived. Both depictions are seriously flawed, at least for my region of study, as according to my data, as well as that of an extensive survey carried out by 'Evidence', a Madurai-based NGO.[39] Indeed, panchayats have, in the localities where they function, been continuously adjudicating as far back as the older villagers could remember, and in many instances beyond that.[40] Furthermore, I have not chanced upon situations of revival of extinct panchayats but have, quite to the contrary, come across villages where no panchayat had been convened for two, six, fifteen or 30 years. Similarly, the Evidence survey report indicates that in 38 per cent of the 167 villages they surveyed no panchayat had been convened for two years (26 per cent) or longer (12 per cent).[41] Hence, the so-called 'discovery' of the existence of caste panchayats does not reflect a recent emergence or revival of village judicial assemblies nor, as far as I can ascertain, any politicization or radicalization of the panchayat over the last decade, as can be seen to be the case for the khap panchayats.[42] According to Tamil villagers with whom I discussed the reaction of the judiciary and correlative representation of the media, this dismay demonstrated the ignorance, and often contempt, of educated urban people in general and the media in particular, they felt, for the norms and practices that govern daily life in an average Indian village in the 21st century. And, true enough, they cited other instances of articles disclosing backward-rural-practices, which are a rather common genre in the columns of the Indian printed press. Indeed, since the mid-1980s at least, every so often a 'backward', or outright 'barbaric', feature of rural life is 'discovered' and revealed by the Press causing shock and disgust among educated city-dwellers.[43] As Thamizan, a panchayattar from Theni district commented: '[they tell us] don't slaughter goats, don't agitate, don't conduct panchayat and so on. If we pass laws to stop this, I feel that this country is heading towards worst times than under the British'.[44]

So, if a generalization must be made, it is that panchayats are a relatively common but a slowly receding feature of village social life. These panchayats are not held secretly and, during the first few years of my PhD fieldwork (2000–2003), men and women, both young and old, talked openly about how they turned to the panchayat to settle a wide range of conflicts. However, in the aftermath of Suganthi's case and with the repeated threats to criminalize the holding of these judicial assemblies, villagers are now sometimes cautious with an outsider who might be a journalist or an activist in search of the another sensational piece to write on the antiquated values and savage practices of the rural folks. However, once the initial reticence is overcome, the conversation on the topic resumes in a fairly normal manner. And, what is more, panchayats have not gone into hiding: it is still possible to witness panchayat session by chance as you walk through the village as they are still generally held in the open (at the mantai, the cavati, inside or outside the temple, under a large tree, etc.).

The depiction of the panchayattars also displays a certain amount of contradictions, as on one hand they are portrayed as 'bored and illiterate old men deriving sadistic pleasure in delivering absurd punishments' and on the other as 'opportunistic young men extorting money from the gullible and the weak'.[45] The profile of panchayattars is indeed a fascinating issue that addresses the question of the transformation of authority in the village setting, which is too vast and complex to be discussed here at any length. The compositions of the panchayats which I have had the opportunity to study are quite varied and showcase the complexities of the reproduction and transformation of village elites. In many instances, the composition of the panchayats reflects the endurance of former agrarian power structures. For example, in a Killiyapattu, as village north of Madurai, it is the former Zamin, an Anuppa Gounder in his late fifties, who still adjudicates conflicts (around, he claims, 30 panchayats a month) on the veranda of his own residence both for his native place but also the 18 villages that were under his father and forefathers' control. Similarly, the current Pramalai Kallar headman adjudicates within the perimeter of his native (sub) nadu and is also called for in the other seven nadus beyond his immediate jurisdiction, which taken together constitutes Kallar Nadu. In the former case, the Zamin pretty much adjudicates alone, though he will consult with other senior members of the locality. In the latter, the caste headman, though given symbolic and ritual pre-eminence, systematically conducts panchayats with four to six lineage headmen. Oppositely, I have met men who have assumed the function of panchayattars because of their education and their professional success and who are often therefore younger than their peers. This democratization, if you can call it that, of the social status of panchayattars is sometimes viewed with ambivalence by the villagers. On the one hand, it lowers the average age of the panchayattars and enhances both their level of education and urban exposure. These minor transformations are sometimes used by villagers to justify that the panchayat is not just a group of illiterate old people imposing an obsolete form of justice. On the other hand, their age may precisely call into question their experience and authority to exercise justice, an area that was previously reserved to certain senior members of important status from the locality.

The specific of Suganthi's case (a divorce case dealt with by the panchayat, the fine, and prostrations) did not cause particular shock among villagers and panchayattars with whom I discussed the case but instead, as we will see, generated many comparisons with the state judiciary. Overall, for both men and women, the motivations to go before a panchayat, instead of the court, is a pragmatic one often based on straightforward criteria proximity, cost and length, as illustrated by the following comment: 'a wealthy person can afford to take a case to the courts and wait for many years in order to get the judgment. But a poor person cannot afford so much time and money to get justice'.[46] In the panchayats of south-central Tamil Nadu it is a standard penalty to impose a fine on the spouse demanding the divorce regardless of issues of gender. The amount imposed by the panchayat in the case of Suganthi (50 000 rupees) appeared excessive to all the panchayattars I have spoken to, who claimed never to have demanded such a sum from a divorcee. During fieldwork, several women speculated that the fact that Suganthi had only her widowed mother to support her and therefore no male relative to defend her during the panchayat that took place in her husband's native village, certainly contributed to the excessive sum of the fine. For instance, in Usilampatti Taluk (Madurai district), the divorce fine rarely exceeds 9,000 or 10,000 rupees and is more often situated somewhere between 200 and 2000 rupees, depending on the income of the spouse asking for divorce. The Evidence survey report also found fines to be a very common form of punishment, actually the most common, awarded by panchayats (161 villages of 167 returning that the panchayats levies fines for various offences and crimes). The report similarly indicates that the maximum fine imposed in the case of divorce was that of 20 000 rupees, and this only in one village out of 161, the average amount being closer to 5 000 rupees, and going as low as 500 rupees. Only 22 villages from the survey report fines exceeding 10 000 rupees and these mostly concern punishments awarded in cases of rape (on average 50 000 rupees). Besides cases such as divorces, which can and are in many instances be handled by a court of law, villagers pointed out that a number of marital issues can only be brought before the panchayat as they would not be receivable before a court of law. For instance, the refusal of the preferential spouse, which is among many sub-castes considered a violation of an inalienable right, gives rise to proceedings before the panchayats. A dispute over the customary right a man has over his sister's daughter could not be dealt with by the district family court. Another common scenario that comes before Panchayattars is that of adjudicating disputes over excessive or ill-honored dowries, a practice prohibited by law since 1983.[47]

One small detail of Suganthi's case elicited the disproval of the 20 panchayattars gathered together in the workshop. The threat to tie Suganthi to the temple post was seen as outrageous. This practice, they said, is reserved to thieves who are thereby temporarily immobilized pending a decision of the panchayat or the arrival of the police, if they have been called. It is also a means of publicly humiliating the thief who will be taunted and insulted by the villagers. Such a threat was perceived as absolutely uncalled for in Suganthi's case. However, the prostrations, which shocked the press, are a fairly common form of penalty awarded by panchayats. When imposed on the accused, they generally serve the purpose of seeking the forgiveness of the victim, the panchayat or even the locality as a whole. By and large, these prostrations were not perceived humiliating or degrading and several villagers pointed out that they are freely performed in other circumstances (namely in front of elders as a mark of respect or as a form of worship in a temple setting). Several panchayattars interviewed were somewhat bemused by the reaction of the Press to the prostrations being described as a violation of human rights. They readily argued that it does not constitute a form of physical abuse as compared to the violence which is said to commonly occurs in police custody. They claimed further that it is not reserved to women but can be equally imposed on men. Regarding the use of prostrations as a mean to reduce the amount of the fine, I have never personally come across such a practice. As Pichaimani, a panchayattar from a village near Dindigul, explained: 'prostrating before everyone is done to reduce the amount of fine. At first the fine may be Rs.5000 and then when the accused prostrates before everyone and apologises, 100 rupees is reduced and so on. [...] Some villages reduce 1000 rupees when the guilty person prostrates once, but there are villages like Alathur where they reduce only in multiples of hundreds. There are even some villages where no such reductions are possible and therefore, the accused have to pay the entire amount'.

Suganthi and her mother were pressured into abiding by the decision of the panchayat (paying a fine of 50 000 rupees) by the threat of excommunication, that is the ultimate caste sanction.[48] Though Suganthi would have not been particularly affected, as she lived in Chennai, her mother would have suffered greatly from this social ostracism The extent of an excommunication may vary in time (for a month, a year or longer) and intensity: villagers may not be allowed to speak to the excommunicated, shopkeepers not allowed to sell products to them, villagers not allowed to hire them as a labourer, they may be denied participation in family functions and rituals, denied participation in village/caste functions and rituals, denied access to the temple, etc. On several occasions, the practice of excommunication was compared by villagers and panchayattars to that of imprisonment. Imprisonment was felt to be a far more brutal and personally damaging form of punishment than social boycott within a specific locality, as one villager put it: 'if you excommunicate somebody because he has harmed us you punish him but you do not cut him off from his home, from work, from his parents and children. He knows every day that he is ostracized for his mistake but can carry on living among those who can help him improve his life and character so he does not repeat the same mistake'.

The feeling among the men and women interviewed was not that their local panchayat was without evident flaws but that in certain circumstances it was certainly the preferable recourse. Overall, they did not feel that greater harm was committed 'under the banian tree' than inside the district court and certainly much less than behind the doors of a police station. Many panchayattars met during this research agreed that the absence of legal recognition of caste panchayats is becoming problematic but feel that though it may not be the ideal forum for justice it is in many regards certainly no worse than the kind of justice meted out in police stations where people's basic rights are violated in the name of law. The response by panchayattars and villagers was unanimous in refuting the categorization of 'their' panchayats as a 'katta panchayat' and instead directed this derogatory label towards criminal gangs mainly operating in urban areas, but also corrupt police officers and politicians whom, I was told with numerous personal tales, intimidate, extort, and brutalize. The public nature of the panchayat was felt to prevent a large number of abuses which occur behind the closed doors of official representatives of law and order.

Over the last decades, other instances of denunciation of practices perceived to be typically rural and utterly backwards have been countered, sometimes successfully by various means of social mobilization which villagers are familiar with (demonstrations, rallies, associations, petitions, etc...). However, in this case, no demonstration was organized, no petition was written up, and delivered to the local district collectorate to retaliate against the scathing depictions by the press or the courts proposition to ban panchayat activities. This uncharacteristic apathy can be explained by several factors. Firstly, as the press adopted the terminology of the court (i.e. 'katta panchayat'), most panchayattars and common villagers I talked to did not feel personally concerned, as 'katta panchayats' are one thing and *their* panchayat another. Secondly, adding to this lack of identification between what was being depicted in the media and what was being practiced under *their* banyan tree, the heterogeneous nature of panchayats in Tamil Nadu (from a geographical, sociological, and structural point of view) made it near to impossible for individual panchayattars to even begin to think of federating. Thirdly, as the attention of the media did not appear subside and it became clear that the so-called 'katta panchayat' was simply a derogatory way of speaking of their own panchayats, it was thought best to 'keep a low profile' and to keep matters inside the locality. When questioned about this unusual display of passiveness, the response was that it would be fruitless and maybe even risky to speak out.

Indeed, one such an attempt was made early on in Suganthi's case in the popular Tamil weekly magazine *Junior Vikatan* in an article titled 'Village panchayats cannot be crushed!'.[49] In this three page feature, several panchayattars spoke out defending their local judicial practices, disputing their appellation as 'katta panchayats' ('which are those [panchayats] in which bias decisions are made by getting money from one party', ibid, p.15) and criticizing the move by the court to ban panchayats.

However, the court reacted swiftly and categorically. Among the panchayattars interviewed, all three who gave their name (others remained anonymous)[50] were summoned to their respective courts (Sivaganga and Madurai) and threatened to be booked for interference with the administration of justice, the argument being that giving a statement to the media justifying the activities of the panchayats was tantamount to criticizing the view of the Court. Thereafter, to the best of my knowledge, neither panchayattars nor other villagers approached the press to 'answer back'.

★★★

In this chapter I have tried to unravel 'the making' of the most recent incarnation of the panchayat which has come to be defined as an iniquitous caste-based institution meting out bad justice. I have tried to demonstrate that the complex nature of the relations between the State and caste customs in matters of judiciary processes and legal reasoning has been lost in translation as complex morphosociological issues have been replaced by damning catchphrases. The trial–*in absentia*–of the caste-panchayats has revealed little or nothing about the coexistence of different legal orders at the village level but betrays instead the ever deepening urban-rural divide, especially in terms of the value ascribed to caste norms which still govern many social relations in the village setting.

One of the latest legislative developments in the trial of Khap and 'Katta' panchayats has been the drafting of a new bill entitled 'The Prohibition of Unlawful Assembly' in 2011. However, as the subtitle of the bill, 'Interference with the Freedom of Matrimonial Alliances', indicates, its sole target is aimed at preventing honor crimes by protecting intra-gotra and inter-caste marriages[51]. It appears that, despite its shocking return from oblivion into the public gaze, the panchayat has failed to capture, once again, that attention of the State.

Notes

1. Pantagruel ii. xxxii.
2. Pur and Moore (2007), Holden (2004), Vincentnathan (1992, 1996) and in collaboration with Lynn Vincentnathan (1994, 2007, 2009), Chowdhry (2004), and Nagaraj (2012).

3. Namely Haryana, Rajasthan, and western Uttar Pradesh.

4. According to Prem Chowdhry (2007:13), the self-appointed mission of a Khap panchayat is to uphold honour (izzat), brotherhood (bhaichara), community (biradri), and village unity (aika). See also Chowdhry (2004), (2007), (2011), Stig Toft Madsen (1991) and Baxi, Rai, and Ali (2006).

5. I will throughout this chapter keep the term 'katta panchayat' in inverted comas, in order to clearly differentiate its meaning and implications from the caste panchayats.

6. *New Indian Express*, Madurai Edition, 10/10/03.

7. *The Hindu*, Madurai Edition, 18/09/03.

8. *New Indian Express*, Madurai Edition, 20/07/05.

9. Hardgrave (1979: 47).

10. Regulation II of 1827, sec. 21; quoted in Roy (1911), p.108. This regulation, applied in the Bombay Presidency, was extended throughout British India by 1859, Galanter (1963), p. 546.

11. Both in the General Census Report and the Report for the Madras Presidency. Census of India, Part I Report, E.A. Gait. pp. 387–395. For the Madras Presidency: Census of India, Volume XII, Madras, Part I Report by J.C. Molony. Government Press 1912.

12. See Dewey (1972).

13. See Bates (2005).

14. There has been recently an attempt to revive the Nyaya Panchayat project but the latest Draft Bill proposed in 2009 was refused. On the topic of Nyaya Panchayat, see Kushawaha (1977), Baxi and Galanter (1979), Meschievitz and Galanter (1982). Mathur (1997), Bandhopadhyay (2005).

15. Dumont and Pocock, (1957), p.25.

16. Inden (1990) and Dirks (2001).

17. It was introduced in the code by the Criminal Law Amendment Act, 1983 (Act 46 of 1983) and states that 'whoever being the husband or relative of the husband of woman, subjects such woman to cruelty shall be punished with the imprisonment for a term which may extend to three years and also be liable to fine. For the purpose of this section, 'cruelty' means: (a) any wilful conduct which is of such nature as is likely to drive the woman to commit suicide or to cause grave injury or danger to life, limb or health (whether mental or physical) of the woman; or (b) harassment of the woman where such harassment is with view to coercing her or any person related to her meet any unlawful demand for any person related to her to meet such demand.' There has been an ongoing controversy over the possible misuse of section 498 A by women seeking to harass their husbands and in-laws, many associations and websites have appeared appealing against its misuse.

18. Significantly, it is not only the law texts that are devoid of references to the panchayat but the Indian Constitution itself has next to nothing to say

about the place and role of the panchayat in democratic India. As Crispin Bates indicates: the only reference to panchayats at all in the Indian Constitution adopted in 1951 is in Part IV [...] (which is non justiciable), and which merely states that 'the state should take steps to organize village panchayats and endow them with such power and authority as may be necessary to enable them to function as units of self-government' (Bates 2005 : 177).

19. Letter No.7932/2003-3 dated 25/11/2003 from the Secretary to Government to the Director General of Police with copy to All the District Collectors. The parenthesis and quote marks around the term katta panchayat are given by author of the letter.

20. Letter No.53140/A/2003-1 dated 02/12/2003 from the Chief Secretary to Government to All Secretaries to Government.

21. Letter No.53140/A/2003-1.

22. In India, the Advocate General is the senior most advisor to the state government on legal matters.

23. Literally 'friend of the court', [...] one that is not a party to a particular litigation but that is permitted by the court to advise it in respect to some matter of law that directly affects the case in question (definition taken from Merriam-Webster dictionary).

24. F.I.R. stands for 'first information report'. It is the written document prepared by the police when they are given information of a cognizable offence. In the case of cognizable offences, the police can arrest the accused without a warrant and can begin investigation without an order from the court.

25. Articles 21, 23, and 25 come under the Fundamental rights (part III): article 21 deals with protection of life and personal liberties, article 23 with prohibition of traffic in human beings and forced labour and article 25 with freedom of conscience and free profession, practice and propagation of religion. Article 51-A comes under Fundamental Duties (part IV A) and deals with the duties of the citizen.

26. This case prompted the Supreme Court to issue guidelines preventing the sexual harassment of women in the workplace. The other cases quoted are : 1992 (1) SCC 221 (Rajangam v. State of Tamil Nadu) , 1994 (6) SCC 260 (Khedat Mazoor Chetna Sangath v. State of Madhya Pradesh, 1995(1) SCC 14 (Delhi Domestic Working Women's Forum v. Union of India), 1995 (3) SCC 743 (citizens for Democracy v. State of Assam) , 1998(1) SCC 1 (Journal Section-Victims of Crime) , 2001 (5) SCC 577 (Centre of Enquiry into Health and Allied Themes (Cewat) v. Union of India), 2002(3) SCC 31 (Death of 25 Chained Inmates in Asylum Fire in T. N., in R.E. v. Union of India), 2002 (7) SCC 39 (Tarun Bora v. State of Assam).

27. Dumont (1966: 218).

28. The term 'caste' is indeed in many contexts, non-grata whether in writing or in speech and therefore substituted for 'community', this both English

and in Tamil. Unfortunately, a context-sensitive comparative research on the usage of the word 'caste', 'community', 'jati' in Tamil is, to the best of my knowledge yet to be done. I am convinced that such a study would offer valuable insight into perception of the place of caste in contemporary Tamil society.

29. In effect, all panchayattars, defendants, and respondents in this case belong to the same subcaste so the issue of caste discrimination could not be factored in.

30. As found in the official correspondence between various government bodies: Letter No.7932/2003-3 dated 25/11/2003 from the Secretary to Government to the Director General of Police; Letter No.53140/A/2003-1 dated 02/12/2003 from the Chief Secretary to Government to All Secretaries to Government; Circular Memorandum Rc.No.257391/Cr.I (1) 2003 dated 04/12/2003 from the Director General of Police to all authorities concerned.

31. To the best of my knowledge there is no literature on the topic of goondas, gangsters, and corrupt politicians involved in fraudulent land deals in Chennai from the late 1990s. I thank my colleague Aurelie Varrel (CNRS-CEIAS) for her insights on this matter.

32. I thank Dr Jean-Luc Chevillard (CNRS-EFEO), Dr Thomas Lehmann (University of Heidelberg), Dr K. Nachimutu (JNU), and Dr A. Murugaiyan (EPHE-INALCO) for taking the time to think over this issue.

33. According to the *West's Encyclopedia of American Law*, 1998, (edition 2):

> The concept of kangaroo court dates to the early nineteenth century. Scholars trace its origin to the historical practice of itinerant judges on the U.S. frontier. These roving judges were paid on the basis of how many trials they conducted, and in some instances their salary depended on the fines from the defendants they convicted. The term *kangaroo court* comes from the image of these judges hopping from place to place, guided less by concern for justice than by the desire to wrap up as many trials as the day allowed.

34. Throughout this chapter, data on Khap panchayats is drawn namely from the in-depth work of Prem Chowdhry's work (2004, 2007a, 2007b, 2011), but also Stig Toft Madsen (1991) and Baxi, Rai, & Ali (2006).

35. This case was extremely important as the court delivered the first capital punishment for an honour killing.

36. On this topic, see Blackburn (1985).

37. Arumugam Servai v. State of Tamil Nadu on 19th of April 2011 (available on indiankanoon.org).

38. I draw my first-hand information from two sources: firstly, from the fieldwork I have been conducting since 2000 in the districts of Madurai and Sivangangai and secondly, from a two day experimental workshop I organized in 2011 in collaboration with S. Ponnarasu and with the help of the EAP 458 team which brought together some 20 panchayattars from the districts of

Madurai, Theni and Dindigul (supported by the IFP, CEIAS-CNRS and Just-India). All names of people and places drawn for my data have been changed. Also of interest are the results of an in-depth research project titled 'Formal and Informal Governance in India' (University of Sussex) conducted between 2001 and 2005 in 30 villages of three districts of Karnataka; see Ananth Pur and Moore (2007).

39. Evidence, conducted an extensive survey in 2010 in 167 villages of 5 districts of south-central Tamil Nadu. Though the purpose of my own study and that of the NGO differ substantially, their purpose was to track down 'Caste panchayats and its violations', we have in numerous instances asked very similar questions to the villagers and, in several cases, in the same villages!

40. I am able to substantiate this statement for at least 20 villages where documents relating to village judicial assemblies going back a century and a half have been digitized (projects EAP 314 ' Rescuing Tamil Customary Law' and EAP 458 'Constituting a Digital Archive of Tamil Agrarian History'). For more information, see the website: http://clac.hypotheses.org/

41. Evidence Study Report, question 3.28, pp. 103–110.

42. For instance, some Khap panchayats have in recent years demanded amendments to the Hindu Marriage Act (1955) to prevent same-gotra marriages (*sagotra*), requested the status of Lok Adalat and, more worryingly defended the principal of honor killings, proposed child marriage as a remedy to prevent rape, etc.

43. Such as female infanticide/foeticide, two-tumbler systems, animal sacrifice, deadly bull races (*jallikattu*), senicide, etc.

44. 'Ennamo ponga, keta vettakkudatu, poratakkudatu, panchayattu pecakudatu, ippati catam potta, vellaikkaran kalattaivitu mocama intu natu poyittirukkonu ninaikku vendi irrukku', interview given in Junior Vikatan, 08th of October 2003, p.1.6

45. Theses depictions are not actual full-length quotes but my own assemblage of different descriptions found in the printed press.

46. Alagappan, expressing himself during the experimental workshop on Tamil customary law. 15th of November 2011.

47. See endnote 17.

48. Numerous ethnographies of the 1960s and 1970s make passing notes or comments on caste excommunication. For more indepth comments see Dumont (1970) and, for an alternative conception, Hayden (1983).

49. 'Nattu panchayattukalai nacukka mutiyatu' Junior Vikatan, 08th of October 2003, pp. 14–16. The term actually used is not '*village* panchayat' but 'nadu panchayat'.

50. K.R.Ramasamy (INC) who, at the time, was M.L.A. of Thiruvadanai Constituency, Periyakaruppan (DMK), Tamilarasan (DMK).

51. ' [...] no person or any group of persons shall gather with an intention to deliberate on, or condemn any marriage, not prohibited by law, on the basis that such marriage has dishonored the caste or community tradition or brought disrepute to all or any of the persons forming part of the assembly or the family or the people of the locality concerned.'

References

Book and Journal Articles

Ananth Pur, K. and Moore, M. 2007. 'Ambiguous Institutions: Traditional Governance and Local Democracy in Rural India'. IDS Working Paper 282. Brighton: Institute of Development Studies of the University of Sussex.

Baird, R.D. 1998. 'Traditional Values, Governmental Values, and Religious Conflict in Contemporary India', *Brigham Young University Law Review*, 2: 337–57.

Bates, C. 2005 .'The Development of the Panchayati Raj', in C. Bates Crispin and B. Subho (eds) *Rethinking Indian Political Institutions*, C., pp.169–84. London: Anthem Press.

Baxi, U, and Galanter, M. 1979. 'Panchayat Justice: An Indian Experiment in Legal Access', in M. Cappelletti and B. Garth (eds) *Access to Justice: Vol. III: Emerging Issues and Perspectives*. Milan: Alphen aan den Rijn: Sijthoff and Noordhoff.

Baxi, P., Shirin M. Rai & Shaheen Sardar Ali. 2006. 'Legacies of Common Law: 'Crimes of Honour' in India and Pakistan', *Third World Quarterly*, 27 (7): 1239–53.

Baxi, Upendra. 1982. *The Crisis of the Indian Legal System: Alternatives in Development: Law*. New Delhi: Vikas.

Benda-Beckmann (von), K. and Benda-Beckmann (von), F.(eds). 2006. Dynamics of Plural Legal order', *The Journal of Legal Pluralism and Unofficial Law* (Special double issue) 53–4.

Blackburn, S. 1985. 'Death and Deification: Folk Cults in Hinduism', *An International Journal for Comparative Historical Studies Chicago*, 24 (3): 255–74

Bonnan, Jean-Claude. 1999. Les Jugements du Tribumal de la Chaudrie de Pondichery : 1766–817. Vol. 1&2. Pondichery: IFP-EFEO.

Bavinck, Maarten, Derek Johnson, Oscar Amarasinghe, Sarah Southwold, and Janet Rubinoff.'Governance of a Patchwork Kind - A comparative Analysis of legal Pluralism in the Management of Fisheries in South Asia', paper presented at the conference of the Commission of Legal Pluralism Legal Pluralist Perspectives on Development and Cultural Diversity. Zurich, Switzerland, August 31 – September 3, 2009.

Chowdhry, P. 2004. 'Caste Panchayats and the Policing of Marriage in Haryana: Enforcing Kinship and Territorial Exogamy', *Contributions to Indian Sociology* 38, (1–2):1–42.

———. 2007. *Contentious Marriages, Eloping Couples: Gender, Caste and Patriarchy in Northern India*. New Delhi: Oxford University Press.

———. 2011. *Political Economy of Production and Reproduction: Caste, Custom and Community in North India*. New Delhi: Oxford University Press.

Cohn, B. S. 1965. 'Anthropological Notes on Disputes and Law in India', *American Anthropologist*, 67 (6): 82–122.

Davis, D. R. Jr. 2009. 'Law in the Mirror of Language: The Madras School of Orientalism on Hindu Law., in Trautmann, T. (ed) *The Madras School of Orientalism: Producing Knowledge in Colonial South India*. Oxford: Oxford University Press.

Dewey, C. 1972. 'Images of the Village Community: A Study in Anglo-Indian Ideology', *Modern Asian Studies*, 6 (03): 291–328.

Dumont, L. 1966. *Homo Hierarchicus: Essai sur le System des Castes*. Paris : Gallimard.

Dumont, L., and D. Pocock. 1957. 'For a Sociology of India', *Contributions to Indian Sociology*, I: 7–22.

Eberhard, C. and N. Gupta (eds.). 2005. 'Legal Pluralism in India', *Indian Socio-Legal Journal*, 31 (Special Issue).

Galanter, M. 1963. 'Law and Caste in Modern India', *Asian Survey*, pp. 544–559.

Hardgrave, R. L. 1979. *India: Government and Politics in a Developing Nation*. *Delhi*: Freeman Book Company.

Hayden, R. M. 1983. 'Excommunication as Everyday Event and Ultimate Sanction: The Nature of Suspension from an Indian Caste', *The Journal of Asian Studies*, 42 (2): 291–307.

———. 1984. 'A Note on Caste Panchayats and Government Courts in India: Different Kinds of Stages for Different Kinds of Performances'. *Journal of Legal Pluralism*, 22: 43–51.

Holden, L. 2003. 'Custom and Law Practices in Central India: Some Case Studies'. *South Asia Research*, 23:115–133.

Kikani, L.T. 1912. *Caste in Courts or Rights and Powers of Castes in Social and Religious Matters as Recognized by Indian Courts*. Rajkot: Ganatra Printng Works

Madsen, S. T. 1991. 'Class, Kinship and Panchayat Justice among Jats of Western U.P', *Anthropos*, 866.

Mathur, S. N. 1997. *Nyaya Panchayats as Instruments of Justice*. Institute of Social Science. New Delhi: Concept Pub. Co.

Mendelsohn, O.1993. 'The Transformation of Authority in Rural India'. *Modern Asian Studies*, 27, (4): 805–842.

Meschievitz, C. and M. Galanter. 1982. 'In Search of Nyaya Panchayats: The Politics of a Moribund Institution', in Abel Richard (ed.) *The Politics of Informal Justice* (volume 2). New York: Academic Press, pp. 47–81.

Nagaraj, V. 2012. 'Local and Customary Forums: Adapting and Innovating Rules and Formal Law', *Indian Journal of Gender Studies*, 17 (3): 429–450.

Roy, Kalpana. 1999. *Encyclopedia of Violence against Women and Dowry Death in India*. New Delhi: Anmol Publication.

Rudolph, S. H. 1961. 'Consensus and Conflict in Indian Politics', *World Politics: A Quarterly Journal of International Relations*, 13 (3): 385–399.

Saraswathi, S. 1973. *The Madras Panchayat System. Volume I. A Historical Survey.* Delhi: Impex India.

Sripaty, Roy. 1911. Customs and Customary Law in British India. Tagore Law Lectures 1908. Calcutta: Hare Press.

Sharafi, M.J. 2008. 'Justice in Many Rooms since Galanter: De-Romanticizing Legal Pluralism Through the Cultural Defense', *Law & Contemporary Problems*, 71: 139–46.

Vincentnathan, G.S. 1966. 'Caste Politics, Violence, and the Panchayat in a South Indian Community', *Comparative Studies in Society and History*, 38 (3): 484–509.

Vincentnathan, L. and Vincentnathan,G. S. 2007. 'Village Courts and the Police: Cooperation and Conflict in Modernizing India', *Police Practice and Research: An International Journal*, 8 (5): 445–59.

Newspaper Articles

'Panchayatdars eat humble pie in HC'. *The Hindu*, 18/09/2003

'Nattu panchayattukalai nacukka mutiyatu'. *Junior Vikatan*, 08/10/2003

'Govt to ban punishment by panchayat'. *New Indian Express*, Madurai Edition, 10/10/2003.

'Village justice system in TN shocks HC'. *Deccan Herald*, Chennai edition, 25/10/2003.

'Outlaw Kangaroo courts, says Madras HC'. *Deccan Herald*, Chennai edition, 14/04/2004.

'Registrar directed to enquire alleged 'katta panchayat'. *The Hindu*, 25/10/2005.

'Devil's Court'. *New Indian Express*, Madurai edition, 20/07/2005.

'Registrar directed to enquire alleged 'katta panchayat'. *The Hindu*, 25/10/2005.

'Officials summoned over katta panchayat'. *The Hindu*, 28/10/2005.

'Katta Panchayat Rampant in Dharmapuri district'. *The Hindu*, 08/02/2006.

'Katta Panchayat excommunicates 5 fishermen's families'. *The Hindu*, 10/06/2006.

'Katta panchayat system prevalent in 30% of villages'. *The Hindu*, 24/11/2006.

'Infant's death: Panchayat slaps fine on activists for reporting barbaric custom'. *The Indian Express*, 31/12/2007.
'The role of village courts in earlier times'. *The Hindu*, 12/09/2007.
'Judget to probe 'katta panchayat''. *The Hindu*, 27/04/2008.
'HC asks police to enforce ban on katta panchayat'. *Times of India*, 19/12/2008.
'Goondaism by 'katta panchayats' continues: Court'. *The Hindu*, 19/12/2008.
'Spreading menace'. *Frontline*, April 11-24 2009.
'Demons and gods'. *Frontline*, August 2009.
'Feudal roots'. *Frontline*, August 15-28, 2009.
'Court directive to SPs on "katta panchayat"'. *The Hindu*, 23/10/2009.
'Take action against katta panchayat gang.' *Express News Service*, 17/12/2009.
'TN katta panchayats rival khaps'. *Deccan Chronicle*. Chennai edition, 16/6/2010.
'Katta panchayat forces Dalits out'. *Express News Service*, 25/7/2010.
'Nyaya panchayat bill rejected'. *Deccan Chronicle*. Chennai edition, 16/5/2010.
'Medieval justice: Kangoroo courts call the shots in TN'. *Times of India*, 16/06/2010.
'Seven honour killings in 12 weeks: Tamil Nadu does it too'. *Tehelka*, Vol 7, Issue 42, 23/10/10.
'Ruling by Decree'. *Frontline*, May 21–June, 2011.
'Law and Honour'. *Frontline*, June 4–17, 2011.

Other Sources

Law Commission of India. Working paper. October 1985. New Delhi.
Evidence (NGO) 2010. A Study report on Caste Panchayat and its Violation. Madurai, Tamil Nadu.
The Nyaya Panchayat Bill 2009.

8

JEFFREY A. REDDING

From 'She-males' to 'Unix'

Transgender Rights and the Productive Paradoxes of Pakistani Policing*

In the summer of 2009, in the midst of a period of heightened judicial activism by Pakistan's higher judiciary, the Supreme Court of Pakistan ordered the Government of Pakistan, and also the governments of

* Generous support for research leading to this chapter was provided by the 'JUST-India' project funded by the French National Research Agency (ANR), and also the Saint Louis University School of Law. Previous drafts of this chapter have been presented at a number of different conferences and venues, including a Centre Jacques Berque conference on 'From the Anthropology of Islamic Law to the Anthropology of Law in the Islamic World: Reflections on the Possibilities for an Anthropology of the Law in Islamic and 'Partly' Islamic Societies' in Rabat, Morocco during January 2011; a University of North Carolina School of Law conference on 'Pluralism in Asia: Exploring How Asian Legal Systems Reflect, Reinforce, and Resist Differences in Identities and Perspectives' in January 2011; and also a public lecture at the Centre d'Etudes de l'Inde et de l'Asie du Sud (CEIAS) in Paris, France during May 2012. I would like to thank the organizers of and participants in these conferences for their very insightful comments, questions, and conversations, and especially Daniela Berti, Devika Bordia, Seval Yildirim, Micah Stanek, Amélie Blom, and Aminah Mohammad-Arif for their particularly detailed feedback. I would also like

Punjab, Sindh, Baluchistan, and the Northwest Frontier[1] provinces to better provide for Pakistan's 'transgendered'[2] citizens. This intervention by the Supreme Court into the social situation facing Pakistani transgendered citizens came as a surprise to many casual observers of Pakistan's political and legal landscape, albeit one that was welcomed by many, and especially those people who saw it as further evidence of the Pakistani higher judiciary's recently renewed interest in deepening democratic values in Pakistan. For other observers, however, the Supreme Court's intervention resulted in as much puzzlement and consternation as it did relief. The Court's finding, for example, that transgenderism is a kind of 'gender disorder'[3] as a predicate for the Court's action on behalf of transgendered individuals—was just one of several aspects of the Court's 'benevolence' that gave many people (including many progressives) cause to worry about what the Court was up to.

While the legal and social issues raised by the Supreme Court of Pakistan's recent actions vis-à-vis transgendered individuals are many, I will focus in this chapter on how and why different conceptions of gender/identity[4] circulated in the events surrounding the Supreme Court's actions. I want to examine not only *how* state actors involved in this litigation articulated, at various times and spaces connected to the events surrounding this litigation, different conceptions of Pakistan's transgendered citizens' gender/identity, but also propose an explanation for *why* these conceptions changed across time and space. Even more particularly, I aim to analyse how and why the gender/identity of the transgendered individuals whose welfare was at issue in the Supreme Court changed from the time they were arrested in a police raid on a

to thank Advocate Muhammad Ali Lasshaari (Lahore) and Professor Osama Siddique (Lahore University of Management Sciences) for the invaluable assistance they provided in relation to this chapter, as well as Robbie Hinz, Leslie Dunlap, and Clifton Martin (all Saint Louis University School of Law) for their very helpful research assistance. All translations in this chapter are mine, though I also benefited (as always) from the Urdu-English translation guidance provided by Ali Faisal Zaidi. For common Urdu terms and names, I have not included diacritics, though I do provide them in other instances. This chapter is dedicated to Gary, for allowing me to see and feel how big and small pictures fit together, for the first time.

wedding party in Rawalpindi, Pakistan, until the time[5] they and their brethren were 'liberated' by the Supreme Court in Islamabad, Pakistan. At different moments in this inter-urban, inter-institutional journey, these transgendered individuals were considered to be anything from 'she-males,' to 'unix,' and also other things as well.

In many ways, these different nomenclatures could be considered the inevitable (and 'innocent') fumbling that any legal system must engage in as it confronts peoples and rights with which it is unfamiliar.[6] Yet, the ramifications of variable uses of nomenclature are important, not least because they result in uncertainty as to whom the Supreme Court of Pakistan's newly-announced 'rights'[7] apply. As Gayatri Reddy has discussed in her recent ethnography of 'transgendered'[8] identities in southern India, the definition of who is a *hijra*—much less a 'real *hijra*'—is a deeply contested and complicated one.[9] Understanding the dynamic and inter-institutional processes which help generate various gender/identities is important then not only as a matter of comprehending the dynamism of all gender/identities, but also as a matter of understanding the difficulties which can accompany the enforcement of gender-premised rights.

In this chapter, I take up this challenge of comprehension and enforcement, focusing on how and why different institutional legal actors in Pakistan—namely, the Pakistani police and the Pakistani higher judiciary together—'produced' different articulations of (trans) gender(ism) at different points in the events surrounding the 2009 litigation at the Supreme Court of Pakistan. Altogether, the different gender/identities which circulated in the events surrounding the litigation at the Supreme Court of Pakistan demonstrate various understandings of gender/identity which are fluid and in flux in contemporary Pakistan, as well as conceptions of gender/identity which are eminently responsive to different and sometimes competing considerations external to 'gender simpliciter'—a paradoxical expression that I use here only to suggest that gender is, in fact, never simple (nor completely 'external'). These competing considerations range from the theoretical—namely, the nature of the rights being claimed by Pakistan's transgendered citizens at the Supreme Court of Pakistan—to the mundane—namely, reporting procedures followed by the Pakistani police in the context of their enforcement of Pakistan's criminal laws. This enforcement of Pakistan's criminal laws by the police against transgendered individuals in Rawalpindi, Pakistan not only instigated the litigation at the Supreme Court, but also structured the initial identification (at least) of these individuals in this litigation. The productivity of this Pakistani police power in relation to gender/identity will thus be a particular focus of this chapter.

The complex ways in which a criminal legal system's operations can help produce a society's conceptions and understandings of gender has been explored in previous literature. For example, Rosalind Morris has argued that 'culturally specific sex/gender systems' must be analyzed taking into account 'changes in [the local] politico-economic order'.[10] And she herself has engaged in such a culturally cognizant political-economic analysis, exploring how the Thai monarchy's 20th-century regulation and criminalization of sartorial affairs impacted the development of Thailand's sex/gender system.[11]

Lawrence Cohen, in his work on 'homosociality' in the Indian city of Varanasi, has sounded similar themes as Morris, warning against 'reduc[ing] understanding to a set of categories ... too easily grounded in a *globalizing* heterosexual/homosexual opposition',[12] and then going on to engage in his own '*local* delineation of hegemonic forms of homosociality and of the multiple sites, modes, and practices of their subversion, introjections, and collapse'.[13] One such local site of homosociality that Cohen has explored in his work is 'Holi cartoon political pornography'[14] depicting male–male sex which is distributed annually during Varanasi's Holi celebrations, the production of which is criminalized by the state.[15]

Gayatri Reddy's recent work on *hijras* living in the southern Indian cities of Hyderabad and Secunderabad is, like Morris and Cohen, also concerned with the interaction of local criminal legal regimes and the (re)production of gender identities and practices.[16] In her work, for example, Reddy has detailed some of the cultural and social epistemologies that both underlay and were reproduced by the British colonial regime's legislation of the Criminal Tribes Act of 1871.[17] This Act, in part, defined the category and criminalized the activities of what it deemed 'eunuchs', describing '[t]he term 'eunuch' [to mean,] for the purposes of this Act,[] all persons of the male sex who admit themselves, or on medical inspection clearly appear, to be impotent'. Moreover, this Act aimed to create 'a register of the names and residences of all eunuchs residing in any town or place ... who are reasonably suspected of kidnapping or castrating children', and also penalized '[a]ny eunuch so registered who has in his charge, or keeps in the house in which he resides, or under his control, any boy who has not completed the age of sixteen years'.[18] As I explain below, the practice of state registration of transgendered individuals, as well as the suspicion that such individuals are prone to kidnapping youth, are prominent themes in the recent litigation at the Supreme Court of Pakistan. Moreover, as Reddy has explained, 'embedded in this construction [of criminal tribes, including eunuchs] was the notion that crime was an inborn, hereditary propensity, passed on to succeeding generations as was caste affiliation'.[19]

This previous literature has clearly demonstrated the gender-productive capabilities of various sorts of criminalization regimes. In this chapter, I aim to build upon this existing literature and its focus on local criminalization regimes and the ways in which they help constitute local sex/gender systems. However, I carry out my analysis of the gender-productive aspects of a particular criminal law system at a more micro-level than that which is typically utilized by other theorists (such as those just mentioned) with their focus on macro-level criminalization and criminal law systems writ large. In particular, I focus in this chapter on how specific institutional reporting practices of a municipal-level police force (embedded *within* Pakistan's criminal legal system writ large) have worked in conjunction—somewhat cooperatively, somewhat conflictually—with the praxis of Pakistan's higher judiciary to produce a range of potential gender/identities for Pakistan's 'transgendered' citizens.

Part I of this chapter first outlines the series of events which culminated in a series of hearings at, and orders from, the Supreme Court of Pakistan during the latter half of 2009 concerning the rights of transgendered individuals in Pakistan. These events began with the Rawalpindi police's raid on a 'suspicious' wedding party in the early morning hours of January 24, 2009. This Part's outline of events is based on a series of documents both filed with and produced by the Supreme Court of Pakistan, media reports, and also an interview with the lawyer who initiated the litigation at the Supreme Court in 2009. As Part I demonstrates, Pakistan's transgendered citizens were subjected to a number of very public changes in gender/identity from the time of the Rawalpindi police raid, to the Supreme Court's initial actions to counter this and other abusive Pakistani police activities, to the Supreme Court's 'final'[20] intervention to improve the overall situation of transgendered people in Pakistan. These changes in gender/identity have not been a focus of the attention that this Pakistani litigation has attracted up until this point, in which the nature of the rights—and not to whom they actually apply—has garnered the most attention.

Part II thus focuses on these changes in gender/identity, commencing an account of the institutional practices and mechanisms which could possibly explain the otherwise rather extraordinary public changes in gender/identity that Pakistan's transgendered individuals experienced from 2009 onwards—institutional practices and mechanisms which will also surely affect the implementation of the rights-regime announced by the Supreme Court of Pakistan via its several judicial orders in this matter. The commencement of an account in this Part relies on an analysis of an internal Urdu-language police report prepared in response to a vigorous public protest of the Rawalpindi police's detention of these transgendered individuals. This Part examines in particular how certain 'everyday' aspects of the Rawalpindi police's investigatory and reporting procedures initially produced the 'she-males' who the Supreme Court then ultimately fashioned into 'unix' as the Court's intervention into the situation of transgendered individuals in Pakistan got extended and widened.

Part III builds on both preceding Parts, suggesting that one can understand the further transformation in identity that Pakistan's transgendered citizens experienced in 2009—from being 'she-males' to being 'unix'—to have occurred as a consequence of their movement from the institutional jurisdiction of the police to the institutional jurisdiction of the Supreme Court with its felt need to fashion these transgendered individuals not so much as subjects of a criminal law system, but rather denizens of a modern, de-gendered, bureaucratic state. This bureaucratic state, however, will ultimately have to interact with Pakistan's police in the future, thereby leaving uncertain which understandings of Pakistan's transgendered individuals' gender/identity will achieve prominence in the future—and where—and which transgendered individuals—if any—will actually be protected by the transgendered rights regime that the Supreme Court of Pakistan has begun to fashion.

Part I: From Rawalpindi to Islamabad

This part outlines the basic series of events that culminated in what some have viewed as a victory for transgender rights in Pakistan,[21] as well as the actual Supreme Court of Pakistan orders which constitute this 'victory'. This outline is important because there has been almost no systematic assembling and analysis of these events in the academic literature before.[22] The description of events I provide in this part is based on a series of English-language filings made at the Supreme Court of Pakistan during 2009 by not only different Pakistani state actors (e.g. the police) but also a lawyer advocating on behalf of Pakistan's trans-gendered citizens, as well as the Supreme Court's own observations and activities as recorded in a series of Court orders that began to be issued that year. The description of events that I provide here also utilizes what I learned from a recent interview that I conducted with the lawyer who initiated the litigation at the Supreme Court in 2009. With respect to all these different kinds of legal materials and sources, two caveats are in order.

First, any examination of legal documents or legal sources in order to ascertain 'what really happened' in a given situation must proceed with a great deal of caution, as the narration of real-life events for the purposes of the legal domain often results in transformations of 'the facts' in order to accommodate legal categories, legal requirements, and legal epistemologies. In this respect, then, no claim is made here—nor could be made here—that the series of events described herein *actually* happened in the specific manner described. It is entirely possible that dates, timings, numbers of individuals, locations of individuals, activities of individuals, etc. have been reduced to writing (or otherwise related) in a way different than how they 'actually' occurred in real life; complete fabrication of some aspects of what happened also cannot be ruled out.

Second, I have been using and will continue to occasionally use and apply in this chapter the term 'transgendered'. The use of this term comes with many complications, and not only because the term is an entirely imprecise one (in English and also other lingual contexts). Different people have different (or no) understanding of it. Moreover, however much precision or imprecision this term can possess, it is impor-tant to note that this exact term never entered the legal discussion in Pakistan that I am describing in this chapter in any significant manner.[23] Instead, terms like 'castrated men' and 'she-male' circulated. On one view then, the series of events that I am describing and analyzing in this chapter has *nothing* to do with 'transgendered' individuals. Of course, this then begs the question as to why I even bother using this term, even if only tentatively. I do so—tentatively—mainly because, as this and the next parts make clear, the terminology that is used to describe the individuals whose welfare becomes litigated at the Supreme Court changed over time and space, from Rawalpindi to Islamabad, from Urdu to English, and from the police station to the court house. In order to provide some sort of foundation for this complex and dynamic discussion, I will use one term—problematic as it is—to sometimes describe these individuals. However, while using this term, I hope also to show the instability of this term (and also 'male' and 'female') by demonstrating the complexity of this term's continuing use by any number of people.

These caveats being stated, according to an English-language report prepared by the Regional Police Officer of Rawalpindi, and filed with the Supreme Court of Pakistan, our story begins in the early morning hours of January 24, 2009, when officers belonging to the city of Rawalpindi's police force received 'secret information'[24] that a marriage ceremony of some sort was going on within their jurisdiction. Rawalpindi is a large city in the north of Pakistan's Punjab province, located just adjacent to Islamabad, the country's capital. According to this police report, after receiving this information, the police entered the building where the marriage ceremony was transpiring and discovered that 'a large number of persons were enjoying themselves by dance of women and castrated men in a vulgar manner'.[25] Also, '[s]ome persons besides the dancing place were busy in gambling through play cards'.[26] Whatever their particular vice, the 'gambling persons', 'dancing women', and 'castrated men' were rounded up and 'remanded to judicial lock up'.[27]

Three days later, a transgendered individual by the name of Almas Shah—also going by the name of 'Boby'—delivered a petition to the Senior Superintendent of Police (SSP) in Rawalpindi, but only after first joining a violent protest of approximately 100 other transgendered individuals outside the SSP's office.[28] Seemingly as a result of this protest, Boby's petition, and press coverage of the entire situation, the District Superintendent of Police in Rawalpindi 'after thorough enquiry recommended that 3 dancing ladies and 5 dancing she males were not involved in any kind of offence and recommended their discharge from the case'.[29] Subsequently, all charges against these 'dancing ladies' and 'she males' were dropped. The other ('not-she' male) suspects, however, were charged under the Punjab Gambling Ordinance and the

Pakistan Penal Code, for crimes relating to gambling and running of non-approved lottery games.[30]

This was not the end of the story, however, and this is where an activist-petitioner by the name of Dr Mohammad Aslam Khaki (as well as Dr Khaki's wife and colleague, Yasmin Haider) got involved. Dr Khaki is an Islamabad-based lawyer (originally from District Muzaffargarh in Pakistan's Punjab province) who, by his own description, is a well-known 'liberal Islamic jurist', also acting as a 'juris consultant' to Pakistan's high-level Federal Shariat Court.[31] Dr. Khaki and the Islamabad-based organization, the Insaaf Welfare Trust, which he and his wife coordinate[32] filed a human rights petition in the Supreme Court of Pakistan on February 6, 2009. According to Dr. Khaki's petition[33] to the Supreme Court, he decided to get involved in this case when he was 'approached by the members of Civil Society [who] have drawn the attention towards the case of molestation, humiliation and arresting [of] the most oppressed section of the society i.e. the Eunuch or people of middle Sex (also called as She males) by the [Rawalpindi] Police'.[34]

Dr Khaki's petition went on to note that 'the Community of the Shemales is the most oppressed section of life whose fundamental rights are infringed by the parents[,] Society[,] and also the government'.[35] With respect to these rights, the petition described how she-males'[36] 'right to live with their parents' gets violated when she-males parents' effectively disown them and "send them to 'Gurus' at birth to live in a separate Society'.[37] The petition also described how 'the members of the Society claiming themselves to be the members of civil or Islamic society' violate she-males' 'right to dignity as enshrined by the Quran as well as by Article 14 of the Constitution of Islamic Republic of Pakistan'.[38] Furthermore, according to the petition, she-males' 'legal & Islamic right to property and inheritance is negated as they are not given such inheritance from their parents' and the petition also lamented that she-males' rights to education and employment are violated by various government practices and policies.[39]

By way of remedy, Dr Khaki's petition asked the Supreme Court to take action against errant officers in the Rawalpindi police force, to direct both government and civil society to take steps to protect she-males and, finally, to direct the federal and provincial governments to 'restore and protect the fundamental rights of the Shemales' in order that they may be restored to—as the petition characterized it—the 'mainstream of life'.[40]

In response, on June 16 (four months later) the Supreme Court ordered the various provincial governments to conduct a census[41] of the numbers, names, and locations of she-males living in each province. Evidencing a degree of hostility and suspicion towards the 'gurus' who typically govern she-male communities,[42] the Court also directed the provincial governments to

> ensure that in future if any child is handed over to the 'Gurus', their particulars should be noted and intimated to the [provincial government] for the purpose of further probe with regard to the status of such child and also to know whether they are voluntarily handed over or under compulsion and in both the situations what offence/crime has been committed by elders/parents by handing over them to such 'Gurus[']'.[43]

In a subsequent hearing one month later, on July 14, the Court heard directly from a she-male whose given name was 'Saleem Iqbal,' but who also went by the name of 'Shazia'. As recounted by the Supreme Court in the order it issued after this hearing, Shazia relayed how her and her brethren get 'involved in false cases and kept in custody by the police, where they are subjected to physical and sexual abuse'.[44] Additionally, Dr Khaki lamented in this hearing that 'on account of [she-males'] sexual features and inclinations, they are not enjoying the status of either male or female but they are nevertheless citizens of this country'.[45] By way of example of how she-males get troublesomely caught in-between traditional gender categories, Dr. Khaki explained how 'while getting [National Identity Card,] the photograph [] is of women but in the relevant column of status they are categorized as male'.[46] Additionally, according to Dr. Khaki, 'there is no scope for she-males to receive higher education as normally they are allowed to attend the classes during childhood but no sooner they start growing up, the schools meant either for males or for females, refuse to admit them'.[47]

In an order issued after this July hearing, the Supreme Court agreed with Dr Khaki and declared that 'she-males are *citizens* of this country and entitled to protection particularly under Articles 4 and 9 of the Constitution'.[48] Article 4 of the Constitution of Pakistan guarantees for any person within Pakistan the 'inalienable right ... [t]o enjoy the protection of law and to be treated in accordance with law'.[49] Article 9 declares that '[n]o person shall be deprived of life or liberty save in accordance with law'.[50] In its order, the Court also went on to warn the police not to engage in 'any highhandedness' with she-males in the future, and also ordered the provincial governments to send to the Court before the next hearing of this constitutional case their recommendations as to how to ensure 'social uplift' of she-males.[51]

At this next hearing, in August of 2009, the Supreme Court devised more concrete remedies for she-males or—as the Court now described them—'eunuchs'.[52] Before doing so, however, the Court first remarked that while there is

> [n]o doubt eunuchs engage themselves in professions, for the purpose of earning for their livelihood, but as per Islamic injunction there should not be element of insult against them. They are creatures of Allah Almighty, therefore, their social life is to be respected. The Federal as well as the Provincial Governments who are responsible to protect the rights of the citizens ... are bound to protect ... eunuch[s] ... under the Constitution of the Islamic Republic of Pakistan.[53]

Per the Constitution then, the Supreme Court at this August hearing ordered the federal and provincial governments to enable eunuchs 'to get education and respectable jobs'.[54] The Supreme Court then directed police departments in the country to 'provid[e] security to eunuchs' in order to protect eunuchs from 'the hands of miscreant person [sic] who exploit them for taking the benefit of their sexual weaknesses'.[55] And finally, with respect to miscreants within Pakistani police departments themselves, the Supreme Court directed police officials to 'ensure that eunuchs are given protection and security and [that] they are not involved un-necessarily in Criminal Cases just to grab money from them'.[56]

The next major hearing in this case did not occur until the fall of 2009, on November 20, 2009.[57] Interestingly, in the order that the Court issued after this November hearing, the Court's nomenclature for the persons whose welfare was at issue changed once again, this time from 'eunuchs' to 'unix'.

In this order, the Court ordered the provincial and federal governments to provide for unix' inheritance rights, franchise rights, and also educational opportunities. As well, the Court begins in this order to describe 'this class of the society' as suffering from a 'gender disorder'.[58] Indeed, on this basis of this understanding of transgenderism, the Court directed the federal and provincial governments to ensure unix employment opportunities, noting that '[a]s the Government has already ensured the jobs to the disable[d] persons ... similar policy can also be adopted for [unix]'.[59]

Even more remarkable, with respect to unix' official registration and the issuance of identity documents, the Court instructed the Pakistani government's National Database and Registration Authority (or 'NADRA') to 'adopt a strategy ... to record [unix'] exact status in the column meant for male or female after undertaking some medical tests based on hormones etc'.[60] Why this concern with the 'exact', hormonal status of various unix? One reason appears to be that the Court had received information 'that in the name of the unix some male and female who ... otherwise have no gender disorder in their bodies have adopted this status and commit crimes on account of which a bad name is brought to unix'.[61] While the source of this information is not clear from Supreme Court documents, Dr. Khaki conveyed to me his own personal experience of taking tea with and giving money to a teenaged 'eunuch' that used to visit his law offices, who was later revealed to be a 'fake' when Dr. Khaki spotted him one day wearing 'normal dress'.[62]

In case anyone was mistaken that the Court was genuinely concerned about a real problem with 'fake unix', the Supreme Court repeated its concern with those 'who in fact are not unix but by using such status are committing the crimes and [as a result of which] the actual unix are being blamed for the same' in a subsequent order issued on December 23, 2009.[63] In this December order, the Court also repeated its earlier concerns and commands with respect to unix'[64] inheritance rights, voting rights, and education and employment opportunities. With respect to these employment opportunities, the Court congratulated Sindh province for employing unix to assist with that province's polio vaccination efforts.[65] And interestingly, the Court also took notice of a report about the Indian state of Bihar's action to put 'eunuchs, also called *kinnars* or *hijras*, in socially useful work'[66] by, namely, 'provid[ing] respectable jobs ... like recovery of taxes from the habitual defaulter'.[67] Pakistan's Sindh province has recently taken this Indian example to heart and, in fact, has hired transgendered individuals in this tax-collecting capacity.[68]

As one can see, the 'transgendered' individuals who were taken into custody by the Rawalpindi police in the early morning hours of January 24, 2009 traversed an incredible amount of ground (for both themselves and their brethren) over the remainder of 2009. Simultaneously, they were transformed themselves, from 'she-males' (in the hands of the Rawalpindi police, Dr. Khaki, and the initial Supreme Court orders) to 'eunuchs' (in later Supreme Court orders) to 'unix' (in even later Supreme Court orders).[69]

Part II: From Urdu to English

There any number of possible explanations available for why the gender/identity of Pakistan's transgendered citizens changed over the course of the various events and judicial hearings described in Part I. The possibility that the Pakistani legal system was exhibiting carelessness and/or 'innocent' fumbling with respect to unfamiliar persons and practices should not be ruled out,[70] as this is characteristic behavior of any legal system. In this part, however, I would like to begin to explore and develop another sort of explanation, one that utilizes a micro-level cultural/contextual—and, in fact, a micro-level institutional jurisdictional—approach to explaining how it is that legal subjects might quite easily be made to experience inconsistent gender/identity as they are moved from the institutional jurisdiction of the Pakistani police *thana* to the institutional jurisdiction of the Pakistani higher judiciary.

This part commences this kind of micro-level analysis by conducting an analysis of a significant Urdu-language document[71] that was also entered into the record in the Supreme Court case, namely an internal Rawalpindi police report prepared in response to the vigorous protest held on January 27, 2009 outside of the Senior Superintendent of Police's office in Rawalpindi on behalf of the still-detained transgendered individuals.[72] This report provides some clues as to the initially puzzling decision by both Dr. Khaki and the Supreme Court to refer to the arrested individuals as 'she-males',[73] in contrast to the (also puzzling) subsequent decision to later recharacterize these individuals as 'eunuchs' and then 'unix'. Indeed, as the next two Parts together attempt to explain, one might understand the initial characterization of these arrested individuals' gender/identity as the consequence of 'everyday' police investigatory and reporting practices directed against private individuals, which later became superseded (or at least complicated) by understandings of gender/identity used by state/public institutions vis-à-vis their own denizens.

In the materials on file with the Supreme Court of Pakistan is an English-language memo, dated March 19, 2009, from the Inspector

General of Police for Punjab province to the Registrar of the Supreme Court of Pakistan. This memo indicates that

[o]n receipt of [the Supreme Court Registrar's earlier] memo [], the matter was referred to Regional Police Officer, Rawalpindi, with the direction to send a report on the complaint. In this connection, the report of the Regional Police Officer, Rawalpindi has been received, which is enclosed for your information, please.[74]

From another memo in the Supreme Court file, it can be surmised that the Supreme Court asked the Inspector General of Police for Punjab to direct the Regional Police Officer[75] of Rawalpindi to prepare a report explaining the events of the early morning hours of January 24, 2009 in Rawalpindi which instigated Dr Khaki's eventual petition to the Supreme Court. The Regional Police Officer's English-language report is then found along with these two memos.

Part of this report was described above in Part I.[76] Generally speaking, this report describes a set of events which transpired on and after approximately 2 a.m. on January 24, 2009 in Rawalpindi. Also referred to in this report is yet another report prepared by the District Superintendent of Police's Legal Operations office, in response to the petition that Boby registered with the Senior Superintendent of Police, Rawalpindi (SSP) on January 27, 2009, after protesting with approximately 100 individuals outside of the Senior Superintendent of Police's office in order to liberate the transgendered individuals who had been detained by the Rawalpindi police on January 24.[77]

This report from the District Superintendent of Police's Legal Operations office is also enclosed in the Supreme Court file. Unlike nearly all of the other materials in this file—the only other exception being a chargesheet, prepared by an Inspector SHO (Station House Officer), against the individuals who were detained in the police raid on the Rawalpindi wedding party and who were eventually charged with gambling-related offenses,[78] and also a couple short Urdu-language newspaper articles—this report is composed in Urdu. Reading this report, one finds that it, like the English-language report prepared for the Supreme Court Registrar by the Regional Police Officer just noted, describes what happened during the early-morning hours of January 24, 2009. However, this Urdu-language report is over 6 pages long, versus the 1.5-page English-language report prepared by the Regional Police Officer.

Part of the difference in length is attributable to this report's inclusion and summarization of different statements collected from different parties who got caught up in the events of the early morning hours of January 24. In this respect, the Legal Operations office's Urdu-language report is different than its English-language counterpart (the Regional Police Officer's report) as the Urdu-language report contains different parties' somewhat diverging 'testimonies' as to what happened on January 24, while the English-language report is devoted to presenting a one-sided 'executive summary' as to 'what really happened' during the early hours of that day.[79]

Another reason for the two different reports' difference in length is that the Legal Operations office's report contains more-detailed information as to the identities of all the different people who were caught up in the events of January 24. And herein lies some clues pertaining to the initial nomenclature choices as to the transgendered individuals who became the subject of Dr Khaki's Supreme Court petition.

In this respect, the Legal Operations office's report—after describing how the Rawalpindi police came to know about, and then raided, the wedding party of a Munir Ahmad, where they found a '*mujra* of women and *hijras* going on in an obscene manner and, in addition, gambling also going on in this place'[80]—lists all of the individuals who were detained at this wedding function. These individuals are divided into different groups, based on the activities they were implicated in, and also seemingly some conceptions of their gender(s). First listed are

> the following individuals whose names and addresses were later found [and who] were busily found to be gambling using a deck of playing cards:
>
> 1) Babar Shehzad, son of Muhammad Gulzar, *qaum* Awan, resident of Malikabad
> 2) Shabir Shah, son of Zaman Shah, *qaum* Syed, resident of 18-G/533, Wah Cantt.
> 3) Muhammad Zahir, son of Muhammad Rafiq, *qaum* Bhati, resident of Malikabad
> 4) Malik Qadir, son of Muhammad Maqsood, *qaum* Bhati, resident of Malikabad
> 5) Shaukat, son of Kala Khan, *qaum* Bhati, resident of Paswal, Taxila

6) Shahid, son of Dawood, *qaum* Awan, resident of Carriage Factory, Rawalpindi
7) Muhammad Basharat, son of Muhammad Banaras, *qaum* Awan, resident of Malikabad
8) Malik Muhammad Asif, son of Kareem, *qaum* Gujar, resident of Ban Bhula
9) Munir Ahmad, son of Maqsood Hamid, resident of Malikabad
10) Zubair Khan, son of Mahmood Khan, resident of Taxila, Rawalpindi[81]

Following the list of these men is a description of money and items that the Rawalpindi police seized at the *mujra*, seeming to implicate the above individuals in some sort of illicit gaming. After this description, the Legal Operations office's report then lists the 'dancing girls'[82] who were also found and detained at the wedding function:

Dancing girls:

1) Musammat Fari, daughter of Shaukat, resident of Qasai Gali, Rawalpindi
2) Musammat Rozi, daughter of Habib, resident of Kotli Sattian, Rawalpindi
3) Musammat Sonia, daughter of Hamid, resident of Qadarabad, Lahore[83]

And immediately following this list of women is another list of the *"hijras"*[84] who were detained at the wedding function, also while dancing:

Hijras:

1) Ali, son of Shah Alam, resident of Mohalla Eid Gah, Rawalpindi
2) Akmal, son of Iqbal, resident of Mohalla Eid Gah, Rawalpindi
3) Ali Ahmad, son of Muhammad Din, resident of Mohalla Eid Gah, Rawalpindi
4) Wahid, son of Nur Ahmad, resident of Mohalla Eid Gah, Rawalpindi
5) Imran, son of Pervez Mahmood, resident of Mohalla Eid Gah, Rawalpindi[85]

Finally included after these three separate lists of gambling men, dancing girls, and *hijras*, is a list of men who were found 'showering'[86] currency notes on the dancing girls and *hijras*[87] during their dance performance, and who were also detained by the police:

1) Muhammad Yusuf, son of Muhammad Rafiq, *qaum* Awan, resident of Khagpur, Taxila
2) Jamal Din, son of Abdallah, resident of [sic] Mohalla Sadiqabad, Taxila
3) Muhammad Jahangir, son of Muhammad Rafiq, *qaum* Rajput, resident of Khagpur, Taxila
4) Babar Shahzad, son of Abdul Qayum, *qaum* Awan, resident of Nawababad, Wah Cantt.
5) Ali Asghar, son of Ghulam Rasool, *qaum* Awan, resident of Nawaababad, Wah Cantt.
6) Zahid, son of Sheer Khan, *qaum* Pathan, resident of Malikabad, Taxila
7) Moin, son of Anayak, resident of Taxila[88]

A number of aspects of this way of identifying and categorizing all these various individuals might be noticed and remarked upon. First is that the Legal Operations office makes some sort of distinction between the dancing girls and the *hijras* seized in the police raid, even though both were implicated in the same activity, 'dancing-singing'.[89] This distinction is made not only by the mere act of separating the seized individuals out into two different groups within the Legal Operations office's report, but also by the way that individuals are identified within and between these two groups. For example, all of the dancing girls' names are preceded by the honorific and (female) gendered '*musmāt*' (or '*musammat*', often abbreviated elsewhere as 'Mst'.), while the *hijras*' names are not so preceded.

As well, the dancing girls are each identified as being the 'daughter'[90] of their respective fathers. The *hijras*, by way of contrast are each identified as being the 'son'[91] of their respective fathers. In identifying each of the *hijras* as the son of a father, the Legal Operations office's report follows the identification pattern it uses in identifying men who were seized both for gambling and for showering currency on the dancing girls and *hijras*. All of the men in these two respective groups of seized individuals are identified as the 'son' of their respective fathers.

Yet, despite this similarity in identification practice used for the gambling men, the showering men, and the *hijras*, it should also be noted that the Legal Operation office's report groups the *hijras* separately from the men throwing currency notes on them. This differentiation *might* be naturalized by viewing the people throwing currency notes into the air as fundamentally different than those upon whom the currency notes land. However, that being said, it is worth stating again that the *hijras* were engaged in some sort of dance and, as the expression goes, 'it takes two to tango'. As a result, this distinction made by the police between the 'showerer' and the 'showeree' appears to be as arbitrary as that found in other criminal law contexts where one finds differential prosecution for the 'insertor' versus the 'insertee'—for example, in relation to the prosecution of anal sex.[92] As arbitrary as this distinction may be, it is nonetheless significant for what it can reveal about the police and how they are 'thinking gender' with respect to the detained *hijras*. For the police, gender here seems to be less a residue of bio-identity, than it is of (purported) activity, as has been witnessed elsewhere in South Asia (and beyond).[93]

Finally, another noteworthy distinction that this Legal Operations office's report makes between the *hijras* and (bio) men detained on January 24 is an attribution of '*qaum*' to the vast majority of arrested men—whether gamblers or 'currency showerers'—while making no such attribution to any of the *hijras*, or any of the dancing girls either.[94] *Qaum* is an Urdu word with many different meanings across different contexts but can be translated here to mean 'community,' or more controversially, 'caste'.[95] Whatever the appropriate translation in this situation, for the Rawalpindi police, *qaum* appears to be an attribution of—or possibly a determiner of—masculinity, and its lack an attribute of—or possibly a determiner of—femininity.[96]

In sum then, the Rawalpindi police distinguished the *hijras* they detained on January 24, 2009 from the other individuals detained that day in ways that have relevance for the perception and description of the gender/identity of these transgendered individuals by later actors in this social and legal controversy. In this respect, the detained dancing girls were distinguished from the detained *hijras* in ways which seem to distinguish the two groups of individuals along metrics pertaining to honor (Mst./not-Mst.) and kinship (daughter/son). Likewise, in describing each detained *hijra* (along with detained men) as a 'son', the Rawalpindi police again seemed to be attributing a masculinized gender to these *hijras*.

Conversely, in the way that the police made a distinction between these *hijras* and the men throwing currency notes on them, the police seemed to be attributing a not-male, or feminized, gender to these *hijras*. This attribution of a feminized gender then seems to get repeated when these *hijras* – in contrast to most of the detained men, but like the detained dancing girls—are not attributed a *qaum*.

In other words, there are some ways in which the patterns of identification used by the police vis-à-vis the detained *hijras* seem to resonate with the patterns of identification used for men detained on the same day, yet there are other ways in which the detained *hijras'* recorded identities seem to resonate more with the patterns of identification used for detained women (i.e. dancing girls). Based simply on these identification patterns found in the police report then, it would be arguably difficult for later actors in this situation to describe the detained *hijras* as either 'male' or 'female'.[97] Indeed, it would seem to be easiest for later actors in this situation to interpret these individuals instead—as they were initially in the English-language materials—as a combination of male and female, for example 'she-males'.[98]

Part III: From the Police *Thana* to the Supreme Court

While the *hijras* that the Rawalpindi police detained in the early morning hours of January 24, 2009, entered the English-language, Supreme Court record as 'she-males,' they were not to remain as such for long. Indeed, ultimately, these *hijras*-cum-'she-males' were to be refashioned by the Supreme Court of Pakistan into 'eunuchs' and then 'unix'. While a fuller exploration of how and why this happened would ideally rely on interviews with some of the Supreme Court judges who adjudicated this matter, this kind of ethnographic material may never be available because of norms concerning the confidentiality of judicial opinion-writing.[99] In the (current) absence of such ethnographic material, one must look for explanations elsewhere. While the explanation that is developed here is necessarily somewhat speculative, it nonetheless raises important questions as to how judicial understandings of gender/identities interact with, relate to, and mutually impact police understandings of gender/identity. As a result, as 'true' or 'false' as the following explanation ends up being, I believe it is nonetheless useful, at the very least because it provides an example of how one might think though the relationship of police practices to judicial priorities with respect to the gender/identities of Pakistan's 'transgendered' citizens— and anyone else too.

This part, then, briefly explores one possible explanation for the transformation in gender/identity that the transgendered individuals who were arrested on January 24, 2009 experienced as they traveled out of Rawalpindi to Islamabad, and from a police *thana* to the Supreme Court, and onwards through a series of hearings at the Court. In what follows, I suggest that as these transgendered individuals moved from the institutional jurisdiction of the police and their 'everyday' procedures for reporting the identity—whether relating to activity, gender, kinship, or *qaum* –of accused individuals, to the institutional jurisdiction of the Supreme Court, that it was inevitable that these transgendered individuals' gender/identity would change. While it was not inevitable (or predictable) that the change would be in the direction of 'unix' per se during this transition, the following discussion suggests that there are reasons to have predicted *some sort* of move away from the Pakistani police's intensely gendered method of identifying individuals to a more generic and (arguably) less gendered way of naming and identifying these transgendered individuals at the Court.

This seems to be especially the case given how the Pakistani state identifies members of its own corps, at least in certain contexts. In this respect, it is worth looking at another identification practice that the Rawalpindi District Superintendent of Police's Legal Operations office deployed in the report discussed in Part II. To recall, this Urdu-language report was written in response to a petition filed at the Senior Superintendent of Police's office after a violent protest outside of this office by over a 100 transgendered individuals, angry over the unjustified detainment of their brethren by the Rawalpindi police. The report is thus structured as an investigation into the events of January 24, 2009, and contains 'testimonies' by various parties implicated in these events. One such set of individuals is the actual police officers who conducted the raid on the wedding function, and who the protesting transgendered individuals wanted disciplined. As such, these police officers are listed in the Legal Operations office's report in the following manner:

Police Officers:

1) Akhtar Ali, I/S.H.O., Taxila Police Station
2) Muhammad Nazir, S.I.
3) Muhammad Akram, S.I.
4) Manzoor Ahmad, A.S.I.

5) Nazeer Ahmad, A.S.I.
6) Shehzad Hussein, 6128/c
7) Muhammad Nawaz, 611/c
8) Sufyan Saqib, 6625/c
9) Namir Mukhtar, 6400/c
10) Majid Ali, 6826/c
11) Zeeshan Sajid, 6860/c
12) Muhammad Ashfaq, 7816/c
13) Tayab Shah, 7140/c
14) Hussein Shehzad, 6942/c
15) Rizwan Akram, 6138/c
16) Yasir Mahmood, 6124/c[100]

As one can see, with the exception of the more-highly-ranked officers (who presumably are easily identified by their rank), all of the lower-ranked police officials are identified by a seemingly generic (badge) number, along with a 'c' denoting their (lower-ranked) 'constable' position.

Given this (seemingly) generic manner of identifying the state's own denizens, it should not be surprising that as the detained transgendered individuals became—through the initiation and progression of the litigation at the Supreme Court—protected wards of the state, that the state would engage in identification practices vis-à-vis them which resemble the ways in which the state identifies its own member-officers. As Part I discussed, this 'state incorporation' of the transgendered individuals whose welfare got litigated in front of the Supreme Court occurred in numerous ways. For example, in one of the first orders that the Supreme Court issued in this matter (on June 16), the Court ordered the provincial governments to conduct a detailed census of the 'she-males' living in each province. Later orders focused on incorporating Pakistan's transgendered citizens into the state's educational system, as well as key areas of state employment, most notably healthcare (e.g. polio vaccination[101]) and tax collection. Moreover, this concern with moving Pakistan's transgendered citizens into the "mainstream"[102] of Pakistani (state) life, coincided with the Court's suspicious attitude toward existing transgendered affiliations and communal practices—for example the phenomenon of 'gurus' exercising leadership over disciples (or 'chēlē')[103] within Pakistani transgender communities.[104] As well, while the Court did also try to more firmly situate transgendered individuals within 'non-state' (or 'private') kinship practices—for example, inheritance—this can be read as an (attempted) exertion of state power and jurisdiction over family law rather than any real deference by the state to non-state kinship structures and practices. In sum, one might view it as less-than-surprising that as the Supreme Court attempted to move Pakistan's transgendered citizens more fully into the domain and jurisdiction (and 'protection') of the state, that state patterns of 'generic' identification would start to surface with more force.

Of course, there are complications to and potential inaccuracies with this explanation as to why the gender/identity of Pakistan's transgendered citizens changed as they moved from the institutional jurisdiction of the police *thana* to the institutional jurisdiction of the Supreme Court. For example, my assumption that the Supreme Court's use of 'eunuchs' (and subsequently 'unix') is a less-gendered, more-generic identifier for transgendered individuals—at least compared to 'she-males'—is potentially controversial.[105] Indeed, considering historical patterns of usage, including most notably the definition of 'eunuch' contained in the Criminal Tribes Act of 1871,[106] one could alternatively understand 'eunuch' as being specifically gendered 'male.'[107] Additionally, my characterization of the state's system of identifying its own denizens—or, more specifically, the state's relatively simple usage of badge numbers in the report described above to identify police officers—as 'generic' may not be entirely accurate; women police officers may be identified in some different manner, if also perhaps with 'generic' numbers.[108] Additional research and dialogue would help shed light on these issues of interpretation.

★ ★ ★

The Supreme Court of Pakistan's recent actions on the behalf of Pakistan's transgendered citizens were groundbreaking, if also problematic. While much remains uncertain about the future course of events in Pakistan with respect to the rights and welfare of transgendered individuals, what is absolutely certain is that the Supreme Court of Pakistan's recent actions have initiated a vigorous public discourse centered on (1) gender/identity (2) public accountability of police authorities, and (3) the responsibilities that the institutions of an Islamic welfare state have towards *all* citizens. Moreover, as the recent actions of the Supreme Court of Pakistan and the Pakistani police together demonstrate, these three discourses are not separate ones; indeed, they are deeply intertwined and imbricated with each other. In this chapter, I have aimed to demonstrate this deep complexity. In the process, this chapter has also suggested that all gender/identities (wherever and whatever) must be understood in substantial part (though not exclusively) as local and contextual and, as a consequence, eminently responsive to particular local institutions' varying needs and social epistemologies. In other words, one can rarely (if ever) comprehend either gender, identity, or criminality using simple or monological paradigms, whether Pakistani or otherwise. Indeed, as the material I have presented and discussed in this chapter suggests, even repressive police practices can ultimately be quite productive.

Notes

1. The (former) Northwest Frontier Province (NWFP) is now known as Khyber Pakhtunkhwa (province).
2. I explain and problematize this use of terminology in Part I *infra*.
3. *See infra* text accompanying notes 58–59.
4. I use this term to indicate that gender is only one possible lens through which to view the identity of transgendered (or any other) people, whether in Pakistan or elsewhere. As Gayatri Reddy has explained somewhat similarly in relation to her work on Indian *hijras*: 'Hijras do not see themselves or others solely through the lens of sexuality; they argue explicitly for the roles of kinship, religion, and class, among others, in their constructions of self-identity' (Reddy 2006: 32–33).
5. See Part I *infra* for my demonstration of the fact that this 'time' was, in reality, an extended one, lasting over several Supreme Court hearings and orders.
6. *See, e.g., infra* note 99.
7. As my discussion in Part I *infra* demonstrates, the actions taken by the Supreme Court of Pakistan pertain to more than the enforcement of liberal-style constitutional rights.
8. See Reddy, *supra* note 4, at 30–34, for discussion of her discomfort at describing her research subjects solely through the lens of gender or sex, whether 'third-gender,' 'third-sex,' or any other kind of solely gender- or sex-premised positionality.
9. *See generally ibid.* at 44–77.

10. *See* Morris (1994: 16–17). In this respect, Morris in her work has also cautioned against using Western/global understandings of (third) genders when trying to understand the *kathoey* of Thailand. She has particularly deplored the tendency of many Western gender theorists to invoke tropes like 'the drag queen' [-] the de facto hero in a global sexual resistance' when thinking about gender outside of the West. *Ibid.* at 16.

11. *See ibid.* at 33–4.

12. *See* Cohen (1995 : 401, emphasis added).

13. *Ibid.* (emphasis added).

14. *Ibid.* at 408.

15. *See ibid.* at 400, 408.

16. *See generally* Reddy, *supra* note 4.

17. *See generally ibid.* at 26–8.

18. Criminal Tribes Act, 1871. §§ 24, 27.

19. Reddy, *supra* note 4, at 27. It should be noticed that despite this posited hereditary account of eunuchs (or, at least, their moral failings), later actions by the colonial authorities resulted in the seizure of 'lands [] granted to [eunuchs] by previous rulers ... *because [eunuchs] could not demonstrate legitimate heritage'*. *Ibid.* at 27 (*citing* Ayres 1992).

20. Since the last Supreme Court of Pakistan order examined in this chapter, the Supreme Court has continued to hold hearings and issue orders with respect to the welfare of transgendered people in Pakistan. Dr. Mohammad Aslam Khaki, interviewed by author, Islamabad, Pakistan, March 10, 2012. Indeed, the Court appears quite intent to continue its supervision of these individuals' welfare. I use the word 'final' here, then, only to indicate the final Supreme Court order which I currently have in my possession. There remains much further research work to be done on additional Supreme Court orders which have been and which will be issued in relation to this litigation.

21. *See, e.g.*, Walsh (2010).

22. *But see* Suhail (2010).

23. The exception that I am able to find in the written record comes from a report filed with the Supreme Court by the Northwest Frontier Province's Social Welfare and Women Development Department. In this report, there are a number of instances of the use of the term 'transgender.' However, in this lengthy report, the use of this term is far outpaced by the use of other related terms. *See infra* note 105.

24. Report prepared by the Regional Police Officer, Rawalpindi for the Inspector General of Police, Punjab, Lahore, at 1 (2009) (on file with author).

25. *Ibid.*

26. *Ibid.*

27. *Ibid.* These are the precise terms used in this report.

28. *See* 'Eunuch protests lead to 3 cops' suspensions', *Daily Times*, January 28, 2009, http://www.dailytimes.com.pk/default.asp?page=2009%5C01%5C28%5Cstory_28-1-2009_pg11_3.

29. Report prepared by the Regional Police Officer, Rawalpindi for the Inspector General of Police, Punjab, Lahore, at 2 (2009) (on file with author). As my description in this Part suggests, while this report from the Regional Police Officer began by referring to 'castrated men,' by the end it was using the term 'she males.' Seeing that this was the only material in the Supreme Court record that ever referred to 'castrated men,' and also seeing that the use of this nomenclature was so temporary, I do not focus in this chapter on the antecedents and implications of the use of the term 'castrated men.' As the focus of the rest of this chapter makes clear, I believe it is more important to concentrate on the use of the term 'she males' (and other nearly-identical iterations of this expression).

30. Specifically, it appears that they were charged under § 5 of the Punjab Gambling Ordinance, and §§ 294-A and 109 of the Pakistan Penal Code. See *ibid.* at 1.

31. Dr. Mohammad Aslam Khaki, interviewed by author, Islamabad, Pakistan, March 10, 2012. For more descriptive information about the Federal Shariat Court, see generally Redding (2004: 759–827).

32. Dr. Khaki described this organization to me as a "pocket trust" which does not accept any outside grants. Dr. Mohammad Aslam Khaki, interviewed by author, Islamabad, Pakistan, March 10, 2012.

33. I refer to this petition here and elsewhere in this chapter as "Dr. Khaki's petition" since Dr. Khaki is the only individual publicly associated with the Insaaf Welfare Trust in the Supreme Court documents which I possess. Dr. Khaki relayed to me, however, that his wife, Yasmin Haider, has also been very much involved in the behind-the-scenes work on this case. *Ibid.*

34. Dr. Mohammad Aslam Khaki v. Senior Superintendent of Police (Operation) Rawalpindi, H/R Constitutional Petition No. 63/2009 ¶ 2 (on file with author). This constitutional petition appears to have been mistakenly labeled with the number '43' in a few of the documents I obtained from the Supreme Court.

35. *Ibid.* ¶ 5.

36. While there are differently punctuated and capitalized versions of this term circulating in the materials related to this Supreme Court case, I will use this iteration of this term in the rest of this chapter unless I am quoting directly from case-related materials.

37. *Ibid.* The petition goes on to argue that she-males' "right for movement is also restricted as they are enslaved by the Gurus." *Ibid.*

38. *Ibid.*

39. *Ibid.*

40. *Ibid.* ¶ 'Prayer.'

41. See also *supra* text accompanying note 18.

42. See also *supra* text accompanying note 18. See Reddy, *supra* note 4, at 156-64 for discussion of guru dynamics in a different South Asian urban context.

43. Human Rights Const. P. No. 63 of 2009, 16.06.2009 Order at 2 (on file with author).

44. Human Rights Case No. 63 of 2009, 14.07.2009 Order ¶ 2 (on file with author).

45. *Ibid.*

46. *Ibid.* ¶ 4.

47. *Ibid.*

48. *Ibid.* ¶ 6 (emphasis added).

49. Pak. Const., art. 4.

50. *Ibid.*, art. 9.

51. Human Rights Case No. 63 of 2009, 14.07.2009 Order, *supra* note 44, at ¶ 6.

52. The Court begins the order that resulted from this hearing by referring to "shemales (eunuchs)" but then transitions to using only "eunuchs" in the rest of the order. See Human Rights Case No. 63 of 2009, 17-08-2009 Order ¶¶ 2-6.

53. *Ibid.* ¶ 5 (original in italics).

54. *Ibid.* ¶ 6. Other 'social uplift' measures that the Court ordered included ones pertaining to eunuchs' health and education. See *ibid.*

55. *Ibid.*

56. *Ibid.*

57. The Court issued a very brief order on November 4, 2009 ordering the Attorney General of Pakistan to "prepare some proposals ... to protect [eunuchs'] right of inheritance in moveable and immovable properties left by their parents/elders and their legal obligations to provide maintenance to them on account of disability to which they are not being treated at par with other citizens of the country." Const. Petition No. 43/2009, 04.11.2009 Order (on file with author).

58. Constitution Petition No. 43 of 2009, 20.11.2009 Order ¶ 2 (on file with author).

59. *Ibid.* ¶ 3.

60. *Ibid.* ¶ 2.

61. *Ibid.* ¶ 5.

62. Dr. Mohammad Aslam Khaki, interviewed by author, Islamabad, Pakistan, March 10, 2012. Dr. Khaki also informed me that one reason that any number of people are 'pretending' to be eunuchs these days is that, according to Dr. Khaki, it is possible to earn 20,000-30,000 Pakistani rupees per month—in

other words, a respectable Pakistani middle-class monthly salary—while begging on the streets, if one is recognized as a eunuch. *Ibid.*

63. Constitutional Petition No. 43 of 2009, 23.12.2009 Order ¶ 7 (on file with author).

64. At the very beginning of this order, the Court refers to "unix/eunuchs," but then in the rest of the order refers exclusively to "unix." See *ibid.* ¶ 1.

65. *Ibid.* ¶ 6.

66. *Ibid.* ¶ 9 (original in italics).

67. *Ibid.*

68. *See* Walsh (2011).

69. In regards the shifting choice of nomenclature used to describe the individuals arrested in Rawalpindi and 'liberated' by the final Supreme Court, it should be noted that—remarkably—two nomenclature choices that one might expect to enter the fray never really did. In particular, the term 'transgendered' never made an appearance in the English-language documents produced by either the Rawalpindi police, Dr. Khaki, or the Supreme Court. But see *supra* note 23. Additionally, the term *hijra* made only a fleeting appearance in such documents in the very final Supreme Court order of 2009, and then more in reference to (ostensibly) comparable persons in India than to the persons in front of the Supreme Court of Pakistan itself. See *supra* text accompanying note 66.

70. See, e.g., *infra* note 99.

71. English is the predominant language in use for the written decisions and records of the Supreme Court (including in this case), and this Urdu-medium report is somewhat anomalous and thus noteworthy.

72. See *supra* text accompanying note 28.

73. Dr. Khaki's initial petition did refer also to 'the Eunuch or people of middle Sex (also called as She males)', *See supra* text accompanying note 34. Otherwise, however, his petition concertedly used the term 'she-males' (or nearly-identical terms).

74. Memo from Inspector General of Police (Punjab, Lahore) to the Registrar of Supreme Court of Pakistan, Islamabad, 19-3/2009 (on file with author).

75. This appears to be the same position/office as the "City Police Officer" who is the actual signatory to the report being discussed here.

76. See *supra* text accompanying notes 24–30.

77. See *supra* text accompanying note 28.

78. See *supra* text accompanying note 30.

79. For example, the former report contains Boby's statement that, upon reaching the police station where her fellow *hijras* were being detained, Manzoor Ahmed (ASI) started beating the detainees in front of Boby while simultaneously announcing: 'You people don't know that Chief Minister

Shahbaz Sharif is very much against you and he has ordered that your functions should not be permitted' (in the original: "tum lōgōṇ kō ma'alūm
nahīṇ keh wazīr-e-a'ala shahbaz sharīf tum lōgōṇ kē sakht khilāf hai aur un
kā ḥukm hē keh tumhēṇ fankshan na karnē di'ē jā'ēṇ '). Report 'minjānib:
ḍapuṭī suparanṭanḍant āf pōlīs lēgal āparēshanz, rāwalpinḍī; bajānib: sēni'ir
suparanṭanḍant-āf pōlīs āparēshanz, Rāwalpinḍī" [From: Deputy Superintendent
of Police, Legal Operations, Rawalpindi; To: Senior Superintendent of Police
Operations, Rawalpindi], at 27 (Feb. 28, 2009) (on file with author). The Regional
Police Officer's English-language report contains no mention of any of this.

80. *Ibid.* at 25.

81. *Ibid.* at 25–26.

82. The term used here is 'ruqāṣā'ēṇ' which can be translated as 'dancing
girls'. In this respect, it is noteworthy in this report that, along with this term,
the generic Urdu word for 'women,' ('auratēṇ) was also used to specifically refer
to these girls/women. See, e.g., *ibid.* at 25–26.

83. Report 'minjānib: ḍapuṭī suparanṭanḍant āf pōlīs lēgal āparēshanz,
rāwalpinḍī; bajānib: sēni'ir suparanṭanḍant āf pōlīs āparēshanz, rāwalpinḍī'
[From: Deputy Superintendent of Police, Legal Operations, Rawalpindi; To:
Senior Superintendent of Police Operations, Rawalpindi], at 28 (Feb. 28, 2009)
(on file with author).

84. Again, this common Urdu term for a specific type of (male-to-female)
transgendered individual is only very rarely used in the English-language documents produced in this case. See *supra* note 69, *infra* note 105.

85. *Ibid.*

86. The expression used in this respect is 'nichhāvar karnā'.

87. The report here again distinguishes dancing girls from *hijras*, as it often
does throughout the report.

88. *Ibid.* at 26–27.

89. The Urdu term used in this respect is 'nāch-gānā', and this compound-
term is used throughout the report to refer to 'dancing-singing.'

90. The Urdu term used in this report in this respect is 'dukhtar'.

91. The Urdu term used in this report in this respect is 'walad'.

92. *See*, e.g., Long (2004).

93. *See*, e.g., People's Union for Civil Liberties-Karnataka, Human rights violations against sexuality minorities in India: A PUCL-K fact finding report about
Bangalore (Bangalore, 2001), http://www.pucl.org/Topics/Gender/20.03/sexual-
minorities.pdf (describing incidents where Bangalore police detained and harassed
hijras seemingly on the basis of their behavior and self-fashioned appearance rather
than on the basis of any 'biological markers' of gender).

94. See *supra* text accompanying notes 81–88. Another similarity in identification practices for the *hijras* and the dancing girls that might be noted in this

report is that all of the dancing girls are identified using only one name (e.g. 'Rozi'), a practice which is generally followed vis-à-vis the *hijras* as well. The majority of detained men, however, are identified with what appears to be both a first name and surname.

95. See Redding (2010: 29, 42–44) for a discussion of different historical interpretations of the word *qaum*. See Yoginder Sikand, 'Islam and Caste Inequality: Among Indian Muslims', http://www.law.emory.edu/ihr/yogi3. html for an exploration of both the existence and appropriateness of caste affiliation (or ascription) amongst Indian Muslims.

96. This gendered aspect to *qaum* does not seem to have received any prior scholarly attention. See Redding, *supra* note 95, for discussion of the general parameters of recent scholarly discussion on *qaum*.

97. Clearly, I am reasoning in this Part from an assumed male/female dichotomy, and attempting to place hijras somewhere in a world defined by two 'poles' called 'male' and 'female'. This is not the only way to 'do gender,' however, and I note the controversial nature of my method here. By way of contrast, one might wonder whether *males* are somewhere in-between the two poles of 'female' and *hijra*. Due to space limitations, I do not engage in this kind of analysis here, though I do hope to return to this and similar issues in future work.

98. But see *supra* note 29.

99. Dr. Khaki himself suggested to me that the term 'unix' entered the Supreme Court record as a result of a mistake of a court clerk who was 'just typing'. Dr. Mohammad Aslam Khaki, interviewed by author, Islamabad, Pakistan, March 10, 2012. However, Dr. Khaki also went on to explain to me that this term persisted in Court discussions for some time because the Supreme Court judges themselves had very little experience with different extant vocabularies concerning transgenderism. *Ibid.* Thus, there is still some question as to the reasons—conscious or otherwise—which motivated the use of a term that is seemingly related not only to the term 'unisex' but also the 'generic' computer operating system known as 'UNIX'.

100. Report 'minjānib: ḍapuṭī suparanṭanḍant āf pōlīs lēgal āparēshanz, rāwalpinḍī; bajānib: sēni'ir suparanṭanḍant āf pōlīs āparēshanz, rāwalpinḍī' [From: Deputy Superintendent of Police, Legal Operations, Rawalpindi; To: Senior Superintendent of Police Operations, Rawalpindi], at 24-25 (Feb. 28, 2009) (on file with author).

101. See *supra* text accompanying note 65.

102. See *supra* text accompanying note 40.

103. Report 'minjānib: ḍapuṭī suparanṭanḍant āf pōlīs lēgal āparēshanz, rāwalpinḍī; bajānib: sēni'ir suparanṭanḍant āf pōlīs āparēshanz, rāwalpinḍī' [From: Deputy Superintendent of Police, Legal Operations, Rawalpindi; To: Senior Superintendent of Police Operations, Rawalpindi], at 27 (Feb. 28, 2009) (on file with author).

104. Dr. Aslam Khaki viewed this 'leadership' as more akin to 'enslavement.' See *supra* note 37. This, however, is a controversial characterization and I avoid using it here.

105. While there is much more that could be said about this assumption, it might be noted in its defense that the Supreme Court chose to use the terms 'eunuchs' and 'unix' even though the Court was presented with a lengthy investigatory report from the Northwest Frontier Province's Social Welfare and Women Development department, detailing a very complex ontology of transgenderism and transgendered identities found in Pakistan. *See generally* Report prepared by the Social Welfare and Women Development Department (N.W.F.P.), Aug. 13, 2009 (on file with author). This report offered the Court with an opportunity to use a wide range of more-specific terms to describe the transgendered individuals whose welfare was being litigated at the Court, including 'Shemale', 'Spiritual *Hijra*', 'Dervish *Hijra*', and 'Pseudo *Hijra*'. See generally *ibid*. While emphasizing the reality of this transgendered diversity, this report also notes that '[i]n our culture, the word '*Hijra*' (Male-to-Female gender dysphoric) is used as an umbrella term that includes all the persons with physical anomaly (impotence)[,] physiological androgyny (intersex), sexual androgyny (homosexual)[,] behavioral androgyny, (personal social anomalies in gender), and psychological androgyny (anomalies in gender identity)'. *Ibid.* at 7. Nonetheless, according to this report, "[t]he usage of the umbrella term *Hijra* for different anomalies of Gender dysphoric needs to be discouraged'. *Ibid.* at 13. In other words then, one defensible interpretation of the Court's use of 'eunuchs' and 'unix' is that the Court not only decided to ignore this report's cautionary advice about the use of generic identifiers, but then also substituted a (relatively) generic identifier of its own choosing. See also Chatterjee (1999: 46, 48–9) for a discussion of the role of 'androgynous' eunuchs in notable Indian Muslim households during the 19[h]-century, thereby suggesting a possible continuity between the contemporary use of this term and historical patterns of gender-generic understanding and usage.

106. See *supra* text accompanying note 18.

107. Considering this, this indicates yet another reason not to consider this Pakistani litigation as concerning 'transgendered' rights generally; left unclear by the decision is its impact on female-to-male transgendered persons.

108. Considering their noted names, all of the police officers listed in the text accompanying *supra* note 100 appear to be male police officers.

References

Ayres, A.C. 1992. A Scandalous Breach of Public Decency: Defining the Decent. Indian Hijras in the Nineteenth and Twentieth Centuries'. B.A. thesis: Harvard University.

Chatterjee, Indrani. 1999. *Gender, Slavery and Law in Colonial India*. New Delhi: Oxford University Press.

Cohen, L. 1995. 'Holi in Banaras and the Mahaland of Modernity', *GLQ: A Journal in Lesbian and Gay Studies*, 2: 399-424.

'Eunuch protests lead to 3 cops' suspensions'. *Daily Times*. January 28, 2009. *http://archives.dailytimes.com.pk/islamabad/28-Jan-2009/eunuch-protest-leads-to-3-cops-suspension* 25/06/2014

Long, Scott. 2004. 'In a Time of Torture: The Assault on Justice in Egypt's Crackdown on Homosexual Conduct'. New York: Human Rights Watch. *http://www.hrw.org/sites/default/files/reports/egypt0304_0.pdf* 25/06/2014

Morris, Rosalind C. 1994. *Three Sexes and Four Sexualities: Redressing the Discourses on Gender and Sexuality in Contemporary Thailand*. Durham, North Carolina: Duke University Press.

People's Union for Civil Liberties-Karnataka. 2001. 'Human rights violations against sexuality minorities in India: A PUCL-K fact finding report about Bangalore', Bangalore. *http://www.pucl.org/Topics/Gender/2003/sexual-minorities.pdf*. 25/06/2014.

Redding, Jeffrey A. 2004. 'Constitutionalizing Islam: Theory and Pakistan', *Virginia Journal of International Law*, 44: 759-827.

———. 2010. 'Beyond Exclusion: A Review of Peter J. Spiro's "Beyond Citizenship"', *Minnesota Law Review Headnotes*, 95: 29-44.

Reddy, Gayatri. 2006. *With Respect to Sex: Negotiating Hijra Identity in South India*. Chicago: University of Chicago Press.

Sikand, Yoginder. 2004. 'Islam and Caste Inequality: Among Indian Muslims'. *http://www.law.emory.edu/ihr/yogi3.html*. 25/06/2014.

Suhail, Sarah. 2010. 'Eunuchs and Rights', *Chay Magazine*. November 28, 2010.*http://chaymagazine.org/2010-society-nov/300-eunuchs-and-rights*. 26/06/2013

Walsh, Declan. 'Harassed, Intimidated, Abused: But now Pakistan's Hijra Transgender Minority Finds Its Voice'. *The Guardian*. January 29, 2010. *http://www.guardian.co.uk/world/2010/jan/29/hijra-pakistan-transgender-rights*. 25/06/2014.

Walsh, Nick Paton. "Pakistan's transgender tribe of tax collectors." *CNN*. April 14, 2011. *http://articles.cnn.com/2011-04-14/world/pakistan.tax.collectors_1_tax-collectors-tax-debtors-tax-deadline?_s=PM:WORLD*. 25/06/2014.

Case Documents (in Alphabetic Order)

Constitutional Petition No. 43 of 2009, 04.11.2009 Order. *On file with author.*

Constitutional Petition No. 43 of 2009, 20.11.2009 Order. *On file with author.*

Constitutional Petition No. 43 of 2009, 23.12.2009 Order. *On file with author.*

Khaki, Dr. Mohammad Aslam, Interview with author, Islamabad, Pakistan. (March 10, 2012). *On file with author.*

Khaki, Dr Mohammad Aslam v. Senior Superintendent of Police (Operation) Rawalpindi, H/R Constitutional Petition No. 63/2009. *On file with author.*

Human Rights Case No. 63 of 2009, 14.07.2009 Order. *On file with author.*

Human Rights Case No. 63 of 2009, 17-08-2009 Order. *On file with author.*

Human Rights Constitutional Petition No. 63. 16.06.2009 Order. (2009). *On file with author.*

Human Rights Constitutional Petition No. 63. 14.07.2009 Order. (2009). *On file with author.*

Memo from Inspector General of Police (Punjab, Lahore) to the Registrar of Supreme Court of Pakistan, Islamabad, 19-3. (2009). *On file with author.*

Report 'minjānib: ḍapuṭī suparanṭanḍant āf pōlīs lēgal āparēshanz, Rāwalpinḍī; bajānib: sēni'ir suparanṭanḍant āf pōlīs āparēshanz, Rāwalpinḍī' [From: Deputy Superintendent of Police, Legal Operations, Rawalpindi; To: Senior Superintendent of Police Operations, Rawalpindi]. (Feb. 28, 2009). *On file with author.*

Report prepared by the Regional Police Officer, Rawalpindi for the Inspector General of Police, Punjab, Lahore. (2009). *On file with author.*

Report prepared by the Social Welfare and Women Development Department. (Aug. 13, 2009). *On file with author.*

9

VÉRONIQUE BOUILLIER

From a Comparative Perspective

Criminal Cases involving South Asian People at French Assize Courts*

In cases of serious offence, French criminal proceedings take place at Courts of Assize. My purpose in writing this essay is to present the sequence of events as they happen during a criminal trial. I highlight the part that the different actors play in the judiciary performance and the differences in proceedings between the French inquisitorial system and the accusatorial or adversarial system as practised in England, the USA, and South Asia.

The cases I followed involved litigants of South Asian origin, who may eventually have been familiar with legal systems based on common law. By observing the interactions between people of foreign origin, culture, and language, and French law courts, we are more conscious of the specificities of the procedure involved, and, I might add, of the many difficulties and misunderstandings that may emerge in

* This essay is part of the ANR programme, 'Justice and Governance in India and South Asia' (http://just-india.net). Research on which this chapter was based was funded by the French National Research Agency (ANR-08-GOUV-064). I am thankful to Daniela Berti and Devika Bordia for their comments on a first draft of this text.

such circumstances. The French administrative and legal system's lack of familiarity with South Asians adds to the difficulties encountered. Examining French criminal proceedings from a different, comparative perspective helps to define their characteristics.

People of South Asian descent residing in France come from various backgrounds. The first group includes people from the former French colony, Pondicherry, who settled in France in the 1950s, while the last to arrive are Nepalese refugees fleeing the civil war. It so happened that the criminal trials I was able to attend during the period 2009–2010 involved Sri Lankan citizens who are Tamil refugees. About 70,000 Sri Lankan refugees have settled in France since the seventies, mainly in Paris and its suburbs, where for the most part they carry out menial tasks in shops or restaurants. Many of them have been granted asylum and have been able to settle as families. However, some are still illegal residents and have difficulties in securing a proper job and lodgings, therefore, leading a secluded and solitary existence. Alcohol is often their only solace and, as I saw in court, unfortunately the primary reason they end up before the Assize.

The case I have chosen to focus on is rather unusual as it involves a Sri Lankan women who was accused of murder and was subsequently found guilty, but which is meaningful and exemplar in its complexity and implications.

Setting of the Trial: The Jury

A trial, lasting a few days, comes after a series of lengthy enquiries that are made under the supervision of an investigating judge and which may take between two and ten years to complete. Most of the time, the person suspected of the crime is held in pre-trial detention; he or she is called *'mis en examen'* (placed under judicial investigation), a linguistic turn that is meant to avoid any presumption of culpability. However, after being committed to the Court of Assize, the suspect becomes 'the accused'.

The Assize courtroom is at the centre of the court buildings. Its theatrical layout is designed to impress: on one side are terraced benches for members of the public, on the opposite side a semi-circular podium for the judiciary actors and in between the dock, with the defence lawyer at the front. Different doors lead to the different spaces, according to a person's status in the trial: entries and exits are subjected to a very strict code. Everything is done to give the impression of solemnity and almost religious reverence. For instance, when the judge enters the courtroom, a bell rings and the solemn voice of the clerk announces: 'Mesdames, Messieurs, la cour!' (i.e., Ladies and Gentlemen, all rise). And everybody stands quickly yet silently. Then, when the jurors and judges have reached their places and are standing behind their seats, the presiding judge declares: 'You can now sit!' Such a ceremony takes place every time the judge exits or breaks for the day.

The Assize is made up of a presiding judge who leads the hearing, two assessors, and six lay jurors (or nine in the case of an appeal).[1] Together they decide on the eventual culpability of the accused and the relevant sentence. The jurors sit on either side of the presiding judge and assessors. Not far from them and on the same level stands the public prosecutor, whose role is to defend the values of society and public interest, hence the name 'advocate general', avocat général at the Court of Assize.[2] On the prosecutor's side, but not on the podium, are the lawyers representing the victims, or the victims themselves: they are called the parties civiles, the civil plaintiffs, and they often intervene during the trial. On the other side of the room, facing them is/are the defence lawyer(s) next to the accused. It is a very hierarchical setup: the lawyers are at ground level, whereas the judges and prosecutor are higher up, on a podium. Even the chairs are subtly arranged, the presiding judge seated in an impressive armchair, whilst the lawyers sit on simple benches.[3]

The main difference with Indian criminal courts is the presence and role of the jury. As members of civil society, potential jurors are first selected from the electoral roll for each circumscription. Then, for each Assize session, which lasts fifteen days, a panel of at least thirty people are selected at random.[4] These potential jurors must be present at the beginning of each new lawsuit, and the presiding judge chooses six (or nine for appeal cases) effective jurors from among these people by drawing lots. Each person receives a number; the presiding judge takes a token from a wooden box placed in front of him and reads aloud the number on the token. The person with the same number stands up and slowly moves to the podium where they sit as juror. However, the prosecutor and the defence lawyer have the right to challenge this selection, the former three times and the latter four times. Contrary to proceedings in the USA, they have no information about the jurors except their name, age, and profession, thus, they may recuse a juror based on the aforementioned, plus their physical appearance.[5] When a person is challenged in this way, they often experience ambivalent feelings: they smile awkwardly, they are spared a difficult and demanding task, yet somehow they feel excluded.

The selected jurors sit on either side of the judges, facing the public and the accused. Before their selection, they are briefed on the role they are to play in the proceedings. In particular, they are told not to show any emotions or feelings, not to react to anything said or shown in court and, if they have any questions, to pass them on in writing to the presiding judge who formats them so that they meet the required juridical neutrality and impartiality.

The jurors are once again informed of the importance of the role they play when they take the oath. The presiding judge reads them the following formula, then each juror stands, raises their right hand and says: 'I swear'. There is no question in secular France of swearing on the Bible or on any sacred symbol.

> You swear and promise to scrupulously examine the charges against X, to not betray the interests of the accused, nor of the society that accuses him, nor of the victim; […] not to be guided by hate or wickedness, nor by fear or affection; to remember that the accused is presumed innocent and that doubt must benefit him; to decide after considering the charges and the means of the defence, according to your conscience and your innermost convictions, with the impartiality and the rightness which befit an honest and free man, and to keep deliberations secret (Code of Criminal Procedure, article 304).

And again, at the very end of the trial, just before going into deliberation, the jury will be reminded to judge the accused 'in all conscience' (*en âme et conscience*). The presiding judge reads them the following rule, quoted from the *Code de procedure pénale* (Code of Criminal Procedure, article 353):

> The law does not require judges to account for the reasons they are convinced, it does not prescribe rules […]; it stipulates that they have to ask themselves in silence and contemplation and to seek, according to their true conscience, what impression the evidence given against the accused and the means of his defence have made on their reason. The law only asks them this one question, which gives the full measure of their duties: 'Are you firmly convinced?'

To appeal to the jurors' conscience, to their inner self is culturally meaningful and reflects a Judaeo-Christian conception of the person, where psychological categories have superficially replaced references to God and to the soul.

Although the prosecutor makes his accusations on behalf of the state and demands application of the law, the jury's position represents society in the objective act of judging: justice is done on behalf of and by the citizens.[6] The proceedings are dictated by the presence of the lay jury—heritage of the French Revolution influenced by the British system based on common law—and its ignorance of the case: everything has to be clarified and didactically explained in order for the jury to decide in all honesty. The way the jury is made up reflects society: a jury in Paris looks different from one in the multicultural suburbs, such as Seine Saint Denis. Prosecutors told me that, when challenging the jurors, they try to make the jury as representative of the *departement*'s population as possible, and they consider that 'there is no better training for citizenship than to be part of the legal process and to be considered representative of society'.[7] In France, the role of the jury in court cases gives rise to many passionate arguments, motivated by political ploys.[8]

Courtrooms are open to the public (in camera excepted). The idea is to make the public part of the judicial procedure, when sentence is passed 'in the name of the French people'. And the sentence must be 'exemplar'. However, the public may be reduced to the families of the litigants, and in some cases in Bobigny, I was actually the only member of the public, which says a lot about the isolation of some of the South Asian people involved.

The First Step: 'Ordonnance de Mise en Accusation', Bill of Indictment

As soon as the jury has been chosen, when everyone is in their proper place, the clerk starts the proceedings by reading aloud the charge against the accused. Known as an '*ordonnance de mise en accusation*', this long text sets out for the court the long process that started with the discovery of the victim and ends with the appearance before the court of the person accused of a criminal offence.

Thus, in an inquisitorial system, the facts are established by the investigating judge (who does not appear in court). Trial proceedings serve to clarify and to give the details of a narrative that is regarded as being fundamentally truthful. This is symbolized by the fact that only one word in French, les faits (the facts), 'indexes both the charges alleged during the investigation as well as the facts established during the trial' (Terrio 2009: 49). Committing the accused for trial before a Court of Assize on the investigating judge's decision, therefore supposes that the investigation has already proved the charges against the accused. In the case of Mrs X, for instance, the ordonnance specifies that: 'the inquiry has helped to establish that Mrs X wilfully killed Mr Y [...] and that she used all the resources available to achieve her goal'.

The bill of indictment begins by establishing the identity of the defendant(s), their name, and their parents' name. This can be confusing in the case of Tamil litigants, since on arrival in France, often as refugees, they generally give their first name, which is registered as their family name (surname). When asked to give their first name, they are hesitant and may give their father's name. Unfamiliar with the Tamil language and its usages, the various administrations mix up the order of the names, which may temporarily benefit the accused. In one case, the presiding judge declared: 'you are unknown in police records under the name X, but under the name Y (recognized as the first name), there is a lot of information!' Another example of this emerged in the case that I develop here: three brothers, the victim's brothers, act as civil plaintiffs. Two have the same family name (written in capitals on the act) as the victim, and the third has this family name written in small capitals as his first name: thus, the family includes four brothers, three Arumugam[9] and one Kanalingam, with Arumugam as his first name.

Once the person's identity has been established, the motive for the accusation is given. The person is placed under judicial investigation (mise en examen) charged with... of victim X. In criminal procedures at the Assize, charges mainly concern rape, incest, or murder. The cases I followed all involved murder, but the charge can vary, for instance, between manslaughter (or 'assault and battery causing death without intention', coups et blessures ayant entraîné la mort sans intention de la donner), 'attempted murder' (tentative d'assassinat), 'murder' (meurtre or homicide volontaire), and 'premeditated murder' (assassinat avec préméditation). According to how it is qualified, the maximum sentences vary from fifteen years to life imprisonment; it therefore happens that, before the trial takes place, lawyers make all efforts to have the charge reclassified by trying to justify that a murder was in fact a case of manslaughter.

The different articles in the Penal Code related to the case are then mentioned as follows: 'Crime listed and punishable according to articles 221–3, etc. of the Criminal Code'. In French trials, judgement is passed according to the Law, as written in the Codes, and precedents are neither mentioned nor used (except in very special cases in order to specify a general rule). The Criminal Code and the Code of Criminal Procedure are the two legal guidebooks to be found on the desk of every magistrate. Every decision must be taken according to the law and must quote the article it is based on. However, the law may change and various amendments are often added.[10]

For instance, in the case of Mrs. X., she was placed under investigation charged with 'assassination, premeditated murder of a male victim who could be Mr. X. The crime was committed on... at ..., on national territory and at an unspecified time.' She was also accused of concealing a dead body (*recel de cadavre*) and of an offence against the integrity of a dead body (*atteinte à l'intégrité d'un cadavre*).

The bill of indictment then goes on to develop the different steps in the investigation. Starting with the discovery of the crime, it explains the different actions undertaken by the police: searches at the scene of the crime, examination of the victim, questioning of the first witnesses, and the eventual arrest of a suspect. The police immediately report to the prosecutor, who asks the *juge d'instruction* (examining magistrate) to investigate; this examining magistrate's task is to conduct judicial investigations of serious offences.[11] Any subsequent police enquiries, hearings with witnesses and suspects, experts' reports come under the supervision of the examining judge, who collects all the data and compiles the dossier.

Let us look at the case in question. The beginning of the description given in the file starts as follows: Around 6 p.m., a few passers-by notice a suitcase floating on the SD canal. They bring it up onto the bank and discover some human remains inside. They call the police who question the people present and the next day they discover more remains in a plastic bag hidden behind a bush. A preliminary medico-legal expertise leads to the reconstitution of the body of 'a person of Asian type'. Police inspectors identify the fingerprints using OFPRA's[12] register of refugees and they are able to give the victim a name.

A judicial inquiry is opened against 'a person or persons unknown' and the investigating judge launches various inquiries. With the name of the victim who is a man, the judicial police is able to discover his place of residence: he was living in the apartment of Mrs X, a widow born in Sri Lanka. After questioning neighbours, they discover that the victim had been in a relationship with Mrs X (as 'concubines') and that they had a young child. Mrs X was arrested and placed in police custody. On searching her bag, they discovered a supermarket receipt for a circular saw. Mrs X, speaking through an interpreter, admitted that she had a relationship with the victim and complained that he had been violent. She first denied the murder, but then confessed. She gave the victim crushed sleeping pills, and then looked for a way of disposing of the body. The report gives many gory details about how she said she had proceeded. At another hearing the next day, she added that she had phoned her young son to ask for his help, without explaining the situation to him. Travelling over night by train, he arrived at his mother's flat and discovered the dying man. Later he helped his mother to dispose of the corpse. They confessed to cutting up the corpse into pieces and to trying to hide them, throwing a suitcase containing the head and trunk into the canal.

After hearing Mrs X's confession that she willingly 'killed' the victim, and since the details of the enquiry confirmed her story, the investigating judge charged Mrs X with Mr. Y's premeditated murder and ordered her indictment before the Court of Assize.

This first narrative of the facts is written in a linear format, with no mention of the questions or dialogues, with no allusion to the fact that every word said by or to the defendant was translated into or from Tamil.[13] It is supposed to be a flat neutral rendering of the process leading to committal before the Assize.

The document I have paraphrased here is read aloud by the bailiff. It is a summary of the investigations and of the alleged charges against the accused. For the lay jury, it is their first contact with the court case.

This reading shows the importance of the relationship between the oral and written word in the French procedure. French proceedings are supposed to be purely oral, and it is quite true that at the time of the trial everything has to be presented orally: the accused, the witnesses, the experts have to explain their position verbally to the jury and the jury must only take into account what they hear during the few days of the trial as elements to help them to decide on the culpability of the accused. Moreover, no record is kept of what is said during the hearing, with the clerk writing only the formal sequence of what happens even when a witness gives new information or when the accused changes his statement.[14] Indeed, the way the prosecutor, the victims', or civil plaintiffs' lawyer and defence lawyer plead the case is a pure moment of oral eloquence, for which there is no written trace.

However, though the lay jurors and the two assessors arrive at the trial with no previous knowledge of the case and gradually make their judgement according to their impression during the hearings, this is not the case for the presiding judge, the prosecutor, and the lawyers. They attend the court laden with enormous files, which contain the records of everything ever done during the investigation.[15]

As an example of this complex relationship between oral debates and written files and the constant shift from one to the other, let us look at the case of witnesses' evidence. After being told to wait outside the courtroom, the witnesses are summoned, one by one when their turn comes, by the bailiff. They enter the room through a special door and are usually very impressed by the imposing decor. It is probably the first time they enter a courtroom.[16] They walk to the middle of the room, to the bar (*à la barre*), and remain standing before the presiding judge who asks them to state their identity and then makes them swear to say 'the whole truth and nothing but the truth'. Then the judge asks every witness to make an 'unprepared statement': 'Tell us what you have to say'. Ordinary witnesses, especially when foreign and ignorant of the judiciary ritual, are very surprised at this: they have been requested to come, and what is more, they have already said everything they know to the investigating judge! They often maintain an awkward silence and the presiding judge has to explain: 'Tell us first what you saw or what you know, and then you will answer our questions'. The witness then tells his story, but, although the discourse is new to the jury who listen eagerly, the presiding judge already has all the witness's previous testimonies in the dossier. And he refers to his files when questioning the witness: 'at a previous hearing with the examining judge, you said so and so... Can you confirm this?' The judge formulates his questions according to what he already knows and he confronts the witness with contradictions or lapses of memory.[17] The situation is rather disconcerting for the witnesses: they are told to explain everything again for the jurors but this is done before the judge who has a record of everything each witness has ever said about the case, and this sometimes gives the impression of a cat playing with a mouse.

Verbal evidence is also required from the police officers in charge of the investigation, but they may be allowed to use their field notes. They made their inquiries at least two or three years ago and, as they have dealt with other cases since then, they can easily make a mistake or forget a detail, even though they have prepared for their hearing. I remember the judge reproaching a young police officer for having come without her notes and for saying something different from her previous statement that had been recorded in the file.

In sum, the investigation is run by an investigating judge who gives orders to the judicial police, hears the witnesses, summons the experts, and produces reams of written files, on which the trial is based.[18] Yet the trial itself is essentially oral: any argument that has not been orally defended before the jurors cannot be taken into consideration. Indeed, this ambiguity between oral and written forms is clearly reflected in the secrecy surrounding the file: even though the public is allowed and even welcome to attend the court case and to listen to all the declarations, access to any of the files, even after the ruling, is impossible.[19] And the few websites that publish decisions only mention a few cases and give only the sentence with no further details.

Defendant

In criminal cases, the accused or defendant is likely to be placed in pre-trial detention. This was the case of Mrs X who was detained in the women's quarters of Fresnes prison. Every day during the trial, when she arrived from the jail she entered the courtroom, handcuffed and surrounded by two policemen. Her handcuffs were removed and, with the policemen still on either side of her, she sat in the dock, which was open only at the front, while the other two sides were closed with glass panels. These security measures were a striking contrast to her frail appearance, as is generally the case with the timid, humble attitude of Sri Lankan defendants.[20] Her lawyer was seated before the dock, close to her, and they talked freely through an interpreter.

The interpreter is an essential character in the assize drama. According to judicial ideology, the litigants must understand the proceedings; hence the presence of an interpreter is required at every stage in the investigations and during the trial itself. In the case of Sri Lankan Tamil speakers, some thirty to fifty interpreters are listed at the different courts or police stations. They are of Sri Lanka or Pondicherry origin, with varying linguistic abilities, and faced with an extremely difficult task. They have to translate both ways, from French to Tamil and Tamil to French. They must be familiar with the strange type of French spoken in courtrooms and must be able to explain in plain Tamil the peculiarities of the judiciary vocabulary. They have to be very fast, especially when translating the bill of indictment: in the case of Mrs X, the interpreter was a young lady, as specifically required by the accused, and the presiding judge allowed her to have a written copy of the bill. Standing close to the accused, she whispered everything that was written. Then, during the debates that followed, she translated all the questions and answers for the accused and for the jury as well as the witnesses' testimonies and experts' reports. She even translated the prosecutor's and attorney's speeches for the accused, which is not the case with all interpreters.

Hearings using the services of an interpreter induce a peculiar and often frustrating situation. The idea of a literal translation is pure fiction since the interpreter has, for instance, to explain or rephrase the questions in order for the accused to fully understand them.[21] On the other hand, the interpreter often tries to convey the replies of the accused as clearly as possible, for on hearing vague or misleading answers the bench is quick to chastise them for a misunderstanding or/and poor translation. '*Monsieur l'interprete*, it needs to be clear', an irritated judge once said aggressively. Thus, what is heard as a stream of Tamil, may be reduced to a few sentences. I remember a long and very passionate explanation between a Sri Lankan suspect and his interpreter about his presence at a given location that was reduced to the mere formula: 'He says it was not him!' For the audience, the time lapse between the explanation or the answer given in Tamil and their understanding of it after translation is also frustrating: bodily attitudes and facial expressions are visible but their meaning is lost.[22] As judges often say: 'Translation makes the hearing void of any emotion'. And whatever the capacities of the interpreter, it is impossible to render the subtleties of the discourse: the hesitations, hedges, or the passionate or pleading tone of voice. The special place the interpreter holds in court becomes evident during the process of questioning: at first, the presiding judge addresses the accused and then the interpreter translates: 'Mrs X, do you think....? Did you, etc.?' Then the points at issue are gradually addressed more and more directly to the interpreter, and it is up to them to form the questions: 'Did Mrs. X recognize that...? Has she been going...?' And in the end the questions become very indirect, with the translator having to find a way of conveying the judge's expectations: 'Ask her if she has anything to say'.

The defendant was given two main occasions to talk freely during the proceedings. At the beginning when she was asked to talk about herself and at the very end, just before the jury's deliberation. The presiding judge's invitation: 'Now Mrs X, tell us who you are, tell us about your childhood, your life and your feelings', might have been somewhat disconcerting for the accused if she had not been prepared by her lawyer for such intrusion into her personal life. As written in the Criminal Code (article 132–24), in the French inquisitorial system judgement concerns the person as well as the facts: 'Courts pronounce sentences according to the circumstances of the offence and to the personality of the perpetrator'.[23] Judges want 'to know the truth', to understand what was done, and that means that the criminal act has to be examined in its context. Judges want to know what induced the person to commit such a crime. This is why the accused was questioned about her life, why witnesses were summoned to describe their personal relationship with the accused and to give their opinion about her character, and why psychological experts were called upon (as we shall see later).

Thus, in her statement, when talking of her childhood, Mrs X explained that she was the eldest of a family of seven, that her parents had been relatively well off until they suffered financial problems: 'My mother said that my father's family put a spell on us and that is why my father changed and started to drink. They were jealous because my father, as the youngest, inherited the family property upon his father's death'. 'We went to Colombo... I took care of my brothers and sisters... Many men wanted to marry me... I was obliged to accept my cousin because he threatened to commit suicide otherwise... My father was mortally burned in his house during the war, and I stayed with him till his death... First I refused any sexual relations with my husband, but my stepmother thought I was barren and wanted him to take another wife... Then I bore two children... My husband started to drink with friends… I became pregnant with my third child, but I tried to get an abortion; I didn't want this child, but it failed'. And in reply to a question from the judge (looking at his files), she answered: 'Yes, it's the son I called to help me, and yes he was born with leg trouble after the abortion attempt'. We see with these few remarks how, when incited by the judge's precise questions, the defendant is led to disclose personal and intimate information.[24]

The Judiciary Discourse: What is Said and What is Expected

When listening to debates in assize courts, I am always surprised at how much importance is attributed to very minor details, which at first do not seem particularly relevant. These details may concern the life of the accused or the facts, such as a detailed timetable of the preceding day's activities or of the persons met. For instance, in a lawsuit concerning a murder caused by a screwdriver, an hour was devoted to discussing the type and size of screwdriver because after the culprit's first narrative, confession and subsequent seizure of the tool, another screwdriver was discovered in the room: even if this one was free of any fingerprints or blood, it was considered important to show it to the jury and to discuss in length with the accused which screwdriver had been taken. A complete set of details is supposed to give a true picture of the situation, and the search for truth is the main purpose of the trial. As previously pointed out, the French legal system constantly refers to the idea of truth.[25] As one presiding judge says: 'We are here to discover the truth', and a prosecutor: 'Perhaps truth will emerge from the debates, which will be quite close to The Truth'. And when there was a slight difference between two of Mrs X's successive answers, she was sternly rebuked: 'You are lying!' Such accusations are also made when the accused or the witnesses diverge from the written statement they gave to the investigating judge. During the trial, the presiding judge and the prosecutor may quote previous statements and ask for explanations: when the accused changes their version of the facts, they make a very bad impression on the jury.[26] In one court case, when a defendant denied a statement, the judge was rather indignant: 'The court has made a mistake, here is your answer…'

How can the defendants know what is expected of them? Coming from a country with an adversarial system of justice, they try to protect themselves by denying the facts or else they hope to negotiate. And seeing that judges (during the investigation process and the trial) ask the same questions again and again, a defendant may infer that the judges are not satisfied with his/her answers and therefore modifies them in order to find a credible story. There is a complete misunderstanding about the purpose of the trial.

What is expected of the accused is their collaboration in the trial, their compliance with the proceedings. This compliance is measured by their acceptance of their culpability. The trial relies on a 'culture of confession', of acknowledged guilt. In this context, to remain silent is to behave badly:[27] 'If the defendant fails to respond, the judge will assume the worst' (Moskovitz 1995: 1135). Mrs X was very voluble and this was a point in her favour: 'She cooperates fully with the justice' says her lawyer.

Problems arise when there are memory lapses. One can well imagine that many years later, when the time of the trial finally arrives, litigants as well as witnesses may have forgotten some details and be confused. This may also be a useful strategy when reprimanded for providing insubstantial answers. Alcohol also serves as a similar device to explain lapses of memory: 'I am sorry, I don't remember, I was drunk!' An excuse that can be shared with the French culture, a common language… though not always: 'You said that you drank whisky, before that you talked about cognac, is that the same thing in Sri Lanka, cognac and whisky? You said you drank cognac at 9 a.m., in France we don't drink cognac at 9 a.m.!'…

Active collaboration during the trial is seen as a way of adhering to the rehabilitative model, the idea that judgement and sentencing are part of a process aimed at the culprit's social reinsertion: the prison is presented (illusorily or hypocritically?) as a place where the culprit will make amends, pay his debt to society and the victims, and prepare to start a new virtuous life. 'Is the culprit mentally fit to stand[28] punishment?' [*accessible à la sanction*] is a question the psychologist has to answer in his report. Confessing culpability, expressing remorse, and showing emotional displays are signs of the (forced) acceptance by the accused of a judiciary system grounded on moral standards, which regards misdeed and punishment as leading to rehabilitation. In this context, the reports made by the penitentiary administration, which are read in court, are of utmost importance. They elucidate the prisoner's behaviour, their obedience, their relationship to others, their efforts to learn. Mrs X for instance benefited from a very positive report stating her trustworthiness and her generous attitude towards other women: she cooked for everyone, other women called her '*maman*', and warders entrusted young psychologically fragile prisoners to her care.

The last opportunity for the accused to express the sort of feelings that are expected of them, is at the end of the trial, just before the jury withdraws. It may happen that with a few vindictive words the accused ruins the lawyer's efforts to influence the jury: he (or she) may find it hard to accept their council's advice and keep a low profile, to ask for clemency and forgiveness instead of claiming to have suffered great wrongdoing. A vengeful Durga is not good in French courts. Mrs X fully understood her lawyer's explanations, and she showed the appropriate emotions: her last redeeming tears and apologies won over the jury, and she therefore benefited from mitigating circumstances.

The place held by the accused during the trial is somewhat paradoxical. He (or she) is of course the centre; everything revolves around him, yet this centre is somehow hollow. The accused is not so much an actor as much as a spectator at his own trial. During the few days of the hearing, various experts, investigators, witnesses speak and are supposed to tell the truth (they swear an oath) about the facts or the person of the accused. A narrative is constructed which is beyond the grasp or the control of the accused, but which claims to tell their truth. Seldom are reports translated for them and seldom are they asked to comment on the psychologist's and psychiatrist's findings. Much depends on the attitude of the presiding judge who organizes the debates and decides whether the accused can talk or not. Interestingly enough, witnesses and experts have to stand before the bench and talk only to the judges, hardly ever looking at the accused. And, even when the defence lawyer questions them, they have to face the judges. In some ways, the accused is left out of the proceedings. Indeed, Mrs X was very upset; she told the interpreter: 'Everybody is talking about me, making comments, and yet I have no right to speak. I can only answer questions. When will I be able to speak?' To which her lawyer answered, anxious about any declarations she might make: 'You will be able to, but you have to talk to me first!'

The role of the lawyer is, of course, to defend the accused using convincing arguments but also, in the event where people know nothing of the French procedural system, to explain what is required of them, what demeanour they must adopt to incite clemency. Defence lawyers at the Court of Assize are usually specialist lawyers; they can be privately hired, but in many cases involving poor litigants, they are appointed by the state. This may benefit the defendant, since pleading before the assize court is one of the duties of the best attorneys, those selected every year after a competitive examination, the twelve *Secretaires de la Conférence* (Conference Secretaries).

Victims

What characterizes the French Assize trial is the presence of both, the public prosecutor who represents society and the wrong it has suffered by the breach of its rules, and the victims, called civil plaintiffs, who are defended by their lawyers.[29]

Various scenarios are possible: either the victim survives and attends the hearing, or if dead, his family acts as plaintiff. It may also happen, especially where illegal and isolated immigrants are concerned, that nobody appears in court; the bench on the side of the civil plaintiff remains empty, and the prosecutor therefore has to defend the victim as well as society, as in trial proceedings in the USA.

During the trial, the place attributed to the victim as a person varies considerably. When nobody is there to represent them, the victim appears strangely absent. Obviously, the trial focuses on the accused, their personality, their actions, and their eventual punishment: the victim is often portrayed merely as a wounded body that is presented to the audience through alarming pictures and descriptions. However, much depends on the victims' social conditions.

In fact, the victim appears to be either an extenuating or aggravating circumstance for the culprit. The defence lawyer's main argument is often based on the victim's violent tendencies or threatening attitude, which forced the accused to react. For instance, Mrs X's defence argued that she had been ill-treated, beaten, and blackmailed by her companion, that in her position she had had no other choice but to get rid of him: his own violence obliged her to kill him! Even though the victim's violence was strongly challenged by the prosecutor, no inquiries had been made about his behaviour. The grievances of the accused were taken for granted 'in this *département* where so many women are ill-treated', 'where to be ill-treated is part of their culture' (in the words of a witness).

However, the lawyer skilfully defended the victim's misfortune when he narrated how the latter had arrived in France, fleeing from the Sri Lankan war: 'He took refuge in France to save his life and he found death!' And at Mrs X's trial, the testimony given by the victim's brothers was received in icy silence as they explained in floods of tears that a small part of the body was missing, and therefore the cremation had been incomplete and their brother's soul was still roaming around discontented. The jurors looked at the accused in a hostile manner. However, when the same brothers answered the defence attorney's question about why they had not looked after the young son of their dead brother and his jailed companion with: 'no question of taking care of the son of a criminal woman!', pity swung to the other side.

Witnesses

The list of witnesses is made public by the presiding judge at the beginning of the hearing. He ascertains with the help of the clerk that every witness has been duly summoned and will be present, and he organizes the order in which they are to be heard. There are three kinds of witnesses: investigating policemen, ordinary civilians who happen to have witnessed the crime, and those related to the accused or to the victim.

The judge summons all the witnesses. They are all supposed to be impartial and to tell 'the truth and nothing but the truth': there is no question here of witnesses for the prosecution or for the defence, no real cross-examination even though the prosecutor and the attorney may ask questions once the judge has finished his questioning, and even though some witnesses may be presented by the defence as 'morality witnesses'.[30]

Witnesses are not allowed in the courtroom before their hearing to prevent them from being influenced.[31] When they are summoned, they are brought before the bench, and they stand 'à la barre', at the witness stand. The presiding judge asks them their name, profession, and age, and then to specify that they are not 'related to the accused or to the victim by birth or marriage and that they are not at his service'; witnesses often feel disconcerted at this question, because they do not really understand it. Then the judge asks them to take an oath: 'Swear to speak without hate and without fear, to tell the whole truth and nothing but the truth. Raise your right hand and say 'I swear''. However, the immediate family (or dependants) are not supposed nor requested to swear impartiality: they do testify but their evidence is regarded with some caution. The case is not the same when the witnesses are also victims, hence civil plaintiffs, for instances of victims of a robbery, a hold-up, or a rape. Here of course they are not supposed to be neutral and they do not swear an oath.

The first to be called to the witness stand are the police officers who discovered the crime then carried out the successive investigations, as requested by the investigating judge or the prosecutor. They are the third persons to speak, after the first presentation of the facts in the indictment and the first declaration by the accused about his or her life. We then come to a more detailed and precise description of the crime and of the different steps that led to charging the accused. The policemen and members of the crime squad give an oral summary of the many written reports they have made, and which the judge and the attorney already know from the files. After giving their evidence, they are questioned by the presiding judge who gets them to confirm some points he/she considers important.

Contrary to the situation in Anglo-American systems, the presiding judge is the leading investigator. He asks questions, gives others the right to talk, or interrupts them, and sometimes arbitrates between defence attorney and prosecutor. Assessors may also ask questions but the jurors have to submit written questions to the judge, who checks their form and neutrality before asking the question himself. Then the prosecutor, the victim's lawyer, and the defence lawyers take turns in asking for further information. Of course, they do this in their party's interest, but questions are usually devoid of any aggressiveness. The aim is not to trick the witness. However, in one trial I attended, the many questions the defence attorney asked the police officer made it clear that some doubt remained as to the presence of the accused: the police said that the wounded victim had given the name of the accused as his aggressor but it emerged that the name had finally been suggested by a third Sri Lankan man present at the scene. Even though evidence given by policemen, who were outsiders to a fight between Sri Lankan compatriots, may sound unbiased, their personal feelings may well come into play. Though police officers, they are also men or women...

I remember a young policewoman testifying very emotionally to the violence that the wife of the accused had suffered, and the terror she had been enduring: 'As a woman I could talk to her', she said with deep empathy.

After the presentation of the evidence by the police, it is the turn of ordinary witnesses, those who were present at the scene. Some are very shy and reluctant to talk, while others like to be the focus of attention and act all-important even though they have nothing to say! Some provide a lot of details, which may seem astonishing if we consider that the events date back a few years (minimum three): the truthfulness of an eyewitness never seems to be challenged nor even doubted by the court, no matter what the findings of psychological studies are.[32]

Some objects are placed under seal and put into boxes on a low table in front of the judges as mute testimonies: the murder weapon, the victim's clothes, objects from which fingerprints or DNA have been taken and analyzed. These boxes are rarely opened but if a party, generally the prosecution, makes the request, the objects are shown to the jurors. It goes without saying that a bloody tee-shirt torn by a knife may impress the jury. Photographs are also shown to the jury. They are pictures of places and the victim's body taken by the police at the scene of the crime. They may also be pictures provided by the accused or by the plaintiff to justify their arguments and to portray 'normal life'. When necessary, the presiding judge circulates these pictures but he may remove the most shocking ones, to spare the jurors: 'They are of no use in trying to establish the truth'. The prosecutor grimaces but does not dare to insist, not wishing to look macabre or indifferent to the jurors' feelings...

Experts

There are two types of expertise: psychological and technical.

Technical Experts

They are asked to make forensic and case-relevant scientific reports. Long used to working for the law, they know how to present their expertise, which they give in written form beforehand for it to be included in the files. They may be called upon by the presiding judge to testify in court, but if they are unavailable, the judge himself may sometimes read the report or they may appear in court via a video link. The description that the forensic expert provides of the dead body can be unbearable, as was the case at Mrs X's trial: the description of the pieces of the corpse and how it was cut up made it difficult for the jurors to maintain an impassive countenance. As for the toxicological expert who, in Mrs X's trial, appeared on a huge video screen, he explained how alcohol and drugs effect a person's behaviour, which seems rather didactic and far from the matter at hand. Thus, the experts both explain their general role and comment on their factual analysis. Their conclusions may be challenged and a counter-expertise called for; this is often the case for ballistic reports. Once I was surprised to see that the forensic expert's conclusion which differed from the testimonies of the accused and the witnesses was simply left out (he stated that the victim should have died two or three minutes after being knifed, yet evidence showed that he succumbed to his injuries after twenty minutes).

Personality Experts

Considering the importance attributed by French law courts to the person and to the background of the accused, it comes as no surprise that three different types of expert are asked to submit reports. The 'personality investigator' (*enquêteur de personnalité*),[33] the psychologist, and the psychiatrist have to meet the accused at least once before the trial and to write a report to explain the latter's character and behaviour which are by definition enigmatic. Cultural factors are often mentioned in these inquiries and reports. Experts ponder the context and the eventual influence of the person's cultural background, even though they are often very ignorant about South Asia in general and of Tamil culture in particular. They mostly rely on information given by the interpreter, who accompanies them during the interviews, which may take place in jail. These experts not only write reports but they also come to the trial where they summarize their report and answer questions.

The 'personality investigator' makes the first report. These investigators may be sociologists, psychologists, or social workers, and they are members of civil associations with official court approval. The investigator first has to question the accused about his or her life and to enter the details under precise headings (childhood, schooling, family relationships...), and then to evaluate his/her social relationships and way of life by visiting the family or friends whose names have been provided by the accused. The investigator makes his report based on the information people give them. The result is very ambiguous. With regards to the political situation in Sri Lanka, for instance, the investigator appeared in court and repeated what a friend of the accused had told him about the war, 'which started when the Singhalese arrived at the beginning of the twentieth century and took power from the Tamils'! Presented as such during the trial, it was regarded by the judiciary as the historical truth. Given the complexity of the Sri Lankan situation, the description is generally limited to: 'He (or she) was harassed in his (or her) country because of civil war'. Other information is sometimes added to this simple statement such as the situation of the diaspora and the complex involvement in semi-mafia groups claiming to work for the LTTE (Tamil Tigers). Another topic that always appears in the report, since it is well known in France, is the 2004 tsunami. All the accused I have ever listen to mention family members as victims of the disaster. They are no doubt reacting to a question put to them by the investigator, but they may make great use of it. For instance, an accused told the investigator that his own parents had died in the tsunami, but at the hearing he said that they were alive. To the bewildered judge (who had the files in front of her), he answered: 'No, not my father and mother, but my father's brother and his wife'. Perhaps this confusion stemmed from the kinship terms. In another case, the psychiatrist was convinced that the defendant showed behavioural problems at every commemoration of the victims of the tsunami.

The report by the personality investigator is followed by the psychologist's report. A psychologist's expertise varies enormously according to their level of competence and training. I have seen experts subject the accused to standard personality tests such as Rorschach or TAT and wonder about the 'paucity' of the answers, without questioning the validity of such an approach in a culturally different context. In the case of Mrs X, on the other hand, the report was made by a psychologist trained in ethno-psychiatry who had taken the trouble to visit the accused three times in jail and to give detailed cultural explanations whenever she found it useful.

She came to the court and explained the mission she had carried out on the orders of the investigating judge. The different points she had to address were as follows:

- To analyze the present state of the personality of the accused
- To define her level of intelligence, manual dexterity, and capacity to concentrate
- To define the personal, family, and socio-cultural elements that might influence the mental structure of the person in question and in particular her notion of family relations, religion, violence, death
- To specify the elements susceptible to explain the motive for the charges against her
- To suggest that she will benefit from psychological treatment.

These guidelines framed the psychologist's examination. She gave a very detailed report of Mrs X's life, from her childhood in Jaffna up to recent events, based on information given by Mrs X and—I would add—which was seen from a rather positive angle.

Furthermore, thanks to her training in anthropology, she paid particular attention to the specific cultural context. She started by explaining the Tamil way of giving names and how the French administration confuses name and surname. Then she presented Mrs X's family's caste (Vellala). She was the only one to mention this. Caste is totally overlooked in French courts. She insisted on Mrs X's exceptional destiny: head of the household when she was ten, practically a mother to her brothers and sisters, married to somebody who wanted to kill himself for her, a working woman in Singapore then in France with her husband and children. There was a first rupture with Tamil tradition when her daughter ran away with a young boy and returned home pregnant. This was the first in a series of misfortunes and breaks with tradition, which ended up with Mrs X running away with a much younger man, abandoning husband and children, and living a secret life with her lover, bearing a son that she had kept hidden. The psychologist explained how transgressive Mrs X's behaviour had become in the Tamil context and how trapped she had felt when violence raised its ugly head once more. She also explained the religious context, the family changing their allegiance according to the circumstances. Mrs X's family was Hindu but her mother had converted to Catholicism when her wish to have a son had been fulfilled 'thanks to the Virgin Mary'. However, the family respected Hindu rituals and also believed in witchcraft: the father's misfortune was due to sorcery, an evil spell that had been cast upon them when their house was built. Again when Mrs X's son married against her will, it was because he was under a spell that his young bride had cast upon him. Finally, Mrs X went to see a Hindu priest in Paris who explained that one of her lover's former female relations had cast a spell on their couple and that he could undo it in exchange for money. She could not afford this and preferred to pray to the Christian God in church. In keeping with her training in ethno-psychiatry, the psychiatrist recommended that Mrs X and her children once again embrace the Hindu religion, that they revive their ancestral traditions according to which it is possible to interpret their series of misfortunes 'as a consequence of neglecting the cult of the Hindu protective deities in order to adopt Christianity', and that 'the Hindu religion might be a therapeutic resource'.

It is in fact thanks to the ethno-psychiatric training that traditional culture is seen as a resource. More often than not psychological comments emphasize what they see as the negative aspect and impact of foreign cultural tradition. An arranged marriage is, for instance, seen as the source of all the family's problems and it is absolutely exceptional to hear, as in Mrs X's case, a social worker or a psychologist explain that, for Tamils, love marriage is the problem; that it does not last, and that parents are much better at finding a suitable partner.

The third category of psychological experts are the psychiatrists. Selected by the investigating judge from a list of certified psychiatrists, they also have to visit the accused prior to the trial, to make a report which they present before the court. Their main task is to assess the mental state and the responsibility of the accused. Of course, it is very difficult for them to judge the mental capacities, the power of reasoning, the linguistic skills of somebody whose language they do not share, and they have to rely entirely on the interpreter. Like the psychologist, they have to answer questions according to specific guidelines. In short, these questions are as follows: does the accused show any psychological or mental disorder and are the facts due to any eventual disorder? At the time of the crime, was his/her judgment impaired, or was he/she suffering from diminished responsibility for his/her acts (*alteration du contrôle des actes*)? If mentally ill, can he/she be cured? Is his/her mental state compatible with detention? Some psychiatrists totally reject such questions and refuse to give precise, definite answers: 'The judiciary uses us. They want us to set the sentence, they want to shirk their responsibility for passing judgment. There is a growing medicalization of the judgement, which is scary'.

Speeches

We are now at the end of the trial: the witnesses have all testified, the experts have given their reports, the accused has had their say, the judges and parties have asked all their questions. We are under the impression that the jurors have made their opinion. Now it is up to the parties' attorneys and the prosecutor to summarize their version of the facts and to justify it in the hope of convincing the jury.

The first to speak is the civil plaintiff's attorney (or attorneys). His role is obviously to cast a slur on the accused and to present the victim (s) in the most favourable light and to defend his memory. He calls on the public's emotions to move the jury to pity.

In Mrs X's trial, the attorney spoke on behalf of the victim's brothers. Standing in front of the bench, near his clients, he first of all spoke about the victim's tragedy, his young age, his refugee status: 'he went to France to escape death'. Then he insisted on the atrocity of the crime, without sparing the family: 'She tore off his limbs'. At this the brothers covered their ears with their hands. He went on vehemently: 'She put the body parts in garbage bags as if they were scraps'. The brothers sobbed. 'They waited a year to get the body back and then it was incomplete'. The lawyer concluded by stigmatizing the accused for her coldness during the hearing and he addressed the jury: 'Just think of the horrifying truth!'

Then another lawyer intervened on behalf of the couple's small child, who had been living in a foster family since the drama. The lawyer belonged to Childhood Protection Services and severely condemned the mother, 'unable to see the needs and sufferings of her son, to respect him and to tell the truth. When he is eighteen, he will have the right to look at the files... and then, how will he ever be able to forgive?'

The plaintiff's lawyers, as we see, argued their case in an emotional way, often in an indignant tone of voice. But they did not demand any particular sentence. This is not their role, but that of the prosecutor.

Then as soon as they had finished, the prosecutor stood up from his desk, eventually arranging some papers in front of him and, as majestically as his age or appearance permitted, launched into his speech. As the guardian of law and order representing the state, his part is to establish the eventual culpability and propose the sentence he thinks fitting. He reminded the audience of the qualification of the crime, and evoked the maximum sentence incurred. His voice echoed, he looked forbidding, the audience shivered, the accused shrank. Then he came back to the case itself, took into account some mitigating circumstances and concluded by asking for the appropriate sentence. The prosecutor is commonly portrayed as a repressive figure, often politically connoted. However, some prosecutors claim to maintain a balance, to provide equal arguments both against and in favour of the accused and to ask for a just penance. As a prosecutor once said: 'I am not relentless. I'm asking for a punishment that will repress a criminal act but which might also, through its leniency, help somebody who has suffered a difficult life, a sad destiny'. And paradoxically, a benign prosecutor makes the task difficult for the defence attorney.[34]

In Mrs X's trial, the prosecutor first addressed the jurors, as is the custom: 'You represent the French nation. You have full responsibility for your choice and you have to judge according to your own individual conscience… You and only you have the power to implement justice!' He went on to summarize his version of the facts: 'We only have Mrs X's version of the facts…And she is lying, she lied about her isolation, about the violence she was submitted to, she could have left…' He gave a horrific description of the crime and of how the corpse was dismembered, adding some gory details about the saw. 'She got herself into a predicament and chose the most gruesome way out'. And he concluded with: 'For such a crime, the sentence can be as much as life imprisonment. However, some elements do swing in her favour and I would like her to have some sort of future. I recommend 25 years' imprisonment, with no safety period, which means that the length of her sentence might be reduced half-way through her prison term.[35] And if we take into account any eventual remission, it actually amounts to much less'.

This calculation infuriated the defence lawyer who accused the prosecutor: 'You cannot talk like that. You have to recommend a sentence, and remission is no part of it; it is not granted systematically. You have recommended 25 years, which means that she will definitely be excluded from society, she will be 71 when she will be released… Sentencing has various purposes: to prevent her from committing other offences (which is no problem here), to punish, and to rehabilitate her... A just punishment allows for some hope'. The lawyer once again referred to the life of the accused, her misfortunes, and her confusion about values in life. She obviously did not deny the culpability of her client, who had admitted her guilt, but she pleaded in such a way to win over and convince the jury by eliciting the subjectivity of the courts and appealing for leniency.[36] The lawyer delivered a very empathic and psychological speech, vividly describing the problems and the dilemma of the accused: 'It is difficult for her to talk. How can she say things in the solemnity of this room... The Tamils do not speak easily about their emotions'.

However, the lawyer succeeded in persuading her client to show some emotion. After listening to the speech for the defence, the presiding judge granted the accused the right to make a final statement. At this Mrs X burst into tears and asked forgiveness: 'I was lost, I apologize, I apologize to my sons for hurting them'. But, still harbouring a lot of resentment, she was unable to apologize to the victim's family.

The few pathetic words pronounced by another culprit were more spontaneous: 'I am very sad that the victim is dead. I apologize. I was too drunk, he made me too angry. We had been getting on well before that. I ask for forgiveness. I am not able to express myself, I am sorry'.

Deliberation, Verdict, and Sentencing

When everybody has had their say, the presiding judge addresses the jurors and explains that they now have to decide on the verdict, which means answering the first question about culpability: 'Is the accused guilty of the charges against her in the indictment act?' If the answer is yes, they have to consider whether there are any mitigating circumstances, and finally they have to decide on the sentence. This part played by the jurors in deciding the prison sentence is specific to continental procedures.[37]

The judge reads to the jurors the moral recommendation detailed above: they have to judge according to their own conscience, to weigh up the defence and prosecution arguments, but they do not have to justify their choice. This last rule may soon change, since for the first time and in conformity with the European Court of Human Right directives, on 24th November 2010 the Court of Assize in Pas-de-Calais asked the jurors to justify their acquittal vote by answering a series of questions regarding the inquiry, evidence, and the motivation of their decision.[38]

Everybody then stands up and the jurors, the presiding judge, and the two assessors adjourn to the deliberation room (*salle des délibérés*), which they have no right to leave before any final decision has been made. The public, the attorneys, and the interpreter leave the courtroom and wait outside until the doors are opened once again for them to hear the final verdict. There is no time limit and everyone starts making assumptions: 'More than five hours... is it in favour of the accused? It means that the jurors are discussing and disagree!'

Deliberations are kept secret. As far as the rules are concerned, note that the presiding judge and the two assessors sit with the six jurors (or nine in the case of appeal) and vote with them, unlike proceedings in the USA.[39] Some people deplore the influence that the magistrate undoubtedly has on lay jurors, which is difficult to evaluate. However, the decision must be taken by a majority of six (eight in the case of an appeal),[40] and by secret ballot, written on a form provided by the court as follows: 'On my honour and in my conscience, my declaration is (yes or no)' (according to Criminal Procedure Code article 357). And prior to the pronouncement of the final verdict, the jurors are each free to give their opinion, the judges being the last to speak.

If the accused is found guilty by a majority of six (two-thirds), the jury discusses the sentence and votes by secret ballot. The sentence must be accepted by a majority and if this is not the case, they vote again, each time reducing the sentence. One problem raised by jurors is that, if you vote for an acquittal, but you are in the minority, you have to decide a jail sentence even though you personally consider the accused innocent.

When the jury and judges have reached an agreement, everyone is called back into the courtroom. The presiding judge reads the verdict and the sentence. This is done in a rather casual manner, without disclosing the number of votes, and talking only about 'the majority as required by law'. This is immediately translated for the accused, who, in the cases I witnessed, stayed calm. Mrs X was relieved since she was sentenced to 15 years' imprisonment instead of the 25 recommended by the prosecutor. Her lawyer was entirely satisfied and they exchanged a few words.

The last part of the trial takes the form of a civil audience. It takes place immediately afterwards, but without the jurors who leave the bench. The presiding judge and assessors decide on the compensatory damages to be paid by the accused to the civil plaintiffs. These may follow any requests expressed by the plaintiffs' lawyers. Generally speaking, in the case of insolvent Sri Lankans, the sums are paid by a state compensation fund. The culprits have to reimburse the sum eventually with the poor salary they earn from their work in jail.

* * *

Proceedings at the Court of Assize are generally seen by the French judiciary as exemplar. They often take place in an unhurried manner, unlike in the lower chambers: the accused and the witnesses are given all the time they need to express themselves. The interpreter does their job free of time pressures without being interrupted, and the jury waits till all the explanations and comments have been translated. The presiding judge addresses the parties respectfully and tries to maintain a well-balanced series of questions. The court ritual gives the impression of a well-oiled process. Neutrality, fairness, and respect for the rights of the parties are essential.

However, is this all merely a facade? Everything depends on the investigation. When the investigation process has been carried out fully, when every testimony has been checked, any inconsistencies resolved, and when a final comparison has been made with the evidence, the accused confesses their crime and the investigating judge produces a coherent narrative, which is seldom contradicted at the hearing. Nevertheless, I have attended a case where the investigations were carried out ineffectively and which were, in my opinion, incomplete. The accused denied every charge even when confronted with factual evidence (such as video tapes attesting to their very presence), yet the defence could only express its doubts. The system makes it impossible for the lawyer to produce an alternative narrative; they are ill-equipped for such an eventuality.

Another question concerns the case of foreigners: 'The ideology of the French criminal justice system relies on the image of the impartial magistrate who applies the law in a constantly uniform manner because he or she is bound by fixed rules and codified statutes. This representation of the law and its application suggest an 'homogeneous model... where all citizens are equal and equally bound by the law' [Hodgson 2005: 21]. It masks the true power relations', writes Terrio (2009: 45).

What is to be done with people 'whose behaviour is still determined by cultural influences from their country of origin', as was said at one of the trials. Their enigmatic attitude may be used by the prosecutor or the defence attorney to build a more exciting narrative than a flat dispute: a politically grounded conflict or the transgression of an exotic taboo over a certain type of behaviour renders the case more interesting and is worth its human and financial cost. It makes for 'a beautiful trial'.

Notes

1. Two additional jurors are selected in the case where a juror cannot fulfil this task. Before the new law of 01/01/2012, the number of jurors was nine and twelve in appeal courts. Note that judging cases for appeal in assize courts has only been made possible since 15 June 2000. In such cases, the trial starts afresh and follows the same procedure as the first trial, the only difference being the number of jurors (and therefore the majority required for the verdict).

2. He represents the Public Prosecution Department (*Ministère Public*), which is also called *le parquet*, a name that alludes to a standing position when talking, contrary to the judges who are 'from the seat', *du siège*. The Prosecutor's office is the authority that exercises public action on behalf of the state. A General Prosecutor nominated by the *Ministre de la justice*, thus under the political authority, runs it. The General Prosecutor nominates the Public Prosecutor (*Procureur de la République*), who is represented in local courts by vice-prosecutors or deputy-prosecutors. The subordination of the prosecutor to the political authority is often denounced as a hindrance to independent justice.

3. This is quite similar to the 'spatialization of hierarchy' described by P. Baxi (in this volume). The inaudibility she refers to is also often experienced, except at Assize courts where microphones are used (if they actually work or are carefully positioned!).

4. Being summoned as a member of a jury is a citizen's duty. However, it is possible to be excused jury service if you provide a medical note or plead incapacity for various personal reasons. This may lead to an overrepresentation of retired elderly people who are interested in legal matters and have more free time (on this point, see the fascinating testimony by the sociologist and selected juror Marcel d'Ans, 2003).

5. Which contrasts with proceedings in the USA as presented in the gripping article by Moskovitz (1995) in which the O.J. Simpson case is retried according to the French legal system and which portrays US lawyers as being indignant. With regards the jury, they claim: 'Aren't we going to *voir dire* the jurors? You

know, ask them a few questions to see if they are biased' (Moskivitz1995: 1124). Then they refer to the use of 'high-priced jury-consultants' (ibid.:1167–68), offices specialized in enquiries into potential jurors, in order to test arguments likely to influence them (see Garapon and Papadopoulos 2003: 187 ff.)

6. On the history of the jury system, see Whitman 2008.

7. See Moskovitz (1995: 1177) where US lawyers insist on the importance of summoning jurors of various origins, more conscious of behavioural differences: 'They bring 'real life' into court deliberations'.

8. After recently advocating the abolition of the lay jury (spring 2010), the previous government declared (January 2012) that it was in favour of extending it to minor cases (Magistrate's Court) where it is a case of personal injury [*atteinte à la personne*], the (misleading?) idea being that a lay jury would be more repressive. Technically speaking, this would have been very difficult to organise considering the number of lawsuits. Note that financial or economic matters were considered to be too complicated (or politically sensitive) to be entrusted to a jury… But this measure was cancelled with the change of the majority in 2013.

9. The names have been changed.

10. See the words ascribed by Moskovitz (1995) to a French judge: 'We do not treat precedent as you do in the United States. In your common-law system, the law evolves through the application of the law to specific facts, so your published decisions are very important in determining what the law is. But in our system, the law is fixed by the Legislature and it is changed by the Legislature, not by the courts' (Moskovitz 1995: 1147).

11. Contrary to the prosecutor, the examining judge is a magistrate independent of the Ministry of Justice, hence of political power.

12. *Office français de protection des réfugiés et apatrides*, the first administrative court in charge of asylum seekers.

13. See S. Mulhern on the MC Ruby case (1998: 118): 'The police reports on the suspects only contain the translation of their replies into French. They do not include the questions in French or their translation into Russian, nor the replies in their mother tongue'. The same situation is denounced very eloquently by J.B. Haviland (2003: 768) who deplores that there is 'no tape recording of the original testimony'.

14. Contrary to the situation described by D. Berti (in this volume), no written transcription of the oral interactions is made during the trial. The only written documents are those drawn up during the investigation.

15. One difference with a trial in the USA, as Moskovitz notes is (1995:1131): 'In the US of America we would never tolerate a judge or a juror who had read a whole detailed report on the case before the trial even began… even a slimeball criminal defendant is entitled to a fact-finder who hasn't already made up his mind'.

16. See the remarks made by S. Terrio (2009: 223) about French courts: 'The intricacies of the court ritual and the opacity of legal language are such that no one instinctively knows how to act, where to stand, or what is expected in terms of appropriate speech'.

17. See McKillop (1997) about 'a French murder case': 'The presiding judge interrogated the accused and the witnesses from their depositions in the dossier and generally sought to have their oral evidence conform to those depositions. Some witnesses simply confirmed their deposition as read out by the presiding judge... The hearing thus became essentially a public review and confirmation of the contents of the dossier' (McKillop1997: 564-65). It appears to be the same in some US trials, like Oliver North's case where 'witnesses were often questioned with reference to the documents and earlier testimonies that were available in the record' (Lynch and Bogen, 1996: 13).

18. 'It could be said that the investigation was the crucial and determinative phase of the whole process and that the hearing simply added a public dimension to the investigation' McKillop (1997: 565).

19. I often met with a refusal when I asked the actors in the judiciary process for access to the files so that I might take the time to read what I had not heard properly (microphones do not always function) or what I had not had time to write down. I express my deepest gratitude to the few who understood my request.

20. They are mostly in keeping with what S. Terrio describes as the attitude requested from defendants: 'They must display a constantly appropriate and properly deferential demeanor' (Terrio 2009: 223). This is not always the case with young recidivists who sometimes behave rather insolently and are expelled from the court by the judge.

21. See Haviland (2003) on the falsehood of 'the verbatim theory 'and the idea of 'the interpreter as a kind of transparent filter' (Haviland 2003: 764-774), later discussed in Conley and O'Barr (2005).

22. Cf. Lynch and Bogen (1996: 49) on body language and assessment of witness credibility. Since body language is also culturally defined, we see how difficult it is for the jury to interpret the defendant's behaviour.

23. This is called the 'principle of personalizing punishments' (*principe de personnalisation des peines*).

24. What S. Terrio calls 'coercive intrusion into private spheres' (2009: 22): 'French courts intrude authoritatively into the personality and the private life of the accused' (Terrio 2009: 45).

25. About the notion of truth and Indian litigants' supposed disregard for it, see D. Berti (conclusion to her article in this volume).

26. 'The court relies heavily on these statements, signed by the defendants, victims, and witnesses and resists any attempts to reframe or retract the version of events presented there' (Terrio 2009: 224).

27. However, the person in police custody or before the investigating judge must be specifically informed of their right to remain silent. See McKillop: 'The accused as a source of information' (McKillop1997: 575-76) and 'A right to silence?' (McKillop 1997: :576-78). On the contrary, the American lawyer is rather indignant when confronted with what they call 'self-incrimination': 'It doesn't seem fair to put a defendant in a position where he has to hang himself by talking' (Moskovitz 1995: 1136).

28. The accused is often kept in pre-trial detention. If the accused is put on probation, a probation officer also has to make a report on how readily the accused submitted to their supervision.

29. This is not the case in trials in the USA. See the humorous exchange between the prosecutor and attorney in the mock process presented in Moskovitz (1995: 1123): [the prosecutor to the attorney] 'What are you doing here? This is my case, a criminal case, not a civil case. You don't belong here. [The Judge]: Ms Clare, we allow the alleged victim to intervene and appear by counsel in our criminal trials. Who has a greater interest in seeing that justice is done than the victim? [Ms Clare, the prosecutor]: The State does, your Honor. I represent the State, she doesn't. That is how it is done in the United States.'

30. See the differences with the case reported by D. Berti in this volume. The question of hostile witness does not exist in French proceedings. Witnesses have to swear to tell the truth, they are not supposed to have interactions with the prosecutor or the lawyers before they enter the courtroom. Any discrepancies between their previous statement, which was taken down by police officers or the investigating judge and recorded, and their oral statement during the trial are often due to lapses of memory and may lead to heated exchanges between the lawyers and the public attorney.

31. The same goes for Indian criminal courts, see P. Baxi (in this volume).

32. Cf. E. Loftus quoted in Conley and O' Barr (2005: 166–170).

33. McKillop prefers not to translate: Personnalité is not easy to translate. It includes personal history (family life [with parents, siblings, spouse, children], schooling, work record, military service), material situation, leisure interests, and character traits (particularly traits indicative of good or bad character)' (Mackillop 1997: 532 n.19).

34. See the words of a continental prosecutor according to Moskovitz: 'Our prosecutors tend to be 'pro-judge' in the sense that they are out to secure justice not to get convictions. For example, every prosecutor has a duty to present to the court all evidence that favors the defendant, and they really do so'. 'Shocking'. 'I am speaking generally of course. Individual prosecutors vary' (1154–55).

35. When no safety period is required, the defendant can be granted parole (liberté conditionnelle) when she has done half of her term of imprisonment. And in the case of good conduct, she is entitled to a reduction in her sentence

of three months for every year. Thus a ten-year sentence can be reduced to seven and a half years, which means that after four years the person can be released on parole.

36. Terrio (2009: 242) underlines that generally in France 'attorneys did not contest the guilt of their client or advise them to plead innocent but rather urged them to confess' (ibid.).

37. In trials in the USA, the jury only decides the verdict. The fact that only the culpability is determined by the jurors explains that in the USA all personal data, such as any previous judiciary records, are absent from the hearings, as they are likely to influence the jury. However, these data are important in determining the sentence, which is the judge's prerogative.

38. Since 1 January 2012, the law requires that the presiding judge drafts a report to justify the decision.

39. Cf. Moskovitz (1995: 1125) who gets the US procurator to express his indignation: 'You are not telling me that the judges go into the room with these lay assessors and deliberate with them? – I am afraid I am. You seem shocked! – Of course I am! What kind of a jury do you have when judges vote with the jurors? [...] - The jurors can outvote the judges – Look Professor, I wasn't born yesterday. When a judge – when three judges – tell the jurors what they think, what juror is going to disagree'. The current French system dates from 1944. Before that, it was the same as in the United States.

40. Lay jurors and magistrates have equal rights.

References

Ans, André-Marcel d'. 2003. 'La Cour d'assises en examen: Reflexion-témoignage d'un juré sociologue', *Droit et Société*, 54.

Conley, John M., and William. M. O'Barr. 2005[1998]. *Just Words. Law, Language and Power*. Chicago: University of Chicago Press.

Code de procedure pénale, version 2010, electronic version.http://www.legifrance. gouv.fr/affichCode.do?cidTexte=LEGITEXT000006071154. 25/06/2014.

Droit et Cultures. 1998. 'Un procès au crible des Sciences Humaines : L'affaire M.C. Ruby'. 1998. *Droit et Cultures*, 36 (2).

Garcia, R. 1993. 'L'Etat Civil à point nommé', *Accueillir* , 191: 28–29.

Garapon, Antoine. 2001. *Bien juger. Essai sur le rituel judiciaire*. Paris: Odile Jacob.

Garapon, Antoine and Iannis Papadopoulos. 2003. *Juger en Amerique et en France*. Paris : Odile Jacob.

Garapon, A. and T. Pech. 1998. 'Mise en récit du process, mise en process du récit', in 'Un process au crible des sciences humaines : L'affaire MC Ruby', *Droit et Cultures*, 36 (2): 149–66.

Haviland, J. B. 2003. 'Ideologies of Language: Some Reflections on Language and U.S. Law', *American Anthropologist*, 105 (4): 764–74.

Hodgson, Jacqueline. 2005. *French Criminal Justice: A Comparative Account of the Investigation and Prosecution of Crime in France.* Portland: Hart Publishing.

Lynch, Michael and David Bogen. 1996. *The Spectacle of History: Speech, Text, and Memory at the Iran-contra Hearings.* Durham and London: Duke University Press.

McKillop, B. 1997. 'Anatomy of a French Murder Case', *American Journal of Comparative Law*, 45: 527–83.

Moskovitz, M. 1995. 'The O.J. Inquisition: A United States Encounter With Continental Criminal Justice', *Vanderbilt Journal of Transnational Law*, 28:1121–95.

Mulhern, S. 1998. 'Les récits constitutifs dans le procès MC Ruby', in Un procès au crible des sciences humaines: L'affaire MC Ruby, *Droit et Cultures*, 36 (2): 113–40.

Terrio, Susan J. 2009. *Judging Mohammed: Juvenile Deliquency, Immigration, and Exclusion at the Paris Palace of Justice.* Stanford: Stanford University Press.

Trouille, H. 1994. 'A Look at French Criminal Procedure', *Criminal Law Review*, October: 735–43.

Whitman, James Q. 2008. *The Origins of Reasonable Doubt: Theological Roots of the Criminal Trial.* New Haven: Yale University Press.

Index

Editors and Contributors

Srimati Basu is Professor of Gender and Women's Studies and Anthropology at the University of Kentucky, working on law, marriage, and violence. She is the author of the monograph *The Trouble with Marriage: Feminists Confront Law and Violence in India* (University of California Press and Orient BlackSwan, New Delhi; 2015) and the co-editor of *Conjugality Unbound: Sexual Economics, State Regulation, and Marital Form in India* (Women Unlimited, 2015). She has previously written about Indian women and inheritance laws in the monograph *She Comes to Take Her Rights: Indian Women, Property and Propriety* (SUNY Press, 1999). She has also written on property, law, marriage, intimacy, violence and popular culture in various anthologies and journals; edited the Dowry and Inheritance volume in the Women Unlimited series Issues in Indian Feminism; and is a contributing blogger to Ms. Magazine Online.

Pratiksha Baxi teaches at the Centre for the Study of Law and Governance, Jawaharlal Nehru University, Delhi. Her book, *Public Secrets of Law: Rape Trials in India* (Oxford University Press, 2014) brings together her interest in sociology of law, feminist theory, and violence. Baxi's research interests include critical perspectives on medical jurisprudence, ethnographies of courts, sociology of violence, gender studies, politics of judicial reform, judicial iconography, courtroom architecture and feminist legal theory.

Daniela Berti is a social anthropologist and 'Chargée de Recherche' research fellow at the National Centre for Scientific Research (CNRS) in France and a member of the Centre for Himalayan Studies (CEH) in Villejuif. Her research in northern India focuses on ritual interactions, politico-ritual roles and practices formerly associated with kingship, on 'Hindutva' entrenchment in local society, and on the ethnography of courts. In collaboration with Gilles Tarabout, she recently coordinated an international team project entitled *Just-India: A Joint Programme on Justice and Governance in India and South Asia* (2009–2013).

Devika Bordia received her PhD in Anthropology from Yale University and has subsequently taught at Trinity College, Hartford, and held fellowships at the Centre National de la Recherche Scientifique, Paris, and the Centre for the Study of Developing Societies, Delhi. She is currently a postdoctoral fellow at the Centre for Modern Indian Studies at the University of Göttingen. Her research focuses on the practices of legal and military institutions in India.

Véronique Bouillier is a social anthropologist and has worked in particular on religious communities in Nepal and India. Her published books and articles largely pertain to the sociological aspects of Hindu asceticism. The study that she is currently conducting on the French judicial system and cultural processes focuses on people of South Asian origin who live in France.

Anthony Good is Emeritus Professor of Social Anthropology at the University of Edinburgh. His research interests cover Tamil Nadu, South India, and Sri Lanka. He frequently acts as an expert witness in asylum appeals involving Sri Lankan Tamils. His recent research concerns uses of expert evidence in British asylum courts, and (with Robert Gibb) a comparative study of asylum processes in the UK and France. His publications include *Worship and the Ceremonial Economy of a Royal South Indian Temple* (2004) and *Anthropology and Expertise in the Asylum Courts* (2007).

Zoé E. Headley is a research fellow in social anthropology (CEIAS-CNRS, Paris) presently based at IFP (Pondicherry). Her recent publications include: 'Caste et ordre social en Inde contemporaine' in Jaffrelot, C. & Naudet, J. *Justifier l'Ordre Social*. PUF: Paris; 'Of dangerous guardians and contested hierarchies: An ethnographic reading of a south Indian copperplate', in Murugaiyan, A., (ed.) *Studies in Tamil Epigraphy: Historical Sources and Multidisciplinary Approach*, Cre-A Publishers, Chennai; 'Caste and Collective Memory in South India', in Clark-Deces, I. (ed.) *A Companion to the Anthropology of India*, Blackwell Publishing, Oxford.

Nicolas Jaoul is a researcher in anthropology at the French National Centre for Scientific Research (CNRS). He is a member of the *Institut de Recherches Interdisciplinaires sur les Enjeux Sociaux* (IRIS, EHESS, Paris). He specializes in the ethnography of the Ambedkarite movement, but also focuses on the relationship of Dalits to Indian democracy as it unfolds in other political movements (Communism, Gandhism, Hindu Nationalism).

Chiara Letizia is a social anthropologist and historian of religions. She is Professor of South Asian Religions at the University of Québec in Montréal and researcher in Cultural Anthropology at the University of Milan Bicocca. She is also a research associate at the School of Anthropology & Museum Ethnography, University of Oxford. Since 1997 she has conducted fieldwork in Nepal on ritual and symbolism, religion and politics, and ethnic and religious activism. Her current research is on the meanings and the shaping of secularism in Nepal. She has published in English, French, and Italian in peer-reviewed journals and edited books.

Jeffrey A. Redding is Associate Professor at Saint Louis University School of Law where he teaches civil procedure and comparative law. His scholarship focuses on the areas of comparative law and religion, Islamic law, legal pluralism, gender, and law and sexuality. He has lectured widely on these topics in the United States, Europe, and South Asia. His research and work in South Asia has been longstanding, and includes work with non-governmental organizations in both Pakistan and India. Professor Redding earned his J.D. from the University of Chicago Law School.